D1355996

EVERYMAN, *I will go with thee,*

and be thy guide,

In thy most need to go by thy side

PHILIP DORMER STANHOPE

Fourth Earl of Chesterfield, born on 22nd
September 1694. Entered House of Commons, 1715; House of Lords, 1726.
Retired from official life, 1755. Died on
24th March 1773.

Lord Chesterfield's Letters to his Son

AND OTHERS

INTRODUCTION BY

R. K. ROOT
Late Professor of English Literature,
Princeton University

DENT: LONDON
EVERYMAN'S LIBRARY
DUTTON: NEW YORK

No. 823 Hardback ISBN 0 460 00823 4

INTRODUCTION

It is one of the strange ironies of capricious fortune that Lord Chesterfield, a man of considerable consequence in his own day, should have attained to permanence of fame only by a body of very intimate personal letters written to his own son, and never intended for the publicity of the printed page. Lord Chesterfield died on 24 March, 1773, at the age of seventy-eight. Early in the following year the bookseller, James Dodsley, displayed for sale in two handsome quarto volumes, at a guinea a volume, "Letters written by the Earl of Chesterfield to his Son, Philip Stanhope, together with several other pieces on various subjects, published by Mrs. Eugenia Stanhope, London, 1774." These letters, carefully preserved by Philip Stanhope, had at his death in 1768 come into the possession of his widow; and now, when Lord Chesterfield, who had shown himself a generous father-in-law, could no longer protest, she sold them to Dodsley for the very considerable sum of £1500. It was a rather ungracious act of Mrs. Eugenia Stanhope; but to her lack of fine sensibility we owe the possession of a very charming book. To Mr. James Dodsley his venture must have been a profitable one; for the book met instant appreciation. It was copiously reviewed in the magazines; the *Monthly Review* ran a serial discussion of it in four monthly instalments from April to July, 1774. Five editions appeared before the end of the year. For contemporaries, in addition to the intrinsic interest which still endures, there was the added zest of catching off his guard in an intimate self-revelation one of the most conspicuous figures of his day. The writer in the *Monthly Review* begins his first instalment thus:

Few characters, among the nobility of this age, and nation, are better known than that of the late ingenious and witty Earl of Chesterfield; who was alike distinguished in the polite, the political, and the learned circles. He was not, perhaps, what some one has styled a "deep genius," but he certainly had a great portion of good sense, and lively parts; he had a perfect knowledge of mankind; he was a complete gentleman, and a delightful companion.

Philip Dormer Stanhope, fourth Earl of Chesterfield, was born in London on 22 September, 1694. When Queen Anne died in 1714, Stanhope, a young man of twenty, was abroad completing his education by the conventional grand tour; but he hurried home at news of the political crisis, and in 1715, before he had quite attained the legal age of twenty-one, he was elected to Parliament as member for St. Germans, Cornwall, as a staunch Whig. His keen interest in literature won him the friendship of Pope and Arbuthnot, Swift, and Addison. "I used to think myself in company as much above me when I was with Mr. Addison and Mr. Pope, as if I had been with all the princes of Europe." [1] In 1726, on the death of his father, he succeeded to the earldom, and took his seat in the House of Lords, which he playfully called "the hospital for incurables."

Lord Chesterfield's active career as politician fell in the reigns of George I (1714–27) and George II (1727–60), perhaps the least worthy sovereigns who have ever sat on the English throne. In the bitter quarrel between George I and his son, Chesterfield threw in his lot with the Prince, in whose household he was gentleman of the bedchamber; but he made the mistake of cultivating the favour of Mrs. Howard, afterwards Countess of Suffolk, chief mistress of the Prince, and so incurring the hostility of the Princess of Wales, afterwards Queen Caroline, which carried with it the enmity of her ally, the all-powerful Walpole. As a result, despite the favour of George II, Chesterfield never attained to the political success which his abilities deserved. But as an accomplished orator he was a commanding figure in the House of Lords.

For four years, from 1728 to 1732, he was British Ambassador at The Hague. There, in the course of a life of gallantry and polite dissipation, he met Mlle du Bouchet, who became the mother of the son to whom the famous letters are addressed. For her maintenance he provided generously throughout his life, and left her in his will the sum of five hundred pounds "as a small reparation for the injury I did her." In 1733 he married Petronilla, Countess of Walsingham, a natural daughter of George I. The marriage was entirely one of convenience. The lady, who was forty years old—a year older than her husband—brought him a large fortune and received in return the prestige of his name. Each continued to maintain a separate establishment; and Chesterfield, though

[1] Letter of 9 October, 1747.

he always treated his wife with the most courteous consideration, did not in any way allow his marriage to interfere with his accustomed freedom.

In 1737 he led in the House of Lords an unsuccessful attack on Walpole's bill for restricting the liberty of the theatre; and in the winter of 1741-2 he was influential in bringing about Walpole's fall. In 1745 he was appointed Lord Lieutenant of Ireland; and, though serious illness limited his active term of office to eight months, his excellent tact and good judgment made his brief administration memorable in the history of eighteenth-century Ireland. From 1746 to 1748, when he resigned the office, he was Secretary of State in Newcastle's ministry. In 1751 he was responsible for securing the adoption by England of the Gregorian calendar. Of his speech on this occasion he writes to his son a month later in a vein of characteristic cynicism:

I was to bring in this bill, which was necessarily composed of law jargon and astronomical calculations, to both which I am an utter stranger. However, it was absolutely necessary to make the House of Lords think that I knew something of the matter; and also to make them believe that they knew something of it themselves, which they do not. For my own part, I could just as soon have talked Celtic or Sclavonian to them as astronomy, and they would have understood me full as well; so I resolved to do better than speak to the purpose, and to please instead of informing them. I gave them, therefore, only an historical account of calendars from the Egyptian down to the Gregorian, amusing them now and then with little episodes; but I was particularly attentive to the choice of my words, to the harmony and roundness of my periods, to my elocution, to my action. This succeeded, and ever will succeed; they thought I informed, because I pleased them; and many of them said that I had made the whole very clear to them, when, God knows, I had not even attempted it. [1]

The last twenty-five years of Chesterfield's life were spent in graceful leisure, in his garden, with his friends, among his books. He suffered severely from gout and from an increasing deafness which ultimately made conversation difficult and embarrassing. On one occasion he invited guests to dinner in the following words:

Lord Chesterfield presents his compliments to Mr. Mallet, and he will be extremely glad to see him and Monsieur de Bussy at dinner next Wednesday; but he desires Mr. Mallet to inform Monsieur de Bussy previously that Lord Chesterfield has been dead

[1] Letter of 18 March, 1751.

these twelve years, and has lost all the advantages of flesh and blood, without acquiring any of the singular privileges of a spirit.[1]

Dr. Maty, who wrote a memoir of Chesterfield for the edition of his Miscellaneous Works, published in 1777, has preserved a famous account of the Earl's last words:

Upon the morning of his decease, and about half an hour before it happened, Mr. Dayrolles called upon him to make his usual visit. When he had entered the room, the *valet de chambre*, opening the curtains of the bed, announced Mr. Dayrolles to his lordship. The Earl found strength enough, in a faint voice, to say, "Give Dayrolles a chair." Those were the last words he was heard to speak.

It was a gracious ending; the fine courtesy and considerateness which had ruled his life was strong in death. In his will he left two years' full wages to all his servants who had been with him five years and more, "whom I consider as unfortunate friends, my equals by Nature, and my inferiors only by the difference of our fortunes."

In the words of the Monthly Reviewer, Lord Chesterfield was not a "deep genius"; but he was a man of fine abilities, who used the advantages which came to him from his rank and great wealth, within the limits possible to complete worldliness, with excellent result.

Philip Stanhope, to whom the famous letters are addressed, was born in 1732. For his education his father made full provision of private tutors, of residence at the Universities of Lausanne and Leipsic, of an extended grand tour on which letters of introduction opened for him the best society of all the capitals. The letters, the grand aim of which is to supplement the boy's more formal education by instruction in the arts of worldly wisdom and in the graces of a fine gentleman, begin when he is a youngster of five living in London under the care of his mother, and continue until he is three-and-thirty and his father an old gentleman of seventy-one. From rather scanty knowledge, one gathers that as boy and young man Philip was not at all a bad sort. He was good-natured, good-looking, sensible, well informed; but, despite all his father's efforts, he never overcame a natural shyness and awkwardness, a brusqueness of speech, and a gaucherie, which did not conduce to success in the diplomatic service, the career which his father had chosen for him. To quick advancement in this service there was also for Philip the bar of his illegi-

[1] W. H. Craig, *Life of Lord Chesterfield*, p. 336.

timacy. He was twice elected Member of Parliament, but was too shy to qualify as an orator. He was appointed in 1756 resident at Hamburg; in 1763 he was envoy to the Diet at Ratisbon; in 1764 he became Resident Minister at the court of Dresden. This career of only moderate success was prematurely terminated by his death in 1768 at the age of thirty-six. It then came to light that Philip Stanhope had for several years been married to a worthy, but undistinguished wife, who had borne him two sons. His father's repeated counsel had in this, at least, succeeded in teaching him the art of discreet concealment under the guise of apparent frankness. Shocked as Lord Chesterfield must have been at the discovery of this imprudent marriage, he accepted the situation gracefully, and made generous provision for the support of his son's widow and the education of her little boys.

Worldling though he was, Chesterfield felt for this boy of his a very deep and tender affection. When Philip was seventeen, his father wrote to him: "Whatever I see or whatever I hear, my first consideration is, whether it can in any way be useful to you."[1] And two years later he writes: "Now that all tumultuous passions and quick sensations have subsided in me, and that I have no tormenting cares nor boisterous pleasures to agitate me, my greatest joy is to consider the fair prospect you have before you, and to hope and believe you will enjoy it."[2] Besides the father's love, there is in the letters also something of the passion of the creative artist, trying to model in a rather intractable medium a perfect work of art—the complete gentleman and courtier. "You have the means, you have the opportunities. Employ them, for God's sake, while you may, and make yourself that all-accomplished man that I wish to have you."[3] There is the same zest of artistry in the letters of worldly advice written between 1749 and 1769 to the young Lord Huntingdon, first published in 1923. These letters are in much the same vein as those to his son, save that in them parental authority gives place to the deference due to a nobleman his equal in all save years and experience. There is more than a little pathos in the affectionate concern of a father to secure for his son the only sort of happiness which his worldly philosophy thought worth while, to counteract as far as might be the harm done to the boy in the matter of his birth, particularly when both his

[1] Letter of 18 November, 1748.   [2] Letter of 13 June, 1751.
[3] Letter of 28 February, 1749.

fatherly affection and the artist's zeal for his art were to be so
largely frustrate. Nor did his other pupil in worldly wisdom,
the Lord Huntingdon, ever attain to any public distinction.
But Chesterfield was not to be discouraged. In his last
years, after the death of his son, he began again with another
Philip Stanhope, his godson and distant cousin who succeeded
him in the earldom. To this boy, from his sixth to his fifteenth
year, he wrote a series of 236 letters, first published in 1890,
containing advice of the same sort. Here again he wrote in
vain; for the fifth Earl of Chesterfield was described by
Madame d'Arblay in her *Diary* [1] as having "as little good
breeding as any man I ever met with."

But in addition to their human interest as the letters of
Lord Chesterfield to his son Philip, the collection has a larger
significance, as it unconsciously reveals the code of conduct
and the habits of thought of a great nobleman and fine gentleman of the court of George II. It has for eighteenth-century
England the same significance as that of Castiglione's *Courtier*
for Italy of the Renaissance. So completely did the book
reflect the temper of the age that it became a manual of
"practical morality," a book of etiquette for fashioning the
manners of ambitious youth, with its maxims arranged
alphabetically for ready reference under such headings as
Rules for Conversation, Friendship, Dignity of Manners,
Pleasure, Employment of Time. In the "advertisement"
to one such compilation which bears a date as late as 1813
the editor declares:

The abilities of Lord Chesterfield, to inculcate such precepts as
should form the mind and fashion the manners of youth, are too
universally admired to need encomium. In the Advice of that
noble Earl to his son, there are to be found such judicious remarks
on men, manners, and things, connected with so intimate a knowledge of the world, that the sentiments, considered as maxims,
form a very valuable system of education.

For an age when most men distrusted any sort of "enthusiasm," and agreed with Pope that good sense is the sum of
all the sciences and the supreme gift of Heaven—an age to
whose ideals our own seems ready in so many respects to
return—the advice of Lord Chesterfield left little to desire.
Yet even to the generation who first read the letters in published form, the cynical frankness of their worldly wisdom
came with something of a shock. The contemporary reviewers

[1] Vol. iv., p. 355.

temper their praise with smug regrets that with so much of good counsel should go so complete a disregard of the virtue of chastity, so low an estimate of the character of women. Dr. Johnson's famous dictum that the *Letters* "teach the morals of a whore and the manners of a dancing-master" is, of course, grossly untrue in both its indictments. Chesterfield regarded dancing as "a very trifling, silly thing," but one "to which people of sense are sometimes obliged to conform"; [1] and it is to polite gallantries rather than promiscuous libertinism that he gives his approval. "I should have thought that Lord ——, at his age, and with his parts and address, need not have been reduced to keeping an opera whore, in such a place as Paris, where so many women of fashion generously serve as volunteers." [2]

It is such passages as this that led the gentle poet Cowper to write of Chesterfield in his *Progress of Error*, written a half-dozen years after the publication of the *Letters*:

> Thou polished and high-finished foe to truth,
> Graybeard corrupter of our listening youth,
> To purge and skim away the filth of vice,
> That so refined it might the more entice,
> Then pour it on the morals of thy son;
> To taint *his* heart was worthy of *thine own*!

But this indictment, like the epigram of Johnson, is at best but an exaggeration of the truth. Chesterfield, who had in his make up nothing of the ascetic reformer, is in this phase of morality as in all others merely accepting the world as he finds it. "We must take most things as they are, we cannot make them what we would, nor often what they should be." [3] If strict continence is not to be expected of a young gentleman of fashion, is it after all so reprehensible that the young gentleman's father should be concerned to "purge and skim away the filth" which inheres in the more degrading associations of the undiscriminating libertine? Nor could Chesterfield, with very good grace, have urged on this natural son of his a virtue to which he himself made no pretence.

If, to notice another charge that has frequently been brought against the *Letters*, there is too much insistence on the externalities of life, on cultivating the Graces, on the duty of "shining," rather than the acquisition of solid worth, it must not be forgotten that the advice is addressed not to youth in general, but to a particular youth, Philip Stanhope, whose

[1] Letter of 19 November, 1745.   [2] Letter of 6 June, 1751.
[3] Letter of 27 May, 1753.

solid qualities were obscured by a natural gaucherie of manner. And this same awkward lad must be trained for the exacting profession of diplomat and courtier. It is with this career in mind that one should read the letter of 16 October, 1747, which inculcates the fine art of subtle flattery—which must never be "abject and criminal flattery" of vice or crime.

And much of the advice needs no apology whatever:

> Speak the language of the company that you are in; and speak it purely, and unlarded with any other. Never seem wiser, nor more learned, than the people you are with. Wear your learning, like your watch, in a private pocket; and do not pull it out and strike it, merely to show that you have one.[1]

There is not only sound counsel, but much shrewd observation, such as the well-known prediction made in the letter of 25 December, 1753, of impending revolution in France:

> The French nation reasons freely, which they never did before, upon matters of religion and government . . . the officers do so too; in short, all the symptoms which I have ever met with in history, previous to great changes and revolutions in Government, now exist, and daily increase in France.[2]

But if so much of Chesterfield's prophecy is of penetrating insight, the sentence which immediately follows is not so happy:

> I am glad of it; the rest of Europe will be the quieter, and have time to recover.

But it is, after all, not so much for the advice and wise observation that one reads Chesterfield's letters as for their unfailing grace and charm. Whatever the subject of the letter, whether it be addressed to the youngster of seven just beginning to read Roman history, to the boy of sixteen, "a fine gentleman, in a scarlet coat laced with gold, a brocade waistcoat, and all other suitable ornaments,"[3] or to the young man of twenty, for whom the doors of the Paris *salons* are opening hospitably—wherever one opens the book, there is the same quality of graceful style, unaffected yet always polished, the fine flower of eighteenth-century civilization. Lord Chesterfield stands revealed in these letters as the embodiment of all that he would have wished to find in his son—"a complete gentleman, and a delightful companion," a finished practitioner of the fine art of graceful living.

R. K. ROOT.

[1] Letter of 22 February, 1748.
[2] A somewhat similar sentiment is expressed in a letter of Chesterfield's to Lord Huntingdon, written 25 November, 1751.
[3] Letter of 3 April, 1747.

SELECT BIBLIOGRAPHY

WORKS. 'An Army in Waxwork,' 'An Essay upon Ears,' and 'An Essay upon Eyes,' in *Fog's Journal*, 1734; Contributions to *Common Sense*, 1737–9; Letters signed 'Geffery Broadbottom' to *Old England*, 1743; (with Edmund Waller) *The Case of Hanover Forces in the Pay of Great Britain, A Vindication, A Further Vindication*, and *The Interest of Hanover Steadily Pursued since the Accession*, 1743; *An Apology for a late Resignation*, 1748; Social topics in *The World*, 1753–6.

Posthumous Publications: *Miscellaneous Works of the late Philip Dormer, Earl of Chesterfield . . . to which are prefixed Memoirs of his Life . . . by M. Maty*, M.D., 2 vols., 4to, London, 1777, and 3 vols., 8vo, Dublin, 1777. The letters to his son first appeared in *Letters written by the Earl of Chesterfield to his Son, Philip Stanhope, together with several other pieces on various subjects, published by Mrs Eugenia Stanhope*, 2 vols., 4to, London, 1774. In 1845 was published *Letters of Philip Dormer Stanhope, Earl of Chesterfield*, edited with notes by Lord Mahon, 4 vols., London, 1845, which includes the letters to his son and to other correspondents. A supplementary volume of *Miscellanies* was added by the same editor in 1853. The edition of John Bradshaw, London and New York, 1892, contains the materials given by Lord Mahon with some new additions. The best edition of Chesterfield's *Letters to his Son* is that of Charles Strachey, with notes by Annette Calthrop, 2 vols., London, 1901.

Chesterfield's *Letters to his Godson and Successor* were first published by the Earl of Carnarvon, Oxford, 1890. *Letters of Lord Chesterfield to Lord Huntingdon* were published by A. F. Steuart, London, 1923. The best complete edition of Lord Chesterfield's *Letters* is that of Professor Bonamy Dobrée, 6 vols. 1932.

Unauthorised Collections of Chesterfield's Witticisms: *The New Foundling Hospital for Wit* (6 parts), 1768–71. *The Humours of the Times*, 1771. *Lord Chesterfield's Witticisms* (chiefly a reprint of the former two), 1773. *Wit à-la-mode*, 1778.

BIOGRAPHY. The first life of Chesterfield is that of Dr Maty prefixed to the *Miscellaneous Works* of 1777. More modern are *Memoirs of the life of Philip Dormer, fourth Earl of Chesterfield, with numerous letters now first published*, by W. Ernst, London, 1893; and the *Life of Lord Chesterfield*, by W. H. Craig, London, 1907, which particularly stresses the political aspects of his career. A good brief sketch of Chesterfield's life is that of Sir Sidney Lee in the *Dictionary of National Biography*, which, however, is not always just to Chesterfield's character. An interesting appraisal of Chesterfield's career is *Chesterfield and his Critics*, by Roger Coxon, London, 1925, which contains a few hitherto unpublished letters to various friends. An important critical essay, which was influential in correcting the unfavourable attitude towards Chesterfield prevalent throughout the nineteenth century, is that of J. Churton Collins, contained in his volume of *Essays and Studies*, London, 1895 (pages 193–262).

SELECT BIBLIOGRAPHY

ACKNOWLEDGMENT

THE two letters to Lord Huntingdon dated November 18, o.s. 1751, and November 21, 1752, are included in this edition by kind permission of the Medici Society.

CONTENTS

CONTENTS

LETTERS TO HIS SON

MY DEAR BOY,

I was pleased with your asking me, the last time I saw you, why I had left off writing; for I looked upon it as a sign that you liked and minded my letters. If that be the case, you shall hear from me often enough; and my letters may be of use to you, if you will give attention to them; otherwise it is only giving myself trouble to no purpose; for it signifies nothing to read a thing once, if one does not mind and remember it. It is a sure sign of a little mind to be doing one thing, and at the same time to be either thinking of another, or not thinking at all. One should always think of what one is about; when one is learning, one should not think of play; and when one is at play, one should not think of one's learning. Besides that, if you do not mind your book while you are at it, it will be a double trouble to you, for you must learn it all over again.

One of the most important points in life is decency; which is to do what is proper and where it is proper; for many things are proper at one time, and in one place, that are extremely improper in another; for example, it is very proper and decent that you should play some part of the day; but you must see that it would be very improper and indecent, if you were to fly your kite, or play at nine pins, while you are with Mr. Maittaire. It is very proper and decent to dance well; but then you must dance only at balls, and places of entertainment; for you would be reckoned a fool, if you were to dance at church, or at a funeral. I hope, by these examples, you understand the meaning of the word *Decency*; which in French is *Bienséance*; in Latin *Decorum*; and in Greek Πρέπον. Cicero says of it, "Sic hoc decorum, quod elucet in vitâ, movet approbationem eorum quibuscum vivitur, ordine et constantiâ et moderatione dictorum omnium atque factorum." By which you see how necessary decency is, to gain the approbation of mankind. Again, as I am sure you desire to gain Mr. Maittaire's approbation, without which you will never have mine; I dare say you will mind and give attention to whatever he says to you, and behave yourself seriously and decently, while you are with him; afterwards play, run, and jump, as much as ever you please.

DEAR BOY,   Bath, October 26, 1739.

Though Poetry differs much from Oratory in many things, yet it makes use of the same figures of Rhetoric; nay, it abounds in metaphors, similes, and allegories; and you may learn the purity of the language, and the ornaments of eloquence, as well by reading verse as prose.   Poetical diction, that is, poetical language, is more sublime and lofty than prose, and takes liberties which are not allowed in prose, and are called Poetical Licences.   This difference between verse and prose you will easily observe, if you read them both with attention.   In verse, things are seldom said plainly and simply, as one would say them in prose; but they are described and embellished; as, for example, what you hear the watchman say often in three words, *a cloudy morning*, is said thus in verse, in the tragedy of *Cato*:

> The dawn is overcast, the morning lowers,
> And heavily in clouds brings on the day.[1]

This is poetical diction, which would be improper in prose, though each word separately may be used in prose.

I will give you here a very pretty copy of verses of Mr. Waller's, which is extremely poetical and full of images.   It is to a lady who played upon the lute.   The lute, by the way, is an instrument with many strings, which are played upon by the fingers.

> Such moving sounds from such a careless touch;
> So little she concerned, and we so much.
> The trembling strings about her fingers crowd,
> And tell their joy, for every kiss, aloud.
> Small force there needs to make them tremble so,
> Touched by that hand, who would not tremble too?
> Here Love takes stand, and, while she charms the ear,
> Empties his quiver on the list'ning dear.
> Music so softens and disarms the mind,
> That not one arrow can resistance find.
> Thus the fair tyrant celebrates the prize,
> And acts herself the triumph of her eyes.
> So Nero, once, with harp in hand, surveyed
> His flaming Rome: and, as it burnt, he played.[2]

Mind all the poetical beauties of these verses.   He supposes the sounds of the strings when she touches them, to be the expres-

---

[1] The opening lines of Addison's *Cato*.

[2] Waller's poem quoted, not very exactly, by Lord Chesterfield, is entitled, *On Hearing my Lady Isabella Playing on the Lute*.   The opening lines run as follows:

> "Such moving sounds from such a careless touch,
> So unconcerned herself, and we so much.
> What art is this, that with so little pains
> Transports us thus, and o'er our spirit reigns?
> The trembling strings about her fingers crowd,
> And tell their joy, for every kiss, aloud.

sion of their joy for kissing her fingers. Then, he compares the trembling of the strings to the trembling of a lover, who is supposed to tremble with joy and awe, when touched by the person he loves. He represents Love (who, you know, is described as a little boy, with a bow, arrows, and a quiver) as standing by her, and shooting his arrows at people's hearts, while her music softens and disarms them. Then he concludes with that fine simile of Nero, a very cruel Roman Emperor, who set Rome on fire, and played on the harp all the while it was burning: for, as love is represented by the poets as fire and flames, so she, while people were burning for love for her, played, as Nero did while Rome, which he had set on fire, was burning. Pray get these verses by heart, against I see you. Adieu.

You will observe that these verses are all long, or heroic verses, that is, of ten syllables, or five feet, for a foot is two syllables.

DEAR BOY,   Bath, November 1, 1739.

Let us return to Oratory, or the art of speaking well; which should never be entirely out of your thoughts, since it is so useful in every part of life, and so absolutely necessary in most. A man can make no figure without it, in Parliament, in the Church, or in the law; and even in common conversation, a man that has acquired an easy and habitual eloquence, who speaks properly and accurately, will have a great advantage over those who speak incorrectly or inelegantly.

The business of Oratory, as I have told you before, is to persuade people; and you easily feel, that to please people is a great step towards persuading them. You must then, consequently, be sensible how advantageous it is for a man who speaks in public, whether it be in Parliament, or in the pulpit, or at the bar (that is, in the courts of law), to please his hearers so much as to gain their attention; which he can never do without the help of oratory. It is not enough to speak the language he speaks in, in its utmost purity, and according to the rules of grammar, but he must speak it elegantly, that is, he must use the best and the most expressive words, and put them in the best order. He should likewise adorn what he says by proper metaphors, similes, and the other figures of rhetoric; and he should enliven it, if he can, by quick and sprightly turns of wit. For example, supposing you had a mind to persuade

Mr. Maittaire to give you a holiday, would you bluntly say to him, "Give me a holiday"? That would certainly not be the way to persuade him to it. But you should endeavour first to please him, and gain his attention, by telling him, that your experience of his goodness and indulgence encouraged you to ask a favour of him; that, if he should not think proper to grant it, at least you hoped he would not take it ill that you asked it.

Then you should tell him what it was you wanted; that it was a holiday, for which you should give your reasons, as that you had such and such a thing to do, or such a place to go to. Then you might urge some argument, why he should not refuse you; as, that you have seldom asked the favour, and that you seldom will; and that the mind may sometimes require a little rest from labour as well as the body. This you may illustrate by a simile, and say, that as the bow is the stronger for being sometimes unstrung and unbent, so the mind will be capable of more attention for being now and then easy and relaxed.

This is a little oration, fit for such a little orator as you; but, however, it will make you understand what is meant by oratory and eloquence; which is to persuade. I hope you will have that talent hereafter in great matters.

DEAR BOY,   November 20, 1739.

As you are now reading the Roman History, I hope you do it with that care and attention which it deserves. The utility of History consists principally in the examples it gives us of the virtues and vices of those who have gone before us; upon which we ought to make the proper observations. History animates and excites us to the love and the practice of virtue; by showing us the regard and veneration that was always paid to great and virtuous men in the times in which they lived, and the praise and glory with which their names are perpetuated, and transmitted down to our times. The Roman History furnishes more examples of virtue and magnanimity, or greatness of mind, than any other. It was a common thing to see their Consuls and Dictators (who, you know, were their chief magistrates) taken from the plough, to lead their armies against their enemies; and, after victory, returning to their plough again, and passing the rest of their lives in modest retirement; a retirement more glorious, if possible, than the victories that preceded it! Many of their greatest men died so poor, that they were buried at the expense of the public.

Curius, who had no money of his own, refused a great sum that the Samnites offered him, saying, that he saw no glory in having money himself, but in commanding those that had. Cicero relates it thus: *Curio ad focum sedenti magnum auri pondus Samnites cum attulissent, repudiati ab eo sunt. Non enim aurum habere præclarum sibi videri, sed iis, qui haberent aurum, imperare.* And Fabricius, who had often commanded the Roman armies, and as often triumphed over their enemies, was found by his fireside, eating those roots and herbs which he had planted and cultivated himself in his own field. Seneca tells it thus: *Fabricius ad focum cœnat illas ipsas radices, quas, in agro repurgando, triumphalis senex vulsit.* Scipio, after a victory he had obtained in Spain, found among the prisoners a young princess of extreme beauty, who, he was informed, was soon to have been married to a man of quality of that country. He ordered her to be entertained and attended with the same care and respect as if she had been in her father's house; and, as soon as he could find her lover, he gave her to him, and added to her portion the money that her father had brought for her ransom. Valerius Maximus says, *Eximiæ formæ virginem accersitis parentibus et sponso inviolatam tradidit, et Juvenis, et Cœlebs, et Victor.* This was a most glorious example of moderation, continence, and generosity, which gained him the hearts of all the people of Spain; and made them say, as Livy tells us, *Venisse Diis simillimum juvenem, vincentem omnia, cum armis, tum benignitate ac beneficiis.*

Such are the rewards that always crown virtue, and such the characters that you should imitate, if you would be a great and a good man, which is the only way to be a happy one! Adieu!

DEAR BOY,   Monday.

I was very sorry that Mr. Maittaire did not give me such an account of you yesterday as I wished and expected. He takes so much pains to teach you, that he well deserves from you the returns of care and attention. Besides, pray consider, now that you have justly got the reputation of knowing much more than other boys of your age do, how shameful it would be for you to lose it, and to let other boys, that are now behind you, get before you. If you would but have attention, you have quickness enough to conceive, and memory enough to retain: but, without attention while you are learning, all the time you employ at your book is thrown away; and your shame will be the greater if you should be ignorant, when you had such opportunities of learning. An ignorant man is insignificant and contemptible; nobody cares for his company, and he can just be said to live, and that is all. There is a very pretty French epigram upon the death of such an ignorant, insignificant fellow; the sting of which is, that all that can be said of him is, that he was once alive, and that he is now dead. This is the epigram, which you may get by heart:

> Colas est mort de maladie,
>   Tu veux que j'en pleure le sort;
> Que diable veux-tu que j'en die?
>   Colas vivoit, Colas est mort.

Take care not to deserve the name of Colas, which I shall certainly give you if you do not learn well; and then that name will get about, and everybody will call you Colas; which will be much worse than Frisky.

You are now reading Mr. Rollin's *Ancient History* [1]: pray remember to have your maps by you when you read it, and desire Monsieur Pelnote to show you, in the maps, all the places you read of. Adieu!

DEAR BOY,   Longford, June 9, 1740.

I write to you now, in the supposition that you continue to deserve my attention as much as you did when I left London, and that Mr. Maittaire would commend you as much now as he did the last time he was with me; for, otherwise, you know very well that I should not concern myself about you. Take care, therefore, that when I come to town I may not find myself mistaken in the good opinion I entertained of you in my absence.

I hope you have got the linnets and bullfinches you so much wanted, and I recommend the bullfinches to your imitation. Bullfinches, you must know, have no natural note of their own, and never sing, unless taught; but will learn tunes better than any other birds. This they do by attention and memory; and you may observe, that, while they are taught, they listen with great care, and never jump about and kick their heels. Now I really think it would be a great shame for you to be outdone by your own bullfinch.

I take it for granted, that, by your late care and attention, you are now perfect in Latin verses, and that you may at present be called, what Horace desired to be called, *Romanæ fidicen*

[1] Charles Rollin, the French historian; born in 1661; died, 1741.

Lyræ. Your Greek too, I dare say, keeps pace with your Latin; and you have all your paradigms *ad ungeum.*

You cannot imagine what alterations and improvements I expect to find every day, now that you are more than *octennis.* And at this age, *non progredi* would be *regredi*, which would be very shameful.

Adieu! Do not write to me; for I shall be in no settled place to receive letters while I am in the country.

DEAR BOY,   Wednesday.

You behaved yourself so well at Mr. Boden's last Sunday, that you justly deserve commendation: besides, you encourage me to give you some rules of politeness and good-breeding, being persuaded that you will observe them.

Know then, that as learning, honour, and virtue are absolutely necessary to gain you the esteem and admiration of mankind, politeness and good-breeding are equally necessary to make you welcome and agreeable in conversation and common life. Great talents, such as honour, virtue, learning, and parts, are above the generality of the world, who neither possess them themselves, nor judge of them rightly in others: but all people are judges of the lesser talents, such as civility, affability, and an obliging, agreeable address and manner; because they feel the good effects of them, as making society easy and pleasing.

Good-sense must, in many cases, determine good-breeding; because the same thing that would be civil at one time, and to one person, may be quite otherwise at another time, and to another person: but there are some general rules of good-breeding that hold always true, and in all cases. As, for example, it is always extremely rude to answer only Yes, or No, to anybody, without adding, Sir, my Lord, or Madam, according to the quality of the person you speak to; as, in French, you must always say, *Monsieur, Milord, Madame,* and *Mademoiselle.* I suppose you know that every married woman is, in French, *Madame,* and every unmarried one is *Mademoiselle.*

It is likewise extremely rude, not to give the proper attention and a civil answer when people speak to you; or to go away, or be doing something else, while they are speaking to you; for that convinces them that you despise them, and do not think it worth your while to hear or answer what they say. I dare say I need not tell you how rude it is, to take the best place in a room, or to seize immediately upon what you like at table, without offering first to help others, as if you considered nobody but yourself. On the contrary, you should always endeavour to procure all the conveniences you can to the people you are with. Besides being civil, which is absolutely necessary, the perfection of good-breeding is, to be civil with ease, and in a gentlemanlike manner. For this, you should observe the French people, who excel in it, and whose politeness seems as easy and natural as any other part of their conversation; whereas the English are often awkward in their civilities, and, when they mean to be civil, are too much ashamed to get it out.

But, pray, do you remember never to be ashamed of doing what is right: you would have a great deal of reason to be ashamed, if you were not civil; but what reason can you have to be ashamed of being civil? And why not say a civil and an obliging thing as easily and as naturally as you would ask what o'clock it is? This kind of bashfulness, which is justly called by the French *mauvaise honte*, is the distinguishing character of an English booby, who is frightened out of his wits when people of fashion speak to him; and, when he is to answer them, blushes, stammers, can hardly get out what he would say, and becomes really ridiculous from a groundless fear of being laughed at: whereas, a real well-bred man would speak to all the Kings in the world with as little concern and as much ease as he would speak to you.

Remember, then, that to be civil, and to be civil with ease (which is properly called good-breeding), is the only way to be beloved and well received in company; that to be ill-bred and rude is intolerable, and the way to be kicked out of company; and that to be bashful is to be ridiculous. As I am sure you will mind and practise all this, I expect that, when you are *novennis*, you will not only be the best scholar, but the best-bred boy in England of your age. Adieu!

DEAR BOY,   Spa, July 25, N.S. 1741.

I have often told you in my former letters (and it is most certainly true) that the strictest and most scrupulous honour and virtue can alone make you esteemed and valued by mankind; that parts and learning can alone make you admired and celebrated by them; but that the possession of lesser talents was most absolutely necessary towards making you liked, beloved, and sought after in private life. Of these lesser talents, good-breeding is the principal and most necessary one, not only as it is very important in itself; but as it adds great lustre to the more solid advantages both of the heart and the mind.

I have often touched upon good-breeding to you before; so that this letter shall be upon the next necessary qualification to it, which is a genteel, easy manner and carriage, wholly free from those odd tricks, ill habits, and awkwardnesses, which even very many worthy and sensible people have in their behaviour. However trifling a genteel manner may sound, it is of very great consequence towards pleasing in private life, especially the women; which, one time or other, you will think worth pleasing; and I have known many a man, from his awkwardness, give people such a dislike of him at first, that all his merit could not get the better of it afterwards. Whereas a genteel manner prepossesses people in your favour, bends them towards you, and makes them wish to like you.

Awkwardness can proceed but from two causes; either from not having kept good company, or from not having attended to it. As for your keeping good company, I will take care of that; do you take care to observe their ways and manners, and to form your own upon them. Attention is absolutely necessary for this, as indeed it is for everything else; and a man without attention is not fit to live in the world. When an awkward fellow first comes into a room, it is highly probable that his sword gets between his legs, and throws him down, or makes him stumble at least; when he has recovered this accident, he goes and places himself in the very place of the whole room where he should not; there he soon lets his hat fall down; and, taking it up again, throws down his cane; in recovering his cane, his hat falls a second time; so that he is a quarter of an hour before he is in order again. If he drinks tea or coffee, he certainly scalds his mouth, and lets either the cup or the saucer fall, and spills the tea or coffee in his breeches. At dinner, his awkwardness distinguishes itself particularly, as he has more to do: there he holds his knife, fork, and spoon differently from other people; eats with his knife to the great danger of his mouth, picks his teeth with his fork, and puts his spoon, which has been in his throat twenty times, into the dishes again. If he is to carve, he can never hit the joint; but, in his vain efforts to cut through the bone, scatters the sauce in everybody's face. He generally daubs himself with soup and grease, though his napkin is commonly stuck through a button-hole, and tickles his chin. When he drinks, he infallibly coughs in his glass, and besprinkles the company. Besides all this, he has strange tricks and gestures; such as snuffing up his nose, making faces, putting his fingers in his nose, or blowing it and looking afterwards in his handkerchief, so as to make the company sick. His hands are troublesome to him, when he has not something in them, and he does not know where to put them; but they are in perpetual motion between his bosom and his breeches: he does not wear his clothes, and in short does nothing, like other people. All this, I own, is not in any degree criminal; but it is highly disagreeable and ridiculous in company, and ought most carefully to be avoided by whoever desires to please.

From this account of what you should not do, you may easily judge what you should do; and a due attention to the manners of people of fashion, and who have seen the world, will make it habitual and familiar to you.

There is, likewise, an awkwardness of expression and words, most carefully to be avoided; such as false English, bad pronunciation, old sayings, and common proverbs; which are so many proofs of having kept bad and low company. For example: if, instead of saying that tastes are different, and that every man has his own peculiar one, you should let off a proverb, and say, That what is one man's meat is another man's poison; or else, Every one as they like, as the good man said when he kissed his cow; everybody would be persuaded that you had never kept company with anybody above footmen and housemaids.

Attention will do all this; and without attention nothing is to be done: want of attention, which is really want of thought, is either folly or madness. You should not only have attention to everything, but a quickness of attention, so as to observe, at once, all the people in the room; their motions, their looks, and their words; and yet without staring at them, and seeming to be an observer. This quick and unobserved observation is of infinite advantage in life, and is to be acquired with care; and, on the contrary, what is called absence, which is a thoughtlessness, and want of attention about what is doing, makes a man so like either a fool or a madman, that, for my part, I see no real difference. A fool never had thought; a madman has lost it; and an absent man is, for the time, without it.

Adieu! Direct your next to me, *chez Monsieur Chabert, Banquier, à Paris*; and take care that I find the improvements I expect at my return.

DEAR BOY,   Spa, August 6, 1741.

I am very well pleased with the several performances you sent me, and still more so with Mr. Maittaire's letter, that accompanied them, in which he gives me a much better account of you than he did in his former. *Laudari à laudato viro*, was always a commendable ambition; encourage that ambition, and continue to deserve the praises of the praiseworthy. While you do so, you shall have whatever you will from me; and when you cease to do so, you shall have nothing.

I am glad you have begun to compose a little; it will give you an habit of thinking upon subjects, which is at least as necessary as reading them: therefore pray send me your thoughts upon this subject:

Non sibi, sed toti genitum se credere mundo.[1]

It is a part of Cato's character in Lucan; who says, that Cato did not think himself born for himself only, but for all mankind. Let me know, then, whether you think that a man is born only for his own pleasure and advantage, or whether he is not obliged to contribute to the good of the society in which he lives, and of all mankind in general. This is certain, that every man receives advantages from society, which he could not have, if he were the only man in the world; therefore, is he not, in some measure, in debt to society? and is he not obliged to do for others what they do for him? You may do this in English or Latin, which you please; for it is the thinking part, and not the language, that I mind in this case.

I warned you, in my last, against those disagreeable tricks and awkwardnesses which many people contract when they are young, by the negligence of their parents, and cannot get quit of them when they are old; such as odd motions, strange postures, and ungenteel carriage. But there is likewise an awkwardness of the mind, that ought to be, and with care may be, avoided: as, for instance, to mistake or forget names; to speak of Mr. What-d'ye-call-him, or Mrs. Thingum, or How-d'ye-call-her, is excessively awkward and ordinary. To call people by improper titles and appellations is so too; as my Lord, for Sir; and Sir, for my Lord. To begin a story or narration, when you are not perfect in it, and cannot go through with it, but are forced, possibly, to say, in the middle of it, "I have forgot the rest," is very unpleasant and bungling. One must be extremely exact, clear, and perspicuous in everything one says; otherwise,

---

[1] *Pharsalia*, ii, 381, "Nec sibi," etc.

instead of entertaining or informing others, one only tires and puzzles them.

The voice and manner of speaking, too, are not to be neglected: some people almost shut their mouths when they speak, and mutter so, that they are not to be understood; others speak so fast, and sputter, that they are not to be understood either; some always speak as loud as if they were talking to deaf people; and others so low that one cannot hear them. All these habits are awkward and disagreeable; and are to be avoided by attention: they are the distinguishing marks of the ordinary people, who have had no care taken of their education. You cannot imagine how necessary it is to mind all these little things; for I have seen many people, with great talents, ill received, for want of having these talents too; and others well received, only from their little talents, and who had no great ones.

Sir,   Saturday.

The fame of your erudition, and other shining qualifications, having reached to Lord Orrery,[1] he desired me, that you might dine with him and his son, Lord Boyle, next Sunday; which I told him you should. By this time, I suppose, you have heard from him; but, if you have not, you must, however, go there between two and three to-morrow, and say, that you come to wait upon Lord Boyle, according to his Lordship's orders, which I informed you of. As this will deprive me of the honour and pleasure of your company at dinner to-morrow, I will hope for it at breakfast, and shall take care to have your chocolate ready.

Though I need not tell one of your age, experience, and knowledge of the world, how necessary good-breeding is, to recommend one to mankind; yet, as your various occupations of Greek and cricket, Latin and pitch-farthing, may possibly divert your attention from this object, I take the liberty of reminding you of it, and desiring you to be very well-bred at Lord Orrery's. It is good-breeding alone that can prepossess people in your favour at first sight; more time being necessary to discover greater talents. This good-breeding, you know, does not consist in low bows and formal ceremony; but in an easy, civil, and respectful behaviour. You will, therefore, take care to answer with complaisance, when you are spoken to; to

[1] John, who succeeded his father in 1731 as fifth Earl of Orrery, and in 1753 succeeded to the Earldom of Cork; born 1707, died 1762.

place yourself at the lower end of the table, unless bid to go higher; to drink first to the lady of the house, and next to the master; not to eat awkwardly or dirtily; not to sit when others stand; and to do all this with an air of complaisance, and not with a grave, sour look, as if you did it all unwillingly. I do not mean a silly, insipid smile, that fools have when they would be civil; but an air of sensible good-humour. I hardly know anything so difficult to attain, or so necessary to possess, as perfect good-breeding; which is equally inconsistent with a stiff formality, an impertinent forwardness, and an awkward bashfulness. A little ceremony is often necessary; a certain degree of firmness is absolutely so; and an outward modesty is extremely becoming: the knowledge of the world, and your own observations, must, and alone can, tell you the proper quantities of each.

Mr. Fitzgerald was with me yesterday, and commended you much; go on to deserve commendations, and you will certainly meet with them. Adieu.

DEAR BOY,   Dublin Castle, November 19, 1745.

I have received your last Saturday's performance, with which I am very well satisfied. I know or have heard of no Mr. St. Maurice; and young Pain, whom I have made an Ensign, was here upon the spot, as were every one of those I have named in these new levies.

Now that the Christmas breaking-up draws near, I have ordered Mr. Desnoyers to go to you, during that time, to teach you to dance. I desire you will particularly attend to the graceful motion of your arms; which, with the manner of putting on your hat, and giving your hand, is all that a gentleman need attend to. Dancing is in itself a very trifling, silly thing; but it is one of those established follies to which people of sense are sometimes obliged to conform; and then they should be able to do it well. And, though I would not have you a dancer, yet, when you do dance, I would have you dance well, as I would have you do everything you do, well.

There is no one thing so trifling, but which (if it is to be done at all) ought to be done well. And I have often told you, that I wished you even played at pitch, and cricket, better than any boy at Westminster. For instance; dress is a very foolish thing; and yet it is a very foolish thing for a man not to be well dressed, according to his rank and way of life; and it is so far from being a disparagement to any man's understanding, that it is rather a proof of it, to be as well dressed as those whom he lives with: the difference in this case, between a man of sense and a fop, is, that the fop values himself upon his dress; and the man of sense laughs at it, at the same time that he knows he must not neglect it: there are a thousand foolish customs of this kind, which, not being criminal, must be complied with, and even cheerfully, by men of sense. Diogenes the Cynic was a wise man for despising them; but a fool for showing it. Be wiser than other people if you can; but do not tell them so.

It is a very fortunate thing for Sir Charles Hotham [1] to have fallen into the hands of one of your age, experience, and knowledge of the world. I am persuaded you will take infinite care of him. Good night.

DEAR BOY,   Bath, October 4, O.S. 1746.

Though I employ so much of my time in writing to you, I confess I have often my doubts whether it is to any purpose. I know how unwelcome advice generally is; I know that those who want it most, like it and follow it least; and I know, too, that the advice of parents, more particularly, is ascribed to the moroseness, the imperiousness, or the garrulity of old age. But then, on the other hand, I flatter myself, that as your own reason, though too young as yet to suggest much to you of itself, is however, strong enough to enable you, both to judge of, and receive plain truths: I flatter myself (I say) that your own reason, young as it is, must tell you, that I can have no interest but yours in the advice I give you; and that consequently, you will at least weigh and consider it well: in which case, some of it will, I hope, have its effect. Do not think that I mean to dictate as a parent; I only mean to advise as a friend, and an indulgent one too: and do not apprehend that I mean to check your pleasures; of which, on the contrary, I only desire to be the guide, not the censor. Let my experience supply your want of it, and clear your way, in the progress of your youth, of those thorns and briars which scratched and disfigured me in the course of mine. I do not, therefore, so much as hint to you, how absolutely dependent you are upon me; that you neither have, nor can have a shilling in the world

---

[1] Lord Chesterfield's nephew, son of Sir Charles and Lady Gertrude Hotham, a lad about the same age as young Stanhope. He succeeded to the baronetcy in 1737, but dying without issue in 1767, it reverted to his uncle, Beaumont.

but from me; and that, as I have no womanish weakness for your person, your merit must, and will, be the only measure of my kindness. I say, I do not hint these things to you, because I am convinced that you will act right, upon more noble and generous principles: I mean, for the sake of doing right, and out of affection and gratitude to me.

I have so often recommended to you attention and application to whatever you learn, that I do not mention them now as duties; but I point them out to you as conducive, nay, absolutely necessary to your pleasures; for can there be a greater pleasure than to be universally allowed to excel those of one's own age and manner of life? And, consequently, can there be anything more mortifying than to be excelled by them? In this latter case, your shame and regret must be greater than anybody's, because everybody knows the uncommon care which has been taken of your education, and the opportunities you have had of knowing more than others of your age. I do not confine the application which I recommend, singly to the view and emulation of excelling others (though that is a very sensible pleasure and a very warrantable pride); but I mean likewise to excel in the thing itself; for, in my mind, one may as well not know a thing at all, as know it but imperfectly. To know a little of anything, gives neither satisfaction nor credit; but often brings disgrace or ridicule.

Mr. Pope says, very truly:

> A little knowledge is a dangerous thing:
> Drink deep, or taste not the Castalian spring.[1]

And what is called a *smattering* of everything, infallibly constitutes a coxcomb. I have often, of late, reflected what an unhappy man I must now have been, if I had not acquired in my youth some fund and taste of learning. What could I have done with myself, at this age, without them? I must, as many ignorant people do, have destroyed my health and faculties by sotting away the evenings; or, by wasting them frivolously in the tattle of women's company, must have exposed myself to the ridicule and contempt of those very women; or, lastly, I must have hanged myself, as a man once did, for weariness of putting on and pulling off his shoes and stockings every day. My books, and only my books, are now left me; and I daily find what Cicero says of learning, to be true: "Hæc studia," says he, "adolescentiam alunt, senectutem oblectant, secundas

---

[1] In the *Essay on Criticism*, 215.

res ornant, adversis perfugium ac solatium præbent, delectant
domi, non impediunt foris, pernoctant nobiscum, peregrinantur,
rusticantur."

I do not mean, by this, to exclude conversation out of the
pleasures of an advanced age; on the contrary, it is a very great
and a very rational pleasure, at all ages; but the conversation
of the ignorant is no conversation, and gives even them
no pleasure: they tire of their own sterility, and have not
matter enough to furnish them with words to keep up a
conversation.

Let me, therefore, most earnestly recommend to you to
hoard up, while you can, a great stock of knowledge; for though,
during the dissipation of your youth, you may not have occasion
to spend much of it, yet, you may depend upon it, that a time
will come when you will want it to maintain you. Public
granaries are filled in plentiful years; not that it is known that
the next, or the second, or third year will prove a scarce one;
but because it is known, that, sooner or later, such a year will
come, in which the grain will be wanted.

I will say no more to you upon this subject; you have
Mr. Harte [1] with you to enforce it; you have Reason to assent
to the truth of it; so that, in short, "you have Moses and the
Prophets; if you will not believe them, neither will you believe,
though one rose from the dead." Do not imagine that the
knowledge which I so much recommend to you, is confined to
books, pleasing, useful, and necessary as that knowledge is: but
I comprehend in it the great knowledge of the world, still more
necessary than that of books. In truth, they assist one another
reciprocally; and no man will have either perfectly, who has
not both. The knowledge of the world is only to be acquired
in the world, and not in a closet. Books alone will never
teach it you; but they will suggest many things to your observation, which might otherwise escape you; and your own

---

[1] The Rev. Walter Harte, M.A., of Oxford, who had been selected by
Lord Chesterfield as travelling tutor to his son, and who will be found
frequently mentioned in the course of this correspondence. The choice,
though made on the recommendation of Lord Lyttelton, was not judicious,
or at least not successful. "We have reason to suspect," says Dr. Maty,
"that Mr. Harte's partiality to Greek, Latin, German law, and Gothic
erudition, rendered him rather remiss in other points." And indeed at
the very outset Lord Chesterfield writes of him: "Cet Anglois est d'une
érudition consommée . . . mais il ne sera guère propre à donner les
manières ou le ton de la bonne compagnie; chose pourtant très nécessaire."
(To Madame de Monconseil, June 24, 1745.)

Harte published a poetical collection called the *Amaranth, a History of
Gustavus Adolphus*, and *Essays on Husbandry*. He died in 1774.

observations upon mankind, when compared with those which you will find in books, will help you to fix the true point.

To know mankind well, requires full as much attention and application as to know books, and, it may be, more sagacity and discernment. I am at this time, acquainted with many elderly people, who have all passed their whole lives in the great world, but with such levity and inattention, that they know no more of it now, than they did at fifteen. Do not flatter yourself, therefore, with the thought that you can acquire this knowledge in the frivolous chit-chat of idle companies; no, you must go much deeper than that. You must look into people, as well as at them. Almost all people are born with all the passions, to a certain degree; but almost every man has a prevailing one, to which the others are subordinate. Search every one for that ruling passion [1]; pry into the recesses of his heart, and observe the different workings of the same passion in different people. And, when you have found out the prevailing passion of any man, remember never to trust him where that passion is concerned. Work upon him by it, if you please; but be upon your guard yourself against it, whatever professions he may make you.

I would desire you to read this letter twice over, but that I much doubt whether you will read once to the end of it. I will trouble you no longer now; but we will have more upon this subject hereafter. Adieu.

I have this moment received your letter from Schaffhausen; in the date of it you forgot the month.

DEAR BOY,   Bath, October 9, O.S. 1746.

Your distress in your journey from Heidelberg to Schaffhausen, your lying upon straw, your black bread, and your broken *Berline*, are proper seasonings for the greater fatigues and distresses which you must expect in the course of your travels; and, if one had a mind to moralise, one might call them the samples of the accidents, rubs, and difficulties, which every man meets with in his journey through life. In this journey, the understanding is the *voiture* that must carry you through; and in proportion as that is stronger or weaker, more or less in repair, your journey will be better or worse; though, at best

Search then the ruling passion; there alone
The wild are constant, and the cunning known.
POPE, *Moral Essays*, I, 274.

you will now and then find some bad roads, and some bad inns. Take care, therefore, to keep that necessary *voiture* in perfect good repair; examine, improve, and strengthen it every day: it is in the power, and ought to be the care, of every man to do it; he that neglects it, deserves to feel, and certainly will feel, the fatal effects of that negligence.

A propos of negligence; I must say something to you upon that subject. You know I have often told you, that my affection for you was not a weak, womanish one; and, far from blinding me, it makes me but more quick-sighted, as to your faults: those it is not only my right, but my duty, to tell you of; and it is your duty and your interest to correct them. In the strict scrutiny which I have made into you, I have (thank God) hitherto not discovered any vice of the heart, or any peculiar weakness of the head; but I have discovered laziness, inattention, and indifference; faults which are only pardonable in old men, who, in the decline of life, when health and spirits fail, have a kind of claim to that sort of tranquillity. But a young man should be ambitious to shine and excel; alert, active, and indefatigable in the means of doing it; and, like Cæsar, *Nil actum reputans, si quid superesset agendum.* You seem to want that *vivida vis animi,* which spurs and excites most young men to please, to shine, to excel. Without the desire and the pains necessary to be considerable, depend upon it, you never can be so; as, without the desire and attention necessary to please, you never can please. *Nullum numen abest, si sit prudentia,* is unquestionably true with regard to everything except poetry; and I am very sure that any man of common understanding may, by proper culture, care, attention, and labour, make himself whatever he pleases, except a good poet.

Your destination is the great and busy world; your immediate object is the affairs, the interests, and the history, the constitutions, the customs, and the manners of the several parts of Europe. In this, any man of common sense may, by common application, be sure to excel. Ancient and Modern History are, by attention, easily attainable. Geography and Chronology the same; none of them requiring any uncommon share of genius or invention. Speaking and writing clearly, correctly, and with ease and grace, are certainly to be acquired, by reading the best authors with care, and by attention to the best living models. These are the qualifications more particularly necessary for you in your department, which you may be possessed of, if you please; and which, I tell you fairly, I shall be very angry with you, if you are not; because, as you have the means in your hands, it will be your own fault only.

If care and application are necessary to the acquiring of those qualifications, without which you can never be considerable, nor make a figure in the world; they are not less necessary with regard to the lesser accomplishments, which are requisite to make you agreeable and pleasing in society. In truth, whatever is worth doing at all is worth doing well; and nothing can be done well without attention: I therefore carry the necessity of attention down to the lowest things, even to dancing and dress. Custom has made dancing sometimes necessary for a young man; therefore mind it while you learn it, that you may learn to do it well, and not be ridiculous, though in a ridiculous act. Dress is of the same nature: you must dress: therefore attend to it; not in order to rival or to excel a fop in it, but in order to avoid singularity, and consequently ridicule. Take great care always to be dressed like the reasonable people of your own age, in the place where you are; whose dress is never spoken of one way or another, as either too negligent or too much studied.

What is commonly called an absent man, is commonly either a very weak, or a very affected man; but be he which he will, he is, I am sure, a very disagreeable man in company. He fails in all the common offices of civility; he seems not to know those people to-day, with whom yesterday he appeared to live in intimacy. He takes no part in the general conversation; but, on the contrary, breaks into it from time to time with some start of his own, as if he waked from a dream. This (as I said before) is a sure indication, either of a mind so weak that it is not able to bear above one object at a time; or so affected, that it would be supposed to be wholly engrossed by, and directed to, some very great and important objects. Sir Isaac Newton,[1] Mr. Locke,[2] and (it may be) five or six more, since the creation of the world, may have had a right to absence, from that intense thought which the things they were investigating required. But if a young man, and a man of the world, who has no such avocations to plead, will claim and exercise that right of absence in company, his pretended right should, in my mind, be turned into an involuntary absence, by his perpetual exclusion out of company. However frivolous a company may be, still, while you are among them, do not show them, by your inattention, that you think them so; but rather take their tone, and conform

---

[1] Born 1642, died 1727.   [2] Born 1632, died 1704.

in some degree to their weakness, instead of manifesting your contempt for them.

There is nothing that people bear more impatiently, or forgive less, than contempt; and an injury is much sooner forgotten than an insult. If, therefore, you would rather please than offend, rather be well than ill spoken of, rather be loved than hated, remember to have that constant attention about you, which flatters every man's little vanity; and the want of which, by mortifying his pride, never fails to excite his resentment, or at least his ill-will. For instance: most people (I might say, all people) have their weaknesses; they have their aversions and their likings, to such or such things; so that if you were to laugh at a man for his aversion to a cat, or cheese (which are common antipathies), or, by inattention and negligence, to let them come in his way, where you could prevent it, he would, in the first case, think himself insulted, and, in the second, slighted; and would remember both. Whereas your care to procure for him what he likes, and to remove from him what he hates, shows him that he is at least an object of your attention; flatters his vanity, and makes him possibly more your friend, than a more important service would have done. With regard to women, attentions still below these are necessary, and, by the custom of the world, in some measure due, according to the laws of good-breeding.

My long and frequent letters, which I send you in great doubt of their success, put me in mind of certain papers, which you have very lately, and I formerly, sent up to kites, along the string, which we called messengers; some of them the wind used to blow away, others were torn by the string, and but few of them got up and stuck to the kite. But I will content myself now, as I did then, if some of my present messengers do but stick to you. Adieu!

DEAR BOY,   London, December 2, O.S. 1746.

I have not, in my present situation,[1] time to write to you, either so much or so often as I used, while I was in a place of much more leisure and profit [2]: but my affection for you must not be judged by the number of my letters; and, though the one lessens, the other, I assure you, does not.

I have just now received your letter of the 25th past, N.S., and, by the former post, one from Mr. Harte; with both which

[1] Secretary of State.   [2] Lord-Lieutenant of Ireland.

I am very well pleased: with Mr. Harte's, for the good account which he gives me of you; with yours, for the good account you give me of what I desired to be informed of. Pray continue to give me further information of the form of government of the country you are now in; which, I hope, you will know most minutely before you leave it. The inequality of the town of Lausanne seems to be very convenient in this cold weather; because going up hill and down will keep you warm.—You say there is a good deal of good company; pray, are you got into it? Have you made acquaintances, and with whom? Let me know some of their names. Do you learn German yet, to read, write, and speak it?

Yesterday, I saw a letter from Monsieur Bochat to a friend of mine, which gave me the greatest pleasure that I have felt this great while; because it gives so very good an account of you. Among other things which Monsieur Bochat says to your advantage, he mentions the tender uneasiness and concern that you showed during my illness; for which (though I will say that you owe it me) I am obliged to you; sentiments of gratitude not being universal, nor even common. As your affection for me can only proceed from your experience and conviction of my fondness for you (for to talk of natural affection is talking nonsense), the only return I desire is, what it is chiefly your interest to make me; I mean, your invariable practice of Virtue, and your indefatigable pursuit of knowledge. Adieu! and be persuaded that I shall love you extremely, while you deserve it; but not one moment longer.

DEAR BOY,   London, December 9, O.S. 1746.

Though I have very little time, and though I write by this post to Mr. Harte, yet I cannot send a packet to Lausanne without a word or two to yourself. I thank you for your letter of congratulation which you wrote me, notwithstanding the pain it gave you. The accident that caused the pain was, I presume, owing to that degree of giddiness which I have sometimes taken the liberty to speak to you of. The post I am now in, though the object of most people's views and desires, was in some degree inflicted upon me; and a certain concurrence of circumstances obliged me to engage in it; but I feel that it requires more strength of body and mind than I have, to go through with it. Were you three or four years older, you should share in my trouble, and I would have taken you into my office; but I hope you will employ those three or four years so well, as to make yourself capable of being of use to me, if I should continue in it so long. The reading, writing, and speaking the modern languages correctly; the knowledge of the laws of nations, and the particular constitution of the Empire; of History, Geography, and Chronology; are absolutely necessary to this business, for which I have always intended you. With these qualifications, you may very possibly be my successor, though not my immediate one.

I hope you employ your whole time, which few people do; and that you put every moment to profit of some kind or other. I call company, walking, riding, etc., employing one's time, and, upon proper occasions, very usefully; but what I cannot forgive in anybody, is sauntering, and doing nothing at all, with a thing so precious as time, and so irrecoverable when lost.

Are you acquainted with any ladies at Lausanne? and do you behave yourself with politeness enough to make them desire your company?

I must finish: God bless you!

DEAR BOY,   London, March 6, O.S. 1747.

Whatever you do, will always affect me, very sensibly, one way or another; and I am now most agreeably affected by two letters, which I have lately seen from Lausanne, upon your subject; the one was from Madame St. Germain, the other from Monsieur Pampigny: they both give so good an account of you, that I thought myself obliged, in justice both to them and to you, to let you know it. Those who deserve a good character, ought to have the satisfaction of knowing that they have it, both as a reward and as an encouragement. They write, that you are not only *décrotté*, but tolerably well-bred; and that the English crust of awkward bashfulness, shyness, and toughness (of which, by the bye, you had your share), is pretty well rubbed off. I am most heartily glad of it; for, as I have often told you, those lesser talents, of an engaging, insinuating manner, an easy good-breeding, a genteel behaviour and address, are of infinitely more advantage than they are generally thought to be, especially here in England. Virtue and learning, like gold, have their intrinsic value; but if they are not polished, they certainly lose a great deal of their lustre: and even polished brass will pass upon more people than rough gold.

What a number of sins does the cheerful, easy good-breeding

of the French frequently cover? Many of them want common sense, many more common learning; but, in general, they make up so much, by their manner, for those defects, that, frequently, they pass undiscovered. I have often said, and do think, that a Frenchman, who, with a fund of virtue, learning, and good sense, had the manners and good-breeding of his country, is the perfection of human nature. This perfection you may, if you please, and I hope you will, arrive at. You know what virtue is: you may have it if you will; it is in every man's power; and miserable is the man who has it not. Good sense God has given you. Learning you already possess enough of, to have, in a reasonable time, all that a man need have. With this, you are thrown out early into the world, where it will be your own fault if you do not acquire all the other accomplishments necessary to complete and adorn your character.

You will do well to make your compliments to Madame St. Germain and Monsieur Pampigny; and tell them how sensible you are of their partiality to you, in the advantageous testimonies which, you are informed, they have given of you here.

Adieu! Continue to deserve such testimonies; and then you will not only deserve, but enjoy, my truest affection.

DEAR BOY,   London, March 27, O.S. 1747.

Pleasure is the rock which most young people split upon; they launch out with crowded sails in quest of it, but without a compass to direct their course, or reason sufficient to steer the vessel; for want of which, pain and shame, instead of Pleasure, are the returns of their voyage. Do not think that I mean to snarl at Pleasure, like a Stoic, or to preach against it, like a parson; no, I mean to point it out, and recommend it to you, like an Epicurean: I wish you a great deal; and my only view is to hinder you from mistaking it.

The character which most young men first aim at is, that of a Man of Pleasure; but they generally take it upon trust; and, instead of consulting their own taste and inclinations, they blindly adopt whatever those, with whom they chiefly converse, are pleased to call by the name of Pleasure; and a *Man of Pleasure*, in the vulgar acceptation of that phrase, means only a beastly drunkard, an abandoned whoremaster, and a profligate swearer and curser. As it may be of use to you, I am not unwilling. though at the same time ashamed, to own, that the vices of my youth proceeded much more from my silly resolution of being what I heard called a Man of Pleasure, than from my own inclinations. I always naturally hated drinking; and yet I have often drunk, with disgust at the time, attended by great sickness the next day, only because I then considered drinking as a necessary qualification for a fine gentleman, and a Man of Pleasure.

The same as to gaming. I did not want money, and consequently had no occasion to play for it; but I thought Play another necessary ingredient in the composition of a Man of Pleasure, and accordingly I plunged into it without desire, at first; sacrificed a thousand real pleasures to it; and made myself solidly uneasy by it, for thirty the best years of my life.

I was even absurd enough, for a little while, to swear, by way of adorning and completing the shining character which I affected; but this folly I soon laid aside, upon finding both the guilt and the indecency of it.

Thus seduced by fashion, and blindly adopting nominal pleasures, I lost real ones; and my fortune impaired, and my constitution shattered, are, I must confess, the just punishment of my errors.

Take warning then by them; choose your pleasures for yourself, and do not let them be imposed upon you. Follow nature, and not fashion: weigh the present enjoyment of your pleasures against the necessary consequences of them, and then let your own common sense determine your choice.

Were I to begin the world again, with the experience which I now have of it, I would lead a life of real, not of imaginary, pleasure. I would enjoy the pleasures of the table, and of wine; but stop short of the pains inseparably annexed to an excess in either. I would not, at twenty years, be a preaching missionary of abstemiousness and sobriety; and I should let other people do as they would, without formally and sententiously rebuking them for it: but I would be most firmly resolved not to destroy my own faculties and constitution, in compliance to those who have no regard to their own. I would play to give me pleasure, but not to give me pain; that is, I would play for trifles, in mixed companies, to amuse myself, and conform to custom: but I would take care not to venture for sums, which, if I won, I should not be the better for; but, if I lost, should be under a difficulty to pay; and, when paid, would oblige me to retrench in several other articles. Not to mention the quarrels which deep play commonly occasions.

I would pass some of my time in reading, and the rest in the company of people of sense and learning, and chiefly those above me; and I would frequent the mixed companies of men and women of fashion, which, though often frivolous, yet they unbend and refresh the mind, not uselessly, because they certainly polish and soften the manners.

These would be my pleasures and amusements, if I were to live the last thirty years over again: they are rational ones; and moreover, I will tell you, they are really the fashionable ones: for the others are not, in truth, the pleasures of what I call people of fashion, but of those who only call themselves so. Does good company care to have a man reeling drunk among them? Or to see another tearing his hair, and blaspheming, for having lost, at play, more than he is able to pay? Or a whoremaster, with half a nose, and crippled by coarse and infamous debauchery? No; these practices, and, much more, those who brag of them, make no part of good company, and are most unwillingly, if ever, admitted into it. A real man of fashion and pleasure observes decency; at least, neither borrows nor affects vices; and, if he unfortunately has any, he gratifies them with choice, delicacy, and secrecy.

I have not mentioned the pleasures of the mind (which are the solid and permanent ones), because they do not come under the head of what people commonly call pleasures, which they seem to confine to the senses. The pleasure of virtue, of charity, and of learning, is true and lasting pleasure; which I hope you will be well and long acquainted with. Adieu!

DEAR BOY,   London, April 3, O.S. 1747.

If I am rightly informed, I am now writing to a fine gentleman, in a scarlet coat laced with gold, a brocade waistcoat, and all other suitable ornaments. The natural partiality of every author for his own works makes me very glad to hear that Mr. Harte has thought this last edition of mine worth so fine a binding; and, as he has bound it in red, and gilt it upon the back, I hope he will take care that it shall be *lettered* too. A showish binding attracts the eye, and engages the attention of everybody: but with this difference, that women, and men who are like women, mind the binding more than the book; whereas men of sense and learning immediately examine the inside, and, if they find that it does not answer the finery on the outside, they throw it by with the greater indignation and contempt. I hope that, when this edition of my works shall be opened and read, the best judges will find connection, consistency, solidity, and spirit in it. Mr. Harte may *recensere* and *emendare*, as much as he pleases; but it will be to little purpose, if you do not co-operate with him. The work will be imperfect.

I thank you for your last information, of our success in the Mediterranean;[1] and you say, very rightly, that a Secretary of State ought to be well informed. I hope, therefore, you will take care that I shall. You are near the busy scene in Italy; and I doubt not but that, by frequently looking at the map, you have all that theatre of the war very perfect in your mind.

I like your account of the salt-works; which shows that you gave some attention while you were seeing them. But, notwithstanding that, by your account, the Swiss salt is (I dare say) very good, yet I am apt to suspect that it falls a little short of the true Attic salt, in which there was a peculiar quickness and delicacy. That same Attic salt seasoned almost all Greece, except Bœotia; and a great deal of it was exported afterwards to Rome, where it was counterfeited by a composition called Urbanity, which in some time was brought to very near the perfection of the original Attic salt. The more you are powdered with these two kinds of salt, the better you will keep, and the more you will be relished.

Adieu! My compliments to Mr. Harte and Mr. Eliot.[2]

DEAR BOY,   London, April 14, O.S. 1747.

If you feel half the pleasure from the consciousness of doing well, that I do from the informations I have lately received in your favour from Mr. Harte, I shall have little occasion to exhort or admonish you any more, to do what your own satisfaction and self-love will sufficiently prompt you to. Mr. Harte tells me that you attend, that you apply to your studies; and that, beginning to understand, you begin to taste them. This pleasure will increase, and keep pace with your attention; so that the balance will be greatly to your advantage.

---

[1] Of this year and the preceding, Coxe observes that "the British flag rode triumphant in the Mediterranean" (*Memoirs of the Pelham Administration* (1829), i, 363). Our cruisers not only intercepted the French trading-vessels, but co-operated with the Austrian armies on shore.

[2] Edward Eliot, born in 1727, for many years M.P. for St. Germans or other places, and in 1784 created Lord Eliot. He died in 1804, and was father of the first Earl of St. Germans, his son having been raised to the peerage in 1815.

You may remember, that I have always earnestly recommended to you to do what you are about, be that what it will; and to do nothing else at the same time. Do not imagine that I mean, by this, that you should attend to, and plod at, your book all day long; far from it: I mean that you should have your pleasures too; and that you should attend to them, for the time, as much as to your studies; and, if you do not attend equally to both, you will neither have improvement nor satisfaction from either. A man is fit for neither business nor pleasure, who either cannot, or does not, command and direct his attention to the present object, and, in some degree, banish, for that time, all other objects from his thoughts. If at a ball, a supper, or a party of pleasure, a man were to be solving, in his own mind, a problem in Euclid, he would be a very bad companion, and make a very poor figure in that company; or if, in studying a problem in his closet, he were to think of a minuet, I am apt to believe that he would make a very poor mathematician. There is time enough for every thing in the course of the day, if you do but one thing at once; but there is not time enough in the year, if you will do two things at a time.

The Pensionary de Witt, who was torn to pieces in the year 1672, did the whole business of the Republic, and yet had time left to go to assemblies in the evening, and sup in company. Being asked how he could possibly find time to go through so much business, and yet amuse himself in the evenings as he did? he answered, "There was nothing so easy; for that it was only doing one thing at a time, and never putting off anything till to-morrow that could be done to-day." This steady and undissipated attention to one object, is a sure mark of a superior genius; as hurry, bustle, and agitation, are the never-failing symptoms of a weak and frivolous mind. When you read Horace, attend to the justness of his thoughts, the happiness of his diction, and the beauty of his poetry; and do not think of Puffendorf [1] *de Homine et Cive*; and, when you are reading Puffendorf, do not think of Madame de St. Germain; nor of Puffendorf, when you are talking to Madame de St. Germain.

Mr. Harte informs me, that he has reimbursed you part of your losses in Germany; and I consent to his reimbursing you the whole, now that I know you deserve it. I shall grudge you nothing, nor shall you want anything that you desire,

[1] Baron Samuel von Puffendorf, the eminent critic and historian, was born in Saxony in 1631, and died in Berlin, 1694.

provided you deserve it: so that, you see, it is in your own power to have whatever you please.

There is a little book which you read here with Monsieur Coderc, entitled, *Manière de bien penser dans les ouvrages d'esprit*, written by Père Bouhours. I wish you would read this book again, at your leisure hours; for it will not only divert you, but likewise form your taste, and give you a just manner of thinking Adieu!

DEAR BOY,   London, June 30, O.S. 1747.

I was extremely pleased with the account, which you gave me in your last, of the civilities that you received in your Swiss progress; and I have wrote, by this post, to Mr. Burnaby, and to the *Avoyer*, to thank them for their parts. If the attention you met with pleased you, as I dare say it did, you will, I hope, draw this general conclusion from it, "That attention and civility please all those to whom they are paid; and that you will please others in proportion as you are attentive and civil to them."

Bishop Burnet [1] has wrote his travels through Switzerland; and Mr. Stanyan, from a long residence there, has written the best account, yet extant, of the Thirteen Cantons; but those books will be read no more, I presume, after you shall have published your account of that country. I hope you will favour me with one of the first copies. To be serious; though I do not desire that you shall immediately turn author, and oblige the world with your travels; yet, wherever you go, I would have you as curious and inquisitive as if you did intend to write them.

I do not mean that you should give yourself so much trouble to know the number of houses, inhabitants, sign-posts, and tomb-stones of every town that you go through; but that you should inform yourself, as well as your stay will permit you, whether the town is free, or whom it belongs to, or in what manner; whether it has any peculiar privileges or customs; what trade or manufactures; and such other particulars as people of sense desire to know. And there would be no manner of harm, if you were to make memorandums of such things, in a paper book, to help your memory. The only way of knowing

---

[1] *Some Letters containing an Account of what seemed most Remarkable in Travelling through Switzerland, Italy, and Germany, in* 1685 *and* 1686 (Rotterdam, 1687).

all these things is, to keep the best company, who can best inform you of them.

I am just now called away; so good-night!

DEAR BOY,   London, July 20, O.S. 1747.

In your Mamma's letter, which goes here enclosed, you will find one from my sister[1] to thank you for the Arquebusade water which you sent her; and which she takes very kindly. She would not show me her letter to you; but told me, that it contained good wishes and good advice; and as I know she will show me your letter, in answer to hers, I send you here enclosed the draught of the letter which I would have you write to her. I hope you will not be offended at my offering you my assistance upon this occasion: because, I presume, that as yet you are not much used to write to ladies.

A propos of letter-writing; the best models that you can form yourself upon, are Cicero, Cardinal d'Ossat, Madame Sévigné,[2] and Comte Bussy Rabutin.[3] Cicero's Epistles to Atticus, and to his familiar friends, are the best examples that you can imitate, in the friendly and the familiar style. The simplicity and clearness of Cardinal d'Ossat's letters, show how letters of business ought to be written: no affected turns, no attempt at wit, obscure or perplex his matter; which is always plainly and clearly stated, as business always should be. For gay and amusing letters, for *enjouement* and *badinage*, there are none that equal Comte Bussy's and Madame Sevigné's. They are so natural, that they seem to be the extempore conversations of two people of wit, rather than letters; which are commonly studied, though they ought not to be so. I would advise you to let that book be one of your itinerant library; it will both amuse and inform you.

I have not time to add any more now; so good night!

DEAR BOY,   London, July 30, O.S. 1747.

It is now four posts since I have received any letter, either from you or from Mr. Harte. I impute this to the rapidity of

---

[1] Lady Gertrude Hotham.
[2] Marie de Rabutin, Marquise de Sévigné, was born in 1626 and died 1696. Her letters were to her daughter, the Comtesse de Grignan.
[3] Roger Rabutin, Comte de Bussy, was born in 1618 and died in 1693.

your travels through Switzerland; which I suppose are by this time finished.

You will have found by my late letters, both to you and to Mr. Harte, that you are to be at Leipsig by next Michaelmas; where you will be lodged in the house of Professor Mascow,[1] and boarded in the neighbourhood of it, with some young men of fashion. The Professor will read you lectures upon *Grotius de Jure Belli et Pacis*, the *Institutes of Justinian*, and the *Jus Publicum Imperii*; which I expect that you shall not only hear, but attend to, and retain. I also expect that you make yourself perfectly master of the German language; which you may very soon do there if you please. I give you fair warning, that at Leipsig I shall have an hundred invisible spies upon you; and shall be exactly informed of everything that you do, and of almost everything that you say. I hope, that, in consequence of those minute informations, I may be able to say of you, what Velleius Paterculus says of Scipio; that, in his whole life, *nihil non laudandum aut dixit, aut fecit, aut sensit.*

There is a great deal of good company in Leipsig, which I would have you frequent in the evenings, when the studies of the day are over. There is likewise a kind of Court kept there, by a Duchess Dowager of Courland,[2] at which you should get introduced. The King of Poland and his Court go likewise to the fair at Leipsig twice a year; and I shall write to Sir Charles Williams, the King's Minister there, to have you presented, and introduced into good company.

But I must remind you, at the same time, that it will be to very little purpose for you to frequent good company, if you do not conform to, and learn, their manners; if you are not attentive to please, and well-bred, with the easiness of a man of fashion. As you must attend to your manners, so you must not neglect your person; but take care to be very clean, well dressed, and genteel; to have no disagreeable attitudes, nor awkward tricks, which many people use themselves to, and then cannot leave them off. Do you take care to keep your

---

[1] There were two brothers Mascow, both Professors of Civil Law, both trained at Leipsig, and both celebrated for their learning. The elder, John James Mascow, was the author of the well-known *History of the Germans* which appeared in 1726. Born 1689, died 1762.

[2] From Betham's *Genealogical Tables* (tab. 575) this lady appears to have been Benigna de Treiden, born 1703, the consort of Ernest John Biren, formerly Duke of Courland, and well known as the favourite of the Empress Anne of Russia.

teeth very clean, by washing them constantly every morning, and after every meal? This is very necessary, both to preserve your teeth a great while, and to save you a great deal of pain. Mine have plagued me long, and are now falling out, merely for want of care when I was of your age. Do you dress well, and not too well? Do you consider your air and manner of presenting yourself, enough, and not too much? neither negligent nor stiff? All these things deserve a degree of care, a second-rate attention; they give an additional lustre to real merit. My Lord Bacon says, that a pleasing figure is a perpetual letter of recommendation. It is certainly an agreeable forerunner of merit, and smooths the way for it.

Remember that I shall see you at Hanover next summer, and shall expect perfection; which if I do not meet with, or at least something very near it, you and I shall not be very well together. I shall dissect and analyse you with a microscope, so that I shall discover the least speck or blemish. This is fair warning, therefore take your measures accordingly. Yours.

DEAR BOY,   London, August 7, O.S. 1747.

I reckon that this letter has but a bare chance of finding you at Lausanne; but I was resolved to risk it, as it is the last that I shall write to you till you are settled at Leipsig. I sent you, by the last post, under cover to Mr. Harte, a letter of recommendation to one of the first people at Munich, which you will take care to present to him in the politest manner: he will certainly have you presented to the Electoral family, and I hope you will go through that ceremony with great respect, good-breeding, and ease.

As this is the first Court that ever you will have been at, take care to inform yourself, if there be any particular customs or forms to be observed, that you may not commit any mistake. At Vienna, men always make courtesies instead of bows, to the Emperor; in France nobody bows at all to the King, nor kisses his hand; but, in Spain and England, bows are made, and hands are kissed. Thus, every Court has some peculiarity or other, which those who go to them ought previously to inform themselves of, to avoid blunders and awkwardnesses.

I have not time to say any more now, than to wish you a good journey to Leipsig, and great attention, both there and in going thither. Adieu!

DEAR BOY,   London, October 9, O.S. 1747.

People of your age have, commonly, an unguarded frankness about them; which makes them the easy prey and bubbles of the artful and the inexperienced: they look upon every knave, or fool, who tells them that he is their friend, to be really so; and pay that profession of simulated friendship, with an indiscreet and unbounded confidence, always to their loss, often to their ruin. Beware, therefore, now that you are coming into the world, of these proffered friendships. Receive them with great civility, but with great incredulity too; and pay them with compliments, but not with confidence. Do not let your vanity, and self-love, make you suppose that people become your friends at first sight, or even upon a short acquaintance. Real friendship is a slow grower; and never thrives, unless ingrafted upon a stock of known and reciprocal merit.

There is another kind of nominal friendship, among young people, which is warm for the time, but, by good luck, of short duration. This friendship is hastily produced, by their being accidentally thrown together, and pursuing the same course of riot and debauchery. A fine friendship, truly! and well cemented by drunkenness and lewdness. It should rather be called a conspiracy against morals and good manners, and be punished as such by the civil magistrate. However, they have the impudence, and the folly, to call this confederacy a friendship. They lend one another money, for bad purposes; they engage in quarrels, offensive and defensive, for their accomplices; they tell one another all they know, and often more too; when, of a sudden, some accident disperses them, and they think no more of each other, unless it be to betray and laugh at their imprudent confidence. Remember to make a great difference between companions and friends; for a very complaisant and agreeable companion may, and often does, prove a very improper and a very dangerous friend.

People will, in a great degree, and not without reason, form their opinion of you, upon that which they have of your friends; and there is a Spanish proverb, which says very justly, *Tell me whom you live with, and I will tell you who you are.* One may fairly suppose, that a man, who makes a knave or a fool his friend, has something very bad to do or to conceal. But, at the same time that you carefully decline the friendship of knaves and fools, if it can be called friendship, there is no occasion to make either of them your enemies, wantonly, and unprovoked; for they are numerous bodies; and I would rather choose a secure neutrality, than alliance, or war, with either of them. You may be a declared enemy to their vices and follies, without being marked out by them as a personal one. Their enmity is the next dangerous thing to their friendship. Have a real reserve with almost everybody, and have a seeming reserve with almost nobody; for it is very disagreeable to seem reserved, and very dangerous not to be so. Few people find the true medium; many are ridiculously mysterious and reserved upon trifles; and many imprudently communicative of all they know.

The next thing to the choice of your friends, is the choice of your company. Endeavour, as much as you can, to keep company with people above you. There you rise, as much as you sink with people below you; for (as I have mentioned before) you are, whatever the company you keep is. Do not mistake, when I say company above you, and think that I mean with regard to their birth; that is the least consideration: but I mean with regard to their merit, and the light in which the world considers them.

There are two sorts of good company; one, which is called the *beau monde*, and consists of those people who have the lead in Courts, and in the gay part of life; the other consists of those who are distinguished by some peculiar merit, or who excel in some particular and valuable art or science. For my own part, I used to think myself in company as much above me, when I was with Mr. Addison and Mr. Pope, as if I had been with all the Princes in Europe. What I mean by low company which should by all means be avoided, is the company of those, who, absolutely insignificant and contemptible in themselves, think they are honoured by being in your company, and who flatter every vice and every folly you have, in order to engage you to converse with them. The pride of being the first of the company, is but too common; but it is very silly, and very prejudicial. Nothing in the world lets down a character more, than that wrong turn.

You may possibly ask me, whether a man has it always in his power to get into the best company? and how? I say, Yes, he has, by deserving it; provided he is but in circumstances which enable him to appear upon the footing of a gentleman. Merit and good-breeding will make their way everywhere. Knowledge will introduce him, and good-breeding will endear him to the best companies; for, as I have often told you, politeness and good-breeding are absolutely necessary to adorn any, or all other good qualities or talents. Without them, no knowledge, no perfection whatsoever, is seen in its best light. The scholar, without good-breeding, is a pedant; the philosopher, a cynic; the soldier, a brute; and every man disagreeable.

I long to hear, from my several correspondents at Leipsig, of your arrival there, and what impression you make on them at first; for I have Arguses, with a hundred eyes each, who will watch you narrowly, and relate to me faithfully. My accounts will certainly be true; it depends on you, entirely, of what kind they shall be. Adieu!

DEAR BOY, London, October 16, O.S. 1747.

The art of pleasing is a very necessary one to possess; but a very difficult one to acquire. It can hardly be reduced to rules; and your own good sense and observation will teach you more of it than I can. "Do as you would be done by," is the surest method that I know of pleasing. Observe carefully what pleases you in others, and probably the same things in you will please others. If you are pleased with the complaisance and attention of others to your humours, your tastes, or your weaknesses, depend upon it, the same complaisance and attention on your part, to theirs, will equally please them. Take the tone of the company that you are in, and do not pretend to give it; be serious, gay, or even trifling, as you find the present humour of the company: this is an attention due from every individual to the majority. Do not tell stories in company; there is nothing more tedious and disagreeable: if by chance you know a very short story, and exceedingly applicable to the present subject of conversation, tell it in as few words as possible; and even then, throw out that you do not love to tell stories; but that the shortness of it tempted you.

Of all things, banish the egotism out of your conversation, and never think of entertaining people with your own personal concerns or private affairs; though they are interesting to you, they are tedious and impertinent to everybody else: besides that, one cannot keep one's own private affairs too secret. Whatever you think your own excellencies may be, do not affectedly display them in company; nor labour, as many people do, to give that turn to the conversation, which may supply you with an opportunity of exhibiting them. If they are real, they will infallibly be discovered, without your pointing them out yourself, and with much more advantage. Never maintain an argument with heat and clamour, though you think or know yourself to be in the right; but give your opinions modestly and coolly, which is the only way to convince; and, if that does not do, try to change the conversation, by saying, with good-humour, "We shall hardly convince one another; nor is it necessary that we should, so let us talk of something else."

Remember that there is a local propriety to be observed in all companies; and that what is extremely proper in one company, may be, and often is, highly improper in another.

The jokes, the *bon-mots*, the little adventures, which may do very well in one company, will seem flat and tedious when related in another. The particular characters, the habits, the cant of one company may give merit to a word, or a gesture, which would have none at all if divested of those accidental circumstances. Here people very commonly err; and fond of something that has entertained them in one company, and in certain circumstances, repeat it with emphasis in another, where it is either insipid, or, it may be, offensive, by being ill-timed or misplaced.

Nay, they often do it with this silly preamble, "I will tell you an excellent thing," or, "I will tell you the best thing in the world." This raises expectations, which when absolutely disappointed, make the relator of this excellent thing look, very deservedly, like a fool.

If you would particularly gain the affection and friendship of particular people, whether men or women, endeavour to find out their predominant excellency, if they have one, and their prevailing weakness, which everybody has; and do justice to the one, and something more than justice to the other. Men have various objects in which they may excel, or at least would be thought to excel; and though they love to hear justice done to them, where they know that they excel, yet they are most and best flattered upon those points where they wish to excel, and yet are doubtful whether they do or not. As for example: Cardinal Richelieu,[1] who was undoubtedly the ablest statesman of his time, or perhaps of any other, had the idle vanity of being thought the best poet too: he envied the great Corneille [2] his reputation, and ordered a criticism to be written upon the *Cid*. Those, therefore, who flattered skilfully, said little to him of his abilities in state affairs, or at least but *en passant*, and as it might naturally occur. But the incense which they gave him—the smoke of which they knew would turn his head

---

[1] 1585-1642.   [2] 1606-84.

in their favour—was as a *bel esprit* and a poet. Why?—
Because he was sure of one excellency, and distrustful as to
the other.

You will easily discover every man's prevailing vanity by
observing his favourite topic of conversation; for every man
talks most of what he has most a mind to be thought to excel
in. Touch him but there, and you touch him to the quick.
The late Sir Robert Walpole [3] (who was certainly an able man)
was little open to flattery upon that head, for he was in no
doubt himself about it; but his prevailing weakness was, to be
thought to have a polite and happy turn to gallantry—of which
he had undoubtedly less than any man living. It was his
favourite and frequent subject of conversation, which proved
to those who had any penetration that it was his prevailing
weakness, and they applied to it with success.

Women have, in general, but one object, which is their
beauty; upon which, scarce any flattery is too gross for them
to follow. Nature has hardly formed a woman ugly enough
to be insensible to flattery upon her person; if her face is so
shocking that she must, in some degree, be conscious of it, her
figure and air, she trusts, make ample amends for it. If her
figure is deformed, her face, she thinks, counterbalances it.
If they are both bad, she comforts herself that she has graces;
a certain manner; a *je ne sçais quoi* still more engaging than
beauty. This truth is evident, from the studied and elaborate
dress of the ugliest woman in the world. An undoubted,
uncontested, conscious beauty is, of all women, the least sensible
of flattery upon that head; she knows it is her due, and is
therefore obliged to nobody for giving it her. She must be
flattered upon her understanding, which, though she may possibly
not doubt of herself, yet she suspects that men may distrust.

Do not mistake me, and think that I mean to recommend to
you abject and criminal flattery: no; flatter nobody's vices or
crimes: on the contrary, abhor and discourage them. But
there is no living in the world without a complaisant indulgence
for people's weaknesses, and innocent, though ridiculous vanities.
If a man has a mind to be thought wiser, and a woman handsomer, than they really are, their error is a comfortable one to
themselves, and an innocent one with regard to other people;
and I would rather make them my friends by indulging them in
it, than my enemies by endeavouring (and that to no purpose)
to undeceive them.

[1] 1676–1745.

There are little attentions, likewise, which are infinitely engaging, and which sensibly affect that degree of pride and self-love, which is inseparable from human nature; as they are unquestionable proofs of the regard and consideration which we have for the persons to whom we pay them. As for example: to observe the little habits, the likings, the antipathies, and the tastes of those whom we would gain; and then take care to provide them with the one, and to secure them from the other; giving them genteelly to understand, that you had observed they liked such a dish or such a room; for which reason you had prepared it: or, on the contrary, that having observed they had an aversion to such a dish, a dislike to such a person, etc., you had taken care to avoid presenting them. Such attention to such trifles flatters self-love much more than greater things, as it makes people think themselves almost the only objects of your thoughts and care.

These are some of the *arcana* necessary for your initiation in the great society of the world. I wish I had known them better at your age; I have paid the price of three-and-fifty years for them, and shall not grudge it if you reap the advantage. Adieu!

DEAR BOY,   London, December 11, O.S. 1747.

There is nothing which I more wish that you should know and which fewer people do know, than the true use and value of Time. It is in everybody's mouth, but in few people's practice. Every fool who slatterns away his whole time in nothings, utters, however, some trite common-place sentence, of which there are millions, to prove at once the value and the fleetness of time. The sun-dials, likewise, all over Europe, have some ingenious inscription to that effect; so that nobody squanders away their time without hearing and seeing, daily, how necessary it is to employ it well, and how irrecoverable it is if lost. But all these admonitions are useless where there is not a fund of good sense and reason to suggest them, rather than receive them. By the manner in which you now tell me that you employ your time, I flatter myself that you have that fund: that is the fund which will make you rich indeed. I do not, therefore, mean to give you a critical essay upon the use and abuse of time; I will only give you some hints with regard to the use of one particular period of that long time which I hope you have before you; I mean the next two years.

Remember, then, that whatever knowledge you do not solidly lay the foundation of before you are eighteen, you will never be master of while you breathe. Knowledge is a comfortable and necessary retreat and shelter for us in an advanced age; and if we do not plant it while young, it will give us no shade when we grow old. I neither require nor expect from you great application to books after you are once thrown out into the great world. I know it is impossible; and it may even, in some cases, be improper: this, therefore, is your time, and your only time, for unwearied and uninterrupted application. If you should sometimes think it a little laborious, consider that labour is the unavoidable fatigue of a necessary journey. The more hours a day you travel, the sooner you will be at your journey's end. The sooner you are qualified for your liberty, the sooner you shall have it; and your manumission will entirely depend upon the manner in which you employ the intermediate time. I think I offer you a very good bargain, when I promise you, upon my word, that, if you will do everything that I would have you do till you are eighteen, I will do everything that you would have me do ever afterwards.

I knew a gentleman, who was so good a manager of his time, that he would not even lose that small portion of it which the calls of nature obliged him to pass in the necessary-house, but gradually went through all the Latin poets in those moments. He bought, for example, a common edition of Horace, of which he tore off gradually a couple of pages, carried them with him to that necessary place, read them first, and then sent them down as a sacrifice to Cloacina; this was so much time fairly gained; and I recommend to you to follow his example. It is better than only doing what you cannot help doing at those moments; and it will make any book which you shall read in that manner, very present to your mind. Books of science, and of a grave sort, must be read with continuity; but there are very many, and even very useful ones, which may be read with advantage by snatches, and unconnectedly; such are all the good Latin poets, except Virgil in his Æneid: and such are most of the modern poets in which you will find many pieces worth reading that will not take up above seven or eight minutes. Bayle's,[1] Moreri's, and other dictionaries, are proper books to take and shut up for the little intervals of

---

[1] Pierre Bayle, author of the *Biographical, Historical and Critical Dictionary*. Born 1647, died 1706. Louis Moreri, a French ecclesiastic, also compiled a biographical dictionary. Born 1643, died 1680.

(otherwise) idle time, that everybody has in the course of the day, between either their studies or their pleasures. Good night!

DEAR BOY,   January 2, O.S. 1748.

I am edified with the allotment of your time at Leipsig; which is so well employed, from morning till night, that a fool would say, you had none left for yourself; whereas, I am sure you have sense enough to know that such a right use of your time is having it all to yourself; nay, it is even more, for it is laying it out to immense interest; which, in a very few years, will amount to a prodigious capital.

Though twelve of your fourteen *commensaux* may not be the liveliest people in the world, and may want (as I easily conceive they do) *le ton de la bonne compagnie, et les grâces*, which I wish you, yet pray take care not to express any contempt, or throw out any ridicule, which, I can assure you, is not more contrary to good manners than to good sense: but endeavour rather to get all the good you can out of them; and something or other is to be got out of everybody. They will, at least, improve you in the German language; and, as they come from different countries, you may put them upon subjects concerning which they must necessarily be able to give you some useful information, let them be ever so dull or disagreeable in general: they will know something, at least, of the laws, customs, government, and considerable families of their respective countries; all which are better known than not, and consequently worth inquiring into. There is hardly anybody good for every thing, and there is scarcely anybody who is absolutely good for nothing. A good chymist will extract some spirit or other out of every substance; and a man of parts will, by his dexterity and management, elicit something worth knowing out of every being he converses with.

As you have been introduced to the Duchess of Courland, pray go there as often as ever your more necessary occupations will allow you. I am told she is extremely well-bred, and has parts. Now, though I would not recommend to you to go into women's company in search of solid knowledge or judgment, yet it has its use in other respects; for it certainly polishes the manners, and gives *une certaine tournure*, which is very necessary in the course of the world, and which Englishmen have generally less of than any people in the world.

I cannot say that your suppers are luxurious, but you must own they are solid; and a quart of soup and two pounds of potatoes will enable you to pass the night without great impatience for your breakfast next morning. One part of your supper (the potatoes) is the constant diet of my old friends and countrymen, the Irish, who are the healthiest and the strongest men that I know in Europe.

As I believe that many of my letters to you and to Mr. Harte have miscarried, as well as some of yours and his to me (particularly one of his from Leipsig, to which he refers in a subsequent one, and which I never received), I would have you, for the future, acknowledge the dates of all the letters which either of you shall receive from me, and I will do the same on my part.

That which I received by the last mail from you was of the 25th November, N.S.; the mail before that brought me yours, of which I have forgot the date, but which enclosed one to Lady Chesterfield; she will answer it soon, and, in the mean time, thanks you for it.

My disorder was only a very great cold, of which I am entirely recovered. You shall not complain for want of accounts from Mr. Grevenkop, who will frequently write you whatever passes here, in the German language and character, which will improve you in both. Adieu!

DEAR BOY,   London, January 15, O.S. 1748.

I willingly accept the New-year's gift which you promise me for next year, and the more valuable you make it, the more thankful I shall be. That depends entirely upon you, and, therefore, I hope to be presented every year with a new edition of you, more correct than the former, and considerably enlarged and amended.

Since you do not care to be an Assessor of the Imperial Chamber, and desire an establishment in England, what do you think of being Greek Professor at one of our Universities? It is a very pretty sinecure, and requires very little knowledge (much less than, I hope, you have already) of that language. If you do not approve of this, I am at a loss to know what else to propose to you, and therefore desire that you will inform me what sort of destination you propose for yourself, for it is now time to fix it, and to take our measures accordingly. Mr. Harte tells me, that you set up for a Πολιτικὸς ἀνήρ: if so, I presume it is in the view of succeeding me in my office, which I will very willingly resign to you whenever you shall call upon me for it. But, if you intend to be the Πολιτικός, or the Βουληφόρος ἀνηρ, there are some trifling circumstances upon which you should previously take your resolution: the first of which is, to be fit for it; and then, in order to be so, make yourself master of ancient and modern history, and languages. To know perfectly the constitution and form of government of every nation, the growth and the decline of ancient and modern empires, and to trace out and reflect upon the causes of both;—to know the strength, the riches, and the commerce of every country;— these little things, trifling as they may seem, are yet very necessary for a politician to know, and which therefore, I presume, you will condescend to apply yourself to.

There are some additional qualifications necessary, in the practical part of business, which may deserve some consideration in your leisure moments—such as, an absolute command of your temper, so as not to be provoked to passion upon any account; patience, to hear frivolous, impertinent, and unreasonable applications; with address enough to refuse, without offending; or, by your manner of granting, to double the obligation;—dexterity enough to conceal a truth, without telling a lie; sagacity enough to read other people's countenances; and serenity enough not to let them discover anything by yours— a seeming frankness, with a real reserve. These are the rudiments of a politician; the world must be your grammar.

Three mails are now due from Holland, so that I have no letters from you to acknowledge. I therefore conclude with recommending myself to your favour and protection when you succeed.   Yours.

Dear Boy,   London, February 13, O.S. 1748.

Your last letter gave me a very satisfactory account of your manner of employing your time at Leipsig. Go on so but for two years more, and I promise you that you will outgo all the people of your age and time. I thank you for your explication of the *Schriftsassen* and *Amptsassen*; and pray let me know the meaning of the *Landsassen*. I am very willing that you should take a Saxon servant, who speaks nothing but German; which will be a sure way of keeping up your German, after you leave Germany. But then, I would neither have that man, nor him whom you have already, put out of livery; which makes them both impertinent and useless. I am sure that, as soon as you shall have taken the other servant, your present man will press extremely to be out of livery, and valet de chambre; which is as much as to say, that he will curl your hair and shave you, but not condescend to do anything else. I therefore advise you never to have a servant out of livery; and, though you may not always think proper to carry the servant who dresses you abroad in the rain and dirt, behind a coach, or before a chair, yet keep it in your power to do so if you please, by keeping him in livery.

I have seen Monsieur and Madame Flemming, who give me a very good account of you, and of your manners; which, to tell you the plain truth, were what I doubted of the most. She told me that you were easy, and not ashamed, which is a great deal for an Englishman at your age.

I set out for the Bath to-morrow, for a month: only to be better than well, and to enjoy in quiet the liberty which I have acquired by the resignation of the seals. You shall hear from me more at large from thence: and now good night to you!

DEAR BOY,   Bath, February 16, O.S. 1748.

The first use that I made of my liberty was to come hither, where I arrived yesterday. My health, though not fundamentally bad, yet, for want of proper attention of late, wanted some repairs, which these waters never fail giving it. I shall drink them a month, and return to London, there to enjoy the comforts of social life, instead of groaning under the load of business. I have given the description of the life that I propose to lead for the future in this motto, which I have put up in the frieze of my library, in my new house [1]:

> Nunc veterum libris, nunc somno, et inertibus horis
> Ducere sollicitæ jucunda oblivia vitæ.

I must observe to you upon this occasion, that the uninterrupted satisfaction which I expect to find in that library will be chiefly owing to my having employed some part of my life well at your age. I wish I had employed it better, and my satisfaction would now be complete; but, however, I planted, while young, that degree of knowledge which is now my refuge and my shelter. Make your plantations still more extensive; they will more than pay you for your trouble.

[1] Chesterfield House in London. The inscription still remains as Lord Chesterfield placed it.

I do not regret the time that I passed in pleasures; they were seasonable, they were the pleasures of youth, and I enjoyed them while young. If I had not, I should probably have overvalued them now, as we are very apt to do what we do not know; but, knowing them as I do, I know their real value, and how much they are generally over-rated. Nor do I regret the time that I have passed in business, for the same reason. Those who see only the outside of it, imagine that it has hidden charms, which they pant after, and nothing but acquaintance can undeceive them. I, who have been behind the scenes, both of pleasure and business, and have seen all the springs and pullies of those decorations which astonish and dazzle the audience, retire, not only without regret, but with contentment and satisfaction.

But what I do, and ever shall, regret, is the time which, while young, I lost in mere idleness, and in doing nothing. This is the common effect of the inconsideracy of youth, against which I beg you will be most carefully upon your guard. The value of moments, when cast up, is immense, if well employed; if thrown away, their loss is irrecoverable. Every moment may be put to some use, and that with much more pleasure than if unemployed.

Do not imagine that by the employment of time I mean an uninterrupted application to serious studies. No; pleasures are, at proper times, both as necessary and as useful; they fashion and form you for the world; they teach you characters, and show you the human heart in its unguarded minutes. But then remember to make that use of them. I have known many people, from laziness of mind, go through both pleasure and business with equal inattention; neither enjoying the one, nor doing the other: thinking themselves men of pleasure, because they were mingled with those who were, and men of business, because they had business to do, though they did not do it. Whatever you do, do it to the purpose; do it thoroughly, not superficially. *Approfondissez*; go to the bottom of things. Anything half done, or half known, is, in my mind, neither done nor known at all. Nay, worse, for it often misleads. There is hardly any place, or any company, where you may not gain knowledge, if you please; almost everybody knows some one thing, and is glad to talk about that one thing. Seek and you will find, in this world as well as in the next. See everything, inquire into everything; and you may excuse your curiosity, and the questions you ask (which otherwise might be thought impertinent), by your manner of asking them; for most things depend a great deal upon the manner. As, for example, *I am afraid that I am very troublesome with my questions; but nobody can inform me so well as you*; or something of that kind.

Now that you are in a Lutheran country, go to their churches, and observe the manner of their public worship; attend to their ceremonies, and inquire the meaning and intention of every one of them; and, as you will soon understand German well enough, attend to their sermons, and observe their manner of preaching. Inform yourself of their church-government—whether it resides in the Sovereign, or in consistories and synods; whence arises the maintenance of their clergy—whether from tithes, as in England, or from voluntary contributions, or from pensions from the state. Do the same thing when you are in Roman Catholic countries; go to their churches, see all their ceremonies, ask the meaning of them, get the terms explained to you—as, for instance, Prime, Tierce, Sexte, Nones, Matins, Angelus, High Mass, Vespers, Compline, etc. Inform yourself of their several religious orders, their founders, their rules, their vows, their habits, their revenues, etc.; but when you frequent places of public worship, as I would have you go to all the different ones you meet with, remember that, however erroneous, they are none of them objects of laughter and ridicule. Honest error is to be pitied, not ridiculed. The object of all the public worships in the world is the same; it is that great eternal Being, who created everything. The different manners of worship are by no means subjects of ridicule; each sect thinks its own the best; and I know no infallible judge, in this world, to decide which is the best. Make the same inquiries, wherever you are, concerning the revenues, the military establishment, the trade, the commerce, and the police of every country. And you would do well to keep a blank-paper book, which the Germans call an *album*; and there, instead of desiring, as they do, every fool they meet with to scribble something, write down all these things, as soon as they come to your knowledge from good authorities.

I had almost forgotten one thing, which I would recommend as an object for your curiosity and information, that is, the administration of justice; which, as it is always carried on in open court, you may, and I would have you, go and see it, with attention and inquiry.

I have now but one anxiety left, which is, concerning you.

I would have you be, what I know nobody is, perfect. As that is impossible, I would have you as near perfection as possible. I know nobody in a fairer way towards it than yourself, if you please. Never were so much pains taken for anybody's education as for yours, and never had anybody those opportunities of knowledge and improvement which you have had, and still have. I hope, I wish, I doubt, and I fear alternately. This only I am sure of—that you will prove either the greatest pain, or the greatest pleasure, of

Yours.

DEAR BOY,   Bath, February 22, O.S. 1748.

Every excellency, and every virtue, has its kindred vice or weakness; and if carried beyond certain bounds, sinks into the one or the other. Generosity often runs into profusion, economy into avarice, courage into rashness, caution into timidity, and so on; insomuch that, I believe, there is more judgment required for the proper conduct of our virtues, than for avoiding their opposite vices. Vice, in its true light, is so deformed, that it shocks us at first sight; and would hardly ever seduce us, if it did not, at first, wear the mask of some virtue. But virtue is, in itself, so beautiful, that it charms us at first sight; engages us more and more upon further acquaintance, and, as with other beauties, we think excess impossible, it is here that judgment is necessary, to moderate and direct the effects of an excellent cause.

I shall apply this reasoning at present, not to any particular virtue, but to an excellency, which, for want of judgment, is often the cause of ridiculous and blameable effects; I mean, great learning—which, if not accompanied with sound judgment, frequently carries us into error, pride, and pedantry. As I hope you will possess that excellency in its utmost extent, and yet without its too common failings, the hints, which my experience can suggest, may probably be useless to you.

Some learned men, proud of their knowledge, only speak to decide, and give judgment without appeal. The consequence of which is, that mankind, provoked by the insult and injured by the oppression, revolt; and, in order to shake off the tyranny, even call the lawful authority in question. The more you know, the modester you should be; and (by the bye) that modesty is the surest way of gratifying your vanity. Even where you are sure, seem rather doubtful; represent, but do not pronounce;

and, if you would convince others, seem open to conviction yourself.

Others, to show their learning, or often from the prejudices of a school education, where they hear nothing else, are always talking of the ancients as something more than men, and of the moderns as something less. They are never without a classic or two in their pockets; they stick to the old good sense; they read none of the modern trash; and will show you plainly that no improvement has been made, in any one art or science, these last seventeen hundred years. I would by no means have you disown your acquaintance with the ancients, but still less would I have you brag of an exclusive intimacy with them. Speak of the moderns without contempt, and of the ancients without idolatry; judge them all by their merits, but not by their age; and, if you happen to have an Elzevir [1] classic in your pocket, neither show it nor mention it.

Some great scholars, most absurdly, draw all their maxims, both for public and private life, from what they call parallel cases in the ancient authors; without considering that, in the first place, there never were, since the creation of the world, two cases exactly parallel; and, in the next place, that there never was a case stated, or even known, by any historian, with every one of its circumstances; which, however, ought to be known, in order to be reasoned from. Reason upon the case itself, and the several circumstances that attend it, and act accordingly; but not from the authority of ancient poets or historians. Take into your consideration, if you please, cases seemingly analogous; but take them as helps only, not as guides. We are really so prejudiced by our educations, that, as the ancients deified their heroes, we deify their madmen: of which, with all due regard to antiquity, I take Leonidas and Curtius to have been two distinguished ones. And yet a solid pedant would, in a speech in Parliament relative to a tax of twopence in the pound upon some commodity or other, quote those two heroes as examples of what we ought to do and suffer for our country. I have known these absurdities carried so far by people of injudicious learning, that I should not be surprised if some of them were to propose, while we are at war with the Gauls, that a number of geese should be kept in the Tower upon account of the infinite advantage which Rome received, *in a parallel case*, from a certain number of geese in the Capitol.

[1] The Elzevir family of printers resided at Amsterdam and Leyden. These beautiful editions were published principally between 1594 and 1680.

This way of reasoning and this way of speaking will always form a poor politician, and a puerile declaimer.

There is another species of learned men, who, though less dogmatical and supercilious, are not less impertinent. These are the communicative and shining pedants, who adorn their conversation, even with women, by happy quotations of Greek and Latin; and who have contracted such a familiarity with the Greek and Roman authors, that they call them by certain names or epithets denoting intimacy. As *old* Homer; that *sly rogue* Horace; *Maro* instead of Virgil; and *Naso*, instead of Ovid. These are often imitated by coxcombs, who have no learning at all, but who have got some names and some scraps of ancient authors by heart, which they improperly and impertinently retail in all companies, in hopes of passing for scholars. If, therefore, you would avoid the accusation of pedantry on one hand, or the suspicion of ignorance on the other, abstain from learned ostentation. Speak the language of the company that you are in; speak it purely, and unlarded with any other. Never seem wiser, nor more learned, than the people you are with. Wear your learning, like your watch, in a private pocket; and do not merely pull it out and strike it merely to show you have one. If you are asked what o'clock it is, tell it; but do not proclaim it hourly and unasked like the watchman.

Upon the whole, remember that learning (I mean Greek and Roman learning) is a most useful and necessary ornament, which it is shameful not to be master of; but, at the same time, most carefully avoid those errors and abuses which I have mentioned, and which too often attend it. Remember, too, that great modern knowledge is still more necessary than ancient; and that you had better know perfectly the present than the old state of Europe; though I would have you well acquainted with both.

I have this moment received your letter of the 17th, N.S. Though I confess there is no great variety in your present manner of life, yet materials can never be wanting for a letter; you see, you hear, or you read, something new every day: a short account of which, with your own reflections thereupon, will make out a letter very well. But since you desire a subject, pray send me an account of the Lutheran establishment in Germany; their religious tenets, their Church government, the maintenance, authority and titles of their clergy.

Vittorio Siri, complete, is a very scarce and very dear book here; but I do not want it. If your own library grows too

voluminous, you will not know what to do with it when you
leave Leipsig. Your best way will be, when you go away from
thence, to send to England, by Hamburg, all the books that you
do not absolutely want. Yours.

DEAR BOY,   Bath, March 9, O.S. 1748.

I must, from time to time, remind you of what I have often
recommended to you, and of what you cannot attend to too
much; *sacrifice to the Graces*.[1] The different effects of the same
things, said or done, when accompanied or abandoned by them,
is almost inconceivable. They prepare the way to the heart;
and the heart has such an influence over the understanding,
that it is worth while to engage it in our interest. It is the whole
of women, who are guided by nothing else: and it has so much to
say, even with men, and the ablest men too, that it commonly
triumphs in every struggle with the understanding. Monsieur
de Rochefoucault,[2] in his *Maxims*, says, that *l'esprit est souvent
la dupe du cœur*. If he had said, instead of *souvent*, *presque
toujours*, I fear he would have been nearer the truth. This
being the case, aim at the heart. Intrinsic merit alone will
not do; it will gain you the general esteem of all; but not the
particular affection, that is, the heart of any. To engage the
affection of any particular person, you must, over and above
your general merit, have some particular merit to that person,
by services done or offered; by expressions of regard and esteem;
by complaisance, attentions, etc., for him: and the graceful
manner of doing all these things opens the way to the heart,
and facilitates, or rather insures, their effects.

From your own observation, reflect what a disagreeable
impression an awkward address, a slovenly figure, an ungraceful
manner of speaking whether stuttering, muttering, monotony,
or drawling, an unattentive behaviour, etc., make upon you, at
first sight, in a stranger, and how they prejudice you against
him, though, for aught you know, he may have great intrinsic
sense and merit. And reflect, on the other hand, how much
the opposites of all these things prepossess you, at first sight,
in favour of those who enjoy them. You wish to find all good

[1] Dr. Hill quotes: "Plato used to say to Xenocrates, the philosopher,
who had a morose and unpolished manner, 'Good Xenocrates, *sacrifice to
the Graces*.'"—PLUTARCH's *Lives*. "Prince Maurice never *sacrificed to the
Graces*, nor conversed amongst men of quality, but had most used the
company of ordinary and inferior men with whom he loved to be very
familiar."—CLARENDON, *History of the Rebellion*.
[2] Francis, Duc de la Rochefoucault, born 1613, died 1680.

qualities in them, and are in some degree disappointed if you
do not. A thousand little things, not separately to be defined,
conspire to form these Graces, this *je ne sçais quoi*, that always
pleases. A pretty person, genteel motions, a proper degree of
dress, an harmonious voice, something open and cheerful in
the countenance, but without laughing; a distinct and properly
varied manner of speaking: all these things, and many others,
are necessary ingredients in the composition of the pleasing *je
ne sçais quoi*, which everybody feels, though nobody can describe.
Observe carefully, then, what displeases or pleases you in
others, and be persuaded, that, in general, the same thing will
please or displease them in you.

Having mentioned laughing, I must particularly warn you
against it: and I could heartily wish that you may often be
seen to smile, but never heard to laugh while you live. Frequent and loud laughter is the characteristic of folly and ill
manners: it is the manner in which the mob express their silly
joy at silly things; and they call it being merry. In my mind
there is nothing so illiberal, and so ill-bred, as audible laughter.
True wit, or sense, never yet made anybody laugh; they are
above it: they please the mind, and give a cheerfulness to the
countenance. But it is low buffoonery, or silly accidents, that
always excite laughter; and that is what people of sense and
breeding should show themselves above. A man's going to sit
down, in the supposition that he had a chair behind him, and
falling down upon his breech for want of one, sets a whole
company a laughing, when all the wit in the world would not
do it; a plain proof, in my mind, how low and unbecoming a
thing laughter is. Not to mention the disagreeable noise that
it makes, and the shocking distortion of the face that it occasions.
Laughter is easily restrained by a very little reflection; but, as
it is generally connected with the idea of gaiety, people do not
enough attend to its absurdity. I am neither of a melancholy,
nor a cynical disposition; and am as willing, and as apt, to be
pleased as anybody; but I am sure that, since I have had the
full use of my reason, nobody has ever heard me laugh.[1] Many
people, at first from awkwardness and *mauvaise honte*, have got
a very disagreeable and silly trick of laughing whenever they
speak: and I know a man of very good parts, Mr. Waller, who

[1] Swift "stubbornly resisted any tendency to laughter."—JOHNSON's
Works, viii, 222. "By no merriment, either of others or of his own, was
Pope ever seen excited to laughter."—Ibid., 312. "There is nothing more
unbecoming a man of quality than to laugh, it is such a vulgar expression
of the passion. Everybody can laugh."—CONGREVE's *Double Dealer*, i, 1

cannot say the commonest thing without laughing; which makes those, who do not know him, take him at first for a natural fool.

This, and many other very disagreeable habits, are owing to *mauvaise honte* at their first setting out in the world. They are ashamed in company, and so disconcerted that they do not know what they do, and try a thousand tricks to keep themselves in countenance; which tricks afterwards grow habitual to them. Some put their fingers in their nose, others scratch their head, others twirl their hats; in short, every awkward, ill-bred body has his trick. But the frequency does not justify the thing; and all these vulgar habits and awkwardness, though not criminal indeed, are most carefully to be guarded against, as they are great bars in the way of the art of pleasing. Remember, that to please, is almost to prevail, or at least a necessary previous step to it. You, who have your fortune to make, should more particularly study this art. You had not, I must tell you, when you left England, *les manières prévenantes*; and I must confess they are not very common in England: but I hope that your good sense will make you acquire them abroad. If you desire to make yourself considerable in the world (as, if you have any spirit, you do), it must be entirely your own doing; for I may very possibly be out of the world at the time you come into it. Your own rank and fortune will not assist you; your merit and your manners can alone raise you to figure and fortune. I have laid the foundations of them, by the education which I have given you; but you must build the superstructure yourself.

I must now apply to you for some informations which I dare say you can, and which I desire you will, give me.

Can the Elector of Saxony put any of his subjects to death for high-treason, without bringing them first to their trial in some Public Court of Justice?

Can he, by his own authority, confine any subject in prison as long as he pleases, without trial?

Can he banish any subject out of his dominions by his own authority?

Can he lay any tax whatsoever upon his subjects without the consent of the States of Saxony? and what are those States? how are they elected? what Orders do they consist of? do the Clergy make part of them? and when, and how often, do they meet?

If two subjects of the Elector's are at law for an estate situated in the Electorate, in what court must this suit be tried?

and will the decision of that court be final, or does there lie an appeal to the Imperial Chamber at Wetzlar?

What do you call the two chief courts, or two chief magistrates, of civil and criminal justice?

What is the common revenue of the Electorate one year with another?

What number of troops does the Elector now maintain? and what is the greatest number that the Electorate is able to maintain?

I do not expect to have all these questions answered at once; but you will answer them in proportion as you get the necessary and authentic informations.

You are, you see, my German oracle; and I consult you with so much faith that you need not, like the oracles of old, return ambiguous answers; especially as you have this advantage over them, too, that I only consult you about past and present, but not about what is to come.

I wish you a good Easter fair at Leipsig. See, with attention, all the shops, drolls, tumblers, rope-dancers, and *hoc genus omne*: but inform yourself more particularly of the several parts of trade there. Adieu!

DEAR BOY,   London, April 1, O.S. 1748.

I have not received any letter, either from you or from Mr. Harte, these three posts, which I impute wholly to accidents between this place and Leipsig; and they are distant enough to admit of many. I always take it for granted that you are well, when I do not hear to the contrary; besides, as I have often told you, I am much more anxious about your doing well, than about your being well; and, when you do not write, I will suppose that you are doing something more useful. Your health will continue while your temperance continues; and, at your age, Nature takes sufficient care of the body, provided she is left to herself, and that intemperance on one hand, or medicines on the other, do not break in upon her. But it is by no means so with the mind, which, at your age particularly, requires great and constant care, and some physic. Every quarter of an hour, well or ill employed, will do it essential and lasting good or harm. It requires, also, a great deal of exercise, to bring it to a state of health and vigour.

Observe the difference there is between minds cultivated and minds uncultivated, and you will, I am sure, think that you cannot take too much pains, nor employ too much of your time in the culture of your own. A drayman is probably born with as good organs as Milton, Locke, or Newton; but, by culture, they are much more above him than he is above his horse. Sometimes, indeed, extraordinary geniuses have broken out by the force of nature, without the assistance of education; but those instances are too rare for anybody to trust to; and even they would make a much greater figure, if they had the advantage of education into the bargain. If Shakespeare's genius had been cultivated, those beauties, which we so justly admire in him, would have been undisguised by those extravagances and that nonsense with which they are frequently accompanied

People are, in general, what they are made, by education and company, from fifteen to five-and-twenty; consider well, therefore, the importance of your next eight or nine years—your whole depends upon them. I will tell you, sincerely, my hopes and my fears concerning you. I think you will be a good scholar, and that you will acquire a considerable stock of knowledge of various kinds; but I fear that you neglect what are called little, though in truth they are very material things; I mean, a gentleness of manners, an engaging address, and an insinuating[1] behaviour; they are real and solid advantages, and none but those who do not know the world treat them as trifles. I am told that you speak very quick, and not distinctly; this is a most ungraceful and disagreeable trick, which you know I have told you of a thousand times; pray attend carefully to the correction of it. An agreeable and distinct manner of speaking adds greatly to the matter; and I have known many a very good speech unregarded, upon account of the disagreeable manner in which it has been delivered, and many an indifferent one applauded, for the contrary reason. Adieu!

DEAR BOY,   London, May 17, O.S. 1748.

I received yesterday your letter of the 16th, N.S., and have in consequence of it, written this day to Sir Charles Williams,[2]

---

[1] *Insinuating* was still used in a good sense.

[2] Sir Charles Hanbury Williams, who was at this time British Minister at the Court of Dresden, and whose name will frequently recur in this correspondence. He was born in 1708, and died insane (it is said by his own hand) on 2 November, 1759. During his lifetime he was not more highly extolled for his skill in diplomacy than for his wit both in conversation and in light pieces of poetry; but the collection of his works, published in 1822, has by no means tended to increase, or even confirm, his reputation.

to thank him for all the civilities he has shown you. Your first setting out at Court has, I find, been very favourable; and his Polish majesty has distinguished you. I hope you received that mark of distinction with respect and with steadiness, which is the proper behaviour of a man of fashion. People of a low obscure education, cannot stand the rays of greatness: they are frightened out of their wits when kings and great men speak to them; they are awkward, ashamed, and do not know what or how to answer; whereas *les honnêtes gens* are not dazzled by superior rank; they know and pay all the respect that is due to it, but they do it without being disconcerted, and can converse just as easily with a King as with any one of his subjects. That is the great advantage of being introduced young into good company, and being used early to converse with one's superiors. How many men have I seen here, who, after having had the full benefit of an English education, first at school and then at the University, when they have been presented to the king, did not know whether they stood upon their heads or their heels! If the King spoke to them, they were annihilated; they trembled, endeavoured to put their hands in their pockets, and missed them, let their hats fall, and were ashamed to take them up; and, in short, put themselves in every attitude but the right, that is, the easy and natural one. The characteristic of a well-bred man is, to converse with his inferiors without insolence, and with his superiors with respect and with ease. He talks to kings without concern; he trifles with women of the first condition, with familarity, gaiety, but respect; and converses with his equals, whether he is acquainted with them or not, upon general, common topics, that are not, however, quite frivolous, without the least concern of mind, or awkwardness of body; neither of which can appear to advantage, but when they are perfectly easy.

The tea-things which Sir Charles Williams has given you, I would have you make a present of to your mamma, and send them to her by Duval, when he returns. You owe her not only duty, but likewise great obligations, for her care and tenderness; and, consequently, cannot take too many opportunities of showing your gratitude.

I am impatient to receive your account of Dresden, and likewise your answers to the many questions that I asked you.

Adieu for this time, and God bless you!

DEAR BOY,   London, June 21, O.S. 1748.

Your very bad enunciation runs so much in my head, and gives me such real concern, that it will be the subject of this, and I believe of many more letters. I congratulate both you and myself that I was informed of it (as I hope) in time to prevent it; and shall ever think myself, as hereafter you will I am sure think yourself, infinitely obliged to Sir Charles Williams for informing me of it. Good God! if this ungraceful and disagreeable manner of speaking had, either by your negligence or mine, become habitual to you, as in a couple of years more it would have been, what a figure would you have made in company or in a public assembly! Who would have liked you in the one, or have attended to you in the other? Read what Cicero and Quintilian say of enunciation, and see what a stress they lay upon the gracefulness of it; nay, Cicero goes further, and even maintains that a good figure is necessary for an orator; and, particularly, that he must not be *vastus*—that is, overgrown and clumsy. He shows by it, that he knew mankind well, and knew the powers of an agreeable figure and a graceful manner.

Men, as well as women, are much oftener led by their hearts than by their understandings. The way to the heart is through the senses; please their eyes and their ears, and the work is half done. I have frequently known a man's fortune decided for ever by his first address. If it is pleasing, people are hurried involuntarily into a persuasion that he has a merit which possibly he has not; as, on the other hand, if it is ungraceful, they are immediately prejudiced against him, and unwilling to allow him the merit which it may be he has. Nor is this sentiment so unjust and unreasonable as at first it may seem; for, if a man has parts, he must know of what infinite consequence it is to him to have a graceful manner of speaking, and a genteel and pleasing address: he will cultivate and improve them to the utmost. Your figure is a good one; you have no natural defect in the organs of speech; your address may be engaging and your manner of speaking graceful if you will; so that if they are not so, neither I nor the world can ascribe it to anything but your want of parts. What is the constant and just observation as to all actors upon the stage? Is it not, that those who have the best sense always speak the best, though they may happen not to have the best voices? They will speak plainly, distinctly, and with the proper emphasis, be their voices ever so bad. Had Roscius spoken *quick, thick,*

and *ungracefully*, I will answer for it, that Cicero would not
have thought him worth the oration which he made in his favour.
Words were given us to communicate our ideas by; and there
must be something inconceivably absurd in uttering them in
such a manner as that either people cannot understand them,
or will not desire to understand them.

I tell you truly and sincerely, that I shall judge of your parts
by your speaking gracefully or ungracefully. If you have parts,
you will never be at rest till you have brought yourself to a
habit of speaking most gracefully, for I aver that it is in your
power. You will desire Mr. Harte, that you may read aloud to
him every day; and that he will interrupt and correct you every
time that you read too fast, do not observe the proper stops,
or lay a wrong emphasis. You will take care to open your
teeth when you speak, to articulate every word distinctly, and
to beg of Mr. Harte, Mr. Eliot, or whomever you speak to, to
remind and stop you if ever you fall into the rapid and unintelligible mutter. You will even read aloud to yourself, and tune
your utterance to your own ear; and read at first much slower
than you need to do, in order to correct yourself of that shameful trick of speaking faster than you ought. In short, you will
make it your business, your study, and your pleasure, to speak
well if you think right. Therefore, what I have said in this
and in my last is more than sufficient if you have sense, and
ten times more would not be sufficient if you have not: so here
I rest it.

Next to graceful speaking, a genteel carriage and a graceful
manner of presenting yourself are extremely necessary, for
they are extremely engaging; and carelessness in these points
is much more unpardonable in a young fellow than affectation.
It shows an offensive indifference about pleasing. I am told
by one here, who has seen you lately, that you are awkward
in your motions, and negligent of your person: I am sorry for
both; and so will you, when it will be too late, if you continue
so some time longer. Awkwardness of carriage is very
alienating; and a total negligence of dress and air is an impertinent insult upon custom and fashion. You remember
Mr. —— very well, I am sure, and you must consequently
remember his extreme awkwardness; which, I can assure you,
has been a great clog to his parts and merit, that have, with
much difficulty, but barely counterbalanced it at last. Many,
to whom I have formerly commended him, have answered me,
That they were sure he could not have parts because he was so

awkward: so much are people, as I observed to you before, taken by the eye.

Women have great influence as to a man's fashionable character; and an awkward man will never have their votes; which, by the way, are very numerous, and much oftener counted than weighed. You should therefore give some attention to your dress, and to the gracefulness of your motions. I believe, indeed, that you have no perfect model for either, at Leipsig, to form yourself upon; but, however, do not get a habit of neglecting either: attend properly to both when you go to Courts, where they are very necessary, and where you will have good masters and good models for both. Your exercises of riding, fencing, and dancing, will civilise and fashion your body and your limbs, and give you, if you will but take it, *l'air d'un honnête homme*.

I will now conclude with suggesting one reflection to you; which is, that you should be sensible of your good fortune in having one who interests himself enough in you to inquire into your faults in order to inform you of them. Nobody but myself would be so solicitous either to know or correct them, so that you might consequently be ignorant of them yourself; for our own self-love draws a thick veil between us and our faults. But when you hear yours from me, you may be sure that you hear them from one who for your sake only desires to correct them; from one whom you cannot suspect of any partiality but in your favour; and from one who heartily wishes that his care of you, as a father, may in a little time render every care unnecessary but that of a friend. Adieu!

P.S.—I condole with you for the untimely and violent death of the tuneful Matzel.[1]

DEAR BOY,   London, July 26, O.S. 1748.

There are two sorts of understandings; one of which hinders a man from ever being considerable, and the other commonly makes him ridiculous; I mean, the lazy mind, and the trifling, frivolous mind. Yours, I hope, is neither. The lazy mind

[1] The reference is to a bullfinch whose death was lamented by Sir Charles Hanbury Williams to young Stanhope, in a letter and an ode. The Ode was first published in vol. iv of Dodsley's *Collection*, 1755; and in Mrs. Stanhope's edition of Chesterfield's *Letters to his Son*, she gives a copy of the letter and the verses, the originals of which were in her possession.

will not take the trouble of going to the bottom of anything; but, discouraged by the first difficulties (and everything worth knowing or having is attended with some), stops short, contents itself with easy, and, consequently, superficial knowledge, and prefers a great degree of ignorance to a small degree of trouble. These people either think, or represent, most things as impossible; whereas few things are so, to industry and activity. But difficulties seem to them impossibilities, or at least they pretend to think them so, by way of excuse for their laziness. An hour's attention to the same object is too laborious for them; they take everything in the light in which it first presents itself, never consider it in all its different views; and, in short, never think it thorough. The consequence of this is, that, when they come to speak upon these subjects before people who have considered them with attention, they only discover their own ignorance and laziness, and lay themselves open to answers that put them in confusion. Do not then be discouraged by the first difficulties, but *contra audentior ito*; and resolve to go to the bottom of all those things which every gentleman ought to know well.

Those arts or sciences, which are peculiar to certain professions, need not be deeply known by those who are not intended for those professions. As for instance; fortification and navigation; of both which, a superficial and general knowledge, such as the common course of conversation, with a very little inquiry on your part, will give you, is sufficient. Though, by the way, a little more knowledge of fortification may be of some use to you; as the events of war, in sieges, make many of the terms of that science occur frequently in common conversations; and one would be sorry to say, like the Marquis de Mascarille, in Molière's *Précieuses Ridicules*, when he hears of *une demie lune: Ma foi, c'étoit bien une lune toute entière.* But those things which every gentleman, independently of profession, should know, he ought to know well, and dive into all the depths of them. Such are languages, history, and geography ancient and modern; philosophy, rational logic, rhetoric; and, for you particularly, the constitutions, and the civil and military state of every country in Europe. This, I confess, is a pretty large circle of knowledge attended with some difficulties, and requiring some trouble; which, however, an active and industrious mind will overcome, and be amply repaid.

The trifling and frivolous mind is always busied, but to little purpose; it takes little objects for great ones, and throws away upon trifles that time and attention, which only important important things deserve. Knick-knacks, butterflies, shells, insects, etc., are the objects of their most serious researches. They contemplate the dress, not the characters, of the company they keep. They attend more to the decorations of a play, than to the sense of it; and to the ceremonies of a Court, more than to its politics. Such an employment of time is an absolute loss of it. You have now, at most, three years to employ, either well or ill; for, as I have often told you, you will be all your life, what you shall be three years hence. For God's sake, then, reflect: will you throw away this time, either in laziness, or in trifles? Or will you not rather employ every moment of it in a manner that must so soon reward you, with so much pleasure, figure, and character? I cannot, I will not, doubt of your choice. Read only useful books; and never quit a subject till you are thoroughly master of it, but read and inquire on till then. When you are in company, bring the conversation to some useful subject, but à portée of that company. Points of history, matters of literature, the customs ot particular countries, the several orders of Knighthood, as Teutonic, Maltese, etc., are surely better subjects of conversation than the weather, dress, or fiddle-faddle stories, that carry no information along with them. The characters of Kings and great men are only to be learned in conversation; for they are never fairly written during their lives. This, therefore, is an entertaining and instructive subject of conversation, and will likewise give you an opportunity of observing how very differently characters are given, from the different passions and views of those who give them.

Never be ashamed nor afraid of asking questions; for if they lead to information, and if you accompany them with some excuse, you will never be reckoned an impertinent or rude questioner. All those things, in the common course of life, depend entirely upon the manner; and in that respect the vulgar saying is true, "That one man may better steal a horse, than another look over the hedge." There are few things that may not be said in some manner or other; either in a seeming confidence, or a genteel irony, or introduced with wit: and one great part of the knowledge of the world consists in knowing when, and where, to make use of these different manners. The graces of the person, the countenance, and the way of speaking, contribute so much to this, that I am convinced, the very same thing, said by a genteel person, in an engaging way, and *gracefully and distinctly* spoken, would please; which would shock, if *muttered* out by an awkward figure, with a sullen, serious countenance. The poets always represent Venus as attended by the three Graces, to intimate that even Beauty will not do without. I think they should have given Minerva three also; for, without them, I am sure, learning is very unattractive. Invoke them, then, *distinctly*, to accompany all your words and motions. Adieu!

P.S.—Since I wrote what goes before, I have received your letter, *of no date*, with the enclosed state of the Prussian forces: of which I hope you have kept a copy; this you should lay in a *porte-feuille*, and add to it all the military establishments that you can get, of other states and kingdoms: the Saxon establishment you may, doubtless, easily find. By the way, do not forget to send me answers to the questions which I sent you some time ago, concerning both the civil and the ecclesiastical affairs of Saxony.

Do not mistake me, and think I only mean that you should speak elegantly with regard to style and the purity of language; but I mean, that you should deliver and pronounce what you say, gracefully and distinctly; for which purpose, I will have you frequently read, very loud, to Mr. Harte, recite parts of orations, and speak passages of plays. For, without a graceful and pleasing enunciation, all your elegancy of style, in speaking, is not worth one farthing.

I am very glad that Mr. Lyttelton approves of my new house, and particularly of my *Canonical* pillars. My bust of Cicero is a very fine one, and well preserved; it will have the best place in my library, unless, at your return, you bring me over as good a modern head of your own; which I should like still better. I can tell you that I shall examine it as attentively as ever antiquary did an old one.

Make my compliments to Mr. Harte, whose recovery I rejoice at.

DEAR BOY,   London, August 30, O.S. 1748.

Your reflections upon the conduct of France, from the Treaty of Munster to this time, are very just; and I am very glad to find by them that you not only read, but that you think and reflect upon what you read. Many great readers load their memories without exercising their judgments, and make lumber-rooms of their heads, instead of furnishing them usefully: facts are heaped upon facts without order or distinction, and may justly be said to compose that

> Rudis indigestaque moles,
> Quam dixere chaos.[1]

Go on, then, in the way of reading that you are in; take nothing for granted upon the bare authority of the author, but weigh and consider in your own mind the probability of the facts and the justness of the reflections. Consult different authors upon the same facts, and form your opinion upon the greater or lesser degree of probability arising from the whole, which, in my mind, is the utmost stretch of historical faith: certainty (I fear) not being to be found. When an historian pretends to give you the causes and motives of the events, compare those causes and motives with the characters and interests of the parties concerned, and judge for yourself whether they correspond or not. Consider whether you cannot assign others more probable; and in that examination do not despise some very mean and trifling causes of the actions of great men; for so various and inconsistent is human nature, so strong and so changeable are our passions, so fluctuating are our wills, and so much are our minds influenced by the accidents of our bodies, that every man is more the man of the day than a regular and consequential character. The best have something bad, and something little; the worst have something good, and sometimes something great; for I do not believe what Velleius Paterculus (for the sake of saying a pretty thing) says of Scipio, *Qui nihil non laudandum aut fecit, aut dixit, aut sensit.* As for the reflections of historians, with which they think it necessary to interlard their histories, or at least to conclude their chapters (and which, in the French histories, are always introduced with a *tant il est vrai*, and in the English, *so true it is*), do not adopt them implicitly upon the credit of the author, but analyse them yourself, and judge whether they are true or not.

But, to return to the politics of France, from which I have digressed:—you have certainly made one farther reflection, of an advantage which France has, over and above its abilities in the cabinet, and the skill of its negotiators; which is (if I may use the expression) its *soleness*, continuity of riches and power within itself, and the nature of its government. Near twenty millions of people, and the ordinary revenue of above thirteen millions sterling a-year, are at the absolute disposal of the Crown.

---

[1] Adapted from Ovid. *Metam.*, I, 7.

This is what no other Power in Europe can say; so that different Powers must now unite to make a balance against France; which union, though formed upon the principle of their common interest, can never be so intimate as to compose a machine so compact and simple as that of one great kingdom, directed by one will, and moved by one interest. The Allied Powers (as we have constantly seen) have, besides the common and declared object of their alliance, some separate and concealed view, to which they often sacrifice the general one; which makes them, either directly or indirectly, pull different ways. Thus, the design upon Toulon failed, in the year 1706, only from the secret view of the House of Austria upon Naples; which made the Court of Vienna, notwithstanding the representations of the other Allies to the contrary, send to Naples the 12,000 men that would have done the business at Toulon. In this last war, too, the same causes had the same effects: the Queen of Hungary, in secret, thought of nothing but recovering Silesia, and what she had lost in Italy; and therefore never sent half that quota, which she promised and we paid for, into Flanders; but left that country to the Maritime Powers to defend as they could. The King of Sardinia's real object was Savona, and all the Riviera di Ponente; for which reason he concurred so lamely in the invasion of Provence: where the Queen of Hungary, likewise, did not send one-third of the force stipulated; engrossed as she was, by her oblique views upon the plunder of Genoa, and the recovery of Naples. Insomuch that the expedition into Provence, which would have distressed France to the greatest degree, and have caused a great detachment from their army in Flanders, failed, shamefully, for want of everything necessary for its success.

Suppose, therefore, any four or five Powers, who, all together, shall be equal, or even a little superior, in riches and strength, to that one Power against which they are united; the advantage will still be greatly on the side of that single Power, because it it is but one. The power and riches of Charles V were, in themselves, certainly superior to those of Francis I; and yet, upon the whole, he was not an overmatch for him. Charles V's dominions, great as they were, were scattered and remote from each other; their constitutions different; and, wherever he did not reside, disturbances arose: whereas the compactness of France made up the difference in the strength. This obvious reflection convinced me of the absurdity of the Treaty of Hanover, in 1725, between France and England, to which the

Dutch afterwards acceded; for it was made upon the apprehensions, either real or pretended, that the marriage of Don Carlos with the eldest Archduchess, now Queen of Hungary, was settled in the Treaty of Vienna, of the same year, between Spain and the late Emperor, Charles VI; which marriage, those consummate politicians said, would revive in Europe the exorbitant power of Charles V. I am sure I heartily wish it had; as, in that case, there had been, what there certainly is not now,—one Power in Europe to counterbalance that of France; and then the Maritime Powers would, in reality, have held the balance of Europe in their hands. Even supposing that the Austrian Power would then have been an overmatch for that of France; which (by the way) is not clear; the weight of the Maritime Powers, then thrown into the scale of France, would infallibly have made the balance at least even. In which case, too, the moderate efforts of the Maritime Powers, on the side of France, would have been sufficient; whereas, now, they are obliged to exhaust and beggar themselves, and that too ineffectually, in hopes to support the shattered, beggared, and insufficient House of Austria.

This has been a long political dissertation, but I am informed that political subjects are your favourite ones; which I am glad of, considering your destination. You do well to get your materials all ready, before you begin your work. As you buy, and (I am told) read, books of this kind, I will point out two or three for your purchase and perusal; I am not sure that I have not mentioned them before; but that is no matter, if you have not got them. *Mémoires pour servir à l'Histoire du 17me Siècle*, is a most useful book for you to recur to, for all the facts and chronology of that century; it is in four volumes octavo, and very correct and exact. If I do not mistake, I have formerly recommended to you, *Les Mémoires du Cardinal de Retz*; however, if you have not yet read them, pray do, and with the attention they deserve. You will there find the best account of a very interesting period of the minority of Louis XIV. The characters are drawn short, but in a strong and masterly manner; and the political reflections are the only just and practical ones, that I ever saw in print; they are all well worth your transcribing. *Le Commerce des Anciens, par Monsieur Huet*,[1] *Evêque d'Avranche*, in one little volume octavo, is worth your perusal,

---

[1] Pierre Daniel Huet was tutor to the Dauphin, and edited sixty-two volumes of the Latin classics, known as the Delphin editions. Born 1630, died 1721.

as commerce is a very considerable part of political knowledge. I need not, I am sure, suggest to you, when you read the course of Commerce, either of the ancients or of the moderns, to follow it upon your map; for there is no other way of remembering Geography correctly, than by looking perpetually in the map for the places one reads of, even though one knows before, pretty nearly, where they are.

Adieu! As all the accounts which I receive of you grow better and better, so I grow more and more affectionately yours.

DEAR BOY,　　　　　　　　　London, September 5, O.S. 1748.

I have received yours, with the enclosed German letter to Mr. Grevenkop, which he assures me is extremely well written, considering the little time that you have applied yourself to that language. As you have now got over the most difficult part, pray go on diligently, and make yourself absolutely master of the rest. Whoever does not entirely possess a language will never appear to advantage, or even equal to himself, either in speaking or writing it: his ideas are fettered, and seem imperfect or confused, if he is not master of all the words and phrases necessary to express them. I therefore desire that you will not fail writing a German letter once every fortnight to Mr. Grevenkop; which will make the writing of that language familiar to you: and, moreover, when you shall have left Germany and be arrived at Turin, I shall require you to write even to me in German, that you may not forget with ease what you have with difficulty learned. I likewise desire that, while you are in Germany, you will take all opportunities of conversing in German, which is the only way of knowing that or any other language accurately. You will also desire your German master to teach you the proper titles and superscriptions to be used to people of all ranks, which is a point so material in Germany, that I have known many a letter returned unopened because one title in twenty has been omitted in the direction.

St. Thomas's day now draws near, when you are to leave Saxony and go to Berlin; and I take it for granted, that if anything is yet wanting to complete your knowledge of the state of that Electorate, you will not fail to procure it before you go away. I do not mean, as you will easily believe, the number of churches, parishes, or towns; but I mean the constitution, the revenues, the troops, and the trade of that

Electorate. A few questions sensibly asked of sensible people will procure you the necessary informations; which I desire you will enter in your little book.

Berlin will be entirely a new scene to you, and I look upon it in a manner as your first step into the great world: take care that step be not a false one, and that you do not stumble at the threshold. You will there be in more company than you have yet been; manners and attentions will therefore be more necessary. Pleasing in company is the only way of being pleased in it yourself. Sense and knowledge are the first and necessary foundations for pleasing in company; but they will by no means do alone, and they will never be perfectly welcome if they are not accompanied with manners and attentions. You will best acquire these by frequenting the companies of people of fashion; but then you must resolve to acquire them in those companies by proper care and observation; for I have known people who, though they have frequented good company all their lifetime, have done it in so inattentive and unobserving a manner as to be never the better for it, and to remain as disagreeable, as awkward, and as vulgar, as if they had never seen any person of fashion. When you go into good company (by good company is meant the people of the first fashion of the place) observe carefully their turn, their manners, their address, and conform your own to them.

But this is not all, neither; go deeper still; observe their characters, and pry, as far as you can, into both their hearts and their heads. Seek for their particular merit, their predominant passion, or their prevailing weakness; and you will then know what to bait your hook with to catch them. Man is a composition of so many and such various ingredients, that it requires both time and care to analyse him; for, though we have all the same ingredients in our general composition, as reason, will, passion, and appetites; yet the different proportions and combinations of them in each individual, produce that infinite variety of characters which in some particular or other distinguishes every individual from another. Reason ought to direct the whole, but seldom does. And he who addresses himself singly to another man's reason, without endeavouring to engage his heart in his interest also, is no more likely to succeed, than a man who should apply only to a King's nominal minister and neglect his favourite.

I will recommend to your attentive perusal, now you are going into the world, two books, which will let you as much into the characters of men as books can do. I mean *Les Réflexions Morales de Monsieur de la Rochefoucault*, and *Les Caractères de La Bruyère*[1]: but remember at the same time that I only recommend them to you as the best general maps to assist you in your journey, and not as marking out every particular turning and winding that you will meet with. There, your own sagacity and observation must come to their aid.

La Rochefoucault is I know blamed, but I think without reason, for deriving all our actions from the source of self-love. For my own part, I see a great deal of truth and no harm at all in that opinion. It is certain that we seek our own happiness in everything we do; and it is as certain that we can only find it in doing well, and in conforming all our actions to the rule of right reason, which is the great law of nature. It is only a mistaken self-love that is a blameable motive, when we take the immediate and indiscriminate gratification of a passion or appetite for real happiness. But am I blameable if I do a good action, upon account of the happiness which that honest consciousness will give me? Surely not. On the contrary, that pleasing consciousness is a proof of my virtue. The reflection which is the most censured in Monsieur de la Rochefoucault's book, as a very ill-natured one, is this: *On trouve dans le malheur de son meilleur ami, quelque chose qui ne déplait pas.* And why not? Why may I not feel a very tender and real concern for the misfortune of my friend, and yet at the same time feel a pleasing consciousness of having discharged my duty to him, by comforting and assisting him to the utmost of my power in that misfortune? Give me but virtuous actions, and I will not quibble and chicane about the motives. And I will give anybody their choice of these two truths, which amount to the same thing: He who loves himself best is the honestest man; or, The honestest man loves himself best.

The characters of La Bruyère are pictures from the life; most of them finely drawn, and highly coloured. Furnish your mind with them first; and when you meet with their likeness, as you will every day, they will strike you the more. You will compare every feature with the original; and both will reciprocally help you to discover the beauties and the blemishes.

As women are a considerable, or at least a pretty numerous

---

[1] Jean de la Bruyère, born 1644, died 1696; employed by Bossuet as tutor to the Duke of Burgundy; author of *Characters in the Manner of Theophrastus*; these were drawn from real persons, and exposed the prevailing follies.

part, of company; and as their suffrages go a great way towards establishing a man's character in the fashionable part of the world (which is of great importance to the fortune and figure he proposes to make in it), it is necessary to please them. I will therefore, upon this subject, let you into certain *arcana*, that will be very useful for you to know, but which you must, with the utmost care, conceal, and never seem to know. Women, then, are only children of a larger growth [1]; they have an entertaining tattle and sometimes wit; but for solid, reasoning good-sense, I never in my life knew one that had it, or who reasoned or acted consequentially for four-and-twenty hours together. Some little passion or humour always breaks in upon their best resolutions. Their beauty neglected or controverted, their age increased, or their supposed understandings depreciated, instantly kindles their little passions, and overturns any system of consequential conduct, that in their most reasonable moments they might have been capable of forming. A man of sense only trifles with them, plays with them, humours and flatters them, as he does with a sprightly, forward child; but he neither consults them about, nor trusts them with, serious matters; though he often makes them believe that he does both; which is the thing in the world that they are proud of; for they love mightily to be dabbling in business (which by the way, they always spoil); and being justly distrustful, that men in general look upon them in a trifling light, they almost adore that man, who talks more seriously to them, and who seems to consult and trust them; I say, who seems, for weak men really do, but wise ones only seem to do it. No flattery is either too high or too low for them. They will greedily swallow the highest, and gratefully accept of the lowest; and you may safely flatter any woman, from her understanding down to the exquisite taste of her fan. Women who are either indisputably beautiful, or indisputably ugly, are best flattered upon the score of their understandings; but those who are in a state of mediocrity, are best flattered upon their beauty, or at least their graces; for every woman who is not absolutely ugly, thinks herself handsome; but, not hearing often that she is so, is the more grateful and the more obliged to the few who tell her so; whereas a decided and conscious beauty looks upon every tribute paid to her beauty, only as her due; but wants to shine, and to be considered on the side of her understanding; and a woman who is ugly enough to know that she is so, knows that she has nothing left for it but her

[1] "Men are but children of a larger growth."—DRYDEN, *All for Love*, iv, i.

understanding, which is consequently (and probably in more senses than one) her weak side.

But these are secrets which you must keep inviolably, if you would not, like Orpheus, be torn to pieces by the whole sex; on the contrary, a man who thinks of living in the great world, must be gallant, polite, and attentive to please the women. They have, from the weakness of men, more or less influence in all Courts; they absolutely stamp every man's character in the *beau monde*, and make it either current, or cry it down, and stop it in payments. It is, therefore, absolutely necessary to manage, please, and flatter them; and never to discover the least marks of contempt, which is what they never forgive; but in this they are not singular, for it is the same with men; who will much sooner forgive an injustice than an insult. Every man is not ambitious, or covetous, or passionate; but every man has pride enough in his composition to feel and resent the least slight and contempt. Remember, therefore, most carefully to conceal your contempt, however just, wherever you would not make an implacable enemy. Men are much more unwilling to have their weaknesses and their imperfections known, than their crimes; and, if you hint to a man that you think him silly, ignorant, or even ill-bred or awkward, he will hate you more, and longer, than if you tell him plainly that you think him a rogue. Never yield to that temptation, which to most young men is very strong, of exposing other people's weaknesses and infirmities, for the sake either of diverting the company, or of showing your own superiority. You may get the laugh on your side by it, for the present; but you will make enemies by it for ever; and even those who laugh with you then will, upon reflection, fear, and consequently hate you; besides that, it is ill-natured, and a good heart desires rather to conceal than expose other people's weaknesses or misfortunes. If you have wit, use it to please, and not to hurt: you may shine like the sun in the temperate zones, without scorching. Here it is wished for: under the line it is dreaded.

These are some of the hints which my long experience in the great world enables me to give you; and which, if you attend to them, may prove useful to you in your journey through it. I wish it may be a prosperous one; at least, I am sure that it must be your own fault if it is not.

Make my compliments to Mr. Harte, who, I am very sorry to hear, is not well. I hope by this time he is recovered.

Adieu!

DEAR BOY,   London, September 13, O.S. 1748.

I have more than once recommended to you the Memoirs of the Cardinal de Retz, and to attend particularly to the political reflections interspersed in that excellent work. I will now preach a little upon two or three of those texts.

In the disturbances at Paris, Monsieur de Beaufort, who was a very popular, though a very weak man, was the Cardinal's tool with the populace. Proud of his popularity, he was always for assembling the people of Paris together, thinking that he made a great figure at the head of them. The Cardinal, who was factious enough, was wise enough, at the same time, to avoid gathering the people together except when there was occasion, and when he had something particular for them to do. However, he could not always check Monsieur de Beaufort, who, having assembled them once very unnecessarily, and without any determined object, they ran riot, would not be kept within bounds by their leaders, and did their cause a great deal of harm; upon which the Cardinal observes, most judiciously, *Que Monsieur de Beaufort ne sçavoit pas, que qui assemble le peuple, l'émeut.*

It is certain that great numbers of people, met together, animate each other, and will do something, either good or bad, but oftener bad; and the respective individuals, who were separately very quiet, when met together in numbers, grow tumultuous as a body, and ripe for any mischief that may be pointed out to them by the leaders; and, if their leaders have no business for them, they will find some for themselves. The demagogues, or leaders of popular factions, should, therefore, be very careful not to assemble the people unnecessarily, and without a settled and well-considered object; besides that, by making those popular assemblies too frequent, they make them likewise too familiar, and consequently, less respected by their enemies. Observe any meetings of people, and you will always find their eagerness and impetuosity rise or fall in proportion to their numbers; when the numbers are very great, all sense and reason seem to subside, and one sudden phrenzy to seize on all, even the coolest of them.

Another very just observation of the Cardinal's is, That the things which happen in our own times, and which we see ourselves, do not surprise us near so much as the things which we read of in times past, though not in the least more extraordinary; and adds, that he is persuaded that, when Caligula made his horse a Consul, the people of Rome, at that time, were not greatly surprised at it, having necessarily been in some degree prepared for it, by an insensible gradation of extravagancies from the same quarter. This is so true, that we read every day, with astonishment, things which we see every day without surprise. We wonder at the intrepidity of a Leonidas, a Codrus, and a Curtius, and are not the least surprised to hear of a sea-captain who has blown up his ship, his crew, and himself, that they might not fall into the hands of the enemies of his country. I cannot help reading of Porsenna and Regulus with surprise and reverence; and yet I remember that I saw, without either, the execution of Shepherd, a boy of eighteen years old, who intended to shoot the late King, and who would have been pardoned, if he would have expressed the least sorrow for his intended crime; but, on the contrary, he declared that if he was pardoned he would attempt it again, that he thought it a duty which he owed his country, and that he died with pleasure for having endeavoured to perform it.[1] Reason equals Shepherd to Regulus; but prejudice, and the recency of the fact, make Shepherd a common malefactor, and Regulus a hero.

Examine carefully, and re-consider all your notions of things; analyse them, and discover their component parts and see if habit and prejudice are not the principal ones; weigh the matter, upon which you are to form your opinion, in the equal and impartial scales of reason. It is not to be conceived how many people, capable of reasoning if they would, live and die in a thousand errors, from laziness; they will rather adopt the prejudices of others, than give themselves the trouble of forming opinions of their own. They say things, at first, because other people have said them, and then they persist in them, because they have said them themselves.

The last observation that I shall now mention of the Cardinal's is: That a secret is more easily kept by a good many people than one commonly imagines. By this he means a secret of importance, among people interested in the keeping of it. And it is certain that people of business know the importance of secrecy, and will observe it, where they are concerned in the event. And the Cardinal does not suppose that anybody is silly enough to tell a secret merely from the desire of telling it, to any one that is not some way or other interested in the keeping of it, and concerned in the event. To go and tell any

---

[1] James Shepherd, apprentice to a coachbuilder in Devonshire Street, was executed at Tyburn in March 1718, on the evidence of a clergyman named Leake, whom he had informed of his intention by letter.

friend, wife, or mistress, any secret with which they have nothing to do, is discovering to them such an unretentive weakness, as must convince them that you will tell it to twenty others, and, consequently, that they may reveal it without the risk of being discovered. But a secret properly communicated, only to those who are to be concerned in the thing in question, will probably be kept by them, though they should be a good many. Little secrets are commonly told again, but great ones generally kept.

Adieu!

DEAR BOY,   Bath, October 12, O.S. 1748.

I came here three days ago, upon account of a disorder in my stomach, which affected my head, and gave me vertigos. I already find myself something better; and, consequently, do not doubt that a course of these waters will set me quite right. But, however, and wherever I am, your welfare, your character, your knowledge, and your morals, employ my thoughts more than anything that can happen to me, or that I can fear or hope for myself. I am going off the stage, you are coming upon it; with me, what has been, has been, and reflection now would come too late; with you, everything is to come, even, in some manner, reflection itself; so that this is the very time when my reflections, the result of experience, may be of use to you, by supplying the want of yours. As soon as you leave Leipsig, you will gradually be going into the great world; where the first impressions that you shall give of yourself will be of great importance to you; but those which you shall receive will be decisive, for they always stick. To keep good company, especially at your first setting out, is the way to receive good impressions. If you ask me what I mean by good company, I will confess to you, that it is pretty difficult to define; but I will endeavour to make you understand it as well as I can.

Good company is not what respective sets of company are pleased either to call or think themselves, but it is that company which all the people of the place call and acknowledge to be good company, notwithstanding some objections which they may form to some of the individuals who compose it. It consists chiefly (but by no means without exception) of people of considerable birth, rank, and character; for people of neither birth nor rank are frequently, and very justly, admitted into it, if distinguished by any peculiar merit, or eminency in any liberal art or science. Nay, so motley a thing is good company, that many people, without birth, rank, or merit, intrude into it by their own forwardness, and others slide into it by the protection of some considerable person; and some even of indifferent characters and morals make part of it. But, in the main, the good part preponderates, and people of infamous and blasted characters are never admitted. In this fashionable good company, the best manners and the best language of the place are most unquestionably to be learnt; for they establish and give the tone to both, which are therefore called the language and manners of good company, there being no legal tribunal to ascertain either.

A company consisting wholly of people of the first quality cannot, for that reason, be called good company, in the common acceptation of the phrase, unless they are, into the bargain, the fashionable and accredited company of the place; for people of the very first quality can be as silly, as ill-bred, and as worthless, as people of the meanest degree. On the other hand, a company consisting entirely of people of very low condition, whatever their merit or parts may be, can never be called good company, and consequently should not be much frequented, though by no means despised.

A company wholly composed of men of learning, though greatly to be valued and respected, is not meant by the words *good company*; they cannot have the easy manners and *tournure* of the world, as they do not live in it. If you can bear your part well in such a company, it is extremely right to be in it sometimes, and you will be but more esteemed in other companies for having a place in that; but then do not let it engross you, for, if you do, you will be only considered as one of the *literati* by profession, which is not the way either to shine or rise in the world.

The company of professed wits and poets is extremely inviting to most young men, who, if they have wit themselves, are pleased with it, and, if they have none, are sillily proud of being one of it; but it should be frequented with moderation and judgment, and you should by no means give yourself up to it. A wit is a very unpopular denomination, as it carries terror along with it; and people in general are as much afraid of a live wit in company as a woman is of a gun, which she thinks may go off of itself, and do her a mischief. Their acquaintance is, however, worth seeking, and their company worth frequenting; but not exclusively of others, nor to such a degree as to be considered only as one of that particular set.

But the company which of all others you should most carefully avoid, is that low company which, in every sense of the word, is low indeed—low in rank, low in parts, low in manners, and low in merit. You will, perhaps, be surprised that I should think it necessary to warn you against such company; but yet I do not think it wholly unnecessary, after the many instances which I have seen of men of sense and rank, discredited, vilified, and undone, by keeping such company. Vanity, that source of many of our follies, and of some of our crimes, has sunk many a man into company in every light infinitely below himself, for the sake of being the first man in it; there he dictates, is applauded, admired; and, for the sake of being the *Coryphæus* of that wretched chorus, disgraces and disqualifies himself soon for any better company. Depend upon it, you will sink or rise to the level of the company which you commonly keep; —people will judge of you, and not unreasonably, by that. There is good sense in the Spanish saying, "Tell me whom you live with, and I will tell you who you are." Make it therefore your business, wherever you are, to get into that company which everybody of the place allows to be the best company, next to their own:—which is the best definition that I can give you of good company. But here, too, one caution is very necessary, for want of which many young men have been ruined, even in good company. Good company (as I have before observed) is composed of a great variety of fashionable people, whose characters and morals are very different, though their manners are pretty much the same.

When a young man, new in the world, first gets into that company, he very rightly determines to conform to and imitate it; but then he too often, and fatally, mistakes the objects of his imitation. He has often heard that absurd term of genteel and fashionable vices. He there sees some people who shine, and who in general are admired and esteemed; and observes that these people are whoremasters, or drunkards, or gamesters; upon which he adopts their vices, mistaking their defects for their perfections, and thinking that they owe their fashion and their lustre to those genteel vices. Whereas it is exactly the reverse, for these people have acquired their reputation by their parts, their learning, their good-breeding, and other real accomplishments; and are only blemished and lowered. in the opinions of all reasonable people, and of their own, in time, by these genteel and fashionable vices. A whoremaster in a flux, or without a nose, is a very genteel person indeed, and well worthy of imitation; a drunkard, vomiting up at night the wine of the day, and stupified by the headache all the next, is, doubtless, a fine model to copy from; and a gamester, tearing his hair and blaspheming, for having lost more than he had in the world, is surely a most amiable character. No; these are allays,[1] and great ones too, which can never adorn any character, but will always debase the best. To prove this, suppose any man, without parts and some other good qualities, to be merely a whoremaster, a drunkard, or a gamester—how will he be looked upon by all sorts of people? Why, as a most contemptible and vicious animal. Therefore it is plain that, in these mixed characters, the good part only makes people forgive, but not approve, the bad.

I will hope, and believe, that you will have no vices; but if, unfortunately, you should have any, at least I beg of you to be content with your own, and to adopt no other body's. The adoption of vice has, I am convinced, ruined ten times more young men than natural inclinations.

As I make no difficulty of confessing my past errors, where I think the confession may be of use to you, I will own that, when I first went to the university, I drank and smoked, notwithstanding the aversion I had to wine and tobacco, only because I thought it genteel, and that it made me look like a man. When I went abroad, I first went to the Hague, where gaming was much in fashion; and where I observed that many people of shining rank and character gamed too. I was then young enough, and silly enough, to believe that gaming was one of their accomplishments; and, as I aimed at perfection, I adopted gaming as a necessary step to it. Thus I acquired, by error, the habit of a vice which, far from adorning my character, has, I am conscious, been a great blemish in it.

Imitate, then, with discernment and judgment, the real perfections of the good company into which you may get; copy their politeness, their carriage, their address, and the easy and well-bred turn of their conversation; but remember, that, let them shine ever so bright, their vices, if they have any, are so many spots, which you would no more imitate than you would make an artificial wart upon your face, because some very handsome man had the misfortune to have a natural one

---

[1] Abatements, drawbacks; obsolete.

upon his; but, on the contrary, think how much handsomer he would have been without it.

Having thus confessed some of my *égaremens*, I will now show you a little of my right side. I always endeavoured to get into the best company wherever I was, and commonly succeeded. There I pleased, to some degree, by showing a desire to please. I took care never to be absent or *distrait*; but, on the contrary, attended to everything that was said, done, or even looked, in company; I never failed in the minutest attentions, and was never *journalier*. These things, and not my *égaremens*, made me fashionable.

Adieu! this letter is full long enough.

DEAR BOY,   Bath, October 19, O.S. 1748.

Having, in my last, pointed out what sort of company you should keep, I will now give you some rules for your conduct in it; rules which my own experience and observation enable me to lay down and communicate to you with some degree of confidence. I have often given you hints of this kind before, but then it has been by snatches; I will now be more regular and methodical. I shall say nothing with regard to your bodily carriage and address, but leave them to the care of your dancing-master, and to your own attention to the best models; remember, however, that they are of consequence.

Talk often, but never long; in that case, if you do not please, at least you are sure not to tire your hearers. Pay your own reckoning, but do not treat the whole company; this being one of the very few cases in which people do not care to be treated, every one being fully convinced that he has wherewithal to pay.

Tell stories very seldom, and absolutely never but where they are very apt, and very short. Omit every circumstance that is not material, and beware of digressions. To have frequent recourse to narrative betrays great want of imagination.

Never hold anybody by the button, or the hand, in order to be heard out; for, if people are not willing to hear you, you had much better hold your tongue than them.

Most long talkers single out some one unfortunate man in company (commonly him whom they observe to be the most silent, or their next neighbour) to whisper, or at least, in a half voice, to convey a continuity of words to. This is excessively ill-bred, and, in some degree, a fraud; conversation-stock being a joint and common property. But, on the other hand, if one of these unmerciful talkers lays hold of you, hear him with patience, and at least seeming attention, if he is worth obliging; for nothing will oblige him more than a patient hearing, as nothing would hurt him more than either to leave him in the midst of his discourse, or to discover your impatience under your affliction.

Take, rather than give, the tone of the company you are in. If you have parts, you will show them, more or less, upon every subject; and, if you have not, you had better talk sillily upon a subject of other people's than of your own choosing.

Avoid as much as you can, in mixed companies, argumentative polemical conversations; which, though they should not, yet certainly do, indispose, for a time, the contending parties towards each other; and, if the controversy grows warm and noisy, endeavour to put an end to it by some genteel levity or joke. I quieted such a conversation hubbub once, by representing to them that, though I was persuaded none there present would repeat, out of company, what passed in it, yet I could not answer for the discretion of the passengers in the street, who must necessarily hear all that was said.

Above all things, and upon all occasions, avoid speaking of yourself, if it be possible. Such is the natural pride and vanity of our hearts, that it perpetually breaks out, even in people of the best parts, in all the various modes and figures of the egotism.

Some abruptly speak advantageously of themselves, without either pretence or provocation. They are impudent. Others proceed more artfully, as they imagine, and forge accusations against themselves, complain of calumnies which they never heard, in order to justify themselves, by exhibiting a catalogue of their many virtues. "They acknowledge it may, indeed, seem odd, that they should talk in that manner of themselves; it is what they do not like, and what they never would have done; no, no torture should ever have forced it from them, if they had not been thus unjustly and monstrously accused. But, in these cases, justice is surely due to one's self, as well as to others; and, when our character is attacked, we may say, in our own justification, what otherwise we never would have said." This thin veil of modesty drawn before vanity, is much too transparent to conceal it, even from very moderate discernment.

Others go more modestly and more slyly still (as they think) to work; but, in my mind, still more ridiculously. They confess themselves (not without some degree of shame and confusion) into all the cardinal virtues; by first degrading them into weaknesses, and then owning their misfortune, in being made up of those weaknesses. "They cannot see people suffer, without sympathizing with, and endeavouring to help them. They cannot see people want, without relieving them; though, truly, their own circumstances cannot very well afford it. They cannot help speaking truth, though they know all the imprudence of it. In short, they know that, with all these weaknesses, they are not fit to live in the world, much less to thrive in it. But they are now too old to change, and must rub on as well as they can." This sounds too ridiculous and *outré*, almost for the stage; and yet, take my word for it, you will frequently meet with it upon the common stage of the world. And here I will observe, by the bye, that you will often meet with characters in nature so extravagant, that a discreet poet would not venture to set them upon the stage in their true and high colouring.

This principle of vanity and pride is so strong in human nature, that it descends even to the lowest objects; and one often sees people angling for praise, where, admitting all they say to be true (which, by the way, it seldom is), no just praise is to be caught. One man affirms that he has rode post an hundred miles in six hours: probably it is a lie; but supposing it to be true, what then? Why, he is a very good post-boy, that is all. Another asserts, and probably not without oaths, that he has drank six or eight bottles of wine at a sitting; out of charity, I will believe him a liar; for, if I do not, I must think him a beast.

Such, and a thousand more, are the follies and extravagancies, which vanity draws people into, and which always defeat their own purpose, and, as Waller says upon another subject:

> Make the wretch the most despised,
> Where most he wishes to be prized.[1]

The only sure way of avoiding these evils is never to speak of yourself at all. But when historically you are obliged to mention yourself, take care not to drop one single word, that can directly or indirectly be construed as fishing for applause. Be your character what it will, it will be known; and nobody will take it upon your own word. Never imagine that anything you can say yourself will varnish your defects, or add lustre to

---

[1] These lines are adapted from Waller's *On Love*. The couplet is:
> "Postures which render him despised,
> Where he endeavours to be prized."

your perfections; but, on the contrary, it may, and nine times in ten will, make the former more glaring, and the latter obscure. If you are silent upon your own subject, neither envy, indignation, nor ridicule will obstruct or allay the applause which you may really deserve; but if you publish your own panegyric, upon any occasion, or in any shape whatsoever, and however artfully dressed or disguised, they will all conspire against you, and you will be disappointed of the very end you aim at.

Take care never to seem dark and mysterious; which is not only a very unamiable character, but a very suspicious one too; if you seem mysterious with others, they will be really so with you, and you will know nothing. The height of abilities is, to have *volto sciolto* and *pensieri stretti* [1]; that is, a frank, open, and ingenuous exterior, with a prudent and reserved interior; to be upon your own guard, and yet, by a seeming natural openness, to put people off theirs. Depend upon it, nine in ten of every company you are in will avail themselves of every indiscreet and unguarded expression of yours, if they can turn it to their own advantage. A prudent reserve is therefore as necessary as a seeming openness is prudent. Always look people in the face when you speak to them; the not doing it is thought to imply conscious guilt; besides that, you lose the advantage of observing by their countenances what impression your discourse makes upon them. In order to know people's real sentiments, I trust much more to my eyes than to my ears; for they can say whatever they have a mind I should hear; but they can seldom help looking what they have no intention that I should know.

Neither retail nor receive scandal willingly; for though the defamation of others may for the present gratify the malignity of the pride of our hearts, cool reflection will draw very disadvantageous conclusions from such a disposition; and in the case of scandal, as in that of robbery, the receiver is always thought as bad as the thief.

Mimicry, which is the common and favourite amusement of little low minds, is in the utmost contempt with great ones. It is the lowest and most illiberal of all buffoonery. Pray, neither practise it yourself, nor applaud it in others. Besides that, the person mimicked is insulted; and, as I have often observed to you before, an insult is never forgiven.

---

[1] This is a favourite maxim of Chesterfield's. It was also the advice given by Sir Henry Wotton to Milton, just before he set out for the Continent, in the letter in which he acknowledges *Comus*.

I need not, I believe, advise you to adapt your conversation to the people you are conversing with; for I suppose you would not, without this caution, have talked upon the same subject and in the same manner to a Minister of state, a Bishop, a philosopher, a Captain, and a woman. A man of the world must, like the chameleon, be able to take every different hue, which is by no means a criminal or abject, but a necessary complaisance, for it relates only to manners, and not to morals.

One word only as to swearing; and that I hope and believe is more than is necessary. You may sometimes hear some people in good company interlard their discourse with oaths, by way of embellishment, as they think; but you must observe, too, that those who do so are never those who contribute in any degree to give that company the denomination of good company. They are always subalterns, or people of low education; for that practice, besides that it has no one temptation to plead, is as silly and as illiberal as it is wicked.

Loud laughter is the mirth of the mob, who are only pleased with silly things; for true wit or good sense never excited a laugh since the creation of the world. A man of parts and fashion is therefore only seen to smile, but never heard to laugh.

But, to conclude this long letter; all the above-mentioned rules, however carefully you may observe them, will lose half their effect if unaccompanied by the Graces. Whatever you say, if you say it with a supercilious, cynical face, or an embarrassed countenance, or a silly, disconcerted grin, will be ill received. If, into the bargain, *you mutter it, or utter it indistinctly and ungracefully*, it will be still worse received. If your air and address are vulgar, awkward, and *gauche*, you may be esteemed indeed if you have great intrinsic merit; but you will never please, and without pleasing you will rise but heavily. Venus, among the ancients, was synonymous with the Graces, who were always supposed to accompany her; and Horace tells us, that even youth, and Mercury, the god of arts and eloquence, would not do without her.

> —*Parum comis* sine te Juventas
> Mercuriusque.[1]

They are not inexorable ladies, and may be had if properly and diligently pursued. Adieu!

[1] *Odes*, I, 30.

Dear Boy,   Bath, October 29, O.S. 1748.

My anxiety for your success increases in proportion as the time approaches of your taking your part upon the great stage of the world. The audience will form their opinion of you upon your first appearance (making the proper allowance for your inexperience), and so far it will be final, that, though it may vary as to the degrees, it will never totally change. This consideration excites that restless attention with which I am constantly examining how I can best contribute to the perfection of that character in which the least spot or blemish would give me more real concern than I am now capable of feeling upon any other account whatsoever.

I have long since done mentioning your great religious and moral duties, because I could not make your understanding so bad a compliment, as to suppose that you wanted or could receive any new instructions upon those two important points. Mr. Harte, I am sure, has not neglected them; besides, they are so obvious to common sense and reason, that commentators may (as they often do) perplex, but cannot make them clearer. My province, therefore, is to supply by my experience your hitherto inevitable inexperience in the ways of the world. People at your age are in a state of natural ebriety, and want rails and *gardefous* wherever they go, to hinder them from breaking their necks. This drunkenness of youth is not only tolerated, but even pleases, if kept within certain bounds of discretion and decency. Those bounds are the point which it is difficult for the drunken man himself to find out; and there it is that the experience of a friend may not only serve, but save him.

Carry with you, and welcome, into company all the gaiety and spirits, but as little of the giddiness of youth as you can. The former will charm, but the latter will often, though innocently, implacably offend. Inform yourself of the characters and situations of the company before you give way to what your imagination may prompt you to say. There are in all companies more wrong heads than right ones, and many more who deserve than who like censure. Should you therefore expatiate in the praise of some virtue, which some in company notoriously want, or declaim against any vice which others are notoriously infected with, your reflections, however general and unapplied, will, by being applicable, be thought personal and levelled at those people. This consideration points out to you sufficiently not to be suspicious and captious yourself, not to suppose that things, because they may, are therefore meant at you. The manners of well-bred people secure one from these indirect and mean attacks; but if, by chance, a flippant woman or a pert coxcomb lets off anything of that kind, it is much better not to seem to understand, than to reply to it.

Cautiously avoid talking of either your own or other people's domestic affairs. Yours are nothing to them, but tedious; theirs are nothing to you. The subject is a tender one; and it is odds but you touch somebody or other's sore place; for in this case there is no trusting to specious appearances, which may be, and often are, so contrary to the real situations of things between men and their wives, parents and their children, seeming friends, etc., that, with the best intentions in the world, one often blunders disagreeably.

Remember, that the wit, humour, and jokes of most mixed companies are local. They thrive in that particular soil, but will not often bear transplanting. Every company is differently circumstanced, has its particular cant and jargon, which may give occasion to wit and mirth within that circle, but would seem flat and insipid in any other, and therefore will not bear repeating. Nothing makes a man look sillier than a pleasantry not relished or not understood; and if he meets with a profound silence when he expected a general applause, or, what is worse, if he is desired to explain the *bon mot*, his awkward and embarrassed situation is easier imagined than described. *A propos* of repeating; take great care never to repeat (I do not mean here the pleasantries) in one company what you hear in another. Things seemingly indifferent may, by circulation, have much graver consequences than you would imagine. Besides, there is a general tacit trust in conversation by which a man is obliged not to report anything out of it, though he is not immediately enjoined secrecy. A retailer of this kind is sure to draw himself into a thousand scrapes and discussions, and to be shyly and uncomfortably received wherever he goes.

You will find, in most good company, some people who only keep their place there by a contemptible title enough,—these are what we call *very good-natured fellows*, and the French *bons diables*. The truth is, they are people without any parts or fancy, and who, having no will of their own, readily assent to, concur in, and applaud whatever is said or done in the company; and adopt, with the same alacrity, the most virtuous or the most criminal, the wisest or the silliest scheme, that happens to be entertained by the majority of the company. This foolish, and often criminal complaisance, flows from a foolish cause,—the want of any other merit. I hope you will hold your place in company by a nobler tenure, and that you will hold it (you can bear a quibble, I believe, yet) *in capite*. Have a will and an opinion of your own, and adhere to them steadily; but then do it with good-humour, good-breeding, and (if you have it) with urbanity; for you have not yet beard enough either to preach or censure.

All other kinds of complaisance are not only blameless, but necessary in good company. Not to seem to perceive the little weaknesses, and the idle but innocent affectations of the company, but even to flatter them in a certain manner, is not only very allowable, but, in truth, a sort of polite duty. They will be pleased with you, if you do; and will certainly not be reformed by you, if you do not. For instance; you will find, in every *groupe* of company, two principal figures, *viz.* the fine lady and the fine gentleman; who absolutely give the law of wit, language, fashion, and taste, to the rest of that society. There is always a strict, and often, for the time being, a tender alliance between these two figures. The lady looks upon her empire as founded upon the divine right of beauty (and full as good a divine right it is, as any King, Emperor, or Pope can pretend to); she requires, and commonly meets with, unlimited passive obedience. And why should she not meet with it? Her demands go no higher than to have her unquestioned pre-eminence in beauty, wit, and fashion, firmly established. Few Sovereigns (by the way) are so reasonable. The fine gentleman's claims of right are, *mutatis mutandis*, the same; and though, indeed, he is not always a wit *de jure*, yet, as he is the wit *de facto* of that company, he is entitled to a share of your allegiance; and everybody expects, at least, as much as they are entitled to, if not something more. Prudence bids you make your court to these joint Sovereigns; and no duty, that I know of, forbids it. Rebellion, here is exceedingly dangerous, and inevitably punished by banishment, and immediate forfeiture of all your wit, manners, taste, and fashion; as, on the other hand, a cheerful submission, not without some flattery, is sure to procure you a strong recommendation, and most effectual pass, throughout all their, and probably the neighbouring dominions. With a moderate share of sagacity, you will, before you have been half an hour in their company, easily discover these two principal figures; both by the deference which you will observe the whole company pay them, and by that easy, careless, and serene air, which their consciousness of power gives them. As in this case, so in all others, aim always at the highest; get always into the highest company, and address yourself particularly to the highest in it. The search after the unattainable philosopher's stone has occasioned a thousand useful discoveries, which otherwise would never have been made.

What the French justly call *les manières nobles*, are only to be acquired in the very best companies. They are the distinguishing characteristics of men of fashion; people of low education never wear them so close but that some part or other of the original vulgarism appears. *Les manières nobles* equally forbid insolent contempt, or low envy and jealousy. Low people in good circumstances, fine clothes, and equipages, will insolently show contempt for all those who cannot afford as fine clothes, as good an equipage, and who have not (as their term is) as much money in their pockets; on the other hand, they are gnawed with envy, and cannot help discovering it, of those who surpass them in any of these articles, which are far from being sure criterions of merit. They are likewise jealous of being slighted, and, consequently, suspicious and captious; they are eager and hot about trifles, because trifles were, at first, their affairs of consequence. *Les manières nobles* imply exactly the reverse of all this. Study them early; you cannot make them too habitual and familiar to you.

Just as I had written what goes before, I received your letter of the 24th, N.S., but I have not received that which you mention from Mr. Harte. Yours is of the kind that I desire, for I want to see your private picture drawn by yourself at different sittings; for though, as it is drawn by yourself, I presume you will take the most advantageous likeness, yet I think I have skill enough in that kind of painting to discover the true features, though ever so artfully coloured or thrown into skilful lights and shades.

By your account of the German play, which I do not know whether I should call tragedy or comedy, the only shining part of it (since I am in a way of quibbling) seems to have been the Fox's tail. I presume, too, that the play has had the same fate with the squib, and has gone off no more. I remember a squib much better applied, when it was made the device of the colours of a French regiment of grenadiers; it was represented bursting with this motto under it: *Peream dum luceam*. I like the description of your *picnic*, where I take it for granted that your cards are only to break the formality of a circle, and your *symposion* intended more to promote conversation than drinking. Such an *amicable collision*, as Lord Shaftesbury very prettily calls it, rubs off and smooths those rough corners which mere nature has given to the smoothest of us. I hope some part, at least, of the conversation is in German. *A propos;* tell me,—do you speak that language correctly, and do you write it with ease? I have no doubt of your mastering the other modern languages, which are much easier, and occur much oftener; for which reason I desire you will apply most diligently to German while you are in Germany, that you may speak and write that language most correctly.

I expect to meet Mr. Eliot in London in about three weeks; after which you will soon see him at Leipsig. Adieu!

DEAR BOY,   London, November 18, O.S. 1748.

Whatever I see or whatever I hear, my first consideration is, whether it can in any way be useful to you. As a proof of this, I went accidentally the other day into a print-shop, where, among many others, I found one print from a famous design of Carlo Maratti, who died about thirty years ago,[1] and was the last eminent painter in Europe; the subject is *il Studio del Disegno,* or the School of Drawing. An old man, supposed to be the master, points to his scholars, who are variously employed, in perspective, geometry, and the observation of the statues of antiquity. With regard to perspective, of which there are some little specimens, he has wrote, *tanto che basti,* that is, *as much as is sufficient*; with regard to geometry, *tanto che basti,* again; with regard to the contemplation of the ancient statues, there is written, *non mai a bastanza,—there never can be enough.* But, in the clouds, at top of the piece, are represented the three Graces, with this just sentence written over them, *senza di noi ogni fatica è vana*; that is, *without us all labour is vain.*

This everybody allows to be true in painting; but all people do not seem to consider, as I hope you will, that this truth is full as applicable to every other art or science; indeed to everything that is to be said or done. I will send you the print itself by Mr. Eliot, when he returns; and I will advise you to make the same use of it that the Roman Catholics say they

[1] Maratti was born at Camerino in Italy in 1625, and died in 1713.

do of the pictures and images of their Saints,—which is, only to remind them of those, for the adoration they disclaim. Nay, I will go farther, and, as the transition from popery to paganism is short and easy, I will classically and poetically advise you to invoke and sacrifice to them every day—and all the day. It must be owned that the Graces do not seem to be natives of Great Britain; and, I doubt, the best of us here have more of the rough than the polished diamond. Since barbarism drove them out of Greece and Rome, they seem to have taken refuge in France, where their temples are numerous, and their worship the established one.

Examine yourself seriously why such and such people please and engage you more than such and such others of equal merit, and you will always find that it is because the former have the Graces and the latter not. I have known many a woman, with an exact shape and a symmetrical assemblage of beautiful features, please nobody; while others, with very moderate shapes and features, have charmed everybody. Why?— Because Venus will not charm so much without her attendant Graces as they will without her. Among men, how often have I seen the most solid merit and knowledge neglected, unwelcome, or even rejected, for want of them! While flimsy parts, little knowledge, and less merit, introduced by the Graces, have been received, cherished, and admired. Even virtue, which is moral beauty, wants some of its charms if unaccompanied by them.

If you ask me how you shall acquire what neither you nor I can define or ascertain, I can only answer,—*by observation*. Form yourself, with regard to others, upon what you feel pleases you in them. I can tell you the importance—the advantage of having the Graces; but I cannot give them you; I heartily wish I could, and I certainly would; for I do not know a better present that I could make you.

To show you that a very wise, philosophical, and retired man thinks upon that subject as I do, who have always lived in the world, I send you, by Mr. Eliot, the famous Mr. Locke's book upon education, in which you will find the stress that he lays upon the Graces, which he calls (and very truly) good-breeding. I have marked all the parts of that book which are worth your attention; for, as he begins with the child, almost from its birth, the parts relative to its infancy would be useless to you. Germany is still less than England the seat of the Graces; however, you had as good not say so while

you are there. But the place which you are going to in a
great degree is; for I have known as many well-bred, pretty
men come from Turin as from any part of Europe. The late
King Victor Amedée took great pains to form such of his
subjects as were of any consideration both to business and
manners. The present King, I am told, follows his example;
this, however, is certain, that in all Courts and Congresses
where there are various foreign ministers, those of the King
of Sardinia are generally the ablest, the politest, and *les plus
déliés*. You will, therefore, at Turin, have very good models
to form yourself upon; and remember, that with regard to the
best models, as well as to the antique Greek statues in the
print, *non mai a bastanza*. Observe every word, look, and
motion of those who are allowed to be the most accomplished
persons there. Observe their natural and careless, but genteel
air; their unembarrassed good-breeding; their unassuming, but
yet unprostituted dignity. Mind their decent mirth, their
discreet frankness, and that *entregent*, which, as much above
the frivolous as below the important and the secret, is the
proper medium for conversation in mixed companies. I will
observe, by the bye, that the talent of that light *entregent* is
often of great use to a foreign minister; not only as it helps
him to domesticate himself in many families, but also as it
enables him to put by and parry some subjects of conversation
which might possibly lay him under difficulties—both what to
say and how to look.

Of all the men that ever I knew in my life (and I knew him
extremely well), the late Duke of Marlborough[1] possessed the
Graces in the highest degree, not to say engrossed them; and,
indeed, he got the most by them, for I will venture (contrary
to the custom of profound historians, who always assign deep
causes for great events) to ascribe the better half of the Duke
of Marlborough's greatness and riches to those Graces. He
was eminently illiterate; wrote bad English, and spelled it
still worse. He had no share of what is commonly called
parts; that is, he had no brightness, nothing shining in his
genius. He had, most undoubtedly, an excellent good plain
understanding, with sound judgment. But these alone would
probably have raised him but something higher than they
found him, which was page to King James the Second's Queen.
There the Graces protected and promoted him; for, while he
was an Ensign of the Guards, the Duchess of Cleveland, then

[1] Born 1650, died 1722.

favourite mistress to King Charles the Second, struck by those very Graces, gave him five thousand pounds, with which he immediately bought an annuity for his life, of five hundred pounds a-year, of my grandfather, Halifax,[1] which was the foundation of his subsequent fortune. His figure was beautiful, but his manner was irresistible, by either man or woman. It was by this engaging, graceful manner, that he was enabled, during all his war, to connect the various and jarring powers of the Grand Alliance, and to carry them on to the main object of the war, notwithstanding their private and separate views, jealousies, and wrongheadednesses. Whatever Court he went to (and he was often obliged to go himself to some resty [2] and refractory ones), he as constantly prevailed, and brought them into his measures. The Pensionary Heinsius, a venerable old minister, grown grey in business, and who had governed the republic of the United Provinces for more than forty years, was absolutely governed by the Duke of Marlborough, as that republic feels to this day. He was always cool, and nobody ever observed the least variation in his countenance; he could refuse more gracefully than other people could grant; and those who went away from him the most dissatisfied as to the substance of their business, were yet personally charmed with him, and, in some degree, comforted by his manner. With all his gentleness and gracefulness, no man living was more conscious of his situation, nor maintained his dignity better.

With the share of knowledge which you have already gotten, and with the much greater which I hope you will soon acquire, what may you not expect to arrive at, if you join all these Graces to it! In your destination particularly, they are, in truth, half your business; for if you can once gain the affections, as well as the esteem, of the Prince or Minister of the Court to which you are sent, I will answer for it that will effectually do the business of the Court that sent you; otherwise it is up-hill work. Do not mistake, and think that these Graces, which I so often and so earnestly recommend to you, should only accompany important transactions, and be worn only *les jours de gala*; no, they should, if possible, accompany every the least thing that you do or say; for, if you neglect them in little things, they will leave you in great ones. I should, for instance, be extremely concerned to see you even drink a

[1] George Savile, the celebrated Marquis of Halifax, born 1633, died 1695; he contributed to the restoration of Charles II, and tendered the crown to William and Mary.

[2] *Resty*, hard to move; it occurs in Milton's prose.

cup of coffee ungracefully, and slop yourself with it, by your awkward manner of holding it; nor should I like to see your coat buttoned, or your shoes buckled awry. But I should be outrageous if I heard you mutter your words unintelligibly, stammer in your speech, or hesitate, misplace, and mistake in your narrations: and I should run away from you with greater rapidity, if possible, than I should now run to embrace you, if I found you destitute of all those Graces, which I have set my heart upon their making you one day, *omnibus ornatum excellere rebus.*

This subject is inexhaustible, as it extends to everything that is to be said or done; but I will leave it for the present, as this letter is already pretty long. Such is my desire, my anxiety for your perfection, that I never think I have said enough, though you may possibly think I have said too much; and though, in truth, if your own good sense is not sufficient to direct you in many of these plain points, all that I or anybody else can say will be insufficient. But where you are concerned, I am the insatiable man in Horace, who covets still a little corner more, to complete the figure of his field. I dread every little corner that may deform mine, in which I would have (if possible) no one defect.

I this moment receive yours of the 17th, N.S., and cannot condole with you upon the secession of your German *commensaux*; who, both by your and Mr. Harte's description, seem to be *des gens d'une aimable absence*; and, if you can replace them by any other German conversation, you will be a gainer by the bargain. I cannot conceive, if you understand German well enough to read any German book, how the writing of the German character can be so difficult and tedious to you, the twenty-four letters being very soon learned; and I do not expect that you should write yet with the utmost purity and correctness, as to the language; what I meant by your writing once a fortnight to Grevenkop, was only to make the written character familiar to you. However, I will be content with one in three weeks or so.

I believe you are not likely to see Mr. Eliot again soon, he being still in Cornwall with his father, who, I hear, is not likely to recover. Adieu!

Dear Boy,   London, January 10, O.S. 1749.

I have received your letter of the 31st December, N.S. Your thanks for my present, as you call it, exceed the value of the present; but the use which you assure me that you will make of it is the thanks which I desire to receive. Due attention to the inside of books, and due contempt for the outside, is the proper relation between a man of sense and his books.

Now that you are going a little more into the world, I will take this occasion to explain my intentions as to your future expenses, that you may know what you have to expect from me, and make your plan accordingly. I shall neither deny nor grudge you any money that may be necessary for either your improvement or your pleasures—I mean, the pleasures of a rational being. Under the head of improvement, I mean the best books and the best masters, cost what they will; I also mean, all the expense of lodgings, coach, dress, servants, etc., which, according to the several places where you may be, shall be respectively necessary to enable you to keep the best company. Under the head of rational pleasures, I comprehend—first, proper charities to real and compassionate objects of it; secondly, proper presents to those to whom you are obliged, or whom you desire to oblige; thirdly, a conformity of expense to that of the company which you keep—as in public spectacles, your share of little entertainments, a few pistoles at games of mere commerce, and other incidental calls of good company. The only two articles which I will never supply are—the profusion of low riot, and the idle lavishness of negligence and laziness.

A fool squanders away, without credit or advantage to himself, more than a man of sense spends with both. The latter employs his money as he does his time, and never spends a shilling of the one, nor a minute of the other, but in something that is either useful or rationally pleasing to himself or others; the former buys whatever he does not want, and does not pay for what he does want. He cannot withstand the charms of a toy-shop; snuff-boxes, watches, heads of canes, etc., are his destruction. His servants and tradesmen conspire with his own indolence to cheat him; and in a very little time he is astonished, in the midst of all the ridiculous superfluities, to find himself in want of all the real comforts and necessaries of life. Without care and method, the largest fortune will not—

and with them, almost the smallest will—supply all necessary expenses. As far as you can possibly, pay ready money for everything you buy, and avoid bills. Pay that money, too, yourself, and not through the hands of any servant, who always either stipulates poundage, or requires a present for his good word, as they call it. Where you must have bills (as for meat and drink, clothes, etc.), pay them regularly every month, and with your own hand. Never, from a mistaken economy, buy a thing you do not want because it is cheap, or, from a silly pride, because it is dear. Keep an account in a book of all that you receive, and of all that you pay; for no man, who knows what he receives and what he pays, ever runs out. I do not mean that you should keep an account of the shillings and half-crowns which you may spend in chair-hire, operas, etc.; they are unworthy of the time, and of the ink, that they would consume. Leave such *minuties* to dull, penny-wise fellows; but remember, in economy, as well as in every other part of life, to have the proper attention to proper objects, and the proper contempt for little ones.

A strong mind sees things in their true proportions; a weak one views them through a magnifying medium, which, like the microscope, makes an elephant of a flea, magnifies all little objects, but cannot receive great ones. I have known many a man pass for a miser, by saving a penny and wrangling for twopence, who was undoing himself at the same time by living above his income, and not attending to essential articles, which were above his *portée*. The sure characteristic of a sound and strong mind is, to find in everything those certain bounds, *quos ultra citraque nequit consistere rectum*.[1] These boundaries are marked out by a very fine line, which only good sense and attention can discover: it is much too fine for vulgar eyes. In manners, this line is good-breeding; beyond it, is troublesome ceremony; short of it, is unbecoming. negligence and inattention. In morals, it divides ostentatious puritanism from criminal relaxation. In religion, superstition from impiety; and, in short, every virtue from its kindred vice or weakness. I think you have sense enough to discover the line: keep it always in your eye, and learn to walk upon it; rest upon Mr. Harte, and he will poise you till you are able to go alone. By the way, there are fewer people who walk well upon that line than upon the slack rope, and therefore a good performer shines so much the more.

[1] Horace, *Satires*, I, i, 107.

Your friend, Comte Pertingue, who constantly inquires after you, has written to Comte Salmour, the Governor of the Academy at Turin, to prepare a room for you there, immediately after the Ascension, and has recommended you to him in a manner which I hope you will give him no reason to repent or be ashamed of. As Comte Salmour's son, now residing at the Hague, is my particular acquaintance, I shall have regular and authentic accounts of all that you do at Turin.

During your stay at Berlin, I expect that you should inform yourself thoroughly of the present state of the civil, military, and ecclesiastical government of the King of Prussia's [1] dominions, particularly of the military, which is upon a better footing in that country than in any other in Europe. You will attend at the reviews, see the troops exercise, and inquire into the numbers of troops and companies in the respective regiments of horse, foot, and dragoons; the numbers and titles of the commissioned and non-commissioned officers in the several troops and companies; and also take care to learn the technical military terms in the German language; for, though you are not to be a military man, yet these military matters are so frequently the subjects of conversation, that you will look very awkwardly if you are ignorant of them. Moreover, they are commonly the objects of negotiation, and, as such, fall within your future profession. You must also inform yourself of the reformation which the King of Prussia has lately made in the law, by which he has both lessened the number and shortened the duration of lawsuits; a great work, and worthy of so great a prince! As he is indisputably the ablest prince in Europe, every part of his government deserves your most diligent inquiry, and your most serious attention. It must be owned that you set out well as a young politician, by beginning at Berlin, and then going to Turin, where you will see the next ablest monarch to that of Prussia; so that, if you are capable of making political reflections, those two princes will furnish you with sufficient matter for them.

I would have you endeavour to get acquainted with Monsieur de Maupertuis,[2] who is so eminently distinguished by all kinds of learning and merit, that one should be both sorry and ashamed of having been even a day in the same place with him, and not

[1] Frederick the Great.
[2] A celebrated mathematician, born 1698, died 1759. In 1736 he was chief of the Academicians in the expedition to Lapland to measure a degree of longitude. Frederick the Great invited him to Berlin in 1740, where he was elected President (for life) of the new Academy.

to have seen him. If you should have no other way of being introduced to him, I will send you a letter from hence. Monsieur Cagnoni, at Berlin, to whom I know you are recommended, is a very able man of business, thoroughly informed of every part of Europe; and his acquaintance, if you deserve and improve it as you should do, may be of great use to you.

Remember to take the best dancing-master at Berlin, more to teach you to sit, stand, and walk gracefully, than to dance finely. The Graces, the Graces! remember the Graces! Adieu!

DEAR BOY,   London, February 7, O.S. 1749.

You are now come to an age capable of reflection, and I hope you will do, what, however, few people at your age do, exert it, for your own sake, in the search of truth and sound knowledge. I will confess (for I am not unwilling to discover my secrets to you) that it is not many years since I have presumed to reflect for myself. Till sixteen or seventeen, I had no reflection; and, for many years after that, I made no use of what I had. I adopted the notions of the books I read, or the company I kept, without examining whether they were just or not; and I rather chose to run the risk of easy error, than to take the time and trouble of investigating truth. Thus, partly from laziness, partly from dissipation, and partly from the *mauvaise honte* of rejecting fashionable notions, I was (as I have since found) hurried away by prejudices, instead of being guided by reason; and quietly cherished error, instead of seeking for truth. But since I have taken the trouble of reasoning for myself, and have had the courage to own that I do so, you cannot imagine how much my notions of things are altered, and in how different a light I now see them, from that in which I formerly viewed them through the deceitful medium of prejudice or authority. Nay, I may possibly still retain many errors, which from long habit, have perhaps grown into real opinions; for it is very difficult to distinguish habits, early acquired and long entertained, from the result of our reason and reflection.

My first prejudice (for I do not mention the prejudices of boys and women, such as hobgoblins, ghosts, dreams, spilling salt, etc.) was my classical enthusiasm, which I received from the books I read, and the masters who explained them to me. I was convinced there had been no common sense nor common honesty in the world for these last fifteen hundred years; but that they were totally extinguished with the ancient Greek and Roman governments. Homer and Virgil could have no faults, because they were ancient; Milton and Tasso could have no merit, because they were modern. And I could almost have said, with regard to the ancients, what Cicero, very absurdly and unbecomingly for a philosopher, says with regard to Plato, *Cum quo errare malim quam cum aliis rectè sentire.* Whereas now, without any extraordinary effort of genius, I have discovered that nature was the same three thousand years ago as it is at present; that men were but men then as well as now; that modes and customs vary often, but that human nature is always the same. And I can no more suppose, that men were better, braver, or wiser, fifteen hundred or three thousand years ago, than I can suppose that the animals or vegetables were better then than they are now.

I dare assert, too, in defiance of the favourers of the ancients, that Homer's hero, Achilles, was both a brute and a scoundrel, and, consequently, an improper character for the hero of an epic poem; he had so little regard for his country, that he would not act in defence of it because he had quarrelled with Agamemnon about a w—e; and then, afterwards, animated by private resentment only, he went about killing people basely, I will call it, because he knew himself invulnerable; and yet, invulnerable as he was, he wore the strongest armour in the world; which I humbly apprehend to be a blunder, for a horse-shoe clapped to his vulnerable heel would have been sufficient. On the other hand, with submission to the favourers of the moderns, I assert, with Mr. Dryden, that the Devil is in truth the hero of Milton's poem; his plan, which he lays, pursues, and at last executes, being the subject of the poem. From all which considerations I impartially conclude, that the ancients had their excellences and their defects, their virtues and their vices, just like the moderns; pedantry and affectation of learning decide clearly in favour of the former; vanity and ignorance, as peremptorily, in favour of the latter.

Religious prejudices kept pace with my classical ones; and there was a time when I thought it impossible for the honestest man in the world to be saved, out of the pale of the Church of England; not considering that matters of opinion do not depend upon the will; and that it is as natural, and as allowable, that another man should differ in opinion from me, as that I should differ from him; and that, if we are both sincere, we are both blameless, and should consequently have mutual indulgence for each other.

The next prejudices I adopted, were those of the *beau monde*; in which, as I was determined to shine, I took what are commonly called the genteel vices to be necessary. I had heard them reckoned so, and, without farther inquiry, I believed it; or, at least, should have been ashamed to have denied it, for fear of exposing myself to the ridicule of those whom I considered as the models of fine gentlemen. But I am now neither ashamed nor afraid to assert, that those genteel vices, as they are falsely called, are only so many blemishes in the character of even a man of the world, and what is called a fine gentleman, and degrade him in the opinions of those very people to whom he hopes to recommend himself by them. Nay, this prejudice often extends so far, that I have known people pretend to vices they had not, instead of carefully concealing those they had.

Use and assert your own reason; reflect, examine, and analyse everything, in order to form a sound and mature judgment; let no οὗτος ἔφα impose upon your conversation, mislead your actions, or dictate your conversation. Be early what, if you are not, you will, when too late, wish you had been. Consult your reason betimes; I do not say that it will always prove an unerring guide, for human reason is not infallible; but it will prove the least erring guide that you can follow. Books and conversation may assist it; but adopt neither blindly and implicitly; try both by that best rule which God has given to direct us,—reason.

Of all the troubles, do not decline, as many people do, that of thinking. The herd of mankind can hardly be said to think; their notions are almost all adoptive; and, in general, I believe it is better that it should be so, as such common prejudices contribute more to order and quiet than their own separate reasonings would do, uncultivated and unimproved as they are. We have many of those useful prejudices in this country, which I should be very sorry to see removed. The good Protestant conviction, that the Pope is both Antichrist and the Whore of Babylon, is a more effectual preservative in this country against Popery than all the solid and unanswerable arguments of Chillingworth. The idle story of the Pretender's having been introduced in a warming-pan into the Queen's bed, though as destitute of all probability as of all foundation, has been much more prejudicial to the cause of Jacobitism than all that Mr. Locke and others have written to show the unreasonableness and absurdity of the doctrines of indefeasible hereditary right and unlimited passive obedience. And that silly, sanguine notion, which is firmly entertained here, that one Englishman can beat three Frenchmen, encourages, and has sometimes enabled, one Englishman, in reality, to beat two.

A Frenchman ventures his life with alacrity *pour l'honneur du Roi*; were you to change the object which he has been taught to have in view, and tell him that it was *pour le bien de la patrie*, he would very probably run away. Such gross, local prejudices prevail with the herd of mankind, and do not impose upon cultivated, informed, and reflecting minds; but then there are notions equally false, though not so glaringly absurd, which are entertained by people of superior and improved understandings, merely for want of the necessary pains to investigate, the proper attention to examine, and the penetration requisite to determine the truth. Those are the prejudices which I would have you guard against by a manly exertion and attention of your reasoning faculty.

To mention one instance of a thousand that I could give you: It is a general prejudice, and has been propagated for these sixteen hundred years, that arts and sciences cannot flourish under an absolute government; and that genius must necessarily be cramped where freedom is restrained. This sounds plausible, but is false in fact. Mechanic arts, as agriculture, manufactures, etc., will indeed be discouraged where the profits and property are, from the nature of the government, insecure. But why the despotism of a government should cramp the genius of a mathematician, an astronomer, a poet, or an orator, I confess I never could discover. It may indeed deprive the poet or the orator of the liberty of treating of certain subjects in the manner they would wish; but it leaves them subjects enough to exert genius upon, if they have it. Can an author with reason complain that he is cramped and shackled if he is not at liberty to publish blasphemy, bawdry, or sedition? all which are equally prohibited in the freest governments if they are wise and well-regulated ones. This is the present general complaint of the French authors; but, indeed, chiefly of the bad ones. No wonder, say they, that England produces so many great geniuses; people there may think as they please, and publish what they think. Very true; but who hinders them from thinking as they please?

If, indeed, they think in a manner destructive of all religion, morality, or good manners, or to the disturbance of the state, an absolute government will certainly more effectually prohibit them from, or punish them for, publishing such thoughts than a free one could do. But how does that cramp the genius of an epic, dramatic, or lyric poet? Or how does it corrupt the eloquence of an orator, in the pulpit or at the bar? The number of good French authors, such as Corneille, Racine, Molière, Boileau, and La Fontaine, who seemed to dispute it with the Augustan age, flourished under the despotism of Louis XIV; and the celebrated authors of the Augustan age did not shine till after the fetters were riveted upon the Roman people by that cruel and worthless Emperor. The revival of letters was not owing, either, to any free government, but to the encouragement and protection of Leo X and Francis I—the one as absolute a Pope, and the other as despotic a Prince, as ever reigned. Do not mistake, and imagine that, while I am only exposing a prejudice, I am speaking in favour of arbitrary power, which from my soul I abhor, and look upon as a gross and criminal violation of the natural rights of mankind. Adieu!

DEAR BOY,   London February 28, O.S. 1749.

I was very much pleased with the account that you gave me of your reception at Berlin; but I was still better pleased with the account which Mr. Harte sent me of your manner of receiving that reception, for he says you behaved yourself to those Crowned Heads with all the respect and modesty due to them, but, at the same time, without being any more embarrassed than if you had been conversing with your equals. This easy respect is the perfection of good-breeding, which nothing but superior good-sense or a long usage of the world can produce; and as, in your case, it could not be the latter, it is a pleasing indication to me of the former.

You will now, in the course of a few months, have been rubbed at three of the considerable Courts of Europe—Berlin, Dresden, and Vienna; so that I hope you will arrive at Turin tolerably smooth, and fit for the last polish. There you may get the best, there being no Court I know of that forms more well-bred and agreeable people. Remember, now, that good-breeding, genteel carriage, address, and even dress (to a certain degree), are become serious objects, and deserve a part of your attention.

The day, if well employed, is long enough for them all; one half of it bestowed upon your studies and your exercises will finish your mind and your body; the remaining part of it, spent in good company, will form your manners and complete your character. What would I not give to have you read Demosthenes critically in the morning, and understand him better than anybody; at noon, behave yourself better than any person at Court; and, in the evenings, trifle more agreeably than anybody in mixed companies! All this you may compass if you please; you have the means, you have the opportunities. Employ them for God's sake, while you may, and make yourself that all-accomplished man that I wish to have you. It entirely depends upon these two years; they are the decisive ones.

I send you here enclosed a letter of recommendation to Monsieur Capello, at Venice, which you will deliver him immediately upon your arrival, accompanying it with compliments from me to him and Madame, both whom you have seen here. He will, I am sure, be both very civil and very useful to you there, as he will also be afterwards at Rome, where he is appointed to go Ambassador. By the way, wherever you are, I would advise you to frequent, as much as you can, the Venetian Ministers, who are always better informed of the Courts they reside at than any other minister—the strict and regular accounts which they are obliged to give to their own government making them very diligent and inquisitive.

You will stay at Venice as long as the Carnival lasts; for though I am impatient to have you at Turin, yet I would wish you to see thoroughly all that is to be seen at so singular a place as Venice, and at so showish a time as the Carnival. You will take also particular care to view all those meetings of the government, which strangers are allowed to see; as the assembly of the Senate, etc.; and likewise to inform yourself of that peculiar and intricate form of government. There are books that give an account of it, among which, the best is *Amelot de la Houssaye*; this I would advise you to read previously; it will not only give you a general notion of that constitution, but also furnish you with materials for proper questions and oral informations upon the place, which are always the best. There are likewise many very valuable remains, in sculpture and paintings, of the best masters, which deserve your attention.

I suppose you will be at Vienna as soon as this letter will get thither; and I suppose, too, that I must not direct above one more to you there. After which my next shall be directed to you at Venice, the only place where a letter will be likely to find you till you are at Turin; but you may, and I desire that you will, write to me from the several places in your way from whence the post goes.

I will send you some other letters, for Venice, to Vienna, or to your banker at Venice; to whom you will, upon your arrival there, send for them; for I will take care to have you so recommended from place to place that you shall not run through them, as most of your countrymen do, without the advantage of seeing and knowing what best deserves to be seen and known; I mean the men and the manners.

God bless you, and make you answer my wishes; I will now say, my hopes! Adieu!

DEAR BOY,   London, April 19, O.S. 1749.

This letter will, I believe, still find you at Venice, in all the dissipation of masquerades, ridottos, operas, etc.; with all my heart; they are decent evening amusements, and very properly succeed that serious application to which I am sure you devote your mornings. There are liberal and illiberal pleasures as well as liberal and illiberal arts. There are some pleasures that degrade a gentleman as much as some trades could do. Sottish drinking, indiscriminate gluttony, driving coaches, rustic sports, such as fox-chases, horse-races, etc., are, in my opinion, infinitely below the honest and industrious professions of a tailor and a shoemaker, which are said to *déroger*.

As you are now in a musical country, where singing, fiddling, and piping are not only the common topics of conversation, but almost the principal objects of attention; I cannot help cautioning you against giving into those (I will call them illiberal) pleasures (though music is commonly reckoned one of the liberal arts), to the degree that most of your countrymen do when they travel in Italy. If you love music, hear it; go to operas, concerts, and pay fiddlers to play to you; but I insist upon your neither piping nor fiddling yourself. It puts a gentleman in a very frivolous, contemptible light; brings him into a great deal of bad company; and takes up a great deal of time, which might be much better employed. Few things would mortify me more, than to see you bearing a part in a concert, with a fiddle under your chin, or a pipe in your mouth.

I have had a great deal of conversation with Comte du Perron, and Comte Lascaris, upon your subject; and I will tell you, very truly, what Comte du Perron (who is, in my opinion, a very pretty man) said of you. *Il a de l'esprit, un sçavoir peu commun à son age, une grande vivacité, et quand il aura pris des manières il sera parfait; car il faut avouer qu'il sent encore le collège; mais cela viendra.* I was very glad to hear, from one whom I think so good a judge, that you wanted nothing but *des manières*; which I am convinced you will now soon acquire in the company which henceforwards you are likely to keep. But I must add, too, that, if you should not acquire them, all the rest will be of very little use to you. By *manières*, I do not mean bare common civility; everybody must have that, who would not be kicked out of company; but I mean engaging, insinuating, shining manners; a distinguished politeness, an almost irresistible address; a superior gracefulness in all you say and do. It is this alone that can give all your other talents their full lustre and value; and, consequently, it is this which should now be the principal object of your attention. Observe minutely, wherever you go, the allowed and established models of good-breeding, and form yourself upon them. Whatever pleases you most, in others, will infallibly please others, in you. I have often repeated this to you; now is your time of putting it in practice.

Pray make my compliments to Mr. Harte; and tell him I have received his letter from Vienna, of the 16th N.S., but that I shall not trouble him with an answer to it till I have received the other letter, which he promises me, upon the subject of one of my last. I long to hear from him after your settlement at Turin; the months that you are to pass there will be very decisive ones for you. The exercises of the Academy, and the manners of Courts, must be attended to and acquired, and, at the same time, your other studies continued. I am sure you will not pass, nor desire, one single idle hour there; for I do not foresee that you can, in any part of your life, put out six months to greater interest, than those next six at Turin.

We will talk hereafter about your stay at Rome, and in other parts of Italy. This only I will now recommend to you; which is, to extract the spirit of every place you go to. In those places, which are only distinguished by classical fame, and valuable remains of antiquity, have your Classics in your hand and in your head; compare the ancient geography, and descriptions, with the modern; and never fail to take notes. Rome will furnish you with business enough of that sort; but then it furnishes you with many other objects well deserving your attention, such as deep ecclesiastical craft and policy. Adieu!

DEAR BOY,   London, May 15, O.S. 1749.

This letter will, I hope, find you settled to your serious studies, and your necessary exercises, at Turin, after the hurry and dissipation of the Carnival at Venice. I mean, that your stay at Turin should, and I flatter myself that it will, be an useful and ornamental period of your education; but, at the same time, I must tell you, that all my affection for you has never yet given me so much anxiety as that which I now feel. While you are in danger, I shall be in fear, and you are in danger at Turin. Mr. Harte will, by his care, arm you as well as he can against it; but your own good sense and resolution can alone make you invulnerable. I am informed, there are now many English at the Academy at Turin; and I fear those are just so many dangers for you to encounter. Who they are I do not know, but I well know the general ill conduct, the indecent behaviour, and the illiberal views of my young countrymen abroad; especially wherever they are in numbers together. Ill - example is of itself dangerous enough, but those who give it seldom stop there; they add their infamous exhortations and invitations; and, if these fail, they have recourse to ridicule; which is harder for one of your age and inexperience to withstand, than either of the former. Be upon your guard, therefore, against these batteries, which will all be played upon you. You are not sent abroad to converse with your own countrymen; among them, in general, you will get little knowledge, no languages, and, I am sure, no manners. I desire that you will form no connections, nor (what they impudently call) friendships, with these people; which are, in truth, only combinations and conspiracies against good morals and good manners.

There is commonly in young people a facility that makes them unwilling to refuse anything that is asked of them; a *mauvaise honte*, that makes them ashamed to refuse; and, at the same time, an ambition of pleasing and shining in the company they keep; these several causes produce the best effect in good company, but the very worst in bad. If people had no vices but their own, few would have so many as they have. For my own part, I would sooner wear other people's clothes than their vices; and they would sit upon me just as well. I hope you will have none; but if ever you have, I beg, at least, they may be all your own. Vices of adoption are, of all others, the most disgraceful and unpardonable. There are degrees in vices as well as in virtues; and I must do my countrymen the justice to say, they generally take their vices in the lowest degree. Their gallantry is the infamous mean debauchery of stews, justly attended and rewarded by the loss of their health, as well as their character. Their pleasures of the table end in beastly drunkenness, low riot, broken windows, and very often (as they well deserve) broken bones. They game for the sake of the vice, not of the amusement; and therefore carry it to excess; undo, or are undone by, their companions. By such conduct, and in such company abroad, they come home, the unimproved, illiberal, and ungentlemanlike creatures that one daily sees them; that is, in the park and in the streets, for one never meets them in good company; where they have neither manners to present themselves, nor merit to be received. But, with the manners of footmen and grooms, they assume their dress too; for you must have observed them in the streets here, in dirty-blue frocks, with oaken sticks in their hands, and their hair greasy and unpowdered, tucked up under hats of an enormous size. Thus finished and adorned by their travels, they become the disturbers of playhouses; they break the windows, and commonly the landlords, of the taverns where they drink; and are at once the support, the terror, and the victims of the bawdy-houses they frequent. These poor mistaken people think they shine, and so they do indeed; but it is as putrefaction shines in the dark.

I am not now preaching to you, like an old fellow, upon either religious or moral texts; I am persuaded you do not want the best instructions of that kind: but I am advising you as a friend, as a man of the world, as one who would not have you old while you are young, but would have you take all the pleasures that reason points out and that decency warrants. I will therefore suppose, for argument's sake (for upon no other account can it be supposed), that all the vices above mentioned were perfectly innocent in themselves; they would still degrade, vilify, and sink those who practised them; would obstruct their rising in the world, by debasing their characters; and give them a low turn of mind and manners, absolutely inconsistent with their making any figure in upper life, and great business.

What I have now said, together with your own good sense, is I hope sufficient to arm you against the seduction, the invitations, or the profligate exhortations (for I cannot call them temptations) of those unfortunate young people. On the other hand, when they would engage you in these schemes, content yourself with a decent but steady refusal; avoid controversy upon such plain points. You are too young to convert them, and I trust too wise to be converted by them. Shun them, not only in reality, but even in appearance, if you would be well received in good company; for people will always be shy of receiving a man who comes from a place where the plague rages, let him look ever so healthy. There are some expressions, both in French and English, and some characters, both in those two and in other countries, which have, I dare say, misled many young men to their ruin. *Une honnête débauche, une jolie débauche; an agreeable rake, a man of pleasure.* Do not think that this means debauchery and profligacy; nothing like it. It means at most the accidental and unfrequent irregularities of youth and vivacity, in opposition to dulness, formality, and want of spirit. A *commerce galant* insensibly formed with a woman of fashion; a glass of wine or two too much unwarily taken in the warmth and joy of good company, or some innocent frolic by which nobody is injured, are the utmost bounds of that life of pleasure which a man of sense and decency, who has a regard for his character, will allow himself, or be allowed by others. Those who transgress them in the hopes of shining, miss their aim, and become infamous, or at least contemptible.

The length or shortness of your stay at Turin will sufficiently inform me (even though Mr. Harte should not) of your conduct there; for, as I have told you before, Mr. Harte has the strictest orders to carry you away immediately from thence upon the first and least symptom of infection that he discovers about you; and I know him to be too conscientiously scrupulous, and too much your friend and mine, not to execute them exactly. Moreover, I will inform you that I shall have constant accounts of your behaviour from Comte Salmour, the governor of the Academy, whose son is now here, and my particular friend. I have also other good channels of intelligence of which I do not apprise you. But, supposing that all turns out well at Turin, yet, as I propose your being at Rome for the jubilee at Christmas, I desire that you will apply yourself diligently to your exercises of dancing, fencing, and riding, at the Academy; as well for the sake of your health and growth, as to fashion and supple you. You must not neglect your dress either, but take care to be *bien mis*.

Pray send for the best operator for the teeth at Turin, where I suppose there is some famous one, and let him put yours in perfect order, and then take care to keep them so afterwards yourself. You had very good teeth, and I hope they are so still; but even those who have bad ones should keep them clean, for a dirty mouth is in my mind ill manners: in short, neglect nothing that can possibly please. A thousand nameless little things, which nobody can describe, but which everybody feels, conspire to form that *whole* of pleasing; as the several pieces of a mosaic work, though separately of little beauty or value, when properly joined, form those beautiful figures which please everybody. A look, a gesture, an attitude, a tone of voice, all bear their parts in the great work of pleasing. The art of pleasing is more particularly necessary in your intended profession than perhaps in any other; it is in truth the first half of your business; for, if you do not please the Court you are sent to, you will be of very little use to the Court you are sent from. Please the eyes and the ears, they will introduce you to the heart; and nine times in ten the heart governs the understanding.

Make your court particularly, and show distinguished attentions, to such men and women as are best at Court, highest in the fashion, and in the opinion of the public; speak advantageously of them behind their backs, in companies who you have reason to believe will tell them again. Express your admiration of the many great men that the House of Savoy has produced; observe, that nature, instead of being exhausted by those efforts, seems to have redoubled them in the persons of the present King and the Duke of Savoy: wonder at this rate where it will end, and conclude that it must end in the government of all Europe. Say this, likewise, where it will probably be repeated; but say it unaffectedly, and, the last especially, with a kind of *enjouement*. These little arts are very allowable, and must be made use of in the course of the world; they are pleasing to one party, useful to the other, and injurious to nobody.

What I have said with regard to my countrymen in general does not extend to them all without exception: there are some who have both merit and manners. Your friend Mr. Stevens is among the latter, and I approve of your connection with him. You may happen to meet with some others, whose friendship may be of great use to you hereafter, either from their superior talents, or their rank and fortune. Cultivate them; but then I desire that Mr. Harte should be judge of those persons.

Adieu, my dear child! Consider seriously the importance of the two next years, to your character, your figure, and your fortune.

DEAR BOY,　　　　　　　　　London, May 22, O.S. 1749.

I recommended to you in my last an innocent piece of art—that of flattering people behind their backs, in presence of those who, to make their own court, much more than for your sake, will not fail to repeat, and even amplify, the praise to the party concerned. This is, of all flattery, the most pleasing, and consequently the must effectual. There are other, and many other, inoffensive arts of this kind, which are necessary in the course of the world, and which he who practises the earliest will please the most, and rise the soonest. The spirits and vivacity of youth are apt to neglect them as useless, or reject them as troublesome; but subsequent knowledge and experience of the world remind us of their importance, commonly when it is too late.

The principal of these things is the mastery of one's temper, and that coolness of mind, and serenity of countenance, which hinder us from discovering, by words, actions, or even looks, those passions or sentiments by which we are inwardly moved or agitated, and the discovery of which gives cooler and abler people such infinite advantages over us, not only in great business, but in all the most common occurrences of life. A man who does not possess himself enough to hear disagreeable things without visible marks of anger and change of countenance, or agreeable ones without sudden bursts of joy and expansion of countenance, is at the mercy of every artful knave or pert coxcomb. The former will provoke or please you by design, to catch unguarded words or looks, by which he will easily decipher the secrets of your heart, of which you should keep the key yourself, and trust it with no man living. The latter will, by his absurdity, and without intending it, produce the same discoveries, of which other people will avail themselves.

You will say, possibly, that this coolness must be constitutional, and consequently does not depend upon the will; and I will allow that constitution has some power over us; but I will maintain, too, that people very often, to excuse themselves, very unjustly accuse their constitutions. Care and reflection, if properly used, will get the better; and a man may as surely get a habit of letting his reason prevail over his constitution, as of letting, as most people do, the latter prevail over the former. If you find yourself subject to sudden starts of passion or madness (for I see no difference between them, but in their duration), resolve within yourself, at least, never to speak one word while you feel that emotion within you. Determine, too, to keep your countenance as unmoved and unembarrassed as possible—which steadiness you may get a habit of by constant attention. I should desire nothing better, in any negotiation, than to have to do with one of these men of warm, quick passions, which I would take care to set in motion. By artful provocations, I would extort rash and unguarded expressions; and, by hinting at all the several things that I could suspect, infallibly discover the true one, by the alteration it occasioned in the countenance of the person. *Volto sciolto con pensieri stretti* is a most useful maxim in business. It is so necessary at some games, such as *Berlan, Quinze*, etc., that a man who had not the command of his temper and countenance would infallibly be undone by those who had, even though they played fair; whereas in business you always play with sharpers, to whom at least you should give no fair advantages. It may be objected, that I am now recommending dissimulation to you; I both own and justify it. It has been long said, *Qui nescit dissimulare nescit regnare*; I go still farther, and say, that without some dissimulation no business can be carried on at all. It is *simulation* that is false, mean, and criminal; that is the cunning which Lord Bacon calls crooked or left-handed wisdom, and which is never made use of but by those who have not true wisdom. And the same great man says, that dissimulation is only to hide our own cards; whereas simulation is put on in order to look into other people's. Lord Bolingbroke, in his *Idea of a Patriot King*,[1] which he has lately published, and which I will send you by the first opportunity, says, very justly, that simulation is a *stiletto*; not only an unjust, but an unlawful weapon, and the use of it is rarely to be excused, never justified: whereas dissimulation is a shield, as secrecy is armour; and it is no more possible to preserve secrecy in business, without some degree of dissimulation, than it is to succeed in business without secrecy. He goes on and says, that those two arts of dissimulation and secrecy are like the alloy mingled with pure ore: a little is necessary, and will not debase the coin below its proper standard; but if more than that little be employed (that is, simulation and cunning), the coin loses its currency and the coiner his credit.

Make yourself absolute master, therefore, of your temper and your countenance—so far, at least, as that no visible change do appear in either, whatever you may feel inwardly.

[1] Published in 1749.

This may be difficult, but it is by no means impossible; and, as a man of sense never attempts impossibilities on one hand, on the other he is never discouraged by difficulties; on the contrary, he redoubles his industry and his diligence, he perseveres, and infallibly prevails at last. In any point, which prudence bids you pursue, and which a manifest utility attends, let difficulties only animate your industry, not deter you from the pursuit. If one way has failed, try another; be active, persevere, and you will conquer. Some people are to be reasoned, some flattered, some intimidated, and some teased into a thing; but, in general, all are to be brought into it at last, if skilfully applied to, properly managed, and indefatigably attacked in their several weak places. The time should likewise be judiciously chosen. Every man has his *mollia tempora*, but that is far from being all day long; and you would choose your time very ill, if you applied to a man about one business, when his head was full of another, or when his heart was full of grief, anger, or any other disagreeable sentiment.

In order to judge of the inside of others, study your own; for men in general are very much alike; and though one has one prevailing passion, and another has another, yet their operations are much the same; and whatever engages or disgusts, pleases or offends you in others, will, *mutatis mutandis*, engage, disgust, please, or offend others in you. Observe, with the utmost attention, all the operations of your own mind, the nature of your own passions, and the various motives that determine your will; and you may, in a great degree, know all mankind. For instance, do you find yourself hurt and mortified, when another makes you feel his superiority, and your own inferiority, in knowledge, parts, rank, or fortune? You will certainly take great care not to make a person whose good-will, good word, interest, esteem, or friendship, you would gain, feel that superiority in you, in case you have it. If disagreeable insinuations, sly sneers, or repeated contradictions tease and irritate you, would you use them where you wished to engage or please? Surely not; and I hope you wish to engage, and please, almost universally. The temptation of saying a smart and witty thing, or *bon mot*, and the malicious applause with which it is commonly received, has made people who can say them, and, still oftener, people who think they can, but cannot, but yet try, more enemies, and implacable ones too, than any one other thing that I know of. When such things, then, shall happen to be said at your expense (as sometimes they certainly will), reflect seriously upon the sentiments of uneasiness, anger, and resentment, which they excite in you; and consider whether it can be prudent, by the same means, to excite the same sentiments in others against you. It is a decided folly, to lose a friend for a jest; but, in my mind, it is not a much less degree of folly, to make an enemy of an indifferent and neutral person for the sake of a *bon mot*. When things of this kind happen to be said of you, the most prudent way is to seem not to suppose that they are meant at you, but to dissemble and conceal whatever degree of anger you may feel inwardly; and, should they be so plain, that you cannot be supposed ignorant of their meaning, to join in the laugh of the company against yourself; acknowledge the hit to be a fair one, and the jest a good one, and play off the whole thing in seeming good humour; but by no means reply in the same way; which only shows that you are hurt, and publishes the victory which you might have concealed. Should the thing said, indeed, injure your honour, or moral character, there is but one proper reply; which I hope you never will have occasion to make.

As the female part of the world has some influence, and often too much, over the male, your conduct, with regard to women (I mean women of fashion, for I cannot suppose you capable of conversing with any others), deserves some share in your reflections. They are a numerous and loquacious body; their hatred would be more prejudicial than their friendship can be advantageous to you. A general complaisance, and attention to that sex, is therefore established by custom, and certainly necessary. But where you would particularly please any one whose situation, interest, or connections can be of use to you, you must show particular preference. The least attentions please, the greatest charm them. The innocent, but pleasing flattery of their persons, however gross, is greedily swallowed, and kindly digested; but a seeming regard for their understandings, a seeming desire of, and deference for, their advice, together with a seeming confidence in their moral virtues, turns their heads entirely in your favour. Nothing shocks them so much as the least appearance of that contempt, which they are apt to suspect men of entertaining of their capacities; and you may be very sure of gaining their friendship, if you seem to think it worth gaining. Here dissimulation is very often necessary, and even simulation sometimes allowable; which, as it pleases them, may be useful to you, and is injurious to nobody.

This torn sheet, which I did not observe when I began upon it, as it alters the figure, shortens too the length of my letter. It may very well afford it; my anxiety for you carries me insensibly to these lengths. I am apt to flatter myself that my experience, at the latter end of my life, may be of use to you at the beginning of yours; and I do not grudge the greatest trouble if it can procure you the least advantage. I even repeat frequently the same things, the better to imprint them on your young, and, I suppose, yet giddy mind; and I shall think that part of my time the best employed, that contributes to make you employ yours well. God bless you, child!

DEAR BOY,   London, July 6, O.S. 1749.

As I am now no longer in pain about your health, which I trust is perfectly restored, and as, by the various accounts I have had of you, I need not be in pain about your learning, our correspondence may for the future turn upon less important points, comparatively, though still very important ones; I mean, the knowledge of the world, decorum, manners, address, and all those (commonly called little) accomplishments, which are absolutely necessary to give greater accomplishments their full value and lustre.

Had I the admirable ring of Gyges, which rendered the wearer invisible; and had I, at the same time, those magic powers, which were very common formerly, but are now very scarce, of transporting myself by a wish to any given place; my first expedition would be to Venice, there to *reconnoitre* you unseen myself. I would first take you in the morning at breakfast with Mr. Harte, and attend to your natural and unguarded conversation with him; from whence I think I could pretty well judge of your natural turn of mind. How I should rejoice if I overheard you asking him pertinent questions upon useful subjects, or making judicious reflections upon the studies of that morning or the occurrences of the former day! Then I would follow you into the different companies of the day, and carefully observe in what manner you presented yourself to, and behaved yourself with, men of sense and dignity: whether your address was respectful and yet easy, your air modest and yet unembarrassed: and I would at the same time penetrate into their thoughts, in order to know whether your first *abord* made that advantageous impression upon their fancies, which a certain address, air, and manners never fail doing. I would afterwards follow you to the mixed companies of the evening, such as assemblies, suppers, etc., and there watch if you trifled gracefully and genteelly; if your good-breeding and politeness made way for your parts and knowledge. With what pleasure should I hear people cry out, *Che garbato cabaliere, com' è pulito, disinvolto, spiritoso!*

If all these things turned out to my mind, I would immediately assume my own shape, become visible, and embrace you: but, if the contrary happened, I would preserve my invisibility, make the best of my way home again, and sink my disappointment upon you and the world. As unfortunately these supernatural powers of genii, fairies, sylphs, and gnomes have had the fate of the oracles they succeeded, and have ceased for some time, I must content myself (till we meet naturally and in the common way) with Harte's written accounts of you, and the verbal ones which I now and then receive from people who have seen you. However, I believe it would do you no harm if you would always imagine that I was present, and saw and heard everything you did and said.

There is a certain concurrence of various little circumstances, which compose what the French call *l'aimable*, and which, now you are entering into the world, you ought to make it your particular study to acquire. Without them, your learning will be pedantry; your conversation often improper—always unpleasant; and your figure, however good in itself, awkward and unengaging. A diamond, while rough, has indeed its intrinsic value; but, till polished, is of no use, and would neither be sought for nor worn. Its great lustre, it is true, proceeds from its solidity and strong cohesion of parts; but, without the last polish, it would remain for ever a dirty rough mineral, in the cabinets of some few curious collectors. You have, I hope, that solidity and cohesion of parts; take now as much pains to get the lustre. Good company, if you make the right use of it, will cut you into shape, and give you the true brilliant polish.

A propos of diamonds: I have sent you, by Sir James Gray, the King's minister, who will be at Venice about the middle of September, my own diamond buckles, which are fitter for your young feet than for my old ones: they will probably adorn you—they would only expose me. If Sir James finds anybody whom he can trust, and who will be at Venice before him, he will send them by that person; but if he should not, and that you should be gone from Venice before he gets there, he will in that case give them to your banker, Monsieur Cornet, to forward to you, wherever you may then be. You are now of an age at which the adorning your person is not only not ridiculous, but proper and becoming. Negligence would imply, either an indifference about pleasing, or else an insolent security of pleasing, without using those means to which others are obliged to have recourse. A thorough cleanliness in your person is as necessary for your own health, as it is not to be offensive to other people. Washing yourself, and rubbing your body and limbs frequently with a flesh-brush, will conduce as much to health as to cleanliness. A particular attention to the cleanliness of your mouth, teeth, hands, and nails, is but common decency, in order not to offend people's eyes and noses.

I send you here enclosed a letter of recommendation to the Duke of Nivernois, the French Ambassador at Rome,[1] who is, in my opinion, one of the prettiest men I ever knew in my life. I do not know a better model for you to form yourself upon: pray observe and frequent him as much as you can. He will show you what manners and graces are. I shall, by successive posts, send you more letters, both for Rome and Naples, where it will be your own fault entirely if you do not keep the very best company.

As you will meet swarms of Germans wherever you go, I desire that you will constantly converse with them in their own language; which will improve you in that language, and be, at the same time, an agreeable piece of civility to them.

Your stay in Italy will, I do not doubt, make you critically master of Italian. I know it may, if you please; for it is a very regular, and consequently a very easy, language. Adieu! God bless you!

DEAR BOY,   London, August 10, O.S. 1749.

Let us resume our reflections upon men, their characters, their manners; in a word, our reflections upon the world. They may help you to form yourself and to know others. A knowledge very useful at all ages, very rare at yours; it seems as if

[1] Louis Jules Mancini, Duc de Nivernois, afterwards ambassador to England. Besides the "manners and graces" for which Lord Chesterfield extols him, he was remarkable for combining, like Lord Chesterfield himself, though in a much less eminent degree, literary taste with political distinction. He wrote poetical imitations of Virgil, Horace, Ovid, Ariosto, and Milton. He was imprisoned in the French Revolution by the Republicans in 1793. He was born in Paris, 1716, and died 1798.

it were nobody's business to communicate it to young men. Their masters teach them, singly, the languages or the sciences of their several departments; and are indeed generally incapable of teaching them the world; their parents are often so too, or at least neglect doing it, either from avocations, indifference, or from an opinion that throwing them into the world (as they call it) is the best way of teaching it them. This last notion is in a great degree true; that is, the world can doubtless never be well known by theory; practice is absolutely necessary; but surely, it is of great use to a young man, before he sets out for that country, full of mazes, windings, and turnings, to have at least a general map of it, made by some experienced traveller.

There is a certain dignity of manners absolutely necessary, to make even the most valuable character either respected or respectable.

Horse-play, romping, frequent and loud fits of laughter, jokes, waggery, and indiscriminate familiarity, will sink both merit and knowledge into a degree of contempt. They compose at most a merry fellow; and a merry fellow was never yet a respectable man. Indiscriminate familiarity either offends your superiors, or else dubs you their dependant, and led captain. It gives your inferiors just, but troublesome and improper claims of equality. A joker is near akin to a buffoon; and neither of them is the least related to wit. Whoever is admitted or sought for in company, upon any other account than that of his merit and manners, is never respected there, but only made use of. We will have such-a-one, for he sings prettily; we will invite such-a-one to a ball, for he dances well; we will have such-a-one at supper, for he is always joking and laughing; we will ask another, because he plays deep at all games, or because he can drink a great deal. These are all vilifying distinctions, mortifying preferences, and exclude all ideas of esteem and regard. Whoever *is had* (as it is called) in company for the sake of any one thing singly, is singly that thing, and will never be considered in any other light; consequently never respected, let his merits be what they will.

This dignity of manners, which I recommend so much to you, is not only as different from pride, as true courage is from blustering, or true wit from joking; but is absolutely inconsistent with it; for nothing vilifies and degrades more than pride. The pretensions of the proud man are oftener treated with sneer and contempt than with indignation; as we offer ridiculously too little to a tradesman who asks ridiculously too much for his goods, but we do not haggle with one who only asks a just and reasonable price.

Abject flattery and indiscriminate assentation degrade, as much as indiscriminate contradiction and noisy debate disgust. But a modest assertion of one's own opinion, and a complaisant acquiescence in other people's, preserve dignity.

Vulgar, low expressions, awkward motions and address, vilify; as they imply, either a very low turn of mind, or low education and low company.

Frivolous curiosity about trifles, and a laborious attention to little objects, which neither require nor deserve a moment's thought, lower a man; who from thence is thought (and not unjustly) incapable of greater matters. Cardinal de Retz, very sagaciously, marked out Cardinal Chigi [1] for a little mind, from the moment that he told him he had wrote three years with the same pen, and that it was an excellent good one still.

A certain degree of exterior seriousness in looks and motions, gives dignity, without excluding wit and decent cheerfulness, which are always serious themselves. A constant smirk upon the face, and a whiffling activity of the body, are strong indications of futility. Whoever is in a hurry, shows that the thing he is about is too big for him. Haste and hurry are very different things.

I have only mentioned some of those things which may and do, in the opinion of the world, lower and sink characters in other respects valuable enough; but I have taken no notice of those that affect and sink the moral characters: they are sufficiently obvious. A man who has patiently been kicked may as well pretend to courage as a man blasted by vices and crimes may to dignity of any kind. But an exterior decency and dignity of manners will even keep such a man longer from sinking than otherwise he would be: of such consequence is the τὸ πρέπον, even though effected and put on! Pray read frequently and with the utmost attention; nay, get by heart, if you can, that incomparable chapter in Cicero's *Offices* upon the τὸ πρέπον, or the *Decorum*. It contains whatever is necessary for the dignity of manners.

In my next I will send you a general map of Courts; a region yet unexplored by you, but which you are one day to inhabit. The ways are generally crooked and full of turnings, sometimes

---

[1] Elected Pope in April 1655, under the name of Alexander VII.

strewed with flowers, sometimes choked up with briers; rotten ground and deep pits frequently lie concealed under a smooth and pleasing surface; all the paths are slippery, and every slip is dangerous. Sense and discretion must accompany you at your first setting out; but notwithstanding those, till experience is your guide, you will every now and then step out of your way or stumble.

Lady Chesterfield has just now received your German letter, for which she thanks you; she says the language is very correct, and I can plainly see the character is well formed, not to say better than your English character. Continue to write German frequently, that it may become quite familiar to you. Adieu!

DEAR BOY, London, September 12, O.S. 1749.

It seems extraordinary, but it is very true, that my anxiety for you increases in proportion to the good accounts which I receive of you from all hands. I promise myself so much from you, that I dread the least disappointment. You are now so near the port, which I have so long wished and laboured to bring you safe into, that my concern would be doubled, should you be shipwrecked within sight of it. The object, therefore, of this letter is (laying aside all the authority of a parent) to conjure you as a friend, by the affection you have for me (and surely you have reason to have some), and by the regard you have for yourself, to go on, with assiduity and attention, to complete that work, which of late you have carried on so well, and which is now so near being finished. My wishes and my plan were to make you shine, and distinguish yourself equally in the learned and the polite world. Few have been able to do it. Deep learning is generally tainted with pedantry, or at least unadorned by manners; as, on the other hand, polite manners, and the turn of the world, are too often unsupported by knowledge, and consequently end contemptibly in the frivolous dissipation of drawing-rooms and *ruelles*. You are now got over the dry and difficult parts of learning; what remains, requires much more time than trouble.

You have lost time by your illness; you must regain it now or never. I therefore most earnestly desire, for your own sake, that, for these next six months, at least six hours every morning, uninterruptedly, may be inviolably sacred to your studies with Mr. Harte. I do not know whether he will require so much, but I know that I do, and hope you will, and consequently prevail with him to give you that time: I own it is a good deal; but when both you and he consider that the work will be so much better and so much sooner done by such an assiduous and continued application, you will neither of you think it too much, and each will find his account in it. So much for the mornings, which, from your own good sense, and Mr. Harte's tenderness and care of you, will, I am sure, be thus well employed. It is not only reasonable, but useful too, that your evenings should be devoted to amusements and pleasures; and therefore I not only allow but recommend, that they should be employed at assemblies, balls, *spectacles*, and in the best companies; with this restriction only, that the consequences of the evenings' diversions may not break in upon the mornings' studies, by breakfastings, visits, and idle parties into the country. At your age, you need not be ashamed, when any of these morning parties are proposed, to say you must beg to be excused, for you are obliged to devote your mornings to Mr. Harte; that I will have it so; and that you dare not do otherwise. Lay it all upon me; though I am persuaded it will be as much your own inclination as it is mine. But those frivolous, idle people, whose time hangs upon their own hands, and who desire to make others lose theirs too, are not to be reasoned with; and indeed it would be doing them too much honour. The shortest, civil answers are the best; *I cannot, I dare not*, instead of *I will not*; for, if you were to enter with them into the necessity of study, and the usefulness of knowledge, it would only furnish them with matter for their silly jests; which, though I would not have you mind, I would not have you invite.

I will suppose you at Rome, studying six hours uninterruptedly with Mr. Harte every morning, and passing your evenings with the best company of Rome, observing their manners and forming your own; and I will suppose a number of idle, sauntering, illiterate English, as there commonly is there, living entirely with one another, supping, drinking, and sitting up late at each others' lodgings; commonly in riots and scrapes when drunk; and never in good company when sober. I will take one of these pretty fellows, and give you the dialogue between him and yourself; such as I dare say it will be on his side, and such as I hope it will be on yours.

Englishman. Will you come and breakfast with me to-morrow? there will be four or five of our countrymen; we have provided chaises, and we will drive somewhere out of town after breakfast.

Stanhope. I am very sorry I cannot; but I am obliged to be at home all morning.

Englishman. Why then, we will come and breakfast with you.

Stanhope. I can't do that either, I am engaged.

Englishman. Well, then, let it be the next day.

Stanhope. To tell you the truth, it can be no day in the morning; for I neither go out, nor see anybody at home before twelve.

Englishman. And what the devil do you do with yourself till twelve o'clock?

Stanhope. I am not by myself, I am with Mr. Harte.

Englishman. Then what the devil do you do with him?

Stanhope. We study different things; we read, we converse.

Englishman. Very pretty amusement, indeed! Are you to take orders, then?

Stanhope. Yes; my father's orders, I believe, I must take.

Englishman. Why, hast thou no more spirit than to mind an old fellow a thousand miles off?

Stanhope. If I don't mind his orders, he won't mind my draughts.

Englishman. What! does the old prig threaten, then? threatened folks live long; never mind threats.

Stanhope. No, I can't say he has ever threatened me in his life; but I believe I had best not provoke him.

Englishman. Pooh! you would have one angry letter from the old fellow, and there would be an end of it.

Stanhope. You mistake him mightily; he always does more than he says. He has never been angry with me yet, that I remember, in his life; but, if I were to provoke him, I am sure he would never forgive me: he would be coolly immovable, and I might beg and pray, and write my heart out, to no purpose.

Englishman. Why, then, he is an old dog, that's all I can say; and pray, are you to obey your dry-nurse too, this same what's his name—Mr. Harte?

Stanhope. Yes.

Englishman. So, he stuffs you all morning with Greek, and Latin, and Logic, and all that. Egad, I have a dry-nurse too, but I never looked into a book with him in my life; I have not so much as seen the face of him this week, and don't care a louse if I never see it again.

Stanhope. My dry-nurse never desires anything of me that is not reasonable, and for my own good; and therefore I like to be with him.

Englishman. Very sententious and edifying, upon my word! At this rate you will be reckoned a very good young man.

Stanhope. Why, that will do me no harm.

Englishman. Will you be with us to-morrow in the evening, then? We shall be ten, with you; and I have got some excellent good wine, and we'll be very merry.

Stanhope. I am very much obliged to you, but I am engaged for all the evening, to-morrow; first at Cardinal Albani's, and then to sup at the Venetian Ambassadress's.

Englishman. How the devil can you like being always with these foreigners? I never go amongst them, with all their formalities and ceremonies. I am never easy in company with them, and I don't know why, but I am ashamed.

Stanhope. I am neither ashamed nor afraid; I am very easy with them, they are very easy with me; I get the language, and I see their characters by conversing with them; and that is what we are sent abroad for. Is it not?

Englishman. I hate your modest women's company—your women of fashion as they call 'em. I don't know what to say to them, for my part.

Stanhope. Have you ever conversed with them?

Englishman. No, I never conversed with them, but I have been sometimes in their company, though much against my will.

Stanhope. But at least they have done you no hurt; which is, probably, more than you can say of the women you do converse with.

Englishman. That's true, I own; but, for all that, I would rather keep company with my surgeon, half the year, than with your women of fashion the year round.

Stanhope. Tastes are different, you know, and every man follows his own.

Englishman. That's true; but thine's a devilish odd one, Stanhope. All morning with thy dry-nurse, all the evening in formal fine company, and all day long afraid of old daddy in England. Thou art a queer fellow, and I am afraid there's nothing to be made of thee.

Stanhope. I am afraid so too.

Englishman. Well, then, good night to you; you have no objection, I hope, to my being drunk to-night, which I certainly will be.

Stanhope. Not in the least; nor to your being sick to-morrow, which you as certainly will be; and so good night too.

You will observe that I have not put into your mouth those good arguments, which upon such an occasion would, I am sure, occur to you; as, piety and affection toward me; regard and friendship for Mr. Harte; respect for your own moral character, and for all the relative duties of man, son, pupil, and citizen. Such solid arguments would be thrown away upon such shallow puppies. Leave them to their ignorance, and to their dirty, disgraceful vices. They will severely feel the effects of them, when it will be too late. Without the comfortable refuge of learning, and with all the sickness and pains of a ruined stomach and a rotten carcase, if they happen to arrive at old age, it is an uneasy and ignominious one. The ridicule which such fellows endeavour to throw upon those who are not like them, is, in the opinion of all men of sense, the most authentic panegyric. Go on, then, my dear child, in the way you are in, only for a year and a half more; that is all I ask of you. After that I promise that you shall be your own master, and that I will pretend to no other title than that of your best and truest friend. You shall receive advice, but no orders, from me; and in truth you will want no other advice but such as youth and inexperience must necessarily require. You shall certainly want nothing that is requisite, not only for your conveniency, but also for your pleasures, which I always desire should be gratified. You will suppose that I mean the pleasures *d'un honnête homme*.

While you are learning Italian, which I hope you do with diligence, pray take care to continue your German, which you may have frequent opportunities of speaking. I would also have you keep up your knowledge of the *Jus Publicum Imperii*, by looking over, now and then, those *inestimable manuscripts*, which Sir Charles Williams, who arrived here last week, assures me you have made upon that subject. It will be of very great use to you, when you come to be concerned in foreign affairs, as you shall be (if you qualify yourself for them) younger than ever any other was; I mean, before you are twenty. Sir Charles tells me that he will answer for your learning; and that he believes you will acquire that address, and those Graces, which are so necessary to give it its full lustre and value. But he confesses that he doubts more of the latter than of the former. The justice which he does Mr. Harte, in his panegyrics of him, makes me hope that there is likewise a great deal of truth in his encomiums of you. Are you pleased with, and proud of, the reputation which you have already acquired? Surely you are, for I am sure I am. Will you do anything to lessen or forfeit it? Surely you will not. And will you not do all you can to extend and increase it? Surely you will. It is only going on for a year and a half longer, as you have gone on for the two years last past, and devoting half the day only to application, and you will be sure to make the earliest figure and fortune in the world, that ever man made. Adieu!

Dear Boy,   London, September 22, O.S. 1749.

If I had faith in philters and love potions, I should suspect that you had given Sir Charles Williams some, by the manner in which he speaks of you, not only to me, but to everybody else. I will not repeat to you what he says of the extent and correctness of your knowledge, as it might either make you vain, or persuade you that you had already enough of what nobody can have too much. You will easily imagine how many questions I asked, and how narrowly I sifted him upon your subject; he answered me, and I dare say with truth, just as I could have wished; till, satisfied entirely with his accounts of your character and learning, I inquired into other matters, intrinsically indeed of less consequence, but still of great consequence to every man, and of more to you than to almost any man; I mean, your address, manners, and air. To these questions, the same truth which he had observed before, obliged him to give me much less satisfactory answers. And, as he thought himself, in friendship both to you and me, obliged to tell me the disagreeable as well as the agreeable truths, upon the same principle I think myself obliged to repeat them to you.

He told me, then, that in company you were frequently most *provokingly* inattentive, absent, and *distrait*. That you came into a room, and presented yourself very awkwardly; that at table you constantly threw down knives, forks, napkins, bread, etc., and that you neglected your person and dress, to a degree unpardonable at any age, and much more so at yours.

These things, however immaterial soever they may seem to people who do not know the world and the nature of mankind, give me, who know them to be exceedingly material, very great concern. I have long distrusted you, and therefore frequently admonished you upon these articles; and I tell you plainly, that I shall not be easy till I hear a very different account of them. I know no one thing more offensive to a company, than that inattention and *distraction*. It is showing them the utmost contempt; and people never forgive contempt. No man is *distrait* with the man he fears, or the women he loves; which is a proof that every man can get the better of that *distraction* when he thinks it worth his while to do so; and, take my word for it, it is always worth his while. For my own part, I would rather be in company with a dead man than with an absent one; for if the dead man gives me no pleasure, at least he shows me no contempt; whereas the absent man, silently indeed, but very plainly, tells me that he does not think me worth his attention. Besides, can an absent man make any observations upon the characters, customs, and manners of the company? No. He may be in the best companies all his lifetime (if they will admit him, which, if I were they, I would not), and never be one jot the wiser. I never will converse with an absent man; one may as well talk to a deaf one. It is, in truth, a practical blunder, to address ourselves to a man who we see plainly neither hears, minds, nor understands us. Moreover, I aver that no man is, in any degree, fit for either business or conversation, who cannot, and does not, direct and command his attention to the present object, be that what it will.

You know, by experience, that I grudge no expense in your education, but I will positively not keep you a flapper. You may read, in Dr. Swift, the description of these flappers, and the use they were to your friends the Laputans; whose minds (Gulliver says) are so taken up with intense speculations, that they neither can speak, nor attend to the discourse of others, without being roused by some external action upon the organs of speech and hearing; for which reason, those people who are able to afford it, always keep a flapper in their family, as one of their domestics, nor ever walk about, or make visits, without him. This flapper is likewise employed diligently to attend his master in his walks, and, upon occasion, to give a soft flap upon his eyes; because he is always so wrapped up in cogitation, that he is in manifest danger of falling down every precipice, and bouncing his head against every post, and, in the streets, of jostling others, or being jostled into the kennel himself. If Christian will undertake this province into the bargain, with all my heart; but I will not allow him any increase of wages upon that score.

In short, I give you fair warning, that when we meet, if you are absent in mind, I will soon be absent in body; for, it will be impossible for me to stay in the room; and if at table you throw down your knife, plate, bread, etc., and hack the wing of a chicken for half an hour, without being able to cut it off, and your sleeve all the time in another dish, I must rise from table to escape the fever you would certainly give me. Good God! how I should be shocked if you came into my room, for the first time, with two left legs, presenting yourself with all the graces and dignity of a tailor, and your clothes hanging upon you like those in Monmouth Street, upon tenter-hooks! whereas I expect, nay require, to see you present yourself with the easy and genteel air of a man of fashion who has kept good company. I expect you not only well dressed, but very well dressed; I expect a gracefulness in all your motions, and something particularly engaging in your address. All this I expect, and all this it is in your power, by care and attention, to make me find; but, to tell you the plain truth, if I do not find it, we shall not converse very much together; for I cannot stand inattention and awkwardness; it would endanger my health.

You have often seen, and I have as often made you observe, L[yttelton]'s [1] distinguished inattention and awkwardness. Wrapped up like a Laputan in intense thought, and possibly sometimes in no thought at all; which, I believe, is very often the case of absent people; he does not know his most intimate acquaintance by sight, or answers them as if they were at cross purposes. He leaves his hat in one room, his sword in another, and would leave his shoes in a third, if his buckles, though awry, did not save them; his legs and arms, by his awkward management of them, seem to have undergone the *question extraordinaire*; and his head, always hanging upon one or other of his shoulders, seems to have received the first stroke upon a block. I sincerely value and esteem him for his parts, learning, and virtue; but, for the soul of me, I cannot love him in company. This will be universally the case, in common life, of every inattentive, awkward man, let his real merit and knowledge be ever so great.

When I was of your age, I desired to shine, as far as I was able, in every part of life; and was as attentive to my manners, my dress, and my air, in company on evenings, as to my books and my tutor in the mornings. A young fellow should be ambitious to shine in everything; and, of the two, always

---

[1] George, in 1757 created Lord, Lyttelton. His worth and his accomplishments, his extensive knowledge, and his unsullied probity, were never adorned by the Graces. Horace Walpole says of him, that he had "the figure of a spectre, and the gesticulations of a puppet!" (*Memoirs of George II*, vol. i, p. 175).

rather overdo than underdo. These things are by no means trifles; they are of infinite consequence to those who are to be thrown into the great world, and who would make a figure or a fortune in it. It is not sufficient to deserve well, one must please well too. Awkward, disagreeable merit, will never carry anybody far. Wherever you find a good dancing-master, pray let him put you upon your haunches; not so much for the sake of dancing, as for coming into a room and presenting yourself genteelly and gracefully. Women, whom you ought to endeavour to please, cannot forgive a vulgar and awkward air and gestures; *il leur faut du brillant*. The generality of men are pretty like them, and are equally taken by the same exterior graces.

I am very glad that you have received the diamond buckles safe: all I desire in return for them, is, that they may be buckled even upon your feet, and that your stockings may not hide them. I should be sorry you were an egregious fop; but I protest that, of the two, I would rather have you a fop than a sloven. I think negligence in my own dress, even at my age, when certainly I expect no advantages from my dress, would be indecent with regard to others. I have done with fine clothes; but I will have my plain clothes fit me, and made like other people's. In the evenings I recommend to you the company of women of fashion, who have a right to attention, and will be paid it. Their company will smooth your manners, and give you a habit of attention and respect; of which you will find the advantage among men.

My plan for you, from the beginning, has been to make you shine, equally in the learned and in the polite world; the former part is almost completed to my wishes, and will, I am persuaded, in a little time more, be quite so. The latter part is still in your power to complete; and I flatter myself that you will do it, or else the former part will avail you very little; especially in your department, where the exterior address and graces do half the business; they must be the harbingers of your merit, or your merit will be very coldly received: all can, and do, judge of the former, few of the latter.

Mr. Harte tells me that you have grown very much since your illness; if you get up to five feet ten, or even nine inches, your figure will, probably, be a good one; and, if well dressed and genteel, will probably please; which is a much greater advantage to a man than people commonly think. Lord Bacon calls it a letter of recommendation.

I would wish you to be the *omnis homo, l'homme universel.* You are nearer it, if you please, than ever anybody was at your age; and if you will but, for the course of this next year only, exert your whole attention to your studies in the morning, and to your address, manners, air, and *tournure* in the evenings, you will be the man I wish you, and the man that is rarely seen.

Our letters go, at best, so irregularly, and so often miscarry totally, that, for greater security, I repeat the same things. So, though I acknowledged by last post Mr. Harte's letter of the 8th September, N.S., I acknowledge it again by this to you. If this should find you still at Verona, let it inform you, that I wish you would set out soon for Naples; unless Mr. Harte should think it better for you to stay at Verona, or any other place on this side Rome, till you go there for the Jubilee. Nay, if he likes it better, I am very willing that you should go directly from Verona to Rome; for you cannot have too much of Rome, whether upon account of the language, the curiosities, or the company. My only reason for mentioning Naples, is for the sake of the climate, upon account of your health; but, if Mr. Harte thinks your health is now so well restored as to be above climate, he may steer your course wherever he thinks proper; and, for aught I know, your going directly to Rome, and consequently staying there so much the longer, may be as well as anything else. I think you and I cannot put our affairs into better hands than in Mr. Harte's; and I will stake his infallibility against the Pope's, with some odds on his side. *A propos* of the Pope; remember to be presented to him before you leave Rome, and go through the necessary ceremonies for it, whether of kissing his slipper or his b—h; for I would never deprive myself of anything that I wanted to do or see, by refusing to comply with an established custom. When I was in Roman Catholic countries, I never declined kneeling in their churches at the elevation, nor elsewhere, when the Host went by. It is a complaisance due to the custom of the place, and by no means, as some silly people have imagined, an implied approbation of their doctrine. Bodily attitudes and situations are things so very indifferent in themselves, that I would quarrel with nobody about them. It may indeed be improper for Mr. Harte to pay that tribute of complaisance, upon account of his character.

This letter is a very long, and possibly a very tedious one; but my anxiety for your perfection is so great, and particularly at this critical and decisive period of your life, that I am only afraid of omitting, but never of repeating, or dwelling too long upon anything that I think may be of the least use to you. Have the same anxiety for yourself that I have for you, and all will do well. Adieu, my dear child!

DEAR BOY,   London, September 27, O.S. 1749.

A vulgar, ordinary way of thinking, acting, or speaking, implies a low education, and a habit of low company. Young people contract it at school, or among servants, with whom they are too often used to converse; but, after they frequent good company, they must want attention and observation very much, if they do not lay it quite aside. And indeed, if they do not, good company will be very apt to lay them aside. The various kinds of vulgarisms are infinite; I cannot pretend to point them out to you; but I will give some samples, by which you may guess at the rest.

A vulgar man is captious and jealous; eager and impetuous about trifles. He suspects himself to be slighted, thinks everything that is said meant at him; if the company happens to laugh, he is persuaded they laugh at him; he grows angry and testy, says something very impertinent, and draws himself into a scrape, by showing what he calls a proper spirit, and asserting himself. A man of fashion does not suppose himself to be either the sole or principal object of the thoughts, looks, or words of the company; and never suspects that he is either slighted or laughed at, unless he is conscious that he deserves it. And if (which very seldom happens) the company is absurd or ill-bred enough to do either, he does not care two-pence, unless the insult be so gross and plain as to require satisfaction of another kind. As he is above trifles, he is never vehement and eager about them; and, wherever they are concerned, rather acquiesces than wrangles. A vulgar man's conversation always savours strongly of the lowness of his education and company. It turns chiefly upon his domestic affairs, his servants, the excellent order he keeps in his own family, and the little anecdotes of the neighbourhood; all which he relates with emphasis, as interesting matters. He is a man gossip.

Vulgarism in language is the next, and distinguishing characteristic of bad company and a bad education. A man of fashion avoids nothing with more care than that. Proverbial expressions and trite sayings are the flowers of the rhetoric of a vulgar man. Would he say that men differ in their tastes; he both supports and adorns that opinion, by the good old saying, as he respectfully calls it, that *what is one man's meat is another man's poison*. If anybody attempts being *smart*, as he calls it, upon him, he gives them *tit for tat*, ay, that he does. He has always some favourite word for the time being; which, for the sake of using often, he commonly abuses: such as *vastly* angry, *vastly* kind, *vastly* handsome, and *vastly* ugly. Even his pronunciation of proper words carries the mark of the beast along with it. He calls the earth, *yearth*; he is *obleiged*, not *obliged*, to you. He goes *to wards*, and not *towards*, such a place. He sometimes affects hard words by way of ornament, which he always mangles, like a learned woman. A man of fashion never has recourse to proverbs and vulgar aphorisms; uses neither favourite words nor hard words; but takes great care to speak very correctly and grammatically, and to pronounce properly; that is, according to the usage of the best companies.

An awkward address, ungraceful attitudes and actions, and a certain left-handiness (if I may use that word) loudly proclaim low education and low company; for it is impossible to suppose that a man can have frequented good company, without having catched something, at least, of their air and motions. A new-raised man is distinguished in a regiment by his awkwardness; but he must be impenetrably dull, if, in a month or two's time, he cannot perform at least the common manual exercise, and look like a soldier. The very accoutrements of a man of fashion are grievous incumbrances to a vulgar man. He is at a loss what to do with his hat, when it is not upon his head; his cane (if unfortunately he wears one) is at perpetual war with every cup of tea or coffee he drinks; destroys them first, and then accompanies them in their fall. His sword is formidable only to his own legs, which would possibly carry him fast enough out of the way of any sword but his own. His clothes fit him so ill, and constrain him so much, that he seems rather their prisoner than their proprietor. He presents himself in company, like a criminal in a court of justice; his very air condemns him; and people of fashion will no more connect themselves with the one, than people of character will with the other. This repulse drives and sinks him into low company; a gulf from whence no man, after a certain age, ever emerged.

Les manières nobles et aisées, la tournure d'un homme de condition, le ton de la bonne compagnie, les Graces, le je ne sçais quoi qui plaît, are as necessary to adorn and introduce your intrinsic merit and knowledge as the polish is to the diamond;

which, without that polish, would never be worn, whatever it might weigh. Do not imagine that these accomplishments are only useful with women; they are much more so with men. In a public assembly, what an advantage has a graceful speaker, with genteel motions, a handsome figure, and a liberal air, over one who shall speak full as much good-sense, but destitute of these ornaments! In business, how prevalent are the Graces, how detrimental is the want of them! By the help of these I have known some men refuse favours less offensively than others granted them. The utility of them in Courts and negotiations is inconceivable. You gain the hearts, and consequently the secrets, of nine in ten that you have to do with, in spite even of their prudence; which will, nine times in ten, be the dupe of their hearts and of their senses. Consider the importance of these things as they deserve, and you will not lose one moment in the pursuit of them.

You are travelling now in a country once so famous both for arts and arms, that (however degenerated at present) it still deserves your attention and reflection. View it, therefore, with care, compare its former with its present state, and examine into the causes of its rise and its decay. Consider it classically and politically, and do not run through it, as too many of your young countrymen do, musically, and (to use a ridiculous word) *knick-knackically*. No piping nor fiddling, I beseech you; no days lost in poring upon almost imperceptible *intaglios* and *cameos*; and do not become a virtuoso of small wares. Form a taste of painting, sculpture, and architecture, if you please, by a careful examination of the works of the best ancient and modern artists; those are liberal arts, and a real taste and knowledge of them become a man of fashion very well. But, beyond certain bounds, the man of taste ends, and the frivolous virtuoso begins.

Your friend Mendes, the good Samaritan, dined with me yesterday. He has more good-nature and generosity than parts. However, I will show him all the civilities that his kindness to you so justly deserves; he tells me that you are taller than I am, which I am very glad of. I desire you may excel me in everything else too; and, far from repining, I shall rejoice at your superiority. He commends your friend Mr. Stevens extremely; of whom, too, I have heard so good a character from other people, that I am very glad of your connection with him. It may prove of use to you hereafter. When you meet with such sort of Englishmen abroad, who, either from their parts or their rank, are likely to make a figure at home, I would advise you to cultivate them, and get their favourable testimony of you here, especially those who are to return to England before you. Sir Charles Williams has puffed you (as the mob call it) here extremely. If three or four more people of parts do the same, before you come back, your first appearance in London will be to great advantage. Many people do, and indeed ought to, take things upon trust; many more do, who need not; and few dare dissent from an established opinion. Adieu!

DEAR BOY,   London, November 14, O.S. 1749.

There is a natural good-breeding which occurs to every man of common sense, and is practised by every man of common good-nature. This good-breeding is general, independent of modes, and consists in endeavours to please and oblige our fellow-creatures by all good offices short of moral duties. This will be practised by a good-natured American savage as essentially as by the best bred European. But, then, I do not take it to extend to the sacrifice of our own conveniences for the sake of other people's. Utility introduced this sort of good-breeding as it introduced commerce, and established a truck[1] of the little *agrémens* and pleasures of life. I sacrifice such a conveniency to you, you sacrifice another to me; this commerce circulates, and every individual finds his account in it upon the whole. The third sort of good-breeding is local, and is variously modified, in not only different countries, but in different towns of the same country. But it must be founded upon the two former sorts: they are the matter to which, in this case, fashion and custom only give the different shapes and impressions. Whoever has the two first sorts will easily acquire this third sort of good-breeding, which depends singly upon attention and observation. It is, properly, the polish, the lustre, the last finishing strokes of good-breeding. It is to be found only in capitals, and even there it varies; the good-breeding of Rome differing in some things from that of Paris; that of Paris, in others, from that of Madrid; and that of Madrid, in many things from that of London.

A man of sense, therefore, carefully attends to the local manners of the respective places where he is, and takes for his models those persons whom he observes to be at the head of

---

[1] *Truck*, an old word for barter, exchange.

the fashion and good-breeding. He watches how they address themselves to their superiors, how they accost their equals, and how they treat their inferiors; and lets none of those little niceties escape him; which are to good-breeding what the last delicate and masterly touches are to a good picture; and of which the vulgar have no notion, but by which good judges distinguish the master. He attends even to their air, dress, and motions, and imitates them liberally, and not servilely; he copies, but does not mimic. These personal graces are of very great consequence: they anticipate the sentiments before merit can engage the understanding; they captivate the heart, and give rise, I believe, to the extravagant notions of charms and philters. Their effects were so surprising that they were reckoned supernatural. The most graceful and best bred men, and the handsomest and genteelest women, give the most philters; and, as I verily believe, without the least assistance of the devil. Pray be not only well-dressed, but shining in your dress; let it have *du brillant*; I do not mean by a clumsy load of gold and silver, but by the taste and fashion of it. Women like and require it; they think it an attention due to them; but on the other hand, if your motions and carriage are not graceful, genteel, and natural, your fine clothes will only display your awkwardness the more.

But I am unwilling to suppose you still awkward; for surely by this time you must have catched a good air in good company. When you went from hence you were not naturally awkward; but your awkwardness was adventitious and Westmonasterial. Leipsig, I apprehend, is not the seat of the Graces; and I presume you acquired none there. But now, if you will be pleased to observe what people of the first fashion do with their legs and arms, heads and bodies, you will reduce yours to certain decent laws of motion. You danced pretty well here, and ought to dance very well before you come home; for what one is obliged to do sometimes one ought to be able to do well. Besides, *la belle danse donne du brillant à un jeune homme.* And you should endeavour to shine.

A calm serenity, negative merit and graces, do not become your age. You should be *alerte, adroit, vif*; be wanted, talked of, impatiently expected, and unwillingly parted with in company. I should be glad to hear half a dozen women of fashion say, *Où est donc le petit Stanhope? Que ne vient-il? Il faut avouer qu'il est aimable.* All this I do not mean singly with regard to women as the principal object; but with regard to men, and with a view of your making yourself considerable. For, with very small variations, the same things that please women please men; and a man whose manners are softened and polished by women of fashion, and who is formed by them to an habitual attention and complaisance, will please, engage, and connect men much easier and more than he would otherwise. You must be sensible that you cannot rise in the world without forming connections and engaging different characters to conspire in your point. You must make them your dependants without their knowing it, and dictate to them while you seem to be directed by them. Those necessary connections can never be formed or preserved but by an uninterrupted series of complaisance, attentions, politeness, and some constraint. You must engage their hearts if you would have their support; you must watch the *mollia tempora,* and captivate them by the *agrémens,* and charms of conversation. People will not be called out to your service only when you want them; and, if you expect to receive strength from them, they must receive either pleasure or advantage from you.

I received in this instant a letter from Mr. Harte, of the 2nd, N.S., which I will answer soon; in the mean time I return him my thanks for it, through you. The constant good accounts which he gives me of you will make me suspect him of partiality, and think him *le médecin tant mieux.* Consider, therefore, what weight any future deposition of his against you must necessarily have with me; as, in that case, he will be a very unwilling, he must consequently be a very important witness. Adieu!

Dear Boy,

My last was upon the subject of good-breeding; but, I think, it rather set before you the unfitness and disadvantages of ill-breeding, than the utility and necessity of good; it was rather negative than positive. This, therefore, shall go further, and explain to you the necessity, which you, of all people living, lie under, not only of being positively actively well-bred, but of shining and distinguishing yourself by your good-breeding. Consider your own situation in every particular, and judge whether it is not essentially your interest, by your own good-breeding to others, to secure theirs to you; and that, let me assure you, is the only way of doing it; for people will repay, and with interest too, inattention with inattention, neglect with neglect, and ill manners with worse; which may engage you in very disagreeable affairs. In the next place, your profession requires, more than any other, the nicest and most distinguished good-breeding. You will negotiate with very little success, if you do not, previously, by your manners, conciliate and engage the affections of those with whom you are to negotiate. Can you ever get into the confidence and the secrets of the Courts where you may happen to reside, if you have not those pleasing, insinuating manners which alone can procure them? Upon my word, I do not say too much when I say, that superior good-breeding, insinuating manners, and genteel address, are half your business.

Your knowledge will have but very little influence upon the mind, if your manners prejudice the heart against you; but, on the other hand, how easily will you dupe the understanding where you have first engaged the heart! and hearts are by no means to be gained by the mere common civility which everybody practises. Bowing again to those who bow to you, answering dryly those who speak to you, and saying nothing offensive to anybody, is such negative good-breeding, that it is only not being a brute; as it would be but a very poor commendation of any man's cleanliness to say that he did not stink. It is an active, cheerful, officious, seduceing good-breeding that must gain you the good-will and first sentiments of the men, and the affections of the women. You must carefully watch and attend to their passions, their tastes, their little humours and weaknesses, and *aller au devant*. You must do it, at the same time, with alacrity and *empressement*, and not as if you graciously condescended to humour their weaknesses.

For instance, suppose you invited anybody to dine or sup with you, you ought to recollect if you had observed that they had any favourite dish, and take care to provide it for them: and, when it came, you should say, *You seemed to me, at such and such a place, to give this dish a preference, and therefore I ordered it. This is the wine that I observed you liked, and therefore I procured some.* The more trifling these things are, the more they prove your attention for the person, and are consequently the more engaging. Consult your own breast, and recollect how these little attentions, when shown you by others, flatter that degree of self-love and vanity, from which no man living is free. Reflect how they incline and attract you to that person, and how you are propitiated afterwards to

all which that person says or does. The same causes will
have the same effects in your favour.

Women, in a great degree, establish or destroy every man's
reputation of good-breeding; you must, therefore, in a manner,
overwhelm them with these attentions; they are used to them,
they expect them; and, to do them justice, they commonly
requite them. You must be sedulous, and rather over-officious
than under, in procuring them their coaches, their chairs, their
conveniencies in public places; not see what you should not
see; and rather assist where you cannot help seeing. Opportunities of showing these attentions present themselves perpetually; but, if they do not, make them. As Ovid advises
his Lover, when he sits in the *Circus* near his mistress, to wipe
the dust off her neck, even if there be none: *Si nullus, tamen
excute nullum.* Your conversation with women should always
be respectful; but, at the same time, *enjoué*, and always
addressed to their vanity. Everything you say or do, should
convince them of the regard you have (whether you have it
or not) for their beauty, their wit, or their merit.

Men have possibly as much vanity as women, though of
another kind; and both art and good-breeding require, that
instead of mortifying, you should please and flatter it, by
words and looks of approbation. Suppose (which is by no
means improbable) that, at your return to England, I should
place you near the person of some one of the Royal Family;
in that situation, good-breeding, engaging address, adorned
with all the graces that dwell at Courts, would very probably
make you a favourite, and, from a favourite, a Minister; but
all the knowledge and learning in the world, without them,
never would. The penetration of Princes seldom goes deeper
than the surface. It is the exterior that always engages their
hearts; and I would never advise you to give yourself much
trouble about their understandings. Princes in general (I mean
those *Porphyrogenets* [1] who are born and bred in purple) are
about the pitch of women; bred up like them, and are to be
addressed and gained in the same manner. They always see,

---

[1] "In the Greek language *purple* and *porphyry* are the same word; and
as the colours of nature are invariable, we may learn that a dark, deep red
was the Tyrian dye which stained the purple of the ancients. An apart-
ment of the Byzantine palace was lined with porphyry; it was reserved
of the use of the pregnant empresses, and the royal birth of their children
was expressed by the appellation of *Porphyrogenite*, or Born in the Purple.
Several of the Roman princes had been blessed with an heir; but this
peculiar surname was first applied to Constantine the Seventh" (A.D. 911).
—GIBBON'S *Decline and Fall*, ch. xlviii.

they seldom weigh. Your lustre, not your solidity, must take them; your inside will afterwards support and secure what your outside has acquired. With weak people (and they undoubtedly are three parts in four of mankind), good-breeding, address, and manners are everything; they can go no deeper; but let me assure you, that they are a great deal even with people of the best understandings.

Where the eyes are not pleased, and the heart is not flattered, the mind will be apt to stand out. Be this right or wrong, I confess I am so made myself. Awkwardness and ill-breeding shock me to that degree, that, where I meet with them, I cannot find in my heart to inquire into the intrinsic merit of that person; I hastily decide in myself, that he can have none; and am not sure, I should not even be sorry to know that he had any. I often paint you in my imagination in your present *lontananza*; and, while I view you in the light of ancient and modern learning, useful and ornamental knowledge, I am charmed with the prospect; but when I view you in another light, and represent you awkward, ungraceful, ill-bred, with vulgar air and manners, shambling towards me with inattention and *distractions*, I shall not pretend to describe to you what I feel; but will do as a skilful painter did formerly, draw a veil before the countenance of the father.

I dare say you know already enough of Architecture to know that the Tuscan is the strongest and most solid of all the Orders; but, at the same time, it is the coarsest and clumsiest of them. Its solidity does extremely well for the foundation and base floor of a great edifice; but if the whole building be Tuscan, it will attract no eyes, it will stop no passengers, it will invite no interior examination; people will take it for granted, that the finishing and furnishing cannot be worth seeing, where the front is so unadorned and clumsy. But if, upon the solid Tuscan foundation, the Doric, the Ionic, and the Corinthian Orders rise gradually with all their beauty, proportions, and ornaments, the fabric seizes the most incurious eye, and stops the most careless passenger, who solicits admission as a favour, nay, often purchases it. Just so will it fare with your little fabric, which, at present, I fear, has more of the Tuscan than of the Corinthian Order. You must absolutely change the whole front, or nobody will knock at the door. The several parts, which must compose this new front, are elegant, easy, natural, superior good-breeding; an engaging address; genteel motions; an insinuating softness in your looks, words, and actions; a spruce, lively air; fashionable dress; and all the glitter that a young fellow should have.

I am sure you would do a great deal for my sake; and therefore consider, at your return here, what a disappointment and concern it would be to me, if I could not safely depute you to do the honours of my house and table; and if I should be ashamed to present you to those who frequent both. Should you be awkward, inattentive, and *distrait*, and happen to meet Mr. L[yttelton] at my table, the consequences of that meeting must be fatal; you would run your heads against each other, cut each other's fingers, instead of your meat, or die by the precipitate infusion of scalding soup.

This is really so copious a subject, that there is no end of being either serious or ludicrous upon it. It is impossible, too, to enumerate or state to you the various cases in good-breeding; they are infinite; there is no situation or relation in the world, so remote or so intimate, that does not require a degree of it. Your own good-sense must point it out to you; your own good-nature must incline, and your interest prompt you to practise it; and observation and experience must give you the manner, the air, and the graces, which complete the whole.

This letter will hardly overtake you till you are at or near Rome. I expect a great deal, in every way, from your six months' stay there. My morning hopes are justly placed in Mr. Harte, and the masters he will give you; my evening ones, in the Roman ladies; pray be attentive to both. But I must hint to you, that the Roman ladies are not *les femmes sçavantes, et ne vous embrasseront point pour l'amour du Grec*.[1] They must have *il garbato, il leggiadro, il disinvolto, il lusinghiero, quel non sò che che piace, che alletta, che incanta*.

I have often asserted, that the profoundest learning, and the politest manners, were by no means incompatible, though so seldom found united in the same person; and I have engaged myself to exhibit you as a proof of the truth of this assertion. Should you, instead of that, happen to disprove me, the concern indeed will be mine, but the loss will be yours. Lord

---

[1] An allusion to a passage in the *Femmes Savantes* of Molière:

"*Philaminte.* Quoi! Monsieur sait du Grec! Ah, permettez de grace "Que pour l'amour du Grec, Monsieur, on vous embrasse!"

But when the turn comes to Henriette, she exclaims to the pedant, *qui veut aussi l'embrasser*:

"Excusez-moi, Monsieur, je n'entends pas le Grec!"—iii, 5.

Bolingbroke [1] is a strong instance on my side of the question; he joins, to the deepest erudition, the most elegant politeness and good-breeding that ever any courtier and man of the world was adorned with. And Pope very justly called him "all-accomplished St. John," with regard to his knowledge and his manners. He had, it is true, his faults; which proceeded from unbounded ambition, and impetuous passions; but they have now subsided by age and experience; and I can wish you nothing better than to be what he is now, without being what he has been formerly. His address pre-engages, his eloquence persuades, and his knowledge informs all who approach him. Upon the whole, I do desire, and insist, that, from after dinner till you go to bed, you make good-breeding, address, and manners, your serious object and your only care. Without them, you will be nobody; with them, you may be anything.

Adieu, my dear child! My compliments to Mr. Harte.

DEAR BOY,   London, November 24, O.S. 1749.

Every rational being (I take it for granted) proposes to himself some object more important than mere respiration and obscure animal existence. He desires to distinguish himself among his fellow-creatures; and, *alicui negotio intentus, præclari facinoris, aut artis bonæ, famam quærit.* Cæsar, when embarking in a storm, said, that it was not necessary he should live; but that it was absolutely necessary he should get to the place to which he was going. And Pliny leaves mankind this only alternative; either of doing what deserves to be written, or of writing what deserves to be read. As for those who do neither, *eorum vitam mortemque juxta æstumo; quoniam de utrâque siletur.* You have, I am convinced, one or both of these objects in view; but you must know, and use the necessary means, or your pursuit will be vain and frivolous. In either case, *sapere est principium et fons;* but it is by no means all. That knowledge may be adorned, it must have lustre as well as weight, or it will be oftener taken for lead than for gold. Knowledge you have, and will have; I am easy upon that article. But my business, as your friend, is not to compliment you upon what you have, but to tell you with freedom what you want; and I must tell you plainly, that I fear you want everything but knowledge.

I have written to you so often of late upon good-breeding, address, *les manières liantes,* the Graces, etc., that I shall confine

[1] Henry St. John, Viscount Bolingbroke, born 1678, died 1751.

this letter to another subject, pretty near akin to them, and which, I am sure, you are full as deficient in—I mean style.

Style is the dress of thoughts; and let them be ever so just, if your style is homely, coarse, and vulgar, they will appear to as much disadvantage, and be as ill received as your person, though ever so well proportioned, would, if dressed in rags, dirt, and tatters. It is not every understanding that can judge of matter, but every ear can and does judge, more or less, of style; and were I either to speak or write to the public, I should prefer moderate matter, adorned with all the beauties and elegances of style, to the strongest matter in the world, ill-worded and ill-delivered. Your business is negotiation abroad, and oratory in the House of Commons at home. What figure can you make in either case, if your style be inelegant, I do not say bad? Imagine yourself writing an office-letter to a Secretary of State, which letter is to be read by the whole Cabinet Council, and very possibly afterwards laid before Parliament; any one barbarism, solecism, or vulgarism in it would, in a very few days, circulate through the whole kingdom, to your disgrace and ridicule. For instance; I will suppose you had written the following letter from the Hague, to the Secretary of State at London; and leave you to suppose the consequences of it.

My Lord,

I *had,* last night, the honour of your Lordship's letter of the 24th; and will *set about doing* the orders contained *therein;* and *if so be* that I can get that affair done by the next post, I will not fail *for to* give your Lordship an account of it by *next post.* I have told the French Minister, *as how, that if* that affair be not soon concluded, your Lordship would think it *all long of him;* and that he must have neglected *for to* have wrote to his Court about it. I must beg leave to put your Lordship in mind, *as how,* that I am now full three quarters in arrear; and if *so be* that I do not very soon receive at least one half year, I shall *cut a very bad figure;* for *this here* place is very dear. I shall be *vastly beholden* to your Lordship for *that there* mark of your favour; and so I *rest,* or *remain,* Your etc.

You will tell me, possibly, that this is a *caricatura* of an illiberal and inelegant style; I will admit it; but assure you, at the same time, that a despatch with less than half these faults would blow you up for ever. It is by no means sufficient to be free from faults in speaking and writing; you must do both correctly and elegantly. In faults of this kind, it is not *ille optimus qui minimis urgetur;* but he is unpardonable who has any at all, because it is his own fault; he need only attend to, observe, and imitate the best authors.

It is a very true saying, that a man must be born a poet, but that he may make himself an orator; and the very first principle of an orator is, to speak his own language particularly, with the utmost purity and elegancy. A man will be forgiven, even great errors, in a foreign language; but in his own, even the least slips are justly laid hold of and ridiculed.

A person of the House of Commons, speaking two years ago upon naval affairs, asserted, that we had then the finest navy *upon the face of the yearth*. This happy mixture of blunder and vulgarism, you may easily imagine, was matter of immediate ridicule; but I can assure you, that it continues so still, and will be remembered as long as he lives and speaks. Another, speaking in defence of a gentleman, upon whom a censure was moved, happily said, that he thought that gentleman was more *liable* to be thanked and rewarded, than censured. You know, I presume, that *liable* can never be used in a good sense.

You have with you three or four of the best English authors, Dryden, Atterbury, and Swift: read them with the utmost care, and with a particular view to their language; and they may possibly correct that *curious infelicity of diction* which you acquired at Westminster. Mr. Harte excepted, I will admit that you have met with very few English abroad, who could improve your style; and with many, I dare say, who speak as ill as yourself, and it may be worse; you must, therefore, take the more pains, and consult your authors, and Mr. Harte, the more. I need not tell you how attentive the Romans and Greeks, particularly the Athenians, were to this object. It is also a study among the Italians and the French; witness their respective academies and dictionaries, for improving and fixing their languages. To our shame be it spoken, it is less attended to here than in any polite country; but that is no reason why you should not attend to it; on the contrary, it will distinguish you the more. Cicero says, very truly, that it is glorious to excel other men in that very article, in which men excel brutes; *speech*.

Constant experience has shown me, that great purity and elegance of style, with a graceful elocution, cover a multitude of faults, in either a speaker or a writer. For my own part, I confess (and I believe most people are of my mind) that if a speaker should ungracefully mutter or stammer out to me the sense of an angel, deformed by barbarisms and solecisms, or larded with vulgarisms, he should never speak to me a second time, if I could help it. Gain the heart, or you gain nothing; the eyes and the ears are the only roads to the heart. Merit and knowledge will not gain hearts, though they will secure them when gained. Pray have that truth ever in your mind. Engage the eyes by your address, air, and motions; soothe the ears, by the elegancy and harmony of your diction; the heart will certainly follow; and the whole man, or woman, will as certainly follow the heart. I must repeat it to you, over and over again, that, with all the knowledge which you may have at present, or hereafter acquire, and with all the merit that ever man had, if you have not a graceful address, liberal and engaging manners, a prepossessing air, and a good degree of eloquence in speaking and writing, you will be nobody; but will have the daily mortification of seeing people, with not one-tenth part of your merit or knowledge, get the start of you, and disgrace you both in company and in business.

You have read Quintilian; the best book in the world to form an orator; pray read *Cicero de Oratore*; the best book in the world to finish one. Translate and retranslate, from and to Latin, Greek, and English; make yourself a pure and elegant English style; it requires nothing but application. I do not find that God has made you a poet; and I am very glad that He has not; therefore, for God's sake, make yourself an orator, which you may do. Though I still call you boy, I consider you no longer as such; and when I reflect upon the prodigious quantity of manure that has been laid upon you, I expect you should produce more at eighteen, than uncultivated soils do at eight-and-twenty.

Pray tell Mr. Harte I have received his letter of the 13th, N.S. Mr. Smith was much in the right, not to let you go, at this time of the year, by sea; in the summer you may navigate as much as you please; as for example; from Leghorn to Genoa, etc. Adieu!

DEAR BOY,   London, December 5, O.S. 1749.

Those who suppose that men in general act rationally because they are called rational creatures, know very little of the world; and, if they act themselves upon that supposition, will, nine times in ten, find themselves grossly mistaken. That man is *animal bipes, implume, risibile,* I entirely agree; but, for the *rationale,* I can only allow it him *in actu primo* (to talk logic), and seldom *in actu secundo*. Thus the speculative cloistered pedant in his solitary cell forms systems of things as they should be, not as they are; and writes as decisively and absurdly upon war, politics, manners and characters, as that pedant talked who was so kind as to instruct Hannibal in the art of war. Such closet politicians never fail to assign the deepest motives for the most trifling actions, instead of often ascribing the greatest actions to the most trifling causes, in which they would be much seldomer mistaken. They read and write of Kings, heroes, and statesmen, as never doing anything but upon the deepest principles of sound policy. But those who see and observe kings, heroes, and statesmen, discover that they have headaches, indigestion, humours and passions, just like other people; every one of which in their turns determine their wills in defiance of their reason.

Had we only read in the Life of Alexander that he burnt Persepolis, it would doubtless have been accounted for from deep policy: we should have been told, that his new conquest could not have been secured without the destruction of that capital, which would have been the constant seat of cabals, conspiracies, and revolts. But, luckily, we are informed at the same time, that this hero, this demi-god, this son and heir of Jupiter Ammon, happened to get extremely drunk . . . and, by way of frolic, destroyed one of the finest cities in the world.

Read men, therefore, yourself; not in books, but in nature. Adopt no systems, but study them yourself. Observe their weaknesses, their passions, their humours; of all which their understandings are, nine times in ten, the dupes. You will then know that they are to be gained, influenced or led, much oftener by little things than by great ones; and consequently you will no longer think those things little which tend to such great purposes.

Let us apply this now to the particular object of this letter; I mean, speaking in and influencing public assemblies. The nature of our constitution makes eloquence more useful and more necessary in this country than in any other in Europe. A certain degree of good-sense and knowledge is requisite for that as well as for everything else; but beyond that, the purity of diction, the elegance of style, the harmony of periods, a pleasing elocution, and a graceful action, are the things which a public speaker should attend to the most; because his audience certainly does, and understands them the best: or rather, indeed, understands little else. The late Lord Chancellor Cowper's strength, as an orator, lay by no means in his reasonings, for he often hazarded very weak ones. But such was the purity and elegance of his style, such the propriety and charms of his elocution, and such the gracefulness of his action, that he never spoke without universal applause: the ears and the eyes gave him up the hearts and the understandings of the audience. On the contrary, the late Lord Townshend [1] always spoke materially, with argument and knowledge, but never pleased. Why? His diction was not only inelegant, but frequently ungrammatical, always vulgar; his cadences false, his voice unharmonious, and his action ungraceful. Nobody heard him with patience; and the young fellows used to joke upon him, and repeat his inaccuracies. The late Duke of Argyle, [2] though the weakest reasoner, was the most pleasing speaker I ever knew in my life; he charmed, he warmed, he forcibly ravished the audience, not by his matter certainly, but by his manner of delivering it. A most genteel figure, a graceful noble air, an harmonious voice, an elegancy of style, and a strength of emphasis, conspired to make him the most affecting, persuasive, and applauded speaker I ever saw. I was captivated like others, but when I came home and coolly considered what he had said, stripped of all those ornaments in which he had dressed it, I often found the matter flimsy, the arguments weak, and I was convinced of the power of those adventitious, concurring circumstances, which ignorance of mankind only calls trifling ones. Cicero in his book *de Oratore*, in order to raise the dignity of that profession which he well knew himself to be at the head of, asserts that a complete orator must be a complete everything, lawyer, philosopher, divine, etc. That would be extremely well, if it were possible, but man's life is not long enough; and I hold him to be the completest orator who speaks the best upon that subject which occurs; whose happy choice of words, whose lively imagination, whose elocution and action adorn and grace his matter, at the same time that they excite the attention and engage the passions of his audience.

You will be of the House of Commons as soon as you are of age; and you must first make a figure there, if you would make a figure, or a fortune, in your country. This you can never do

[1] Charles, second Viscount Townshend, born 1674, was Lord Lieutenant of Ireland, 1717.

[2] John, the second and celebrated duke, of whom Thomson says:

"From his rich tongue
Persuasion flows and wins the high debate."

without that correctness and elegancy in your own language, which you now seem to neglect, and which you have entirely to learn. Fortunately for you, it is to be learned. Care and observation will do it; but do not flatter yourself, that all the knowledge, sense, and reasoning in the world will ever make you a popular and applauded speaker, without the ornaments and the graces, of style, elocution, and action. Sense and argument, though coarsely delivered, will have their weight in a private conversation, with two or three people of sense; but in a public assembly they will have none, if naked and destitute of the advantages I have mentioned. Cardinal de Retz observes, very justly, that every numerous assembly is mob, influenced by their passions, humours, and affections, which nothing but eloquence ever did, or ever can engage. This is so important a consideration for every body in this country, and more particularly for you, that I earnestly recommend it to your most serious care and attention.

Mind your diction, in whatever language you either write or speak; contract a habit of correctness and elegance. Consider your style, even in the freest conversation, and most familiar letters. After, at least, if not before you have said a thing, reflect if you could not have said it better. Where you doubt of the propriety or elegancy of a word or a phrase, consult some good dead or living authority in that language. Use yourself to translate from various languages into English; correct those translations till they satisfy your ear, as well as your understanding. And be convinced of this truth, That the best sense and reason in the world will be as unwelcome in a public assembly, without these ornaments, as they will in public companies, without the assistance of manners and politeness. If you will please people, you must please them in their own way; and as you cannot make them what they should be, you must take them as they are. I repeat it again, they are only to be taken by *agrémens*, and by what flatters their senses' and their hearts. Rabelais first wrote a most excellent book, which nobody liked; then, determined to conform to the public taste, he wrote *Gargantua and Pantagruel*, which everybody liked, extravagant as it was. Adieu!

DEAR BOY,　　　　　　　　London, December 9, O.S. 1749.

It is now above forty years since I have never spoken nor written one single word, without giving myself at least one moment's time to consider, whether it was a good one or a bad one, and whether I could not find out a better in its place. An unharmonious and rugged period, at this time, shocks my ears; and I, like all the rest of the world, will willingly exchange, and give up some degree of rough sense, for a good degree of pleasing sound. I will freely and truly own to you, without either vanity or false modesty, that whatever reputation I have acquired as a speaker, is more owing to my constant attention to my diction, than to my matter, which was necessarily just the same as other people's. When you come into Parliament, your reputation as a speaker will depend much more upon your words, and your periods, than upon the subject. The same matter occurs equally to everybody of common sense, upon the same question; the dressing it well, is what excites the attention and admiration of the audience.

It is in Parliament that I have set my heart upon your making a figure; it is there that I want to have you justly proud of yourself, and to make me justly proud of you. This means that you must be a good speaker there; I use the word *must*, because I know you may if you will. The vulgar, who are always mistaken, look upon a speaker and a comet with the same astonishment and admiration, taking them both for preternatural phenomena. This error discourages many young men from attempting that character; and good speakers are willing to have their talent considered as something very extraordinary, if not a peculiar gift of God to His elect. But let you and I [*sic*] analyse and simplify this good speaker; let us strip him of those adventitious plumes, with which his own pride, and the ignorance of others have decked him, and we shall find the true definition of him to be no more than this:— A man of good common sense, who reasons justly, and expresses himself elegantly on that subject upon which he speaks. There is, surely, no witchcraft in this. A man of sense, without a superior and astonishing degree of parts, will not talk nonsense upon any subject; nor will he, if he has the least taste or application, talk inelegantly. What then does all this mighty art and mystery of speaking in Parliament amount to? Why, no more than this, That the man who speaks in the House of Commons, speaks in that House, and to four hundred people, that opinion, upon a given subject, which he would make no difficulty of speaking in any house in England, round the fire, or at table, to any fourteen people whatsoever; better judges, perhaps, and severer critics of what he says, than any fourteen gentlemen of the House of Commons.

I have spoken frequently in Parliament, and not always without some applause; and therefore I can assure you, from my experience, that there is very little in it. The elegancy of the style, and the turn of the periods, make the chief impression upon the hearers. Give them but one or two round and harmonious periods in a speech, which they will retain and repeat, and they will go home as well satisfied, as people do from an opera, humming all the way one or two favourite tunes that have struck their ears and were easily caught. Most people have ears, but few have judgment; tickle those ears, and, depend upon it, you will catch their judgments, such as they are.

Cicero, conscious that he was at the top of his profession (for in his time eloquence was a profession), in order to set himself off, defines, in his treatise *de Oratore*, an orator to be such a man as never was, or never will be; and by this fallacious argument, says, that he must know every art and science whatsoever, or how shall he speak upon them? But with submission to so great an authority, my definition of an orator is extremely different from, and, I believe, much truer than his. I call that man an orator, who reasons justly, and expresses himself elegantly upon whatever subject he treats. Problems in geometry, equations in algebra, processes in chymistry, and experiments in anatomy, are never, that I have heard of, the objects of eloquence; and therefore I humbly conceive, that a man may be a very fine speaker, and yet know nothing of geometry, algebra, chymistry, or anatomy. The subjects of all parliamentary debates, are subjects of common sense singly.

Thus I write whatever occurs to me, that I may contribute either to form or inform you. May my labour not be in vain! and it will not, if you will but have half the concern for yourself, that I have for you. Adieu!

DEAR BOY,   London, December 19, O.S. 1749.

The knowledge of mankind is a very useful knowledge for everybody—a most necessary one for you, who are destined to an active public life. You will have to do with all sorts of characters; you should, therefore, know them thoroughly in order to manage them ably. This knowledge is not to be gotten systematically, you must acquire it yourself by your own observation and sagacity: I will give you such hints as I think may be useful landmarks in your intended progress.

I have often told you (and it is most true) that, with regard to mankind, we must not draw general conclusions from certain particular principles, though, in the main, true ones. We must not suppose, that because a man is a rational animal, he will, therefore, always act rationally; or, because he has such or such a predominant passion, that he will act invariably and consequentially in the pursuit of it. No; we are complicated machines; and though we have one main-spring that gives motion to the whole, we have an infinity of little wheels, which, in their turns, retard, precipitate, and sometimes stop that motion. Let us exemplify: I will suppose ambition to be (as it commonly is) the predominant passion of a minister of state, and I will suppose that minister to be an able one; will he, therefore, invariably pursue the object of that predominant passion? May I be sure that he will do so and so, because he ought? Nothing less. Sickness, or low spirits, may damp this predominant passion; humour and peevishness may triumph over it; inferior passions may at times surprise it and prevail. Is this ambitious statesman amorous? indiscreet and unguarded confidences, made in tender moments, to his wife or his mistress, may defeat all his schemes. Is he avaricious? some great lucrative object suddenly presenting itself may unravel all the work of his ambition. Is he passionate? contradiction and provocation (sometimes, it may be, too, artfully intended) may extort rash and inconsiderate expressions, or actions, destructive of his main object. Is he vain and open to flattery? an artful flattering favourite may mislead him; and even laziness may, at certain moments, make him neglect or omit the necessary steps to that height which he wants to arrive at. Seek first, then, for the predominant passion of the character which you mean to engage and influence, and address yourself to it; but without defying or despising the inferior passions; get them in your interest too, for now and then they will have their turns. In many cases you may not have it in your power to contribute to the gratification of the prevailing passion; then take the next best to your aid. There are many avenues to every man, and when you cannot get at him through the great one, try the serpentine ones, and you will arrive at last.

There are two inconsistent passions, which, however, frequently accompany each other, like man and wife; and which, like man and wife too, are commonly clogs upon each other. I mean ambition and avarice: the latter is often the true cause of the former; and then is the predominant passion. It seems to have been so in Cardinal Mazarin; who did anything, submitted to anything, and forgave anything, for the sake of plunder. He loved and courted power like an usurer, because it carried profit along with it. Whoever should have formed his opinion, or taken his measures singly, from the ambitious part of Cardinal Mazarin's character, would have found himself often mistaken. Some, who had found this out, made their fortunes by letting him cheat them at play. On the contrary, Cardinal Richelieu's prevailing passion seems to have been ambition, and his immense riches only the natural consequences of that ambition gratified; and yet, I make no doubt, but that ambition had now and then its turn with the former, and avarice with the latter. Richelieu (by the way) is so strong a proof of the inconsistency of human nature, that I cannot help observing to you, that while he absolutely governed both his King and his country, and was, in a great degree, the arbiter of the fate of all Europe, he was more jealous of the great reputation of Corneille than of the power of Spain; and more flattered with being thought (what he was not) the best poet, than with being thought (what he certainly was) the greatest statesman in Europe; and affairs stood still while he was concerting the criticism upon the *Cid*. Could one think this possible if one did not know it to be true?

Though men are all of one composition, the several ingredients are so differently proportioned in each individual, that no two are exactly alike; and no one at all times like himself. The ablest man will sometimes do weak things; the proudest man mean things; the honestest man ill things; and the wickedest man good ones. Study individuals then, and if you take (as you ought to do) their outlines from their prevailing passion, suspend your last finishing strokes till you have attended to and discovered the operations of their inferior passions, appetites, and humours. A man's general character may be that of the honestest man of the world: do not dispute it; you might be thought envious or ill-natured; but, at the same time, do not take this probity upon trust, to such a degree as to put your life, fortune, or reputation in his power. This honest man may happen to be your rival in power, in interest, or in love; three passions that often put honesty to most severe trials, in which it is too often cast: but first analyse this honest man yourself; and then you will be able to judge how far you may, or may not, with safety trust him.

Women are much more like each other than men; they have, in truth, but two passions, vanity and love; these are their universal characteristics. An Agrippina may sacrifice them to ambition, or a Messalina to lust, but such instances are rare; and in general, all they say and all they do tends to the gratification of their vanity or their love. He who flatters them most pleases them best; and they are most in love with him who they think is the most in love with them. No adulation is too strong for them; no assiduity too great; no simulation of passion too gross: as, on the other hand, the least word or action that can possibly be construed into a slight or contempt, is unpardonable, and never forgotten. Men are, in this respect, tender too, and will sooner forgive an injury than an insult. Some men are more captious than others; some are always wrong-headed; but every man living has such a share of vanity as to be hurt by marks of slight and contempt. Every man does not pretend to be a poet, a mathematician, or a statesman, and considered as such; but every man pretends to common sense, and to fill his place in the world with common decency; and consequently does not easily forgive those negligences, inattentions, and slights, which seem to call in question or utterly deny him both these pretensions.

Suspect, in general, those who remarkably affect any one virtue; who raise it above all others, and who, in a manner, intimate that they possess it exclusively. I say suspect them, for they are commonly impostors; but do not be sure that they are always so; for I have sometimes known saints really religious, blusterers really brave, reformers of manners really honest, and prudes really chaste. Pry into the recesses of their hearts yourself, as far as you are able, and never implicitly adopt a character upon common fame; which, though generally right as to the great outlines of characters, is always wrong in some particulars.

Be upon your guard against those, who, upon very slight acquaintance, obtrude their unasked and unmerited friendship and confidence upon you; for they probably cram you with them only for their own eating: but, at the same time, do not roughly reject them upon that general supposition. Examine further, and see whether those unexpected offers flow from a warm heart and a silly head, or from a designing head and a cold heart; for knavery and folly have often the same symptoms. In the first case there is no danger in accepting them, *valeant quantum valere possunt*. In the latter case it may be useful to seem to accept them, and artfully to turn the battery upon him who raised it.

There is an incontinency of friendship among young fellows, who are associated by their mutual pleasures only, which has, very frequently, bad consequences. A parcel of warm hearts and inexperienced heads, heated by convivial mirth, and possibly a little too much wine, vow, and really mean at the time, eternal friendship to each other, and indiscreetly pour out their whole souls in common, and without the least reserve. These confidences are as indiscreetly repealed as they were made: for new pleasures and new places soon dissolve this ill-cemented connection; and then very ill uses are made of these rash confidences. Bear your part, however, in young companies; nay, excel if you can in all the social and convivial joy and festivity that become youth. Trust them with your love-tales, if you please, but keep your serious views secret. Trust those only to some tried friend more experienced than yourself, and who, being in a different walk of life from you, is not likely to become your rival; for I would not advise you to depend so much upon the heroic virtue of mankind as to hope or believe that your competitor will ever be your friend, as to the object of that competition.

These are reserves and cautions very necessary to have, but very imprudent to show; the *volto sciolto* should accompany them. Adieu!

DEAR BOY,

Great talents and great virtues (if you should have them) will procure you the respect and the admiration of mankind; but it is the lesser talents, the *leniores virtutes*, which must procure you their love and affection. The former, unassisted and unadorned by the latter, will extort praise; but will at the same time excite both fear and envy; two sentiments absolutely incompatible with love and affection.

Cæsar had all the great vices, and Cato all the great virtues that men could have. But Cæsar had the *leniores virtutes* which Cato wanted; and which made him beloved even by his enemies, and gained him the hearts of mankind in spite of their reason; while Cato was not even beloved by his friends, notwithstanding the esteem and respect which they could not refuse to his virtues; and I am apt to think that if Cæsar had wanted, and Cato possessed, those *leniores virtutes*, the former would not have attempted (at least with success), and the latter could have protected, the liberties of Rome.   Mr. Addison, in his *Cato*, says of Cæsar (and I believe with truth):

> Curse on his virtues, they've undone his country.

By which he means those lesser but engaging virtues of gentleness, affability, complaisance, and good-humour. The knowledge of a scholar, the courage of a hero, and the virtue of a Stoic, will be admired; but if the knowledge be accompanied with arrogance, the courage with ferocity, and the virtue with inflexible severity, the man will never be loved. The heroism of Charles XII of Sweden (if his brutal courage deserves that name) was universally admired, but the man nowhere beloved. Whereas Henry IV of France, who had full as much courage, and was much longer engaged in wars, was generally beloved upon account of his lesser and social virtues. We are all so formed, that our understandings are generally the dupes of our hearts, that is, of our passions; and the surest way to the former is through the latter, which must be engaged by the *leniores virtutes* alone, and the manner of exerting them. The insolent civility of a proud man is (for example), if possible, more shocking than his rudeness could be; because he shows you, by his manner, that he thinks it mere condescension in him; and that his goodness alone bestows upon you what you have no pretence to claim. He intimates his protection instead of his friendship, by a gracious nod instead of an usual bow; and rather signifies his consent that you may, than his invitation that you should, sit, walk, eat or drink with him.

The costive liberality of a purse-proud man insults the distresses it sometimes relieves; he takes care to make you feel your own misfortunes, and the difference between your situation and his; both which he insinuates to be justly merited: yours by your folly, his by his wisdom. The arrogant pedant does not communicate but promulgates his knowledge: he does not give it you, but he inflicts it upon you; and is (if possible) more desirous to show you your own ignorance than his own learning. Such manners as these, not only in the particular instances which I have mentioned, but likewise in all others, shock and revolt that little pride and vanity which every man has in his heart, and obliterate in us the obligation for the favour conferred, by reminding us of the motive which produced, and the manner which accompanied it.

These faults point out their opposite perfections, and your own good sense will naturally suggest them to you.

But besides these lesser virtues, there are, what may be called the lesser talents or accomplishments, which are of great use to adorn and recommend all the greater; and the more so, as all people are judges of the one, and but few are of the other. Everybody feels the impression which an engaging address, an agreeable manner of speaking, and an easy politeness, makes upon them; and they prepare the way for the favourable reception of their betters. Adieu!

DEAR BOY,   London, January 8, O.S. 1750.

I have seldom or never written to you upon the subject of Religion and Morality: your own reason, I am persuaded, has given you true notions of both; they speak best for themselves; but, if they wanted assistance, you have Mr. Harte at hand, both for precept and example; to your own reason, therefore, and to Mr. Harte, shall I refer you, for the reality of both; and confine myself, in this letter, to the decency, the utility, and the necessity, of scrupulously preserving the appearances of both. When I say the appearances of religion, I do not mean that you should talk or act like a missionary, or an enthusiast, nor that you should take up a controversial cudgel against whoever attacks the sect you are of; this would be both useless and unbecoming your age; but I mean that you should by no means seem to approve, encourage, or applaud, those libertine notions, which strike at religions equally, and which are the poor threadbare topics of half wits, and minute philosophers. Even those who are silly enough to laugh at their jokes, are still wise enough to distrust and detest their characters; for, putting moral virtues at the highest, and religion at the lowest, religion must still be allowed to be a collateral security, at least, to virtue; and every prudent man will sooner trust to two securities than to one.

Whenever, therefore, you happen to be in company with those pretended *esprits forts*, or with thoughtless libertines, who laugh at all religion, to show their wit, or disclaim it, to complete their riot; let no word or look of yours intimate the least approbation; on the contrary, let a silent gravity express your dislike; but enter not into the subject, and decline such unprofitable and indecent controversies. Depend upon this truth, That every man is the worse looked upon, and the less trusted, for being thought to have no religion; in spite of all the pompous and specious epithets he may assume, of *esprit fort*, freethinker, or moral philosopher; and a wise atheist (if such a thing there is) would, for his own interest, and character in this world, pretend to some religion.

Your moral character must be not only pure, but, like Cæsar's wife, unsuspected. The least speck or blemish upon it is fatal. Nothing degrades and vilifies more, for it excites and unites detestation and contempt. There are, however, wretches in the world profligate enough to explode all notions of moral good and evil; to maintain that they are merely local, and depend entirely upon the customs and fashions of different countries: nay, there are still, if possible, more unaccountable wretches; I mean those who affect to preach and propagate such absurd and infamous notions, without believing them themselves. These are the devil's hypocrites. Avoid as much as possible the company of such people, who reflect a degree of discredit and infamy upon all who converse with them. But as you may, sometimes, by accident, fall into such company, take great care that no complaisance, no good-humour, no warmth of festal mirth, ever make you seem even to acquiesce, much less to approve or applaud, such infamous doctrines. On the other hand; do not debate, nor enter into serious argument, upon a subject so much below it: but content yourself with telling those *Apostles*, that you know they are not serious; that you have a much better opinion of them than they would have you have; and that, you are very sure, they would not practise the doctrine they preach. But put your private mark upon them, and shun them for ever afterwards.

There is nothing so delicate as your moral character, and nothing which it is your interest so much to preserve pure. Should you be suspected of injustice, malignity, perfidy, lying, etc., all the parts and knowledge in the world will never procure you esteem, friendship, or respect. A strange concurrence of circumstances has sometimes raised very bad men to high stations; but they have been raised like criminals to a pillory, where their persons and their crimes, by being more conspicuous, are only the more known, the more detested, and the more pelted and insulted. If, in any case whatsoever, affectation and ostentation are pardonable, it is in the case of morality; though, even there, I would not advise you to a pharisaical pomp of virtue. But I will recommend to you a most scrupulous tenderness for your moral character, and the utmost care not to say or do the least thing that may, ever so slightly, taint it. Show yourself, upon all occasions, the advocate, the friend, but not the bully, of Virtue. Colonel Chartres,[1] whom you have certainly heard of (who was, I believe, the most notorious blasted rascal in the world, and who had, by all sorts of crimes, amassed immense wealth), was so sensible of the disadvantage of a bad character, that I heard him once say, in his impudent profligate manner, that, though he would not give one farthing for virtue, he would give ten thousand pounds for a character; because he should get a hundred thousand by it: whereas he was so blasted that he had no longer an opportunity of cheating people. It is possible then that an honest man can neglect what a wise rogue would purchase so dear?

There is one of the vices above-mentioned, into which people of good education, and, in the main, of good principles, some-times fall, from mistaken notions of skill, dexterity, and self-defence; I mean Lying: though it is inseparately attended with more infamy and loss than any other. The prudence and necessity of often concealing the truth, insensibly seduces people to violate it. It is the only art of mean capacities, and the only refuge of mean spirits. Whereas·concealing the truth, upon proper occasions, is as prudent and as innocent, as telling a lie, upon any occasion, is infamous and foolish. I will state you a case in your own department. Suppose you are employed at a foreign Court, and that the Minister of that Court is absurd or impertinent enough to ask you what your instructions are, Will you tell him a lie; which, as soon as found out, and found out it certainly will be, must destroy your credit, blast your character, and render you useless there? No. Will you tell him the truth then, and betray your trust? As certainly, No. But you will answer with firmness, That you are surprised at such a question; that you are persuaded he does not expect an answer to it; but that, at all events, he certainly will not have one. Such an answer will give him confidence in you; he will conceive an opinion of your veracity, of which opinion you may afterwards make very honest and fair advantages. But if, in negotiations, you are looked upon as a liar, and a trickster, no confidence will be placed in you, nothing will be communi-cated to you, and you will be in the situation of a man who has been burnt in the cheek; and who, from that mark, cannot after-

[1] Francis Chartres, so frequently and deservedly lashed by Pope. He died in 1731, aged sixty-two. The populace at his funeral raised a riot, almost tore the body out of the coffin, and cast dead dogs into the grave along with it. See a note to Roscoe's edition of Pope, vol. v, p. 326, ed. 1824. See Pope's *Imitations of Horace*, I, vi, 120.

wards get an honest livelihood if he would, but must continue a thief.

Lord Bacon very justly makes a distinction between Simulation and Dissimulation, and allows the latter rather than the former; but still observes, that they are the weaker sort of politicians who have recourse to either. A man who has strength of mind, and strength of parts, wants neither of them. "Certainly," says he, "the ablest men that ever were, have all had an openness and frankness of dealing, and a name of certainty and veracity; but then, they were like horses well-managed; for they could tell, passing well, when to stop, or turn: and at such times, when they thought the case indeed required dissimulation, if then they used it, it came to pass that the former opinion spread abroad, of their good faith and clearness of dealing, made them almost invisible."

There are people who indulge themselves in a sort of lying, which they reckon innocent, and which in one sense is so; for it hurts nobody but themselves. This sort of lying is the spurious offspring of vanity, begotten upon folly: these people deal in the marvellous; they have seen some things that never existed; they have seen other things which they never really saw, though they did exist, only because they were thought worth seeing. Has anything remarkable been said or done in any place, or in any company? they immediately present and declare themselves eye or ear witnesses of it. They have done feats themselves, unattempted, or at least unperformed by others. They are always the heroes of their own fables; and think that they gain consideration, or at least present attention, by it. Whereas, in truth, all they get is ridicule and contempt, not without a good degree of distrust; for one must naturally conclude, that he who will tell any lie from idle vanity, will not scruple telling a greater for interest. Had I really seen anything so very extraordinary as to be almost incredible, I would keep it to myself, rather than, by telling it, give any one body room to doubt for one minute of my veracity. It is most certain, that the reputation of chastity is not so necessary for a woman, as that of veracity is for a man; and with reason; for it is possible for a woman to be virtuous, though not strictly chaste; but it is not possible for a man to be virtuous without strict veracity. The slips of the poor women are sometimes mere bodily frailties; but a lie in a man is a vice of the mind, and of the heart. For God's sake, be scrupulously jealous of the purity of your moral character; keep it immaculate,

*F 823

unblemished, unsullied; and it will be unsuspected. Defamation and calumny never attack, where there is no weak place; they magnify, but they do not create.

There is a very great difference between that purity of character, which I so earnestly recommend to you, and the Stoical gravity and austerity of character, which I do by no means recommend to you. At your age, I would no more wish you to be a Cato than a Clodius. Be, and be reckoned a man of pleasure, as well as a man of business. Enjoy this happy and giddy time of your life; shine in the pleasures, and in the company of people of your own age. This is all to be done, and indeed only can be done, without the least taint to the purity of your moral character: for those mistaken young fellows, who think to shine by an impious or immoral licentiousness, shine only from their stinking, like corrupted flesh in the dark. Without this purity, you can have no dignity of character; and without dignity of character, it is impossible to rise in the world.

You must be respectable, if you will be respected. I have known people slattern away their character, without really polluting it; the consequence of which has been, that they have become innocently contemptible; their merit has been dimmed, their pretensions unregarded, and all their views defeated. Character must be kept bright, as well as clean. Content yourself with mediocrity in nothing. In purity of character, and in politeness of manners, labour to excel all, if you wish to equal many. Adieu!

MY DEAR FRIEND,   London, January 18, O.S. 1750.

I consider the solid part of your little edifice as so near being finished and completed, that my only remaining care is about the embellishments; and that must now be your principal care too. Adorn yourself with all those graces and accomplishments, which, without solidity, are frivolous; but without which, solidity is, to a great degree, useless. Take one man, with a very moderate degree of knowledge, but with a pleasing figure, a prepossessing address, graceful in all that he says and does, polite, *liant*, and, in short, adorned with all the lesser talents; and take another man, with sound sense and profound knowledge, but without the above-mentioned advantages; the former will not only get the better of the latter, in every pursuit of every kind, but in truth there will be no sort of competition between them. But can every man acquire these advantages? I say Yes, if he please; supposing he is in a situation, and in circumstances, to frequent good company. Attention, observation, and imitation, will most infallibly do it.

When you see a man, whose first *abord* strikes you, prepossesses you in his favour, and makes you entertain a good opinion of him, you do not know why: analyse that *abord*, and examine, within yourself, the several parts that compose it; and you will generally find it to be the result, the happy assemblage, of modesty unembarrassed, respect without timidity, a genteel, but unaffected attitude of body and limbs, an open, cheerful, but unsmirking countenance, and a dress, by no means negligent, and yet not foppish. Copy him, then, not servilely, but as some of the greatest masters of painting have copied others; insomuch, that their copies have been equal to the originals, both as to beauty and freedom. When you see a man, who is universally allowed to shine as an agreeable well-bred man, and a fine gentleman (as for example, the Duke de Nivernois), attend to him, watch him carefully; observe in what manner he addresses himself to his superiors, how he lives with his equals, and how he treats his inferiors. Mind his turn of conversation, in the several situations of morning visits, the table, and the evening amusements. Imitate, without mimicking him; and be his duplicate, but not his ape. You will find that he takes care never to say or do anything that can be construed into a slight, or a negligence; or that can, in any degree, mortify people's vanity and self-love; on the contrary, you will perceive that he makes people pleased with him, by making them first pleased with themselves: he shows respect, regard, esteem, and attention, where they are severally proper; he sows them with care, and he reaps them in plenty.

These amiable accomplishments are all to be acquired by use and imitation; for we are, in truth, more than half what we are, by imitation. The great point is, to choose good models, and to study them with care. People insensibly contract, not only the air, the manners, and the vices, of those with whom they commonly converse, but their virtues too, and even their way of thinking. This is so true, that I have known very plain understandings catch a certain degree of wit, by constantly conversing with those who had a great deal. Persist, therefore, in keeping the best company, and you will insensibly become like them; but if you add attention and observation, you will very soon be one of them. This inevitable contagion of company, shows you the necessity of keeping the best, and avoiding all other; for in every one, something will stick. You have hitherto, I confess, had very few opportunities of keeping polite company. Westminster school is, undoubtedly, the seat of illiberal manners and brutal behaviour. Leipsig, I suppose, is not the seat of refined and elegant manners. Venice, I believe, has done something; Rome, I hope, will do a great deal more; and Paris will, I dare say, do all that you want: always supposing, that you frequent the best companies, and in the intention of improving and forming yourself; for, without that intention, nothing will do.

I here subjoin a list of all those necessary, ornamental accomplishments (without which, no man living can either please or rise in the world) which hitherto I fear you want, and which only require your care and attention to possess.

To speak elegantly, whatever language you speak in; without which, nobody will hear you with pleasure, and, consequently, you will speak to very little purpose.

An agreeable and distinct elocution; without which nobody will hear you with patience; this everybody may acquire, who is not born with some imperfection in the organs of speech. You are not; and therefore it is wholly in your power. You need take much less pains for it than Demosthenes did.

A distinguished politeness of manners and address; which common sense, observation, good company, and imitation, will infallibly give you, if you will accept of it.

A genteel carriage, and graceful motions, with the air of a man of fashion. A good dancing-master, with some care on your part, and some imitation of those who excel, will soon bring this about.

To be extremely clean in your person, and perfectly well dressed, according to the fashion, be that what it will. Your negligence of dress, while you were a schoolboy, was pardonable, but would not be so now.

Upon the whole, take it for granted, that, without these accomplishments, all you know, and all you can do, will avail you very little. Adieu!

MY DEAR FRIEND,   London, January 25, O.S. 1750.

It is so long since I have heard from you, that I suppose Rome engrosses every moment of your time; and if it engrosses it in the manner I could wish, I willingly give up my share of it. I would rather *prodesse quam conspici*. Put out your time but to good interest, and I do not desire to borrow much of it. Your studies, the respectable remains of antiquity, and your evenings' amusements, cannot, and indeed ought not, to leave you much time to write. You will probably never see Rome again; and therefore you ought to see it well now: by seeing it well, I do not mean only the buildings, statues, and paintings; though they undoubtedly deserve your attention; but I mean seeing into the constitution and government of it. But these things certainly occur to your own common sense.

How go your pleasures at Rome? Are you in fashion there; that is, do you live with the people who are? The only way of being so yourself, in time. Are you domestic enough in any considerable house to be called *le petit Stanhope*? Has any woman of fashion and good-breeding taken the trouble of abusing and laughing at you amicably to your face? Have you found a good *décrotteuse*? For these are the steps by which you must rise to politeness. I do not presume to ask if you have any attachment, because I believe you will not make me your *confident*; but this I will say eventually, that if you have one, *il faut bien payer d'attentions et de petits soins*, if you would have your sacrifice propitiously received. Women are not so much taken by beauty as men are, but prefer those men who show them the most attention.

> Would you engage the lovely fair?
>   With gentlest manners treat her;
> With tender looks and graceful air,
>   In softest accents greet her.
>
> Verse were but vain, the Muses fail,
>   Without the Graces' aid;
> The God of Verse could not prevail
>   To stop the flying maid.
>
> Attention by attentions gain,
>   And merit care by cares;
> So shall the nymph reward your pain,
>   And Venus crown your prayers.[1]

Probatum est.

A man's address and manner weighs much more with them than his beauty; and without them, the *Abbati* and the *Monsignori* will get the better of you. This address and manner should be exceedingly respectful, but at the same time easy and unembarrassed. Your chit-chat or *entregent* with them, neither can nor ought to be very solid; but you should take

[1] These three stanzas are by Lord Chesterfield himself.

care to turn and dress up your trifles prettily, and make them every now and then convey indirectly some little piece of flattery. A fan, a ribband, or a head-dress, are great materials for gallant dissertations, to one who has got *le ton léger et aimable de la bonne compagnie.* At all events, a man had better talk too much to women than too little; they take silence for dulness, unless where they think the passion they have inspired occasions it; and in that case they adopt the notion, that

> Silence in love betrays more woe
> Than words—though ne'er so witty;
> The beggar that is dumb, we know,
> Deserves a double pity.

A propos of this subject; what progress do you make in that language in which Charles V said that he would choose to speak to his mistress?[1] Have you got all the tender diminutives in *etta, ina,* and *ettina;* which I presume he alluded to? You already possess, and I hope take care not to forget, that language which he reserved for his horse.[2] You are absolutely master too, of that language in which he said he would converse with men; French. But in every language, pray attend carefully to the choice of your words and to the turn of your expression: indeed, it is a point of very great consequence. To be heard with success, you must be heard with pleasure: words are the dress of thoughts, which should no more be presented in rags, tatters, and dirt than your person should. By the way, do you mind your person and your dress sufficiently? Do you take great care of your teeth? Pray have them put in order by the best operator at Rome. Are you be-laced, be-powdered, and be-feathered, as other young fellows are, and should be? At your age, *il faut du brillant, et même un peu de fracas, mais point de médiocre, il faut un air vif, aisé et noble. Avec les hommes, un maintien respectueux et en même tems respectable ; avec les femmes, un caquet léger enjoué, et badin, mais toujours fort poli.*

To give you an opportunity of exerting your talents, I send you here enclosed a letter of recommendation from Monsieur Villettes to Madame de Simonetti at Milan, a woman of the first fashion and consideration there; and I shall in my next send you another from the same person to Madame Clerici at the same place. As these two ladies' houses are the resort of all the people of fashion at Milan,[3] those two recommendations

---

[1] Italian.   [2] German.

[3] Of a shortly subsequent period, Monsieur Dutens writes: "Il y a beaucoup de grandes maisons riches à Milan. Dans le temps que j'y étois les maisons Litta, Clerici, etc., y faisoient la première figure."—*Mem d'un Voyageur,* vol. i, p. 327.

will introduce you to them all. Let me know in due time if you have received these two letters, that I may have them renewed in case of accidents.

Adieu! my dear friend! study hard; divert yourself heartily: distinguish carefully between the pleasures of a man of fashion and the vices of a scoundrel: pursue the former and abhor the latter, like a man of sense.

My Dear Friend,   London, February 5, O.S. 1750.

Very few people are good economists of their fortune, and still fewer of their time; and yet of the two the latter is the most precious. I heartily wish you to be a good economist of both; and you are now of an age to begin to think seriously of these two important articles. Young people are apt to think they have so much time before them, that they may squander what they please of it, and yet have enough left; as very great fortunes have frequently seduced people to a ruinous profusion: fatal mistakes! always repented of, but always too late! Old Mr. Lowndes,[1] the famous Secretary of the Treasury in the reigns of King William, Queen Anne, and King George the First, used to say, *take care of the pence, and the pounds will take care of themselves*. To this maxim, which he not only preached but practised, his two grandsons at this time owe the very considerable fortunes that he left them.

This holds equally true as to time; and I most earnestly recommend to you the care of those minutes and quarters of hours, in the course of the day, which people think too short to deserve their attention; and yet, if summed up at the end of the year, would amount to a very considerable portion of time. For example: you are to be at such a place at twelve, by appointment; you go out at eleven to make two or three visits first; those persons are not at home; instead of sauntering away that intermediate time at a coffee-house, and possibly alone, return home, write a letter, beforehand, for the ensuing post, or take up a good book; I do not mean Descartes, Malebranche, Locke, or Newton, by way of dipping; but some book of rational amusement; and detached pieces, as Horace, Boileau, Waller, La Bruyère, etc. This will be so much time saved, and by no means ill employed. Many people lose a great deal of time by

[1] William Lowndes, who represented St. Mawes and other places. He is chiefly remarkable for his elaborate speech in the case of Ashby and White, 25 January, 1704.

reading, for they read frivolous and idle books; such as the absurd romances of the two last centuries, where characters that never existed are insipidly displayed, and sentiments that were never felt pompously described; the Oriental ravings and extravagances of the Arabian Nights and Mogul Tales; or the new flimsy *brochures* that now swarm in France, of Fairy Tales, *Réflexions sur le Cœur et l'Esprit, Metaphysique de l'Amour, Analyse de Beaux Sentiments*; and such sort of idle frivolous stuff, that nourishes and improves the mind just as much as whipped cream would the body. Stick to the best established books in every language; the celebrated poets, historians, orators or philosophers. By these means (to use a city metaphor) you will make fifty *per cent.* of that time of which others do not make above three or four, or probably nothing at all.

Many people lose a great deal of their time by laziness; they loll and yawn in a great chair, tell themselves that they have not time to begin anything then, and that it will do as well another time. This is a most unfortunate disposition, and the greatest obstruction to both knowledge and business. At your age, you have no right nor claim to laziness; I have, if I please, being *emeritus*. You are but just listed in the world, and must be active, diligent, indefatigable. If ever you propose commanding with dignity, you must serve up to it with diligence. Never put off till to-morrow what you can do to-day.

Despatch is the soul of business; and nothing contributes more to Despatch, than Method. Lay down a method for everything, and stick to it inviolably, as far as unexpected incidents may allow. Fix one certain hour and day in the week for your accounts, and keep them together in their proper order; by which means they will require very little time, and you can never be much cheated. Whatever letters and papers you keep, docket and tie them up in their respective classes, so that you may instantly have recourse to any one. Lay down a method also for your reading, for which you allot a certain share of your mornings; let it be in a consistent and consecutive course, and not in that desultory and immethodical manner, in which many people read scraps of different authors, upon different subjects.

Keep a useful and short common-place book of what you read, to help your memory only, and not for pedantic quotations. Never read History without having maps, and a chronological book, or tables, lying by you, and constantly recurred to; without which, History is only a confused heap of facts.

One method more I recommend to you by which I have found great benefit, even in the most dissipated part of my life; that is, to rise early, and at the same hour every morning, how late soever you may have sat up the night before. This secures you an hour or two, at least, of reading or reflection, before the common interruptions of the morning begin; and it will save your constitution, by forcing you to go to bed early, at least one night in three.

You will say, it may be, as many young people would, that all this order and method is very troublesome, only fit for dull people, and a disagreeable restraint upon the noble spirit and fire of youth. I deny it; and assert, on the contrary, that it will procure you, both more time and more taste for your pleasures; and, so far from being troublesome to you, that, after you have pursued it a month, it would be troublesome to you to lay it aside.

Business whets the appetite, and gives a taste of pleasures, as exercise does to food; and business can never be done without method; it raises the spirits for pleasures; and a *spectacle*, a ball, an assembly, will much more sensibly affect a man who has employed, than a man who has lost, the preceding part of the day; nay, I will venture to say, that a fine lady will seem to have more charms, to a man of study or business, than to a saunterer. The same listlessness runs through his whole conduct, and he is as insipid in his pleasures, as inefficient in everything else.

I hope you earn your pleasures, and consequently taste them; for, by the way, I know a great many men, who call themselves Men of Pleasure, but who, in truth, have none. They adopt other people's indiscriminately, but without any taste of their own. I have known them often inflict excesses upon themselves, because they thought them genteel; though they sat as awkwardly upon them as other people's clothes would have done. Have no pleasures but your own, and then you will shine in them. What are yours? Give me a short history of them. *Tenez-vous votre coin à table, et dans les bonnes compagnies? y brillez vous du côté de la politesse, de l'enjouement, du badinage? Etes-vous galant? Filez-vous le parfait amour? Est-il question de fléchir par vos soins et par vos attentions les rigueurs de quelque fière Princesse?* You may safely trust me; for, though I am a severe censor of vice and folly, I am a friend and advocate for pleasures, and will contribute all in my power to yours.

There is a certain dignity to be kept up, in pleasures as well as in business. In love, a man may lose his heart with dignity; but if he loses his nose, he loses his character into the bargain. At table, a man may with decency have a distinguishing palate; but indiscriminate voraciousness degrades him to a glutton. A man may play with decency; but if he games he is disgraced. Vivacity and wit make a man shine in company; but trite jokes and loud laughter reduce him to buffoon. Every virtue, they say, has its kindred vice; every pleasure, I am sure, has its neighbouring disgrace. Mark carefully, therefore, the line that separates them, and rather stop a yard short, than step an inch beyond it.

I wish to God that you had as much pleasure in following my advice, as I have in giving it you; and you may the easier have it, as I give you none that is inconsistent with your pleasure. In all that I say to you, it is your interest alone that I consider: trust to my experience; you know you may to my affection. Adieu!

I have received no letter yet from you or Mr. Harte.

My DEAR FRIEND,   London, February 8, O.S. 1750.

You have, by this time, I hope and believe, made such a progress in the Italian language, that you can read it with ease; I mean the easy books in it: and indeed, in that, as well as in every other language, the easiest books are generally the best; for, whatever author is obscure and difficult in his own language, certainly does not think clearly. This is, in my opinion, the case of a celebrated Italian author; to whom the Italians, from the admiration they have of him, have given the epithet of *il divino*; I mean, Dante. Though, I formerly knew Italian extremely well, I could never understand him; for which reason I had done with him, fully convinced that he was not worth the pains necessary to understand him.

The good Italian authors are, in my mind, but few; I mean authors of invention; for there are, undoubtedly, very good historians, and excellent translators. The two poets worth your reading, and I was going to say, the only two, are Tasso and Ariosto. Tasso's *Gierusalemme Liberata* is altogether unquestionably a fine poem, though it has some low, and many false thoughts in it: and Boileau very justly makes it the mark of a bad taste, to compare *le clinquant du Tasse, à l'or de Virgile.*

The image, with which he adorns the introduction of his Epic Poem, is low and disgusting; it is that of a froward, sick, puking child, who is deceived into a dose of necessary physic by *du bonbon*. The verses are these:

> Cosi all' egro fanciul porgiamo aspersi
> Di soave licor gli orli del vaso:
> Succhi amari ingannato intanto ei beve,
> E dall' inganno suo vita riceve.

However, the poem, with all its faults about it, may justly be called a fine one.

If fancy, imagination, invention, description, etc., constitute a poet, Ariosto is, unquestionably, a great one. His *Orlando*, it is true, is a medley of lies and truths, sacred and profane wars, loves, enchantments, giants, mad heroes, and adventurous damsels; but then, he gives it you very fairly for what it is, and does not pretend to put it upon you for the true *Epopée*, or Epic Poem. He says:

> Le Donne, i Cavalier, l'arme, gli amori,
> Le cortesie, l'audaci imprese, io canto.

The connections of his stories are admirable, his reflections just, his sneers and ironies incomparable, and his painting excellent. When Angelica, after having wandered over half the world alone with Orlando, pretends, notwithstanding,

> ——— ch' el fior virginal cosi avea salvo,
> Come se lo portò dal matern' alvo.

The Author adds, very gravely:

> Forse era ver, ma non però credibile
> A chi del senso suo fosse signore.

Astolpho's being carried to the moon, by St. John, in order to look for Orlando's lost wits, at the end of the 34th book, and the many lost things that he finds there, is a most happy extravagancy, and contains, at the same time, a great deal of sense. I would advise you to read this poem with attention. It is also, the source of half the tales, novels, and plays that have been written since.

The *Pastor Fido* of Guarini is so celebrated, that you should read it; but in reading it, you will judge of the great propriety of the characters. A parcel of shepherds and shepherdesses, with the *true pastoral simplicity*, talk metaphysics, epigrams, *concetti*, and quibbles, by the hour, to each other.

The *Aminta del Tasso* is much more what it is intended to be, a Pastoral; the shepherds, indeed, have their *concetti*, and their antitheses; but are not quite so sublime and abstracted as those in *Pastor Fido*. I think that you will like it much the best of the two.

Petrarca is, in my mind, a sing-song love-sick poet; much admired, however, by the Italians; but an Italian, who should think no better of him than I do, would certainly say, that he deserved his *Laura* better than his *Lauro*; and that wretched quibble would be reckoned an excellent piece of Italian wit.

The Italian prose-writers (of invention I mean) which I would recommend to your acquaintance, are Machiavelli and Boccaccio the former, for the established reputation which he has acquired, of a consummate politician (whatever my own private sentiments may be of either his politics or his morality), the latter, for his great invention, and for his natural and agreeable manner of telling his stories.

Guicciardini, Bentivoglio, Davila, etc., are excellent historians, and deserve being read with attention. The nature of History checks, a little, the flights of Italian imaginations; which, in works of invention, are very high indeed. Translations curb them still more; and their translations of the Classics are incomparable; particularly the first ten, translated in the time of Leo the Xth, and inscribed to him, under the title of the *Collana*. That original *Collana* has been lengthened since; and, if I mistake not, consists, now, of one hundred and ten volumes.

From what I have said, you will easily guess that I meant to put you upon your guard; and not to let your fancy be dazzled and your taste corrupted by the *concetti*, the quaintnesses, and false thoughts which are too much the characteristics of the Italian and Spanish authors. I think you are in no great danger, as your taste has been formed upon the best ancient models, the Greek and Latin authors of the best ages, who indulge themselves in none of the puerilities I have hinted at. I think I may say with truth, that true wit, sound taste, and good sense, are now as it were engrossed by France and England. Your old acquaintances, the Germans, I fear, are a little below them; and your new acquaintances, the Italians, are a great deal too much above them. The former, I doubt, crawl a little; the latter, I am sure, very often fly out of sight.

I recommended to you, a good many years ago, and I believe

you then read, *La Manière de Bien Penser dans les Ouvrages d'Esprit, par le Père Bouhours*; and I think it is very well worth your reading again, now that you can judge of it better. I do not know any book that contributes more to form a true taste; and you find there, into the bargain, the most celebrated passages both of the ancients and the moderns; which refresh your memory with what you have formerly read in them separately. It is followed by a book much of the same size, by the same author entitled *Suite des Pensées Ingénieuses*.

To do justice to the best English and French authors, they have not given into that false taste; they allow no thoughts to be good that are not just and founded upon truth. The age of Louis XIV was very like the Augustan; Boileau, Molière, La Fontaine, Racine, etc., established the true and exposed the false taste. The reign of King Charles II (meritorious in no other respect) banished false taste out of England, and proscribed puns, quibbles, acrostics, etc. Since that, false wit has renewed its attacks and endeavoured to recover its lost empire, both in England and France, but without success; though I must say with more success in France than in England; Addison, Pope, and Swift having vigorously defended the rights of good sense; which is more than can be said of their contemporary French authors; who have of late had a great tendency to *le faux brillant, le raffinement, et l'entortillement*. And Lord Roscommon would be more in the right now than he was then, in saying, that:

> The English bullion of one sterling line,
> Drawn to French wire, would through whole pages shine.

Lose no time, my dear child, I conjure you, in forming your taste, your manners, your mind, your everything; you have but two years time to do it in; for whatever you are, to a certain degree, at twenty, you will be, more or less, all the rest of your life. May it be a long and happy one. Adieu!

London, March 8, O.S. 1750.

Young as you are, I hope you are in haste to live; by living, I mean living with lustre and honour to yourself, with utility to society, doing what may deserve to be written, or writing what may deserve to be read; I should wish both. Those who consider life in that light will not idly lavish one moment. The present moments are the only ones we are sure of, and as such the most valuable; but yours are doubly so at your age, for the credit, the dignity, the comfort, and the pleasure of all your future moments depend upon the use you make of your present ones.

I am extremely satisfied with your present manner of employing your time; but will you always employ it as well? I am far from meaning always in the same way, but I mean as well in proportion in the variation of age and circumstances. You now study five hours every morning; I neither suppose that you will, nor desire that you should, do so for the rest of your life. Both business and pleasure will justify and equally break in upon those hours; but then, will you always employ the leisure they leave you in useful studies? If you have but an hour, will you improve that hour, instead of idling it away? While you have such a friend and monitor with you as Mr. Harte, I am sure you will; but, suppose that business and situations should, in six or seven months, call Mr. Harte away from you, tell me truly, what may I expect and depend upon from you when left to yourself? May I be sure that you will employ some part of every day in adding something to that stock of knowledge which he will have left you? May I hope that you will allot one hour in the week to the care of your own affairs, to keep them in that order and method which every prudent man does?

But, above all, may I be convinced that your pleasures, whatever they may be, will be confined within the circle of good company and people of fashion? Those pleasures I recommend to you; I will promote them, I will pay for them; but I will neither pay for, nor suffer, the unbecoming, disgraceful, and degrading pleasures (they cannot be called pleasures) of low and profligate company. I confess, the pleasures of high life are not always strictly philosophical; and I believe a Stoic would blame my indulgence; but I am yet no Stoic, though turned of five-and-fifty, and I am apt to think that you are rather less so at eighteen. The pleasures of the table among people of the first fashion may indeed sometimes, by accident, run into excesses; but they will never sink into a continual course of gluttony and drunkenness. The gallantry of high life, though not strictly justifiable, carries, at least, no external marks of infamy about it. Neither the heart nor the constitution is corrupted by it; neither nose nor character lost by it; manners, possibly, improved. Play, in good company, is only play, and not gaming, not deep, and consequently not dangerous, nor dishonourable. It is only the inter-acts of other amusements.

This, I am sure, is not talking to you like an old man, though it is talking to you like an old friend. These are not hard conditions to ask of you. I am certain you have sense enough to know how reasonable they are on my part, how advantageous they are on yours; but have you resolution enough to perform them? Can you withstand the examples and the invitations of the profligate, and their infamous missionaries? For I have known many a young fellow seduced by a *mauvaise honte*, that made him ashamed to refuse. These are resolutions which you must form, and steadily execute for yourself, whenever you lose the friendly care and assistance of your Mentor. In the mean time, make a greedy use of him; exhaust him, if you can, of all his knowledge; and get the prophet's mantle from him, before he is taken away himself.

You seem to like Rome. How do you go on there? Are you got into the inside of that extraordinary government? Has your Abbate Foggini discovered many of those mysteries to you? Have you made an acquaintance with some eminent Jesuits? I know no people in the world more instructive. You would do very well to take one or two such sort of people home with you to dinner every day; it would be only a little *minestra* and *macaroni* the more; and a three or four hours' conversation *de suite* produces a thousand useful informations, which short meetings and snatches at third places do not admit of; and many of those gentlemen are by no means unwilling to dine *gratis*. Whenever you meet with a man eminent in any way, feed him, and feed upon him at the same time; it will not only improve you, but give you a reputation of knowledge, and of loving it in others.

I have been lately informed of an Italian book, which I believe may be of use to you, and which, I dare say, you may get at Rome; written by one Alberti, about fourscore or a hundred years ago, a thick quarto. It is a classical description of Italy; from whence, I am assured, that Mr. Addison, to save himself trouble, has taken most of his remarks and classical references.[1] I am told that it is an excellent book for a traveller in Italy.

What Italian books have you read, or are you reading? Ariosto I hope is one of them. Pray apply yourself diligently

---

[1] Addison's *Travels in Italy* have called forth a different criticism from Macaulay: "They abound with classical quotations happily introduced, but his quotations, with scarcely a single exception, are taken from Latin verse. . . . Even his notions of the political and military affairs of the Romans seem to be derived from poets and poetasters" (*Edinburgh Review*, No. clvi, p. 198. *Essay on Life and Writings of Addison*, 1843).

to Italian; it is so easy a language, that speaking it constantly, and reading it often, must, in six months more, make you perfectly master of it; in which case you will never forget it; for we only forget those things of which we know but little.

But, above all things, to all that you learn, to all that you say, and to all that you do, remember to join *the Graces*. All is imperfect without them; with them, everything is at least tolerable. Nothing could hurt me more than to find you unattended by them. How cruelly should I be shocked, if, at our first meeting, you should present yourself to me without them! Invoke them, and sacrifice to them every moment; they are always kind, where they are assiduously courted. For God's sake, aim at perfection in every thing; *Nil actum reputans si quid superesset agendum*. Adieu. Yours, most tenderly.

My Dear Friend,   London, March 19, O.S. 1750.

I acknowledge your last letter of the 24th February, N.S. In return for your earthquake, I can tell you that we have had, here, more than our share of earthquakes, for we had two very strong ones in eight-and-twenty days. They really do too much honour to our cold climate; in your warm one, they are compensated by favours from the sun, which we do not enjoy.

I did not think that the present Pope [1] was a sort of man to build seven modern little chapels at the expense of so respectable a piece of antiquity as the Colliseum. However, let his Holiness's taste of *virtu* be ever so bad, pray get somebody to present you to him, before you leave Rome; and without hesitation kiss his slipper, or whatever else the *étiquette* of that Court requires. I would have you see all these ceremonies; and I presume that you are, by this time, ready enough at Italian to understand and answer *il Santo Padre* in that language. I hope, too, that you have acquired address, and usage enough of the world, to be presented to anybody, without embarrassment or disapprobation. If that is not yet quite perfect, as I cannot suppose it is entirely, custom will improve it daily, and habit at last complete it. I have for some time

---

[1] Prospero Lambertini, who reigned from 1740 to 1758 under the title of Benedict XIV. Even Voltaire owns of him that he was "aimé de la Chrétienté pour la douceur et la gaieté de son caractère" (*Siècle de Louis XIV*, ch. xxxvi).

told you, that the great difficulties are pretty well conquered. You have acquired knowledge, which is the *principium et fons*; but you have now a variety of lesser things to attend to, which collectively make one great and important object. You easily guess that I mean the Graces, the air, address, politeness, and, in short, the whole *tournure* and *agrémens* of a man of fashion; so many little things conspire to form that *tournure*, that though separately they seem too insignificant to mention, yet aggregately they are too material, for me (who think for you down to the very lowest things) to omit.

For instance: do you use yourself to carve, eat, and drink genteelly, and with ease? Do you take care to walk, sit, stand, and present yourself gracefully? Are you sufficiently upon your guard against awkward attitudes, and illiberal, ill-bred, and disgusting habits; such as scratching yourself, putting your fingers in your mouth, nose, and ears? Tricks always acquired at schools, often too much neglected afterwards; but, however, extremely ill-bred and nauseous. For I do not conceive that any man has a right to exhibit, in company, any one excrement, more than another. Do you dress well, and think a little of the *brillant* in your person? That too is necessary, because it is *prévenant*. Do you aim at easy, engaging, but at the same time civil or respectful manners, according to the company you are in? These, and a thousand other things, which you will observe in people of fashion, better than I can describe them, are absolutely necessary for every man; but still more for you, than for almost any man living. The showish, the shining, the engaging parts of the character of a fine gentleman, should (considering your destination) be the principal objects of your present attention.

When you return here, I am apt to think that you will find something better to do, than to run to Mr. Osborne's at Gray's Inn, to pick up scarce books. Buy good books, and read them; the best books are the commonest, and the last editions are always the best, if the editors are not blockheads; for they may profit of the former. But take care not to understand editions and title-pages too well. It always smells of pedantry, and not always of learning. What curious books I have, they are indeed but few, shall be at your service. I have some of the old *Collana*, and the Machiavel of 1550. Beware of the *Bibliomanie*.

In the midst of either your studies or your pleasures, pray never lose view of the object of your destination; I mean the political affairs of Europe. Follow them politically, chronologically, and geographically, through the newspapers, and trace up the facts which you meet with there to their sources; as for example: consult the treaties of *Neustadt* and *Abo*, with regard to the disputes, which you read of every day in the public papers, between Russia and Sweden. For the affairs of Italy, which are reported to be the objects of present negotiations, recur to the Quadruple Alliance of the year 1718, and follow them down through their several variations to the Treaty of Aix-la-Chapelle, 1748; in which (by the bye) you will find the very different tenures by which the Infant Don Philip, your namesake, holds Parma and Placentia. Consult, also, the Emperor Charles the Sixth's Act of Cession of the kingdoms of Naples and Sicily, in 1736. The succession to the kingdoms of Naples and Sicily being a point, which upon the death of the present King of Spain, is likely to occasion some disputes, do not lose the thread of these matters; which is carried on with great ease, but, if once broken, is resumed with difficulty.

Pray tell Mr. Harte that I have sent his packet to Baron Firmian, by Count Einsiedeln, who is gone from hence this day for Germany, and passes through Vienna in his way to Italy, where he is in hopes of crossing upon you somewhere or other. Adieu, my friend!

Χάριτες, Χάριτες.

MY DEAR FRIEND,   London, March 29, O.S. 1750.

You are now, I suppose, at Naples, in a new scene of *virtù*, examining all the curiosities of Herculaneum, watching the eruptions of Mount Vesuvius, and surveying the magnificent churches and public buildings by which Naples is distinguished. You have a Court there into the bargain, which, I hope, you frequent and attend to. Polite manners, a versatility of mind, a complaisance even to enemies, and the *volto sciolto*, with the *pensieri stretti*, are only to be learned at Courts; and must be well learned by whoever would either shine or thrive in them. Though they do not change the nature, they smooth and soften the manners of mankind. Vigilance, dexterity, and flexibility supply the place of natural force; and it is the ablest mind, not the strongest body, that prevails there. Monsieur and Madame Fogliani will, I am sure, show you all the politeness of Courts; for I know no better bred people than they are. Domesticate yourself there while you stay at Naples, and lay aside the English coldness and formality. You have also a letter to Comte Mahony, whose house I hope you frequent, as it is the resort of the best company. His sister, Madame Bulkeley, is now here, and had I known of your going so soon to Naples, I would have got you, *ex abundantiâ*, a letter from her to her brother. The conversation of the moderns in the evening, is full as necessary for you, as that of the ancients in the morning.

You would do well, while you are at Naples, to read some very short history of that kingdom. It has had great variety of masters, and has occasioned many wars; the general history of which will enable you to ask many proper questions, and to receive useful information in return. Inquire into the manner and form of that government; for constitution it has none, being an absolute one; but the most absolute governments have certain customs and forms, which are more or less observed by their respective tyrants. In China it is the fashion for the Emperors, absolute as they are, to govern with justice and equity; as in the other Oriental monarchies it is the custom to govern by violence and cruelty. The King of France, as absolute in fact, as any of them, is by custom only more gentle; for I know of no constitutional bar to his will. England is now the only monarchy in the world that can properly be said to have a constitution; for the people's rights and liberties are secured by laws. I cannot reckon Sweden and Poland to be monarchies, those two Kings having little more to say than the Doge of Venice. I do not presume to say anything of the constitution of the Empire to you, who are *jurisperitorum Germanicorum facile princeps*.

When you write to me, which, by the way, you do pretty seldom, tell me rather whom you see, than what you see. Inform me of your evening transactions and acquaintances; where, and how you pass your evenings; what English people you meet with, and a hint of their characters; what people of learning you have made acquaintance with; and, if you will trust me with so important an affair, what *belle passion* inflames you. I interest myself most in what personally concerns you most; and this is a very critical year in your life. To talk like a virtuoso, your canvas is, I think, a good one, and *Raphael Harte* has drawn the outlines admirably; nothing is now wanting but the colouring of Titian, and the graces, the *morbidezza*, of Guido; but that is a great deal. You must get them soon, or you will never get them at all. *Per la lingua Italiana sono sicuro ch' ella n' è adesso professore, a segno tale ch' io non ardisca dirle altra cosa in quella lingua se non.—Addio.*

MY DEAR FRIEND,   London, April 26, O.S. 1750.

As your journey to Paris approaches, and as that period will, one way or another, be of infinite consequence to you, my letters will henceforwards be principally calculated for that meridian. You will be left there to your own discretion, instead of Mr. Harte's; and you will allow me, I am sure, to distrust a little the discretion of eighteen. You will find in the Academy a number of young fellows much less discreet than yourself. These will all be your acquaintances; but look about you first and inquire into their respective characters, before you form any connections among them; and *cæteris paribus*, single out those of the most considerable rank and family. Show them a distinguishing attention; by which means you will get into their respective houses, and keep the best company. All those French young fellows are excessively *étourdis*; be upon your guard against scrapes and quarrels; have no corporal pleasantries with them, no *jeux de main*, no *coups de chambrière*, which frequently bring on quarrels. Be as lively as they, if you please, but at the same time be a little wiser than they. As to letters, you will find most of them ignorant; do not reproach them with that ignorance, nor make them feel your superiority. It is not their fault they are all bred up for the army; but, on the other hand, do not allow their ignorance and idleness to break in upon those morning hours which you may be able to allot to your serious studies. No breakfastings with them, which consume a great deal of time; but tell them (not magisterially and sententiously) that you will read two or three hours in the morning, and that for the rest of the day you are very much at their service. Though, by the way, I hope you will keep wiser company in the evenings.

I must insist upon your never going to what is called the English coffee-house at Paris, which is the resort of all the scrub English, and also of the fugitive and attainted Scotch and Irish: party quarrels and drunken squabbles are very frequent there; and I do not know a more degrading place in all Paris. Coffee-houses and taverns are by no means creditable at Paris. Be cautiously upon your guard against the infinite number of fine-dressed and fine-spoken *chevaliers d'industrie* and *aventuriers*, which swarm at Paris, and keep everybody civilly at arm's length, of whose real character or rank you are not previously informed. Monsieur le Comte or Monsieur le Chevalier in a handsome laced coat, *et très bien mis*, accosts you at the play, or some other public place; he conceives at first sight an infinite regard for you, he sees that you are a stranger of the first distinction, he offers you his services, and wishes nothing more ardently than to contribute as far as may be in his little power, to procure you *les agrémens de Paris*. He is acquainted with some ladies of condition, *qui préfèrent une petite société agréable, et des petits soupers aimables d'honnêtes gens, au tumulte et à la dissipation de Paris*; and he will, with the greatest pleasure imaginable, have the honour of introducing you to these ladies of quality. Well, if you were to accept of this kind offer, and go with him, you would find, *au troisième*, a handsome, and painted p—d strumpet, in a tarnished silver or gold second-hand robe, playing a sham party at cards for *livres* with three or four sharpers, well-dressed enough, and dignified by the titles of Marquis, Comte, and Chevalier. The lady receives you in the most polite and gracious manner, and with all those *complimens de routine* which every French woman has equally. Though she loves retirement and shuns *le grand monde*, yet she confesses herself obliged to the Marquis for having procured her so inestimable, so accomplished an acquaintance as yourself; but her concern is how to amuse you, for she never suffers play at her house for above a *livre*; if you can amuse yourself with that low play till supper, *à la bonne heure*. Accordingly you sit down to that little play, at which the good company take care that you shall win fifteen or sixteen *livres*, which gives them an opportunity of celebrating both your good luck and your good play. Supper comes up, and a good one it is, upon the strength of your being to pay for it.

La Marquise en fait les honneurs au mieux, talks sentiments, *mœurs, et morale*; interlarded with *enjouement,* and accompanied with some oblique ogles, which bid you not despair in time. After supper, *pharaon, lansquenet,* or *quinze* happen accidentally to be mentioned; the Chevalier proposes playing at one of them for half-an-hour, the Marquise exclaims against it, and vows she will not suffer it, but is at last prevailed upon, by being assured *que ce ne sera que pour des riens*. Then the wished-for moment is come, the operation begins; you are cheated, at best, of all the money in your pocket, and if you stay late, very probably robbed of your watch and snuff-box;

possibly murdered for greater security. This, I can assure you, is not an exaggerated, but a literal description of what happens every day to some raw and inexperienced stranger at Paris. Remember to receive all these civil gentlemen, who take such a fancy to you at first sight, very coldly, and take care always to be previously engaged, whatever party they propose to you.

You may happen sometimes, in very great and good companies, to meet with some dexterous gentlemen, who may be very desirous, and also very sure, to win your money if they can but engage you to play with them. Therefore, lay it down as an invariable rule never to play with men, but only with women of fashion, at low play, or with women and men mixed. But at the same time, whenever you are asked to play deeper than you would, do not refuse it gravely and sententiously, alleging the folly of staking what would be very inconvenient for one to lose, against what ones does not want to win; but parry those invitations ludicrously, *et en badinant.* Say that if you were sure to lose you might possibly play, but that as you may as well win, you dread *l'embarras des richesses* ever since you have seen what an incumbrance they were to poor Harlequin, and that therefore you are determined never to venture the winning above two louis a-day: this sort of light trifling way of declining invitations to vice and folly, is more becoming your age, and at the same time more effectual than grave philosophical refusals. A young fellow who seems to have no will of his own, and who does everything that is asked of him, is called a very good-natured, but at the same time is thought a very silly, young fellow. Act wisely, upon solid principles and from true motives, but keep them to yourself, and never talk sententiously. When you are invited to drink, say you wish you could, but that so little makes you both drunk and sick, *que le jeu ne vaut pas la chandelle.*

Pray show great attention, and make your court to Monsieur de la Guérinière[1]; he is well with Prince Charles,[2] and many people of the first distinction at Paris; his commendations will raise your character there, not to mention that his favour will be of use to you in the Academy itself. For the reasons which

---

[1] François Robichon de la Guérinière. M. Weiss calls him, "l'un des hommes les plus habiles que la France ait produits dans l'art de soigner et de dresser les chevaux." He published two works on that subject: *L'Ecole de Cavalerie* (Paris, 1733), and *Les Eléments de Cavalerie* (Paris, 1740).—M.

[2] Perhaps Prince Charles of Lorraine, brother-in-law of Maria Theresa.

I mentioned to you in my last, I would have you be *interne* in the Academy for the first six months; but after that, I promise you that you shall have lodgings of your own *dans un hôtel garni*, if in the mean time I hear well of you, and that you frequent, and are esteemed in, the best French companies. You want nothing now, thank God, but exterior advantages, that last polish, that *tournure du monde*, and those graces which are so necessary to adorn and give efficacy to the most solid merit. They are only to be acquired in the best companies, and better in the best French companies than in any other. You will not want opportunities, for I shall send you letters that will establish you in the most distinguished companies, not only of the *beau monde*, but of the *beaux esprits* too. Dedicate, therefore, I beg of you, that whole year to your own advantage and final improvement, and do not be diverted from those objects by idle dissipations, low seduction, or bad example. After that year, do whatever you please; I will interfere no longer in your conduct. For I am sure both you and I shall be safe then. Adieu.

My Dear Friend,   London, April 30, O.S. 1750.

Mr. Harte, who in all his letters gives you some dash of panegyric, told me in his last a thing that pleases me extremely; which was, that at Rome you had constantly preferred the established Italian assemblies, to the English conventicles set up against them by dissenting English ladies. That shows sense, and that you know what you are sent abroad for. It is of much more consequence to know the *mores multorum hominum* than the *urbes*. Pray continue this judicious conduct wherever you go, especially at Paris, where, instead of thirty, you will find above three hundred English herding together, and conversing with no one French body.

The life of *les Milords Anglois* is regularly, or if you will, irregularly, this. As soon as they rise, which is very late, they breakfast together, to the utter loss of two good morning hours. Then they go by coachfuls to the Palais, the Invalides, and Notre-Dame; from thence to the English coffee-house, where they make up their tavern party for dinner. From dinner, where they drink quick, they adjourn in clusters to the play, where they crowd up the stage, drest up in very fine clothes, very ill made by a Scotch or Irish tailor. From the play to the tavern again, where they get very drunk, and where they either quarrel among themselves, or sally forth, commit some riot in the streets, and are taken up by the watch. Those who do not speak French before they go, are sure to learn none there. Their tender vows are addressed to their Irish laundress, unless by chance some itinerant English - woman, eloped from her husband, or her creditors, defrauds her of them. Thus, they return home, more petulant, but not more informed, than when they left it; and show, as they think, their improvement, by affectedly both speaking and dressing in broken French.

Hunc tu Romane *caveto.*

Connect yourself, while you are in France, entirely with the French; improve yourself with the old, divert yourself with the young; conform cheerfully to their customs, even to their little follies, but not to their vices. Do not however remonstrate or preach against them, for remonstrances do not suit your age. In French companies in general, you will not find much learning, therefore take care not to brandish yours in their faces. People hate those who make them feel their own inferiority. Conceal all your learning carefully, and reserve it for the company of *les Gens d'Eglise,* or *les Gens de Robe;* and even then let them rather extort it from you than find you over-willing to draw it. You are then thought, from that seeming unwillingness, to have still more knowledge than it may be you really have, and with the additional merit of modesty into the bargain.

A man who talks of, or even hints at, his *bonnes fortunes,* is seldom believed, or if believed, much blamed; whereas a man who conceals with care is often supposed to have more than he has, and his reputation of discretion gets him others. It is just so with a man of learning; if he affects to show it, it is questioned, and he is reckoned only superficial; but if afterwards it appears that he really has it, he is pronounced a pedant. Real merit of any kind, *ubi est non potest diu celari;* it will be discovered, and nothing can depreciate it, but a man's exhibiting it himself. It may not always be rewarded as it ought; but it will always be known. You will in general find the women of the *beau monde* at Paris more instructed than the men, who are bred up singly for the army, and thrown into it at twelve or thirteen years old; but then that sort of education, which makes them ignorant of books, gives them a great knowledge of the world, an easy address, and polite manners.

Fashion is more tyrannical at Paris than in any other place

in the world; it governs even more absolutely than their King, which is saying a great deal. The least revolt against it is punished by proscription. You must observe, and conform to all the *minuties* of it, if you will be in fashion there yourself; and if you are not in fashion, you are nobody. Get therefore, at all events, into the company of those men and women *qui donnent le ton*; and though at first you should be admitted upon that shining theatre only as a *persona muta*, persist, persevere, and you will soon have a part given you. Take great care never to tell in one company what you see or hear in another, much less to divert the present company at the expense of the last; but let discretion and secrecy be known parts of your character. They will carry you much farther, and much safer, than more shining talents. Be upon your guard against quarrels at Paris; honour is extremely nice there, though the asserting of it is exceedingly penal. Therefore *point de mauvaises plaisanteries, point de jeux de main, et point de raillerie piquante.*

Paris is the place in the world where, if you please, you may the best unite the *utile* and the *dulce.* Even your pleasures will be your improvements, if you take them with the people of the place, and in high life. From what you have hitherto done everywhere else, I have just reason to believe, that you will do every thing you ought at Paris. Remember that it is your decisive moment; whatever you do there will be known to thousands here, and your character there, whatever it is, will get before you hither. You will meet with it at London. May you and I both have reason to rejoice at that meeting! Adieu.

MY DEAR FRIEND,　　　　　　London, May 8, O.S. 1750.

At your age the love of pleasures is extremely natural, and the enjoyment of them not unbecoming; but the danger, at your age, is mistaking the object, and setting out wrong in the pursuit. The character of a man of pleasure dazzles young eyes; they do not see their way to it distinctly, and fall into vice and profligacy. I remember a strong instance of this a great many years ago. A young fellow, determined to shine as a man of pleasure, was at the play, called the *Libertine Destroyed,* a translation of *le Festin de Pierre* of Molière's. He was so struck with what he thought the fine character of the Libertine, that he swore he would be the *Libertine Destroyed.* Some friends asked him, whether he had not better content himself with being only the Libertine, without being *destroyed*? to which he answered with great warmth, "No, for that being destroyed was the perfection of the whole." This, extravagant as it seems in this light, is really the case of many an unfortunate young fellow, who, captivated by the name of pleasures, rushes indiscriminately, and without taste, into them all, and is finally *destroyed*. I am not stoically advising, nor parsonically preaching to you, to be a Stoic at your age; far from it; I am pointing out to you the paths to pleasures, and am endeavouring only to quicken and heighten them for you. Enjoy pleasures, but let them be your own, and then you will taste them: but adopt none; trust to nature for genuine ones. The pleasures that you would feel, you must earn; the man who gives himself up to all, feels none sensibly. Sardanapalus, I am convinced, never in his life felt any. Those only who join serious occupations with pleasures, feel either as they should do. Alcibiades, though addicted to the most shameful excesses, gave some time to philosophy and some to business. Julius Cæsar joined business with pleasure so properly, that they mutually assisted each other; and, though he was the husband of all the wives at Rome, he found time to be one of the best scholars, almost the best orator, and absolutely the best general there.

An uninterrupted life of pleasures is as insipid as contemptible. Some hours given every day to serious business, must whet both the mind and the senses, to enjoy those of pleasure. A surfeited glutton, an emaciated sot, and an enervated rotten whoremaster never enjoy the pleasures to which they devote themselves; they are only so many human sacrifices to false gods. The pleasures of low life are all of this mistaken, merely sensual, and disgraceful nature; whereas those of high life, and in good company (though possibly in themselves not more moral), are more delicate, more refined, less dangerous, and less disgraceful; and, in the common course of things, not reckoned disgraceful at all. In short, pleasure must not, nay, cannot, be the business of a man of sense and character; but it may be, and is, his relief, his reward.

It is particularly so with regard to the women, who have the utmost contempt for those men, that, having no character nor consideration with their own sex, frivolously pass their whole time in *ruelles*, and at *toilettes*. They look upon them as their lumber, and remove them whenever they can get better furniture. Women choose their favourites more by the ear than by any other of their senses, or even their understandings. The man whom they hear the most commended by the men, will always be the best received by them. Such a conquest flatters their vanity, and vanity is their universal, if not their strongest passion. A distinguished shining character is irresistible with them; they crowd to, nay, they even quarrel for, the danger, in hopes of the triumph. Though by the way (to use a vulgar expression), she who conquers, only catches a tartar, and becomes the slave of her captive. *Mais c'est là leur affaire.*

Divide your time between useful occupations and elegant pleasures. The morning seems to belong to study, business, or serious conversations with men of learning and figure; not that I exclude an occasional hour at a *toilette*. From sitting down to dinner, the proper business of the day is pleasure, unless real business, which must never be postponed for pleasure, happens accidentally to interfere. In good company, the pleasures of the table are always carried to a certain point of delicacy and gratification, but never to excess and riot. Plays, operas, balls, suppers, gay conversations in polite and cheerful companies, properly conclude the evenings; not to mention the tender looks that you may direct, and the sighs that you may offer, upon these several occasions, to some propitious or unpropitious female deity; whose character and manners will neither disgrace nor corrupt yours. This is the life of a man of real sense and pleasure; and by this distribution of your time, and choice of your pleasures, you will be equally qualified for the busy, or the *beau monde*. You see I am not rigid, and do not require that you and I should be of the same age. What I say to you, therefore, should have the more weight, as coming from a friend, not a father. But, low company, and their low vices, their indecent riots, and profligacy, I never will bear, nor forgive.

I have lately received two volumes of Treatises, in German and Latin, from Hawkins, with your orders, under your own hand, to take care of them for you, which orders I shall most dutifully and punctually obey; and they wait for you in my library, together with your great collection of rare books, which your Mamma sent me upon removing from her old house.

I hope you not only keep up, but improve in your German, for it will be of great use to you when you come into business, and the more so, as you will be almost the only Englishman who either can speak or understand it. Pray speak it constantly to all Germans, wherever you meet them, and you will meet multitudes of them at Paris. Is Italian now become easy and familiar to you? Can you speak it with the same fluency that you can speak German? You cannot conceive what an advantage it will give you, in negotiations, to possess Italian, German, and French, perfectly, so as to understand all the force and *finesse* of those three languages. If two men of equal talents negotiate together, he who best understands the language in which the negotiation is carried on, will infallibly get the better of the other. The signification and force of one single word is often of great consequence in a treaty, and even in a letter.

Remember the *Graces*, for without them *ogni fatica è vana*. Adieu.

MY DEAR FRIEND,   London, May 17, O.S. 1750.

Your apprenticeship is near out, and you are soon to set up for yourself; that approaching moment is a critical one for you, and an anxious one for me. A tradesman who would succeed in his way must begin by establishing a character of integrity and good manners; without the former, nobody will go to his shop at all; without the latter, nobody will go there twice. This rule does not exclude the fair arts of trade. He may sell his goods at the best price he can within certain bounds. He may avail himself of the humour, the whims, and the fantastical tastes of his customers; but what he warrants to be good must be really so, what he seriously asserts must be true, or his first fraudulent profits will soon end in a bankruptcy. It is the same in higher life, and in the great business of the world. A man who does not solidly establish and really deserve a character of truth, probity, good manners, and good morals, at his first setting out in the world, may impose and shine like a meteor for a very short time, but will very soon vanish, and be extinguished with contempt.

People easily pardon, in young men, the common irregularities of the senses; but they do not forgive the least vice of the heart. The heart never grows better by age; I fear rather worse, always harder.[1] A young liar will be an old one, and a young knave will only be a greater knave as he grows older. But should a bad young heart, accompanied with a good head (which, by the way, very seldom is the case), really reform in a more advanced age from a consciousness of its folly, as well as of its guilt, such a conversion would only be thought prudential

[1] "I believe men may be generally observed to grow less tender as they advance in age."—*The Rambler*, No. 78.

and political, but never sincere. I hope in God, and I verily believe, that you want no moral virtue. But the possession of all the moral virtues, *in actu primo*, as the logicians call it, is not sufficient; you must have them *in actu secundo* too; nay, that is not sufficient neither; you must have the reputation of them also.

You character in the world must be built upon that solid foundation, or it will soon fall, and upon your own head. You cannot, therefore, be too careful, too nice, too scrupulous, in establishing this character at first, upon which your whole depends. Let no conversation, no example, no fashion, no *bon mot*, no silly desire of seeming to be above, what most knaves and many fools call prejudices, ever tempt you to avow, excuse, extenuate, or laugh at the least breach of morality; but show upon all occasions, and take all occasions to show, a detestation and abhorrence of it. There, though young, you ought to be strict; and there only, while young, it becomes you to be strict and severe. But there too, spare the persons while you lash the crimes. All this relates, as you easily judge, to the vices of the heart, such as lying, fraud, envy, malice, detraction, etc.; and I do not extend it to the little frailties of youth, flowing from high spirits and warm blood. It would ill become you, at your age, to declaim against them, and sententiously censure a gallantry, an accidental excess of the table, a frolic, an inadvertency; no, keep as free from them yourself as you can, but say nothing against them in others. They certainly mend by time, often by reason; and a man's worldly character is not affected by them, provided it be pure in all other respects.

To come now to a point of much less, but yet of very great consequence, at your first setting out. Be extremely upon your guard against vanity, the common failing of inexperienced youth; but particularly against that kind of vanity that dubs a man a coxcomb; a character which, once acquired, is more indelible than that of the priesthood. It is not to be imagined by how many different ways vanity defeats its own purposes. One man decides peremptorily upon every subject, betrays his ignorance upon many, and shows a disgusting presumption upon the rest. Another desires to appear successful among the women; he hints at the encouragement he has received from those of the most distinguished rank and beauty, and intimates a particular connection with some one; if it is true, it is ungenerous; if false, it is infamous; but in either case he destroys the reputation he wants to get. Some flatter their vanity by little extraneous objects which have not the least relation to themselves; such as being descended from, related to, or acquainted with, people of distinguished merit, and eminent characters. They talk perpetually of their grandfather such-a-one, their uncle such-a-one, and their intimate friend Mr. such-a-one, with whom, possibly they are hardly acquainted. But admitting it all to be as they would have it, what then? Have they the more merit for these accidents? Certainly not. On the contrary, their taking up adventitious, proves their want of intrinsic merit; a rich man never borrows. Take this rule for granted, as a never-failing one; that you must never seem to affect the character in which you have a mind to shine. Modesty is the only sure bait when you angle for praise. The affectation of courage will make even a brave man pass only for a bully; as the affectation of wit will make a man of parts pass for a coxcomb. By this modesty I do not mean timidity and awkward bashfulness. On the contrary, be inwardly firm and steady, know your own value, whatever it may be, and act upon that principle; but take great care to let nobody discover that you do know your own value. Whatever real merit you have other people will discover; and people always magnify their own discoveries, as they lessen those of others.

For God's sake, revolve all these things seriously in your thoughts before you launch out alone into the ocean of Paris. Recollect the observations that you have yourself made upon mankind, compare and connect them with my instructions, and then act systematically and consequentially from them; not *au jour la journée*. Lay your little plan now, which you will hereafter extend and improve by your own observations, and by the advice of those who can never mean to mislead you; I mean Mr. Harte and myself.

My Dear Friend,   London, June 5, O.S. 1750.

I have received your picture, which I have long waited for with impatience; I wanted to see your countenance, from whence I am very apt, as I believe most people are, to form some general opinion of the mind. If the painter has taken you, as well as he has done Mr. Harte (for his picture is by far the most like I ever saw in my life), I draw good conclusions from your countenance, which has both spirit and *finesse* in it. In bulk you are pretty well increased since I saw you; if your height is not increased in proportion, I desire that you will make haste to complete it. Seriously, I believe that your exercises at Paris will make you shoot up to a good size; your legs, by all accounts, seem to promise it. Dancing excepted, the wholesome part is the best part of those academical exercises. *Ils dégraissent leur homme.* *A propos* of exercises; I have prepared everything for your reception at Monsieur de la Guérinière's, and your room, etc. will be ready at your arrival. I am sure you must be sensible how much better it will be for you to be *interne* in the Academy, for the first six or seven months at least, than to be *en hôtel garni*, at some distance from it, and obliged to go to it every morning, let the weather be what it will, not to mention the loss of time too; besides, by living and boarding in the Academy, you will make an acquaintance with half the young fellows of fashion at Paris; and in a very little while be looked upon as one of them in all French companies; an advantage that has never yet happened to any one Englishman that I have known. I am sure you do not suppose that the difference of the expense, which is but a trifle, has any weight with me in this resolution. You have the French language so perfectly, and you will acquire the French *tournure* so soon, that I do not know anybody likely to pass his time so well at Paris as yourself. Our young countrymen have generally too little French, and too bad address, either to present themselves, or be well received in the best French companies; and, as a proof of it, there is no one instance of an Englishman's having ever been suspected of a gallantry with a French woman of condition, though every French woman of condition is more than suspected of having a gallantry. But they take up with the disgraceful and dangerous commerce of prostitutes, actresses, dancing-women, and that sort of trash; though, if they had common address, better achievements would be extremely easy. *Un arrangement*, which is in plain English a gallantry, is, at Paris, as necessary a part of a woman of fashion's establishment, as her house, table, coach, etc. A young fellow must therefore be a very awkward one to be reduced to, or of a very singular taste, to prefer drabs and danger to a commerce (in the course of the world not disgraceful) with a woman of health, education, and rank.

Nothing sinks a young man into low company, both of women and men, so surely as timidity, and diffidence of himself. If he thinks that he shall not, he may depend upon it, he will not please. But with proper endeavours to please, and a degree of persuasion that he shall, it is almost certain that he will. How many people does one meet with everywhere, who with very moderate parts, and very little knowledge, push themselves pretty far, singly by being sanguine, enterprising and persevering? They will take no denial from man or woman; difficulties do not discourage them; repulsed twice or thrice, they rally, they charge again, and nine times in ten prevail at last. The same means will much sooner, and more certainly, attain the same ends, with your parts and knowledge. You have a fund to be sanguine upon, and good forces to rally. In business (talents supposed) nothing is more effectual, or successful, than a good, though concealed, opinion of one's self, a firm resolution, and an unwearied perseverance. None but madmen attempt impossibilities; and whatever is possible, is one way or another to be brought about. If one method fails, try another, and suit your methods to the characters you have to do with.

At the treaty of the Pyrenees, which Cardinal Mazarin, and Don Louis de Haro concluded, *dans l'Isle des Faisans*, the latter carried some very important points by his constant and cool perseverance. The Cardinal had all the Italian vivacity and impatience; Don Louis all the Spanish phlegm and tenaciousness. The point which the Cardinal had most at heart was, to hinder the re-establishment of the Prince of Condé, his implacable enemy; but he was in haste to conclude, and impatient to return to Court; where absence is always dangerous. Don Louis observed this, and never failed at every conference to bring the affair of the Prince of Condé upon the *tapis*. The Cardinal for some time refused even to treat upon it; Don Louis, with the same *sang froid* as constantly persisted, till he at last prevailed; contrary to the intentions and the interest both of the Cardinal and of his Court.[1] Sense must distinguish between what is impossible, and what is only difficult; and spirit and perseverance will get the better of the latter. Every man is to be had one way or another, and every woman almost any way.

I must not omit one thing, which is previously necessary to this, and indeed to everything else; which is attention, a flexibility of attention; never to be wholly engrossed by any past or future object, but instantly directed to the present one, be

[1] The secret dispatches of Cardinal Mazarin during his conferences with Don Louis de Haro were published in two volumes at Amsterdam in 1693. Those which are numbered 12, 15, 17, 22, 24, 29, 30, 34, 35, 36, 64, 69, 74, 77, 78, 79, 82, 87, 88, 92, 93, 94, contain the progress of the negotiation relative to the Prince de Condé.

it what it will. An absent man can make but few observations; and those will be disjointed and imperfect ones, as half the circumstances must necessarily escape him. He can pursue nothing steadily, because his absences make him lose his way. They are very disagreeable, and hardly to be tolerated in old age; but in youth, they cannot be forgiven. If you find that you have the least tendency to them, pray watch yourself very carefully, and you may prevent them now; but if you let them grow into a habit, you will find it very difficult to cure them hereafter; and a worse distemper I do not know.

I heard with great satisfaction the other day, from one who has been lately at Rome, that nobody was better received in the best companies than yourself. The same thing, I dare say, will happen to you at Paris; where they are particularly kind to all strangers, who will be civil to them, and show a desire of pleasing. But they must be flattered a little, not only by words, but by a seeming preference given to their country, their manners, and their customs; which is but a very small price to pay for a very good reception. Were I in Africa, I would pay it to a negro for his good-will. Adieu.

MY DEAR FRIEND,   London, July 9, O.S. 1750.

I should not deserve that appellation in return from you, if I did not freely and explicitly inform you of every corrigible defect, which I may either hear of, suspect, or at any time discover in you. Those who in the common course of the world will call themselves your friends; or whom, according to the common notions of friendship, you may possibly think such, will never tell you of your faults, still less of your weaknesses. But on the contrary, more desirous to make you their friend, than to prove themselves yours, they will flatter both, and, in truth, not be sorry for either. Interiorly, most people enjoy the inferiority of their best friends. The useful and essential part of friendship, to you, is reserved singly for Mr. Harte and myself; our relations to you stand pure, and unsuspected of all private views. In whatever we say to you, we can have no interest but yours. We can have no competition, no jealousy, no secret envy or malignity. We are therefore authorised to represent, advise, and remonstrate; and your reason must tell you that you ought to attend to, and believe us.

I am credibly informed, that there is still a considerable hitch or hobble in your enunciation; and that when you speak fast, you sometimes speak unintelligibly. I have formerly and frequently laid my thoughts before you so fully upon this subject, that I can say nothing new upon it now. I must therefore only repeat, that your whole depends upon it. Your trade is to speak well both in public and in private. The manner of your speaking is full as important as the matter, as more people have ears to be tickled, than understandings to judge. Be your productions ever so good, they will be of no use, if you stifle and strangle them in their birth. The best compositions of Corelli,[1] if ill executed and played out of tune, instead of touching, as they do when well performed, would only excite the indignation of the hearers, when murdered by an unskilled performer. But to murder your own productions, and that *coram populo*, is a *Medean cruelty*, which Horace absolutely forbids. Remember of what importance Demosthenes, and one of the Gracchi, thought *enunciation*; read what stress Cicero, and Quintilian lay upon it; even the herb-women at Athens were correct judges of it. Oratory with all its graces, that of enunciation in particular, is full as necessary in our government, as it ever was in Greece or Rome.

No man can make a fortune or a figure in this country, without speaking, and speaking well, in public. If you will persuade, you must first please; and if you will please, you must tune your voice to harmony, you must articulate every syllable distinctly, your emphases and cadences must be strongly and properly marked; and the whole together must be graceful and engaging; if you do not speak in that manner, you had much better not speak at all. All the learning you have, or ever can have, is not worth one groat without it. It may be a comfort, and an amusement to you in your closet, but can be of no use to you in the world. Let me conjure you therefore, to make this your only object, till you have absolutely conquered it, for that is in your power; think of nothing else, read and speak for nothing else.

Read aloud, though alone, and read articulately and distinctly, as if you were reading in public, and on the most important occasion. Recite pieces of eloquence, declaim scenes of tragedies

[1] A celebrated composer and violin-player, who was born in 1653, and died in 1713. According to M. Fayolle, "Le caractère de Corelli était doux, aimable, et tout-à-fait conforme au style de sa musique. Un jour qu'il jouait du violon dans une assemblée nombreuse il s'aperçut que chacun se mettait à causer. Il posa doucement son violon au milieu du salon disant qu'il craignait d'interrompre la conversation. Ce fut une leçon pour les auditeurs."

to Mr. Harte, as if he were a numerous audience. If there is any particular consonant which you have a difficulty in articulating, as I think you had with the *R*, utter it millions and millions of times, till you have uttered it right. Never speak quick, till you have first learned to speak well. In short, lay aside every book and every thought, that does not directly tend to this great object, absolutely decisive of your future fortune and figure.

The next thing necessary in your destination, is writing correctly, elegantly, and in a good hand too; in which three particulars, I am sorry to tell you, that you hitherto fail. Your handwriting is a very bad one, and would make a scurvy figure in an office book of letters, or even in a lady's pocket-book. But that fault is easily cured by care, since every man who has the use of his eyes and of his right hand can write whatever hand he pleases. As to the correctness and elegancy of your writing, attention to grammar does the one, and to the best authors the other. In your letter to me of the 27th of June, N.S., you omitted the date of the place, so that I only conjectured from the contents that you were at Rome.

Thus I have, with the truth and freedom of the tenderest affection, told you all your defects, at least all that I know or have heard of. Thank God they are all very curable, they must be cured, and I am sure you will cure them. That once done, nothing remains for you to acquire, or for me to wish, but the turn, the manners, the address, and the graces of the polite world; which experience, observation, and good company will insensibly give you. Few people at your age have read, seen, and known so much as you have, and consequently few are so near as yourself to what I call perfection, by which I only mean, being very near as well as the best. Far, therefore, from being discouraged by what you still want, what you already have should encourage you to attempt, and convince you that by attempting you will inevitably obtain it. The difficulties which you have surmounted were much greater than any you have now to encounter. Till very lately your way has been only through thorns and briars; the few that now remain are mixed with roses.

Pleasure is now the principal remaining part of your education. It will soften and polish your manners; it will make you pursue and at last overtake the Graces. Pleasure is necessarily reciprocal; no one feels who does not at the same time give it. To be pleased, one must please. What pleases you in others, will in general please them in you. Paris is indisputably the seat of the Graces; they will even court you, if you are not too coy. Frequent and observe the best companies there, and you will soon be naturalized among them; you will soon find how particularly attentive they are to the correctness and elegancy of their language, and to the graces of their enunciation; they would even call the understanding of a man in question, who should neglect, or not know the infinite advantages arising from them. *Narrer, réciter, déclamer bien,* are serious studies among them, and well deserve to be so everywhere. The conversations, even among the women, frequently turn upon the elegancies, and minutest delicacies of the French language. An *enjouement,* a gallant turn prevails in all their companies, to women, with whom they neither are, nor pretend to be, in love; but should you (as may very possibly happen) fall really in love there, with some women of fashion and sense (for I do not suppose you capable of falling in love with a strumpet) and that your rival, without half your parts or knowledge, should get the better of you, merely by dint of manners, *enjouement, badinage,* etc., how would you regret not having sufficiently attended to those accomplishments which you despised as superficial and trifling, but which you would then find of real consequence in the course of the world! And men, as well as women, are taken by these external graces. Shut up your books then now as a business, and open them only as a pleasure; but let the great book of the world be your serious study; read it over and over, get it by heart, adopt its style, and make it your own.

When I cast up your account as it now stands, I rejoice to see the balance so much in your favour; and that the items *per contra* are so few, and of such a nature that they may be very easily cancelled. By way of debtor and creditor, it stands thus:

Creditor.	By French.	Debtor.	To English.
	German.		Enunciation.
	Italian.		Manners.
	Latin.		
	Greek.		
	Logic.		
	Ethics.		
	History.		
Jus-	Naturæ.		
	Gentium.		
	Publicum.		

This, my dear friend, is a very true account, and a very encouraging one for you. A man who owes so little, can clear it off in a very little time, and if he is a prudent man will; whereas a man, who by long negligence owes a great deal, despairs of ever being able to pay; and therefore never looks into his accounts at all.

When you go to Genoa, pray observe carefully all the *environs* of it, and view them with somebody who can tell you all the situations and operations of the Austrian army, during that famous siege, if it deserves to be called one [1]; for in reality the town never was besieged, nor had the Austrians any one thing necessary for a siege. If Marquis Centurioni, who was last winter in England, should happen to be there, go to him with my compliments, and he will show you all imaginable civilities.

I could have sent you some letters to Florence, but that I knew Mr. Mann [2] would be of more use to you than all of them. Pray make him my compliments. Cultivate your Italian, while you are at Florence, where it is spoken in its utmost purity, but ill-pronounced.

Pray save me the seed of some of the best melons you eat, and put it up dry in paper. You need not send it me; but Mr. Harte will bring it in his pocket when he comes over. I should likewise be glad of some cuttings of the best figs, especially *il Fico gentile*, and the Maltese; but as this is not the season for them, Mr. Mann will, I dare say, undertake that commission, and send them to me at the proper time by Leghorn.

Adieu. Endeavour to please others, and divert yourself as much as ever you can, *en honnête et galant homme*.

P.S. I send you the enclosed to deliver to Lord Rochford,[3] upon your arrival at Turin.

DEAR FRIEND,   London, October 22, O.S. 1750.

This letter will, I am persuaded, find you, and I hope safely, arrived at Montpellier; from whence I trust that Mr. Harte's

---

[1] In 1747. It was, as Lord Chesterfield truly intimates, less a siege than a blockade.—M.

[2] Sir Horace Mann. From 1740 till his death in 1786 he was British Envoy at Florence, and nearly as long, the correspondent of Horace Walpole. The poet Gray and Walpole were on a visit with him in 1739–40, and Gray sent him a parcel of books, of which he gives a list in a letter enclosed in one to John Chute, July 1742.

[3] William Henry, fourth Earl of Rochford, had been sent in 1749 as Envoy Extraordinary to the King of Sardinia. In 1766, he was appointed Ambassador at Paris, and in 1768 Secretary of State. He died in 1781.

indisposition will, by being totally removed, allow you to get to Paris before Christmas. You will there find two people, who, though both English, I recommend in the strongest manner possible to your attention, and advise you to form the most intimate connections with them both, in their different ways. The one is a man whom you already know something of, but not near enough; it is the Earl of Huntingdon[1]; who, next to you, is the truest object of my affection and esteem, and who (I am proud to say it) calls me and considers me as his adopted father. His parts are as quick as his knowledge is extensive; and if quality were worth putting into account, where every other item is so much more valuable, his is the first almost in this country: the figure he will make soon after he returns to it will, if I am not more mistaken than ever I was in my life, equal his birth and my hopes. Such a connection will be of infinite advantage to you; and I can assure you that he is extremely disposed to form it upon my account; and will, I hope and believe, desire to improve and cement it upon your own.

In our Parliamentary government, connections are absolutely necessary; and, if prudently formed, and ably maintained, the success of them is infallible. There are two sorts of connections, which I would always advise you to have in view. The first I will call equal ones; by which I mean those where the two connecting parties reciprocally find their account, from pretty near an equal degree of parts and abilities. In those, there must be a freer communication; each must see that the other is able, and be convinced that he is willing to be of use to him. Honour must be the principle of such connections; and there must be a mutual dependence, that present and separate interest shall not be able to break them. There must be a joint system of action; and in case of different opinions, each must recede a little, in order at last to form an unanimous one. Such, I hope, will be your connection with Lord Huntingdon. You will both come into Parliament at the same time; and if you have an equal share of abilities and application, you

[1] Francis Hastings succeeded as tenth Earl of Huntingdon in 1746, and died unmarried in 1789. Lord Chesterfield's will contains the following injunctions with regard to him: "I desire that my Noble Friend, Francis Earl of Huntingdon, and Sir Charles Hotham" (who had in 1771 succeeded Sir Beaumont in the baronetcy) "shall have absolute direction of the education of my godson Philip Stanhope, until he shall attain the age of twenty-one years; as I know no persons more capable of giving him the sentiments and manners of a gentleman."

and he, with other young people, whom you will naturally associate, may form a band which will be respected by any administration, and make a figure in the public. The other sort of connections I call unequal ones; that is, where the parts are all on one side, and the rank and fortune on the other. Here, the advantage is all on one side; but that advantage must be ably and artfully concealed. Complaisance, an engaging manner, and a patient toleration of certain airs of superiority, must cement them. The weaker party must be taken by the heart, his head giving no hold; and he must be governed by being made to believe that he governs. These people, skilfully led, give great weight to their leader. I have formerly pointed out to you a couple that I take to be proper objects for your skill; and you will meet with many more, for they are very rife.

The other person, whom I recommend to you, is a woman; not as a woman, for that is not immediately my business; besides, I fear she is turned of fifty. It is Lady Hervey,[1] whom I directed you to call upon at Dijon; but who, to my great joy, because to your great advantage, passes all this winter at Paris. She has been bred all her life at Courts; of which she has acquired all the easy good-breeding, and politeness, without the frivolousness. She has all the reading that a woman should have; and more than any woman need have; for she understands Latin perfectly well, though she wisely conceals it. As she will look upon you as her son, I desire that you will look upon her as my delegate; trust, consult, and apply to her without reserve. No woman ever had, more than she has, *le ton de la parfaitement bonne compagnie, les manières engageantes, et le je ne sçais quoi qui plaît.* Desire her to reprove and correct any, and every, the least error and inaccuracy in your manners, air, address, etc. No woman in Europe can do it so well; none will do it more willingly, or in a more proper and obliging way. In such a case she will not put you out of countenance, by telling you of it in company; but either intimate it by some sign, or wait for an opportunity when you are alone together. She is also in the best French company, where she will not only introduce, but *puff* you, if I may use so low a word. And I can assure you, that it is no little help in the *beau monde*, to be puffed there by a fashionable woman. I send you the enclosed billet

---

[1] The celebrated Mary Lepel married, in 1720, John, Lord Hervey, eldest son of the Earl of Bristol, and the *Sporus* of Pope. She died in 1768. A volume of her letters to the Rev. Edmund Morris, tutor to one of her sons, was published in 1821.

to carry her, only as a certificate of the identity of your person, which I take it for granted she could not know again.

You would be so much surprised to receive a whole letter from me, without any mention of the exterior ornaments necessary for a gentleman, as manners, elocution, air, address, graces, etc., that to comply with your expectations, I will touch upon them; and tell you, that, when you come to England, I will show you some people whom I do not care to name, raised to the highest stations, simply by those exterior and adventitious ornaments; whose parts would never have entitled them to the smallest office in the excise. Are they then necessary, or worth acquiring, or not? You will see many instances of this kind at Paris, particularly a glaring one, of a person raised to the highest posts and dignities in France, as well as to be absolute sovereign of the *beau monde*, singly by the graces of his person and address; by woman's chit-chat, accompanied with important gestures; by an imposing air, and pleasing *abord*.[1] Nay, by these helps he even passes for a wit, though he hath certainly no uncommon share of it. I will not name him, because it would be very imprudent in you to do it. A young fellow, at his first entrance into the *beau monde* must not offend the king *de facto* there. It is very often more necessary to conceal contempt than resentment, the former being never forgiven, but the latter sometimes forgot.

There is a small quarto book, entitled *Histoire Chronologique de la France*, lately published by Le Président Hénault [2]; a man of parts and learning, with whom you will probably get acquainted at Paris. I desire that it may always lie upon your table, for your recourse as often as you read history. The chronology, though chiefly relative to the history of France, is not singly confined to it; but the most interesting events of all the rest of Europe are also inserted, and many of them adorned by short, pretty, and just reflections. The new edition of *les Mémoires de Sully*, in three quarto volumes,[3] is also

---

[1] The Maréchal de Richelieu (note in the edition of 1774).

[2] Le Président Hénault is well known by the chronology which Lord Chesterfield mentions. In 1765, Horace Walpole describes him as follows at a supper at Madame du Deffand's: "The President is very near deaf and much nearer superannuated. He sits by the table; the mistress of the house, who formerly was his, inquires after every dish on the table, is told who has eaten of which, and then bawls the bills of fare of every individual into the President's ears" (To the Hon. H. Conway, October 6, 1765).

[3] The *Œconomies Royales* as written by Sully, and as printed in 1638, adopt throughout the cumbrous fiction of the second person—the secretaries of Sully recounting to their master, under his dictation, all that he

extremely well worth your reading, as it will give you a clearer
and truer notion of one of the most interesting periods of the
French history, than you can yet have formed, from all the
other books you may have read upon the subject.   That
prince, I mean Henry the Fourth, had all the accomplishments
and virtues of a hero and of a king; and almost of a man.
The last are the more rarely seen; may you possess them all!
Adieu!

Pray make my compliments to Mr. Harte, and let him know
that I have this moment received his letter of the 12th, N.S.,
from Antibes.   It requires no immediate answer; I shall therefore delay mine till I have another from him.   Give him the
enclosed, which I have received from Mr. Eliot.

MY DEAR FRIEND,   London, November 1, O.S. 1750.

I hope this letter will not find you still at Montpellier, but
rather be sent after you from thence to Paris, where I am
persuaded that Mr. Harte could find as good advice for his leg
as at Montpellier, if not better; but if he is of a different opinion,
I am sure you ought to stay there as long as he desires.

While you are in France, I could wish that the hours you allot
for historical amusement should be entirely devoted to the
history of France.   One always reads history to most advantage
in that country to which it is relative; not only books, but persons
being ever at hand to solve the doubts and clear up difficulties.
I do by no means advise you to throw away your time in ran-
sacking, like a dull antiquarian, the minute and unimportant
parts of remote and fabulous times.   Let blockheads read
what blockheads wrote.   A general notion of the history of
of France, from the conquest of that country by the Franks,
to the reign of Louis XI, is sufficient for use, consequently
sufficient for you.   There are, however, in those remote times,
some remarkable eras that deserve more particular attention;
I mean those in which some notable alterations happened in

has seen and done!   In 1745 the Abbé de l'Ecluse undertook the revision
of these memoirs, and by judiciously restoring the first person and omitting
some of the *longueurs*—

"We've not so good a word but have the thing"

—has made them one of the most agreeable historical works to be found
in any language.   The edition referred to by Lord Chesterfield is that of
1747, with "London" on the title page, but really printed in Paris.   Since,
and by reason of, that publication, says Sismondi, "la réputation de Sully
a grandi de nouveau" (*Hist. des Français*, vol. xxiii, p. 478).

the constitution and form of government. As for example, the settlement of Clovis in Gaul, and the form of government which he then established; for, by the way, that form of government differed in this particular from all the other Gothic governments, that the people, neither collectively nor by representatives, had any share in it. It was a mixture of monarchy and aristocracy; and what were called the States-General of France consisted only of the nobility and clergy till the time of Philip le Bel, in the very beginning of the fourteenth century; who first called the people to those assemblies, by no means for the good of the people, who were only amused by this pretended honour, but, in truth, to check the nobility and clergy, and induce them to grant the money he wanted for his profusion; this was a scheme of Enguerrand de Marigny, his minister, who governed both him and his kingdom to such a degree, as to be called the coadjutor and governor of the kingdom. Charles Martel laid aside these assemblies, and governed by open force. Pepin restored them, and attached them to him, and with them the nation; by which means he deposed Childeric, and mounted the throne. This is a second period worth your attention. The third race of kings, which begins with Hugues Capet, is a third period.

A judicious reader of history will save himself a great deal of time and trouble, by attending with care only to those interesting periods of history which furnish remarkable events and make eras; going slightly over the common run of events. Some people read history as others read the *Pilgrim's Progress*; giving equal attention to, and indiscriminately loading their memories with every part alike. But I would have you read it in a different manner: take the shortest general history you can find of every country, and mark down in that history the most important periods; such as conquests, changes of kings, and alterations of the form of government, and then have recourse to more extensive histories or particular treatises relative to these great points. Consider them well, trace up their causes, and follow their consequences. For instance, there is a most excellent though very short history of France by Le Gendre. Read that with attention, and you will know enough of the general history; but when you find there such remarkable periods as are above mentioned, consult Mezeray and other the best and minutest historians, as well as political treatises upon those subjects. In later times, memoirs, from those of Philip de Comines down to the innumerable ones in the reign of Louis XIV, have been of great use, and thrown great light upon particular parts of history.

Conversation in France, if you have the address and dexterity to turn it upon useful subjects, will exceedingly improve your historical knowledge; for people there, however classically ignorant they may be, think it a shame to be ignorant of the history of their own country; they read that if they read nothing else, and having often read nothing else, are proud of having read that, and talk of it willingly; even the women are well instructed in that sort of reading. I am far from meaning by this that you should always be talking wisely, in company, of books, history, and matters of knowledge. There are many companies which you will and ought to keep, where such conversations would be misplaced and ill-timed; your own good sense must distinguish the company and the time. You must trifle with triflers, and be serious only with the serious; but dance to those who pipe. *Cur in theatrum Cato severe venisti?* was justly said to an old man; how much more so would it be to one of your age? From the moment that you are dressed and go out, pocket all your knowledge with your watch, and never pull it out in company unless desired; the producing of the one unasked, implies that you are weary of the company; and the producing of the other unrequired, will make the company weary of you. Company is a republic[1] too jealous of its liberties to suffer a dictator even for a quarter of an hour; and yet in that, as in all republics, there are some few who really govern, but then it is by seeming to disclaim, instead of attempting to usurp the power; that is the occasion in which manners, dexterity, address, and the undefinable *je ne sais quoi* triumph; if properly exerted their conquest is sure, and the more lasting for not being perceived. Remember that this is not only your first and greatest, but ought to be almost your only object while you are in France.

I know that many of your countrymen are apt to call the freedom and vivacity of the French, petulancy and ill-breeding; but should you think so, I desire upon many accounts that you will not say so. I admit that it may be so, in some instances of *petits maîtres étourdis*, and in some young people unbroken to the world; but I can assure you, that you will find it much otherwise with people of a certain rank and age, upon whose

[1] "One evening, in a circle of wits, Goldsmith found fault with me for talking of Johnson as entitled to the honour of unquestionable superiority. 'Sir,' said he, 'you are for making a monarchy of what should be a republic.'"—BOSWELL's *Life of Johnson.*

model you will do very well to form yourself. We call their steady assurance impudence. Why? Only because what we call modesty is awkward bashfulness, and *mauvaise honte*. For my part, I see no impudence, but, on the contrary, infinite utility and advantage, in presenting one's self with the same coolness and unconcern, in any and every company; till one can do that, I am very sure that one can never present one's self well. Whatever is done under concern and embarrassment must be ill-done; and, till a man is absolutely easy and unconcerned in every company, he will never be thought to have kept good, nor be very welcome in it. A steady assurance, with seeming modesty, is possibly the most useful qualification that a man can have in every part of life. A man would certainly not make a very considerable fortune and figure in the world, whose modesty and timidity should often, as bashfulness always does, put him in the deplorable and lamentable situation of the pious Æneas, when, *obstupuit, steteruntque comæ, et vox faucibus hæsit.* Fortune, as well as women,

> ———born to be controlled,
> Stoops to the forward and the bold.

Assurance and intrepidity, under the white banner of seeming modesty, clear the way for merit, that would otherwise be discouraged by difficulties in its journey; whereas barefaced impudence is the noisy and blustering harbinger of a worthless and senseless usurper.

You will think that I shall never have done recommending to you these exterior worldly accomplishments, and you will think right, for I never shall; they are of too great consequence to you for me to be indifferent or negligent about them—the shining part of your future figure and fortune depends now wholly upon them. These are the acquisitions which must give efficacy and success to those you have already made. To have it said and believed that you are the most learned man in England, would be no more than was said and believed of Dr. Bentley; but to have it said at the same time that you are also the best bred, most polite, and agreeable man in the kingdom, would be such a happy composition of a character, as I never yet knew any one man deserve, and which I will endeavour, as well as ardently wish, that you may. Absolute perfection is, I well know, unattainable; but I know, too, that a man of parts may be unweariedly aiming at and arrive pretty near it. Try, labour, persevere. Adieu.

My Dear Friend,   London, November 8, O.S. 1750.

Before you get to Paris, where you will soon be left to your own discretion, if you have any, it is necessary that we should understand one another thoroughly; which is the most probable way of preventing disputes. Money, the cause of much mischief in the world, is the cause of most quarrels between fathers and sons; the former commonly thinking that they cannot give too little, and the latter that they cannot have enough; both equally in the wrong. You must do me the justice to acknowledge, that I have hitherto neither stinted nor grudged any expense that could be of use or real pleasure to you; and I can assure you, by the way, that you have travelled at a much more considerable expense than I did myself, but I never so much as thought of that while Mr. Harte was at the head of your finances, being very sure that the sums granted were scrupulously applied to the uses for which they were intended. But the case will soon be altered, and you will be your own receiver and treasurer. However, I promise you that we will not quarrel singly upon the *quantum,* which shall be cheerfully and freely granted; the application and appropriation of it will be the material point, which I am now going to clear up, and finally settle with you. I will fix, or even name, no settled allowance, though I well know in my own mind what would be the proper one; but I will first try your drafts, by which I can in a good degree judge of your conduct. This only I tell you in general, that, if the channels through which my money is to go are the proper ones, the source shall not be scanty; but should it deviate into dirty, muddy and obscure ones (which, by the bye, it cannot do for a week without my knowing it), I give you fair and timely notice, that the source will instantly be dry. Mr. Harte, in establishing you at Paris, will point out to you those proper channels; he will leave you there upon the foot of a man of fashion, and I will continue you upon the same. You will have your coach, your valet de chambre, your own footman, and a valet de place—which, by the way, is one servant more than I had. I would have you well dressed, by which I mean, dressed as the generality of people of fashion are—that is, not to be taken notice of, for being either more or less fine than other people; it is by being well dressed, not finely dressed, that a gentleman should be distinguished. You must frequent *les spectacles,* which expense I shall willingly supply. You must play, *à des petits jeux de commerce,* in mixed companies; that article is trifling; I shall pay it cheerfully. All the other articles of pocket-money are very inconsiderable at Paris, in comparison of what they are here—the silly custom of giving money wherever one dines or sups, and the expensive importunity of subscriptions, not being yet introduced there. Having thus reckoned up all the decent expenses of a gentleman, which, I will most readily defray, I come now to those which I will neither bear nor supply. The first of these is gaming, which, though I have not the least reason to suspect you of, I think it necessary eventually to assure you that no consideration in the world shall ever make me pay your play-debts; should you ever urge to me that your honour is pawned, I should most immovably answer you, that it was your honour, not mine, that was pawned, and that your creditor might even take the pawn for the debt.

Low company and low pleasures are always much more costly than liberal and elegant ones. The disgraceful riots of a tavern are much more expensive, as well as dishonourable, than the (sometimes pardonable) excesses in good company. I must absolutely hear of no tavern scrapes and squabbles.

I come now to another and very material point; I mean women; and I will not address myself to you upon this subject, either in a religious, a moral, or a parental style. I will even lay aside my age, remember yours, and speak to you, as one man of pleasure, if he had parts too, would speak to another. I will, by no means, pay for whores, and their never-failing consequences, surgeons; nor will I, upon any account, keep singers, dancers, actresses, and *id genus omne*; and, independently of the expense, I must tell you, that such connections would give me, and all sensible people, the utmost contempt for your parts and address: a young fellow must have as little sense as address, to venture, or more properly to sacrifice his health, and ruin his fortune, with such sort of creatures; in such a place as Paris especially, where gallantry is both the profession and the practice of every woman of fashion. To speak plainly, I will not forgive your understanding c—s and p—s; nor will your constitution forgive them you. These distempers, as well as their cures, fall nine times in ten upon the lungs. This argument, I am sure, ought to have weight with you; for I protest to you, that if you meet with any such accident, I would not give one year's purchase for your life.

Lastly, there is another sort of expense that I will not allow, only because it is a silly one; I mean the fooling away your money in baubles at toyshops. Have one handsome snuff-box (if you take snuff) and one handsome sword; but then no more very pretty and very useless things.

By what goes before, you will easily perceive that I mean to allow you whatever is necessary, not only for the figure, but for the pleasures of a gentleman, and not to supply the profusion of a rake. This, you must confess, does not savour of either the severity or parsimony of old age. I consider this agreement between us as a subsidiary treaty on my part for services to be performed on yours. I promise you, that I will be as punctual in the payment of subsidies as England has been during the last war; but then I give you notice at the same time, that I require a much more scrupulous execution of the treaty on your part than we met with on that of our Allies; or else that payment will be stopped. I hope that all I have now said was absolutely unnecessary, and that sentiments more worthy and more noble than pecuniary ones, would of themselves have pointed out to you the conduct I recommend; but, in all events, I resolved to be once for all explicit with you, that in the worst that can happen, you may not plead ignorance, and complain that I had not sufficiently explained to you my intentions.

Having mentioned the word rake, I must say a word or two more on that subject, because young people too frequently, and always fatally, are apt to mistake that character for that of a man of pleasure; whereas, there are not in the world two characters more different. A rake is a composition of all the lowest, most ignoble, degrading, and shameful vices; they all conspire to disgrace his character and to ruin his fortune; while wine and the pox contend which shall soonest and most effectually destroy his constitution. A dissolute, flagitious footman or porter makes full as good a rake as a man of the first quality. By the bye, let me tell you that in the wildest part of my youth I never was a rake, but, on the contrary, always detested and despised the character.

A man of pleasure, though not always so scrupulous as he should be, and as one day he will wish he had been, refines at least his pleasures by taste, accompanies them with decency, and enjoys them with dignity. Few men can be men of pleasure, every man may be a rake. Remember that I shall know everything you say or do at Paris, as exactly as if, by the force of magic, I could follow you everywhere, like a Sylph or a Gnome, invisible myself. Seneca says, very prettily, that one should ask nothing of God, but what one should be willing that men should know; nor of men, but what one should be willing that

God should know; I advise you to say or do nothing at Paris, but what you would be willing that I should know. I hope, nay I believe, that will be the case. Sense, I dare say, you do not want; instruction, I am sure, you have never wanted; experience, you are daily gaining; all which together must inevitably (I should think) make you both *respectable et aimable*, the perfection of a human character. In that case nothing shall be wanting on my part, and you shall solidly experience all the extent and tenderness of my affection for you; but dread the reverse of both! Adieu.

P.S. When you get to Paris, after you have been to wait on Lord Albemarle,[1] go to see Mr. Yorke,[2] whom I have particular reasons for desiring that you should be well with, as I shall hereafter explain to you. Let him know that my orders, and your own inclinations, conspired to make you desire his friendship and protection.

MY DEAR FRIEND,

I have sent you so many preparatory letters for Paris, that this, which will meet you there, shall only be a summary of them all.

You have hitherto had more liberty than anybody of your age ever had; and I must do you the justice to own, that you have made a better use of it than most people of your age would have done; but then, though you had not a jailer, you had a friend with you. At Paris, you will not only be unconfined, but unassisted. Your own good sense must be your only guide; I have great confidence in it, and am convinced that I shall receive just such accounts of your conduct at Paris as I could wish; for I tell you beforehand, that I shall be most minutely informed of all that you do, and almost of all that you say there. Enjoy the pleasures of youth, you cannot do better; but refine and dignify them like a man of parts; let them raise and not sink, let them adorn and not vilify, your character; let them, in short, be the pleasures of a gentleman, and taken with your equals at least, but rather with your superiors, and those chiefly French.

[1] William Anne, second Earl of Albemarle, died in December 1754, as ambassador at Paris.
[2] Joseph, third son of Lord Chancellor Hardwicke, was at this time Secretary of Embassy at Paris, but became, in 1751, envoy at the Hague. He was created Lord Dover in 1788, and died without issue in 1792.

Inquire into the characters of the several academicians before you form a connection with any of them; and be most upon your guard against those who make the most court to you.

You cannot study much in the Academy; but you may study usefully there, if you are an economist of your time, and bestow only upon good books those quarters and halves of hours, which occur to everybody in the course of almost every day; and which, at the year's end, amount to a very considerable sum of time.

Let Greek, without fail, share some part of every day: I do not mean the Greek poets, the catches of Anacreon, or the tender complaints of Theocritus, or even the porter-like language of Homer's heroes; of whom all smatterers in Greek know a little, quote often, and talk of always; but I mean Plato, Aristoteles, Demosthenes, and Thucydides, whom none but adepts know. It is Greek that must distinguish you in the learned world, Latin alone will not. And Greek must be sought to be retained, for it never occurs like Latin. When you read history, or other books of amusement, let every language you are master of have its turn; so that you may not only retain, but improve in, every one. I also desire that you will converse in German and Italian with all the Germans and the Italians with whom you converse at all. This will be a very agreeable and flattering thing to them, and a very useful one to you.

Pray apply yourself diligently to your exercises; for though the doing them well is not supremely meritorious, the doing them ill is illiberal, vulgar, and ridiculous.

I recommend theatrical representations to you, which are excellent at Paris. The tragedies of Corneille and Racine, and the comedies of Molière, well attended to, are admirable lessons, both for the heart and the head. There is not, nor ever was, any theatre comparable to the French. If the music of the French operas does not please your Italian ear, the words of them, at least, are sense and poetry, which is much more than I can say of any Italian opera that I ever read or heard in my life.

I send you the enclosed letter of recommendation to Marquis Matignon, which I would have you deliver to him as soon as you can; you will, I am sure, feel the good effects of his warm friendship for me and Lord Bolingbroke, who has also wrote to him upon your subject. By that, and by the other letters which I have sent you, you will be at once so thoroughly introduced into the best French company, that you must take some pains if you will keep bad; but that is what I do not suspect you of.

You have, I am sure, too much right ambition to prefer low and disgraceful company to that of your superiors both in rank and age. Your character, and consequently your fortune, absolutely depends upon the company you keep, and the turn you take at Paris. I do not, in the least, mean a grave turn; on the contrary, a gay, a sprightly, but, at the same time, an elegant and liberal one.

Keep carefully out of all scrapes and quarrels. They lower a character extremely, and are particularly dangerous in France, where a man is dishonoured by not resenting an affront, and utterly ruined by resenting it. The young Frenchmen are hasty, giddy, and petulant; extremely national and *avantageux*. Forbear from any national jokes or reflections, which are always improper, and commonly unjust. The colder northern nations generally look upon France as a whistling, singing, dancing, frivolous nation; this notion is very far from being a true one, though many *petits maîtres* by their behaviours seem to justify it; but those very *petits maîtres*, when mellowed by age and experience, very often turn out very able men. The number of great generals and statesmen, as well as excellent authors, that France has produced is an undeniable proof that it is not that frivolous, unthinking, empty nation that northern prejudices suppose it. Seem to like and approve of everything at first, and I promise you that you will like and approve of many things afterwards.

I expect that you will write to me constantly once every week, which I desire may be every Thursday; and that your letters may inform me of your personal transactions; not of what you see, but of whom you see, and what you do.

Be your own monitor, now that you will have no other. As to enunciation, I must repeat it to you again and again, that there is no one thing so necessary; all other talents, without that, are absolutely useless, except in your own closet.

It sounds ridiculously to bid you study with your dancing-master; and yet I do. The bodily carriage and graces are of infinite consequence to everybody, and more particularly to you.

Adieu for this time, my dear child. Yours tenderly.

MY DEAR FRIEND,   London, November 12, O.S. 1750.

You will possibly think that this letter turns upon strange, little trifling objects; and you will think right, if you consider them separately; but if you take them aggregately, you will be convinced that, as parts, which conspire to form that whole, called the exterior of a man of fashion, they are of importance. I shall not dwell now upon those personal graces, that liberal air, and that engaging address, which I have so often recommended to you; but descend still lower—to your dress, cleanliness, and care of your person.

When you come to Paris, you must take care to be extremely well dressed, that is, as the fashionable people are. This does by no means consist in the finery, but in the taste, fitness, and manner of wearing your clothes; a fine suit ill-made, and slatternly or stiffly worn, far from adorning, only exposes the awkwardness of the wearer. Get the best French tailor to make your clothes, whatever they are, in the fashion, and to fit you, and then wear them; button them or unbutton them, as the genteelest people you see do. Let your man learn of the best *friseur* to do your hair well, for that is a very material part of your dress. Take care to have your stockings well gartered up, and your shoes well buckled; for nothing gives a more slovenly air to a man than ill-dressed legs.

In your person you must be accurately clean; and your teeth, hands, and nails should be superlatively so. A dirty mouth has real ill consequences to the owner, for it infallibly causes the decay, as well as the intolerable pain of the teeth; and it is very offensive to his acquaintance, for it will most inevitably stink. I insist therefore that you wash your teeth the first thing that you do every morning, with a soft sponge and warm water, for four or five minutes, and then wash your mouth five or six times. Mouton, whom I desire you will send for upon your arrival at Paris, will give you an opiate, and a liquor to be used sometimes. Nothing looks more ordinary, vulgar, and illiberal, than dirty hands, and ugly, uneven and ragged nails. I do not suspect you of that shocking, awkward trick of biting yours; but that is not enough; you must keep the ends of them smooth and clean—not tipped with black, as the ordinary people's always are. The ends of your nails should be small segments of circles, which, by a very little care in the cutting, they are very easily brought to; every time that you wipe your hands, rub the skin round your nails backwards, that it may not grow up and shorten your nails too much. The cleanliness of the rest of your person, which by the way will conduce greatly to your health, I refer from time to time to the bagnio. My mentioning these particulars arises (I freely own) from some suspicion that the hints are not unnecessary;

for when you were a schoolboy, you were slovenly and dirty above your fellows. I must add another caution, which is, that upon no account whatever you put your fingers, as too many people are apt to do, in your nose or ears. It is the most shocking, nasty, vulgar rudeness that can be offered to company; it disgusts one, it turns one's stomach; and, for my own part, I would much rather know that a man's fingers were actually in his breech, than see them in his nose. Wash your ears well every morning, and blow your nose in your handkerchief whenever you have occasion; but, by the way, without looking at it afterwards.

There should be in the least, as well as in the greatest parts of a gentleman, *les manières nobles*. Sense will teach you some, observation others; attend carefully to the manners, the diction, the motions, of people of the first fashion, and form your own upon them. On the other hand, observe a little those of the vulgar, in order to avoid them; for though the things which they say or do may be the same, the manner is always totally different; and in that, and nothing else, consists the characteristic of a man of fashion. The lowest peasant speaks, moves, dresses, eats, and drinks, as much as a man of the first fashion; but does them all quite differently; so that by doing and saying most things in a manner opposite to that of the vulgar, you have a great chance of doing and saying them right. There are graduations in awkwardness and vulgarism, as there are in everything else. *Les manières de robe*, though not quite right, are still better than *les manières bourgeoises*; and these, though bad, are still better than *les manières de campagne*. But the language, the air, the dress, and the manners of the Court, are the only true standard *des manières nobles, et d'un honnête homme*. *Ex pede Herculem* is an old and true saying, and very applicable to our present subject; for a man of parts, who has been bred at Courts, and used to keep the best company, will distinguish himself, and is to be known from the vulgar, by every word, attitude, gesture, and even look. I cannot leave these seeming *minuties*, without repeating to you the necessity of your carving well, which is an article, little as it is, that is useful twice every day of one's life; and the doing it ill is very troublesome to one's self, and very disagreeable, often ridiculous, to others.

Having said all this, I cannot help reflecting what a formal dull fellow, or a cloistered pedant, would say, if they were to see this letter; they would look upon it with the utmost contempt, and say that surely a father might find much better topics for advice to a son. I would admit it, if I had given you, or that you were capable of receiving no better; but if sufficient pains have been taken to form your heart and improve your mind, and, as I hope, not without success, I will tell those solid gentlemen, that all these trifling things, as they think them, collectively form that pleasing *je ne sçais quoi*, that *ensemble*, which they are utter strangers to, both in themselves and others. The word *aimable* is not known in their language, or the thing in their manners. Great usage of the world, great attention, and a great desire of pleasing, can alone give it; and it is no trifle.

It is from old people's looking upon these things as trifles, or not thinking of them at all, that so many young people are so awkward and so ill-bred. Their parents, often careless and unmindful of them, give them only the common run of education — as school, university, and then travelling — without examining, and very often without being able to judge if they did examine, what progress they make in any one of these stages. Then they carelessly comfort themselves, and say, that their sons will do like other people's sons; and so they do, that is, commonly very ill. They correct none of the childish, nasty tricks, which they get at school; nor the illiberal manners which they contract at the university; nor the frivolous and superficial pertness, which is commonly all that they acquire by their travels. As they do not tell them of these things, nobody else can; so they go on in the practice of them, without ever hearing, or knowing, that they are unbecoming, indecent and shocking.

For, as I have often formerly observed to you, nobody but a father can take the liberty to reprove a young fellow grown up, for those kind of inaccuracies and improprieties of behaviour. The most intimate friendship, unassisted by the paternal superiority, will not authorise it. I may truly say, therefore, that you are happy in having me for a sincere, friendly, and quick-sighted monitor. Nothing will escape me; I shall pry for your defects, in order to correct them, as curiously as I shall seek for your perfections, in order to applaud and reward them; with this difference only, that I shall publicly mention the latter, and never hint at the former, but in a letter to, or a *tête-à-tête* with you. I will never put you out of countenance before company, and I hope you will never give me reason to be out of countenance for you, as any one of the above-mentioned defects would make me. *Prætor non curat de minimis* was a maxim in the Roman law, for causes only of a certain value were tried by him; but there were inferior jurisdictions, that took cognizance of the smallest. Now I shall try you, not only as a Prætor in the greatest, but as Censor in lesser, and as the lowest magistrate in the least cases.

I have this moment received Mr. Harte's letter of the 1st November, New Style; by which I am very glad to find that he thinks of moving towards Paris, the end of this month, which looks as if his leg were better; besides, in my opinion, you both of you only lose time at Montpellier; he would find better advice, and you better company, at Paris. In the meantime, I hope you go into the best company there is at Montpellier, and there always is some at the Intendant's or the Commandant's. You will have had full time to have learned *les petites chansons Languedociennes*, which are exceeding pretty ones, both words and tunes. I remember, when I was in those parts, I was surprised at the difference which I found between the people on one side, and those on the other side of the Rhône. The Provenceaux were, in general, surly, ill-bred, ugly, and swarthy: the Languedociens the very reverse; a cheerful, well-bred, handsome people. Adieu! Yours most affectionately.

P.S. Upon reflection, I direct this letter to Paris; I think you must have left Montpellier before it could arrive there.

MY DEAR FRIEND,   London, November 19, O.S. 1750.

I was very glad to find, by your letter of the 12th, N.S., that you had informed yourself so well of the state of the French marine at Toulon, and of the commerce at Marseilles; they are objects that deserve the inquiry and attention of every man, who intends to be concerned in public affairs. The French are now wisely attentive to both; their commerce is incredibly increased within these last thirty years; they have beaten us out of great part of our Levant trade; their East-India trade has greatly affected ours; and, in the West Indies, their Martinico establishment supplies, not only France itself, but in the greatest part of Europe, with sugars; whereas our islands, as Jamaica, Barbadoes, and the Leeward, have now no other market for theirs but England. New France, or Canada, has also greatly lessened our fur and skin trade. It is true (as you say) that we have no treaty of commerce subsisting (I do not say *with Marseilles*) but with France. There was a treaty of commerce made, between England and France, immediately after the treaty of Utrecht; but the whole treaty was conditional, and to depend upon the Parliament's enacting certain things, which were stipulated in two of the articles; the Parliament, after a very famous debate, would not do it; so the treaty fell to the ground; however, the outlines of that treaty are, by mutual and tacit consent, the general rules of our commerce with France. It is true too, that our commodities, which go to France, must go in our bottoms; the French having imitated, in many respects, our famous Act of Navigation, as it is commonly called. This Act was made in the year 1652, in the Parliament held by Oliver Cromwell. It forbids all foreign ships to bring into England any merchandise or commodities whatsoever, that were not of the growth and produce of that country to which those ships belonged, under penalty of the forfeiture of such ships. This Act was particularly levelled at the Dutch; who were, at that time, the carriers of almost all Europe, and got immensely by freight.

Upon this principle, of the advantages arising from freight, there is a provision in the same Act, that even the growth and produce of our own colonies in America shall not be carried from thence to any other country in Europe, without first touching in England; but this clause has lately been repealed, in the instances of some perishable commodities, such as rice, etc., which are allowed to be carried directly from our American colonies to other countries. The Act also provides, that two-thirds, I think, of those who navigate the said ships shall be British subjects. There is an excellent, and little book, written by the famous Monsieur Huet, Evêque d'Avranches, *sur le Commerce des Anciens*, which is very well worth your reading, and very soon read. It will give you a clear notion of the rise and progress of commerce. There are many other books which take up the history of commerce where Monsieur d'Avranches leaves it, and bring it down to these times: I advise you to read some of them with care; commerce being a very essential part of political knowledge in every country, but more particularly in this, which owes all its riches and power to it.

I come now to another part of your letter, which is the orthography, if I may call bad spelling *orthography*. You spell induce, *enduce*; and grandeur, you spell grand*ure*; two faults, of which few of my house-maids would have been guilty. I must tell you, that orthography, in the true sense of the word, is so absolutely necessary for a man of letters, or a gentleman, that one false spelling may fix a ridicule upon him for the rest of his life; and I know a man of quality, who never recovered the ridicule of having spelled *wholesome* without the *w*.

Reading with care will secure everybody from false spelling; for books are always well spelled, according to the orthography of the times. Some words are indeed doubtful, being spelled differently by different authors of equal authority, but those are few; and in those cases every man has his option, because he may plead his authority either way; but where there is but one right way, as in the two words above-mentioned, it is unpardonable and ridiculous for a gentleman to miss it: even a woman of a tolerable education would despise, and laugh at a lover, who should send her an ill-spelled *billet-doux*. I fear, and suspect, that you have taken it into your head, in most cases, that the Matter is all, and the Manner little or nothing. If you have, undeceive yourself, and be convinced that, in everything, the Manner is full as important as the Matter. If you speak the sense of an angel, in bad words, and with a disagreeable utterance, nobody will hear you twice, who can help it. If you write epistles as well as Cicero, but in a very bad hand, and very ill-spelled, whoever receives, will laugh at them; and if you had the figure of Adonis, with an awkward air and motions, it will disgust instead of pleasing. Study Manner therefore in everything, if you would be anything. My principal inquiries of my friends at Paris concerning you, will be relative to your Manner of doing whatever you do. I shall not inquire whether you understand Demosthenes, Tacitus, or the *jus publicum imperii*; but I shall inquire whether your utterance is pleasing, your style not only pure but elegant, your manners noble and easy, your air and address engaging; in short, whether you are a gentleman, a man of fashion, and fit to keep good company or not; for, till I am satisfied in these particulars, you and I must by no means meet; I could not possibly stand it. It is in your power to become all this at Paris, if you please. Consult with Lady Hervey and Madame Monconseil upon all these matters, and they will speak to you, and advise you freely. Tell them, that *bisogna compatire ancora*, that you are utterly new in the world, that you are desirous to form yourself, that you beg they will reprove, advise, and correct you, that you know that none can do it sc well, and that you will implicitly follow their directions. This, together with your careful observation of the manners of the best company, will really form you.

Abbé Guasco,[1] a friend of mine, will come to you as soon as he knows of your arrival at Paris; he is well received in the best companies there, and will introduce you to them. He will be desirous to do you any service he can; he is active and curious, and can give you information upon most things. He is a sort of *complaisant* of the President Montesquieu, to whom you have a letter.

I imagine that this letter will not wait for you very long at Paris, where I reckon you will be in about a fortnight. Adieu!

My Dear Friend,   London, January 3, O.S. 1751.

By your letter of the 5th, N.S., I find that your *début* at Paris has been a good one; you are entered into good company, and I dare say you will not sink into bad. Frequent the houses where you have been once invited, and have none of that shyness which makes most of our countrymen strangers where they might be intimate and domestic if they pleased. Wherever you have a general invitation to sup when you please, profit of it with decency, and go every now and then. Lord Albemarle will, I am sure, be extremely kind to you; but his house is only a dinner house, and, as I am informed, frequented by no French people. Should he happen to employ you in his bureau, which I much doubt, you must write a better hand than your common one, or you will get no credit by your manuscripts; for your hand is at present an illiberal one; it is neither a hand of business nor of a gentleman, but the hand of a schoolboy writing his exercise, which he hopes will never be read.

Madame de Monconseil gives me a favourable account of you, and so do Marquis de Matignon and Madame du Boccage; they all say that you desire to please, and consequently promise me that you will; and they judge right; for whoever really desires to please, and has (as you have now) the means of

---

[1] Octavien de Guasco, a native of Pignerol, in 1712 became a canon of Tournay, and a member of the Académie des Inscriptions, to which he contributed several interesting essays. He was also the author of an *Histoire du Pape Clement V*, and the translator of Cantemir into Italian—but these works have remained unpublished.

learning how, certainly will please; and that is the great point of life; it makes all other things easy. Whenever you are with Madame de Monconseil, Madame du Boccage, or other women of fashion, with whom you are tolerably free, say frankly and naturally: *Je n'ai point d'usage du monde, j'y suis encore bien neuf, je souhaiterois ardemment de plaire, mais je ne sçais guères comment m'y prendre; ayez la bonté, Madame, de me faire part de votre secret de plaire à tout le monde. J'en ferai ma fortune, et il vous en restera pourtant toujours plus qu'il ne vous en faut.* When, in consequence of this request, they shall tell you of any little error, awkwardness, or impropriety, you should not only feel but express the warmest acknowledgment. Though nature should suffer, and she will at first hearing them, *Que la critique la plus sévère, est à votre égard la preuve la plus marquée de leur amitié.* Madame du Boccage tells me particularly to inform you, *Qu'il me fera toujours plaisir et honneur de me venir voir; il est vrai qu'à son âge le plaisir de causer est froid, mais je tâcherai de lui faire connoissance avec des jeunes gens, etc.* Make use of this invitation, and as you live in a manner next door to her, step in and out there frequently. Monsieur du Boccage will go with you, he tells me, with great pleasure, to the plays, and point out to you whatever deserves your knowing there. This is worth your acceptance too; he has a very good taste. I have not yet heard from Lady Hervey upon your subject, but as you inform me that you have already supped with her once, I look upon you as adopted by her; consult her in all your little matters; tell her any difficulties that may occur to you; ask her what you should do or say in such cases; she has *l'usage du monde en perfection*, and will help you to acquire it. Madame de Berkenrode *est pétrie de grâces*, and your quotation is very applicable to her. You may be there, I dare say, as often as you please, and I would advise you to sup there once a week.

You say, very justly, that as Mr. Harte is leaving you, you shall want advice more than ever; you shall never want mine; and as you have already had so much of it, I must rather repeat than add to what I have already given you; but that I will do, and add to it occasionally, as circumstances may require. At present, I shall only remind you of your two great objects, which you should always attend to: they are Parliament and foreign affairs. With regard to the former, you can do nothing, while abroad, but attend carefully to the purity, correctness, and elegancy of your diction, the clearness and gracefulness of your utterance, in whatever language you speak. As for the

Parliamentary knowledge, I will take care of that, when you come home. With regard to foreign affairs, everything you do abroad may and ought to tend that way. Your reading should be chiefly historical; I do not mean of remote, dark, and fabulous history, still less of jimcrack natural history of fossils, minerals, plants, etc., but I mean the useful, political, and constitutional history of Europe, for these last three centuries and a half. The other thing necessary for your foreign object, and not less necessary than either ancient or modern knowledge, is a great knowledge of the world, manners, politeness, address, and *le ton de la bonne compagnie.* In that view, keeping a great deal of good company is the principal part to which you are now to attend.

It seems ridiculous to tell you, but it is most certainly true, that your dancing-master is at this time the man in all Europe of the greatest importance to you. You must dance well, in order to sit, stand, and walk well; and you must do all these well, in order to please. What with your exercises, some reading, and a great deal of company, your day is, I confess, extremely taken up; but the day, if well employed, is long enough for everything; and I am sure you will not slattern away one moment of it in inaction. At your age people have strong and active spirits, alacrity and vivacity in all they do; are *impigri*, indefatigable, and quick. The difference is, that a young fellow of parts exerts all those happy dispositions in the pursuit of proper objects; endeavours to excel in the solid, and in the showish parts of life; whereas a silly puppy, or a dull rogue, throws away all his youth and spirits upon trifles, when he is serious, or upon disgraceful vices, while he aims at pleasures. This, I am sure, will not be your case; your good sense and your good conduct hitherto are your guarantees with me for the future. Continue only at Paris as you have begun, and your stay there will make you, what I have always wished you to be; as near perfection as our nature permits.

Adieu, my dear; remember to write to me once a week, not as to a father, but without reserve as to a friend.

My Dear Friend,   London, January 28, O.S. 1751.

A bill for ninety pounds sterling, was brought me, the other day, said to be drawn upon me by you; I scrupled paying it at first, not upon the account of the sum, but because you had sent me no letter of advice, which is always done in those transactions; and still more, because I did not perceive that you had signed it. The person who presented it desired me to look again, and that I should discover your name at the bottom; accordingly I looked again, and with the help of my magnifying glass, did perceive, that what I had first taken only for somebody's mark was, in truth, your name written in the worst and smallest hand I ever saw in my life. I cannot write quite so ill, but it was something like this [here he imitates it]. However, I paid it at a venture; though I would almost rather lose the money, than that signature should be yours. All gentlemen, and all men of business, write their names always in the same way, that their signature may be so well known as not to be easily counterfeited; and they generally sign in a larger character than their common hand; whereas your name was in a less, and a worse hand than your common writing. This suggested to me the various accidents which may very probably happen to you while you write so ill.

For instance, if you were to write in such a character to the Secretary's office, your letter would immediately be sent to the decipherer, as containing matters of the utmost secrecy, not fit to be trusted to the common character. If you were to write to an antiquarian, he (knowing you to be a man of learning) would certainly try it by the Runic, Celtic, or Sclavonian alphabet; never suspecting it to be a modern character. And, if you were to send a *poulet* to a fine woman, in such a hand, she would think that it really came from the *poulaillier*, which, by the bye, is the etymology of the word, *poulet*; for Henry the fourth of France used to send *billets-doux* to his mistresses, by his *poulaillier*, under pretence of sending them chickens; which gave the name of *poulets* to those short, but expressive, manuscripts.

I have often told you, that every man who has the use of his eyes and of his hand, can write whatever hand he pleases; and it is plain that you can, since you write both the Greek and German characters, which you never learned of a writing master, extremely well, though your common hand which you learned of a master, is an exceeding bad and illiberal one, equally unfit for business or common use. I do not desire that you should write the laboured, stiff character of a writing master; a man of business must write quick and well, and that depends singly upon use. I would therefore advise you to get some very good writing-master at Paris, and apply to it for a month only, which will be sufficient; for, upon my word, the writing of a genteel plain hand of business is of much more importance than you think. You will say, it may be, that when you write so very ill, it is because you are in a hurry? a man of sense may be in haste, but can never be in a hurry, because he knows, that whatever he does in a hurry he must necessarily do very ill. He may be in haste to despatch an affair, but he will take care not to let that haste hinder his doing it well. Little minds are in a hurry, when the object proves (as it commonly does) too big for them; they run, they hare, they puzzle, confound, and perplex, themselves; they want to do everything at once, and never do it at all. But a man of sense takes the time necessary for doing the thing he is about well: and his haste to despatch a business, only appears by the continuity of his application to it: he pursues it with a cool steadiness, and finishes it before he begins any other. I own your time is much taken up, and you have a great many different things to do; but remember, that you had much better do half of them well, and leave the other half undone, than do them all indifferently. Moreover, the few seconds that are saved in the course of the day, by writing ill instead of well, do not amount to an object of time, by any means equivalent to the disgrace or ridicule of writing such a scrawl. Consider, that if your very bad writing could furnish me with matter of ridicule, what will it not do to others, who do not view you in the same light that I do.

There was a Pope, I think it was Pope Chigi,[1] who was justly ridiculed for his attention to little things, and his inability in great ones; and therefore called *maximus in minimis*, and *minimus in maximis*. Why? Because he attended to little things, when he had great ones to do. At this particular period of your life, and at the place you are now in, you have only little things to do; and you should make it habitual to you to do them well, that they may require no attention from you when you have, as I hope you will have, greater things to mind. Make a good hand-writing familiar to you now, that you may hereafter have nothing but your matter to think of, when you have occasion to write to kings and ministers. Dance, dress, and present yourself habitually well now, that you may have none of those little things to think of hereafter, and which will be all necessary to be done well occasionally, when you will have greater things to do.

[1] Alexander VII.

As I am eternally thinking of everything that can be relative to you, one thing has occurred to me which I think necessary to mention, in order to prevent the difficulties which it might otherwise lay you under; it is this—as you get more acquaintance at Paris, it will be impossible for you to frequent your first acquaintances so much as you did while you had no others. As for example, at your first *début* I suppose you were chiefly at Madame Monconseil's, Lady Hervey's, and Madame du Boccage's. Now that you have got so many other houses, you cannot be at theirs so often as you used; but pray take care not to give them the least reason to think that you neglect or despise them for the sake of new and more dignified and shining acquaintances, which would be ungrateful and imprudent on your part, and never forgiven on theirs. Call upon them often, though you do not stay with them so long as formerly; tell them that you are sorry you are obliged to go away, but that you have such and such engagements, with which good-breeding obliges you to comply; and insinuate that you would rather stay with them. In short, take care to make as many personal friends, and as few personal enemies as possible. I do not mean by personal friends, intimate and confidential friends, of which no man can hope to have half a dozen in the whole course of his life; but I mean friends in the common acceptation of the word, that is, people who speak well of you, and who would rather do you good than harm, consistently with their own interest and no farther. Upon the whole, I recommend to you again and again *les Grâces*. Adorned by them, you may, in a manner, do what you please; it will be approved of; without them your best qualities will lose half their efficacy. Endeavour to be fashionable among the French, which will soon make you fashionable. Monsieur de Matignon already calls you *le petit François*. If you can get that name generally at Paris it will put you *à la mode*. Adieu! my dear child.

My Dear Friend,   London, February 11, O.S. 1751.

When you go to the play, which I hope you do often, for it is a very instructive amusement, you must certainly have observed the very different effects which the several parts have upon you, according as they are well or ill acted. The very best tragedy of Corneille's, if well spoken and acted, interests, engages, agitates, and affects your passions. Love,

terror, and pity, alternately possess you. But if ill spoken and
acted, it would only excite your indignation or your laughter.
Why? It is still Corneille's; it is the same sense, the same
matter, whether well or ill acted. It is then merely the manner
of speaking and acting that makes this great difference in the
effects. Apply this to yourself, and conclude from it, that if
you would either please in a private company, or persuade in
a public assembly, air, looks, gestures, graces, enunciation,
proper accents, just emphasis, and tuneful cadences, are full
as necessary as the matter itself. Let awkward, ungraceful,
inelegant, and dull fellows say what they will in behalf of their
solid matter and strong reasonings, and let them despise all
those graces and ornaments, which engage the senses and
captivate the heart; they will find (though they will possibly
wonder why) that their rough unpolished matter, and their
unadorned, coarse, but strong arguments, will neither please
nor persuade, but, on the contrary, will tire our attention and
excite disgust. We are so made, we love to be pleased better
than to be informed; information is, in a certain degree, mortifying, as it implies our previous ignorance; it must be sweetened
to be palatable.

To bring this directly to you; know that no man can make a
figure in this country, but by Parliament. Your fate depends
upon your success there as a speaker; and, take my word for
it, that success depends much more upon manner than matter.
Mr. Pitt,[1] and Mr. Murray, the Solicitor-General,[2] uncle to
Lord Stormont, are, beyond comparison, the best speakers;
why? Only because they are the best orators. They alone
can inflame or quiet the House; they alone are so attended to
in that numerous and noisy assembly, that you might hear a
pin fall while either of them is speaking. Is it that their matter
is better, or their arguments stronger, than other people's?
Does the House expect extraordinary informations from them?
Not in the least; but the House expects pleasure from them,
and therefore attends; finds it, and therefore approves. Mr. Pitt,
particularly, has very little Parliamentary knowledge; his matter
is generally flimsy, and his arguments often weak: but his
eloquence is superior, his action graceful, his enunciation just
and harmonious; his periods are well turned, and every word

---

[1] William Pitt, born 1708, Earl of Chatham 1766, died 1778.
[2] William Murray, born at Perth 1705, Solicitor-General 1742, Chief
Justice, with the title of Earl of Mansfield, 1756. In the riots in London
in 1780 his house in Bloomsbury Square, with his valuable library, was
burnt. Died 1793.

he makes use of is the very best, and the most expressive that can be used in that place. This, and not his matter, made him Paymaster, in spite of both King and ministers. From this, draw the obvious conclusion.

The same thing holds full as true in conversation, where even trifles, elegantly expressed, well looked, and accompanied with graceful action, will ever please, beyond all the home-spun, unadorned sense in the world. Reflect, on one side, how you feel within yourself, while you are forced to suffer the tedious, muddy, and ill-turned narration of some awkward fellow, even though the fact may be interesting; and on the other hand, with what pleasure you attend to the relation of a much less interesting matter, when elegantly expressed, genteelly turned, and gracefully delivered. By attending carefully to all these *agrémens* in your daily conversation, they will become habitual to you, before you come into Parliament; and you will have nothing then to do but to raise them a little when you come there. I would wish you to be so attentive to this object, that I would not have you speak to your footman but in the very best words that the subject admits of, be the language which it will. Think of your words, and of their arrangement, before you speak; choose the most elegant, and place them in the best order. Consult your own ear, to avoid cacophony; and what is very near as bad, monotony. Think also of your gesture and looks, when you are speaking even upon the most trifling subjects. The same things differently expressed, looked, and delivered, cease to be the same things. The most passionate lover in the world cannot make a stronger declaration of love than the *Bourgeois Gentilhomme* does in this happy form of words, *Mourir d'amour me font belle Marquise vos beaux yeux*.[1] I defy anybody to say more; and yet I would advise nobody to say that; and I would recommend to you rather to smother and conceal your passion entirely than to reveal it in these words. Seriously, this holds in everything, as well as in that ludicrous instance. The French, to do them justice, attend very minutely to the purity, the correctness and the elegancy of their style, in conversation, and in their letters. *Bien narrer* is an object of their study; and though they sometimes carry it to affectation, they never sink into inelegancy, which is much the worst extreme of the two. Observe them, and form your French style upon theirs; for elegancy in one language will reproduce

---

[1] M. Jourdain is taught five ways in which this sentiment can be expressed, but this is not one of them. See Act II, Scene vi.

itself in all. I knew a young man, who being just elected a member of Parliament, was laughed at for being discovered, through the keyhole of his chamber door, speaking to himself in the glass, and forming his looks and gestures. I could not join in that laugh, but on the contrary, thought him much wiser than those who laughed at him; for he knew the importance of those little graces in a public assembly, and they did not. Your person (which I am told by the way is not ill-turned), whether in a laced coat, or a blanket, is specifically the same; but yet, I believe, you choose to wear the former; and you are in the right, for the sake of pleasing more.

The worst-bred man in Europe, if a lady let fall her fan, would certainly take it up and give it to her; the best-bred man in Europe could do no more. The difference however would be considerable; the latter would please by doing it gracefully; the former would be laughed at for doing it awkwardly. I repeat it, and repeat it again, and shall never cease repeating it to you, air, manners, graces, style, elegancy, and all those ornaments, must now be the only objects of your attention; it is now, or never, that you must acquire them. Postpone, therefore, all other considerations; make them now your serious study; you have not one moment to lose. The solid and the ornamental united are undoubtedly best; but were I reduced to make an option, I should, without hesitation, choose the latter.

I hope you assiduously frequent Marcel, and carry graces from him; nobody had more to spare than he had formerly. Have you learned to carve? for it is ridiculous not to carve well. A man who tells you gravely that he cannot carve, may as well tell you that he cannot blow his nose; it is both as necessary and as easy.

Make my compliments to Lord Huntingdon, whom I love and honour extremely, as I dare say you do; I will write to him soon, though I believe he has hardly time to read a letter; and my letters to those I love are, as you know by experience, not very short ones; this is one proof of it, and this would have been longer, if the paper had been so. Good night then, my dear child.

MY DEAR FRIEND,   London, February 28, O.S. 1751.

This epigram in Martial:

> Non amo te, Sabidi, nec possum dicere quare,
> Hoc tantum possum dicere, non amo te;

has puzzled a great many people; who cannot conceive how it

is possible not to love anybody, and yet not to know the reason why. I think I conceive Martial's meaning very clearly, though the nature of epigram, which is to be short, would not allow him to explain it more fully; and I take it to be this: "O Sabidis, you are a very worthy deserving man; you have a thousand good qualities, you have a great deal of learning; I esteem, I respect, but for the soul of me I cannot love you, though I cannot particularly say why. You are not amiable; you have not those engaging manners, those pleasing attentions, those graces, and that address, which are absolutely necessary to please, though impossible to define. I cannot say it is this or that particular thing that hinders me from loving you, it is the whole together; and upon the whole you are not agreeable."

How often have I, in the course of my life, found myself in this situation, with regard to many of my acquaintance, whom I have honoured and respected without being able to love? I did not know why, because, when one is young, one does not take the trouble, nor allow oneself the time, to analyse one's sentiments, and to trace them up to their source. But subsequent observation and reflection have taught me why. There is a man, whose moral character, deep learning, and superior parts, I acknowledge, admire, and respect; but whom it is impossible for me to love, that I am almost in a fever whenever I am in his company. His figure (without being deformed) seems made to disgrace or ridicule the common structure of the human body. His legs and arms are never in the position which, according to the situation of his body, they ought to be in; but constantly employed in committing acts of hostility upon the Graces. He throws anywhere, but down his throat, whatever he means to drink; and only mangles what he means to carve. Inattentive to all the regards of social life, he mis-times or mis-places everything. He disputes with heat, and indiscriminately; mindless of the rank, character and situation of the several gradations of familiarity or respect; he is exactly the same to his superiors, his equals, and his inferiors; and therefore, by a necessary consequence, absurd to two of the three. Is it possible to love such a man? No. The utmost I can do for him, is to consider him a respectable Hottentot.[1]

[1] "This character has been generally understood to be meant for Dr. Johnson; and I have no doubt that it was," says Boswell. "But I remember when the literary property of Lord Chesterfield's Letters was contested in the court of session in Scotland, and Mr. Henry Dundas, one of the counsel for the proprietors, read this character as an exhibition of Johnson,

I remember that when I came from Cambridge, I had acquired among the pedants of an illiberal seminary a sauciness of literature, a turn to satire and contempt, and a strong tendency to argumentation and contradiction. But I had been but a very little in the world, before I found that this would by no means do; and I immediately adopted the opposite character; I concealed what learning I had; I applauded often without approving; and I yielded commonly, without conviction. *Suaviter in modo* was my law and my prophets; and if I pleased (between you and me) it was much more owing to that than to any superior knowledge or merit of my own.

A propos, the word *pleasing* puts one in mind of Lady Hervey: pray tell her, that I declare her responsible to me for your pleasing; that I consider her as a pleasing Falstaff, who not only pleases herself, but is the cause of pleasing in others; that I know she can make anything of anybody; and that, as your governess, if she does not make you please, it must be only because she will not, and not because she cannot. I hope you are, *du bois dont on en fait*; and if so, she is so good a sculptor, that I am sure she can give you whatever form she pleases. A versatility of manners is as necessary in social, as a versatility of parts is in political life. One must often yield, in order to prevail: one must humble one's-self, to be exalted; one must, like St. Paul, become all things to all men, to gain some; and (by the way) men are taken by the same means, *mutatis mutandis*, that women are gained; by gentleness, insinuation, and submission; and these lines of Mr. Dryden's will hold to a minister as well as to a mistress.

> The prostrate lover, when he lowest lies,
> But stoops to conquer, and but kneels to rise.[1]

Lord Hailes, one of the judges, maintained, with some warmth, that it was not intended as a portrait of Johnson, but of a late noble lord, distinguished for abstruse science. I have heard Johnson himself talk of the character, and say that it was meant for George, Lord Lyttelton, in which I could by no means agree; for his lordship had nothing of that violence which is a conspicuous feature in the composition. Finding that my illustrious friend could not bear to have it supposed that it might be meant for him, I said laughingly that there was one *trait* which unquestionably did not belong to him—*he throws his meat anywhere but down his throat.* 'Sir,' said he, 'Lord Chesterfield never saw me eat in his life!'" (*Life of Dr. Johnson*, ad ann. 1754). Dr. Birkbeck Hill, however, has shown (*Dr. Johnson, his Friends, his Critics*) that Dr. Johnson was not intended in this passage, but Mr. (afterwards Lord) Lyttelton.

[1] Dryden's *Amphitryon*, Act III; another version is "submits to conquer." Goldsmith's comedy, *She Stoops to Conquer*, was first acted on March 15, 1773.

In the course of the world, the qualifications of the cameleon are often necessary; nay, they must be carried a little farther, and exerted a little sooner; for you should, to a certain degree, take the hue of either the man or the woman that you want, and wish to be upon terms with. *A propos,* Have you yet found out at Paris any friendly and hospitable Madame de Lursay, *qui veut bien se charger du soin de vous éduquer?* And have you had any occasion of representing to her, *qu'elle faisoit donc des nœuds?* But I ask your pardon, Sir, for the abruptness of the question, and acknowledge that I am meddling with matters that are out of my department. However, in matters of less importance I desire to be *de vos secrets le fidèle dépositaire.* Trust me with the general turn and colour of your amusements at Paris. Is it *le fracas du grand monde, comédies, bals, opéras, cour,* etc.? Or is it *des petits sociétés moins bruyantes mais pas pour cela moins agréables?*

Where are you the most *établi?* Where are you *le petit Stanhope? Voyez-vous encore jour à quelque arrangement honnête?* Have you made any acquaintance among the young Frenchmen who ride at your Academy; and who are they? Send me this sort of chit-chat in your letters, which, by the bye, I wish you would honour me with somewhat oftener. If you frequent any of the myriads of polite Englishmen who infest Paris, who are they? Have you finished with Abbé Nollet,[1] and are you *au fait* of all the properties and effects of *air?* Were I inclined to quibble, I would say, that the effects of air, at least, are best to be learned of Marcel. If you have quite done with l'Abbé Nollet, ask my friend l'Abbé Sallier[2] to recommend to you some meagre philomath, to teach you a little geometry and astronomy; not enough to absorb your attention, and puzzle your intellects, but only enough, not to be grossly ignorant of either. I have of late been a sort of an *astronome malgré moi,* by bringing last Monday, into the House of Lords, a bill for reforming our present Calendar, and taking the New Style. Upon which occasion I was obliged to talk some astronomical jargon, of which I did not understand one word, but got it by heart, and spoke it by rote from a master. I wished that I had known a little more of it myself; and so

---

[1] Jean Antoine Nollet (born 1700, died 1770) was lecturer on experimental philosophy to the Duke of Savoy, and afterwards professor of physics in Paris.

[2] Claude Sallier (born 1685, died 1761) was an active and distinguished member of the Académie des Inscriptions, to which he contributed a great number of interesting essays.

much I would have you know. But the great and necessary knowledge of all is, to know yourself and others: this knowledge requires great attention and long experience; exert the former, and may you have the latter! Adieu.

P.S. I have this moment received your letters of the 27th February, and the 2d March, N.S. The seal shall be done as soon as possible. I am glad that you are employed in Lord Albemarle's bureau; it will teach you, at least the mechanical part of that business, such as folding, entering, and docketing letters; for you must not imagine that you are into the *fin fin* of the correspondence, nor indeed is it fit that you should at your age. However, use yourself to secrecy as to the letters you either read or write, that in time you may be trusted with *secret, very secret, separate, apart,* etc. I am sorry that this business interferes with your riding; I hope it is but seldom; but I insist upon its not interfering with your dancing-master, who is at this time the most useful and necessary of all the masters you have or can have.

MY DEAR FRIEND,

I mentioned to you, some time ago, a sentence, which I would most earnestly wish you always to retain in your thoughts and observe in your conduct. It is *suaviter in modo, fortiter in re.* I do not know any one rule so unexceptionally useful and necessary in every part of life. I shall therefore take it for my text to-day; and as old men love preaching, and I have some right to preach to you, I here present you with my sermon upon these words. To proceed then regularly and *pulpitically*; I will first show you, my beloved, the necessary connexion of the two members of my text, *suaviter in modo, fortiter in re.* In the next place, I shall set forth the advantages and utility resulting from a strict observance of the precept contained in my text; and conclude with an application of the whole. The *suaviter in modo* alone would degenerate and sink into a mean, timid complaisance, and passiveness, if not supported and dignified by the *fortiter in re*; which would also run into impetuosity and brutality if not tempered and softened by the *suaviter in modo*; however, they are seldom united. The warm choleric man with strong animal spirits despises the *suaviter in modo*, and thinks to carry all before him by the *fortiter in re.* He may, possibly, by great accidents, now and then succeed, when he has only weak and timid people to deal with; but his general fate will be to shock, offend, be hated, and fail. On the other hand, the cunning, crafty man, thinks to gain all ends by the *suaviter in modo* only: *he becomes all things to all men*; he seems to have no opinion of his own, and servilely adopts the present opinion of the present person; he insinuates himself only into the esteem of fools, but is soon detected, and surely despised by everybody else. The wise man (who differs as much from the cunning as from the choleric man) alone joins the *suaviter in modo* with the *fortiter in re*.

Now to the advantages arising from the strict observance of this precept. If you are in authority, and have a right to command, your commands delivered *suaviter in modo* will be willingly, cheerfully, and consequently well obeyed; whereas, if given only *fortiter*, that is brutally, they will rather, as Tacitus says, be interpreted than executed. For my own part, if I bid my footman bring me a glass of wine in a rough, insulting manner, I should expect that in obeying me he would contrive to spill some of it upon me; and I am sure I should deserve it. A cool, steady resolution should show, that where you have a right to command you will be obeyed; but, at the same time, a gentleness in the manner of enforcing that obedience should make it a cheerful one, and soften, as much as possible, the mortifying consciousness of inferiority. If you are to ask a favour, or even to solicit your due, you must do it *suaviter in modo*, or you will give those who have a mind to refuse you either, a pretence to do it by resenting the manner; but, on the other hand, you must, by a steady perseverance and decent tenaciousness, show the *fortiter in re*.

The right motives are seldom the true ones of men's actions, especially of kings, ministers, and people in high stations; who often give to importunity, and fear what they would refuse to justice or to merit. By the *suaviter in modo* engage their hearts, if you can; at least, prevent the pretence of offence; but take care to show enough of the *fortiter in re* to extort from their love of ease, or their fear, what you might in vain hope for from their justice or good-nature. People in high life are hardened to the wants and distresses of mankind as surgeons are to their bodily pains; they see and hear of them all day long, and even of so many simulated ones, that they do not know which are real and which not. Other sentiments are therefore to be applied to than those of mere justice and humanity; their favour must be captivated by the *suaviter in modo*; their love of ease disturbed by unwearied importunity, or their fears wrought upon by a decent intimation of implacable, cool resentment; this is the true *fortiter in re*. This precept is the only way I know in the world of being loved without being despised, and feared without being hated. It constitutes the dignity of character, which every wise man must endeavour to establish.

Now to apply what has been said, and so conclude.

If you find that you have a hastiness in your temper, which unguardedly breaks out into indiscreet sallies or rough expressions, to either your superiors, your equals, or your inferiors, watch it narrowly, check it carefully, and call the *suaviter in modo* to your assistance; at the first impulse of passion be silent till you can be soft. Labour even to get the command of your countenance so well, that those emotions may not be read in it; a most unspeakable advantage in business. On the other hand, let no complaisance, no gentleness of temper, no weak desire of pleasing on your part, no wheedling, coaxing, nor flattery, on other people's, make you recede one jot from any point that reason and prudence have bid you pursue; but return to the charge, persist, persevere, and you will find most things attainable that are possible. A yielding, timid meekness is always abused and insulted by the unjust and the unfeeling; but when sustained by the *fortiter in re*, is always respected, commonly successful. In your friendships and connections, as well as in your enmities, this rule is particularly useful; let your firmness and vigour preserve and invite attachments to you; but, at the same time, let your manner hinder the enemies of your friends and dependants from becoming yours; let your enemies be disarmed by the gentleness of your manner, but let them feel at the same time the steadiness of your just resentment; for there is great difference between bearing malice, which is always ungenerous, and a resolute self-defence, which is always prudent and justifiable. In negotiations with foreign Ministers, remember the *fortiter in re*; give up no point, accept of no expedient, till the utmost necessity reduces you to it, and even then dispute the ground inch by inch; but then, while you are contending with the minister *fortiter in re*, remember to gain the man by the *suaviter in modo*. If you engage his heart, you have a fair chance for imposing upon his understanding, and determining his will. Tell him in a frank and gallant manner that your ministerial wrangles do not lessen your personal regard for his merit; but that, on the contrary, his zeal and ability in the service of his master increase it; and that of all things you desire to make a good friend of so good a servant. By these means you may and will very often be a gainer; you never can be a loser.

Some people cannot gain upon themselves to be easy and civil to those who are either their rivals, competitors, or opposers, though, independently of those accidental circumstances, they would like and esteem them. They betray a shyness and an awkwardness in company with them, and catch at any little thing to expose them; and so, from temporary and only occasional opponents, make them their personal enemies. This is exceedingly weak and detrimental, as indeed is all humour in business; which can only be carried on successfully by unadulterated good policy and right reasoning. In such situations I would be more particularly and *noblement* civil, easy, and frank, with the man whose designs I traversed; this is commonly called generosity and magnanimity, but is, in truth, good sense and policy.

The manner is often as important as the matter, sometimes more so; a favour may make an enemy, and an injury may make a friend, according to the different manner in which they are severally done. The countenance, the address, the words, the enunciation, the Graces, add great efficacy to the *suaviter in modo*, and great dignity to the *fortiter in re*; and consequently they deserve the utmost attention.

From what has been said I conclude with this observation: that gentleness of manners, with firmness of mind, is a short but full description of human perfection, on this side of religious and moral duties; that you may be seriously convinced of this truth, and show it in your life and conversation, is the most sincere and ardent wish of,   Yours.

MY DEAR FRIEND,   London, March 18, O.S. 1751.

I acquainted you in a former letter that I had brought a bill into the House of Lords, for correcting and reforming our present calendar, which is the Julian, and for adopting the Gregorian. I will now give you a more particular account of that affair, from which reflections will naturally occur to you that I hope may be useful, and which I fear you have not made. It was notorious, that the Julian calendar was erroneous, and had overcharged the solar year with eleven days. Pope Gregory

XIII corrected this error; his reformed calendar was immediately received by all the Catholic Powers of Europe, and afterwards adopted by all the Protestant ones, except Russia, Sweden, and England. It was not, in my opinion, very honourable for England to remain in a gross and avowed error, especially in such company; the inconvenience of it was likewise felt by all those who had foreign correspondences, whether political or mercantile. I determined, therefore, to attempt the reformation; I consulted the best lawyers, and the most skilful astronomers, and we cooked up a bill for that purpose. But then my difficulty began; I was to bring in this bill, which was necessarily composed of law jargon and astronomical calculations, to both which I am an utter stranger. However, it was absolutely necessary to make the House of Lords think that I knew something of the matter, and also to make them believe that they knew something of it themselves, which they do not. For my own part, I could just as soon have talked Celtic or Sclavonian to them as astronomy, and they would have understood me full as well; so I resolved to do better than speak to the purpose, and to please instead of informing them. I gave them, therefore, only an historical account of calendars, from the Egyptian down to the Gregorian, amusing them now and then with little episodes; but I was particularly attentive to the choice of my words, to the harmony and roundness of my periods, to my elocution, to my action. This succeeded, and ever will succeed; they thought I informed, because I pleased them; and many of them said, that I had made the whole very clear to them, when, God knows, I had not even attempted it. Lord Macclesfield, who had the greatest share in forming the bill, and who is one of the greatest mathematicians and astronomers in Europe,[1] spoke afterwards with infinite knowledge, and all the clearness that so intricate a matter would admit of; but as his words, his periods, and his utterance were not near so good as mine, the preference was most unanimously, though most unjustly, given to me.

This will ever be the case; every numerous assembly is *mob*, let the individuals who compose it be what they will. Mere reason and good sense is never to be talked to a mob; their passions, their sentiments, their senses, and their seeming interests, are alone to be applied to. Understanding they have collectively none; but they have ears and eyes, which must be

[1] George, second Earl of Macclesfield. In November 1751 he was unanimously elected President of the Royal Society. He died in 1764.

flattered and seduced; and this can only be done by eloquence, tuneful periods, graceful action, and all the various parts of oratory.

When you come into the House of Commons, if you imagine that speaking plain and unadorned sense and reason will do your business, you will find yourself most grossly mistaken. As a speaker, you will be ranked only according to your eloquence, and by no means according to your matter; everybody knows the matter almost alike, but few can adorn it. I was early convinced of the importance and powers of eloquence, and from that moment I applied myself to it. I resolved not to utter one word, even in common conversation, that should not be the most expressive and the most elegant that the language could supply me with for that purpose; by which means I have acquired such a certain degree of habitual eloquence, that I must now really take some pains, if I would express myself very inelegantly. I want to inculcate this known truth into you, which you seem by no means to be convinced of yet—that ornaments are at present your only objects. Your sole business now is to shine, not to weigh. Weight without lustre is lead. You had better talk trifles elegantly, to the most trifling woman, than coarse inelegant sense to the most solid man. You had better return a dropped fan genteelly, than give a thousand pounds awkwardly; and you had better refuse a favour gracefully, than grant it clumsily. Manner is all in everything; it is by manner only that you can please, and consequently rise. All your Greek will never advance you from Secretary to Envoy, or from Envoy to Ambassador; but your address, your manner, your air, if good, very probably may. Marcel can be of much more use to you than Aristotle. I would, upon my word, much rather that you had Lord Bolingbroke's style and eloquence, in speaking and writing, than all the learning of the Academy of Sciences, the Royal Society, and the two Universities united.

Having mentioned Lord Bolingbroke's style, which is, undoubtedly, infinitely superior to anybody's, I would have you read his works, which you have, over and over again, with particular attention to his style. Transcribe, imitate, emulate it, if possible; that would be of real use to you in the House of Commons, in negotiations, in conversation; with that, you may justly hope to please, to persuade, to seduce, to impose; and you will fail in those articles, in proportion as you fall short of it. Upon the whole, lay aside, during your year's residence at Paris, all thoughts of all that dull fellows call solid, and exert your utmost care to acquire what people of fashion call shining. *Prenez l'éclat et le brillant d'un galant homme.*

Among the commonly-called little things to which you do not attend, your handwriting is one, which is indeed shamefully bad, and illiberal; it is neither the hand of a man of business, nor of a gentleman, but of a truant schoolboy; as soon, therefore, as you have done with Abbé Nollet, pray get an excellent writing-master, since you think that you cannot teach yourself to write what hand you please; and let him teach you to write a genteel, legible, liberal hand, and quick, not the hand of a *procureur*, or a writing-master, but that sort of hand in which the first *commis* in foreign bureaus commonly write; for I tell you truly, that were I Lord Albemarle, nothing should remain in my bureau written in your present hand. From hand to arms the transition is natural;—is the carriage and motion of your arms so too? The motion of the arms is the most material part of a man's air, especially in dancing; the feet are not near so material. If a man dances well from the waist upwards, wears his hat well, and moves his head properly, he dances well. Do the women say that you dress well? for that is necessary, too, for a young fellow. Have you *un goût vif*, or a passion for any body? I do not ask for whom; an Iphigenia would both give you the desire, and teach you the means to please.

In a fortnight or three weeks you will see Sir Charles Hotham at Paris, in his way to Toulouse, where he is to stay a year or two. Pray be very civil to him, but do not carry him into company, except presenting him to Lord Albemarle; for, as he is not to stay at Paris above a week, we do not desire that he should taste of that dissipation: you may show him a play and an opera. Adieu, my dear child!

MY DEAR FRIEND,   London, March 25, O.S. 1751.

What a happy period of your life is this! Pleasure is now, and ought to be, your business. While you were younger, dry rules, and unconnected words, were the unpleasant objects of your labours. When you grow older, the anxiety, the vexations, the disappointments, inseparable from public business, will require the greatest share of your time and attention; your pleasures may, indeed, conduce to your business, and **your** business will quicken your pleasures; but still your time must, at least, be divided; whereas now it is wholly your own, and cannot be so well employed as in the pleasures of a gentleman. The world is now the only book you want, and almost the only one you ought to read; that necessary book can only be read in company, in public places, at meals, and in *ruelles*. You must be in the pleasures, in order to learn the manners of good company. In premeditated, or in formal business, people conceal, or at least endeavour to conceal, their characters; whereas pleasures discover them, and the heart breaks out through the guard of the understanding. Those are often propitious moments for skilful negotiators to improve. In your destination particularly, the able conduct of pleasures is of infinite use; to keep a good table, and to do the honours of it gracefully, and *sur le ton de la bonne compagnie*, is absolutely necessary for a foreign minister. There is a certain light chit-chat, useful to keep off improper and too serious subjects, which is only to be learned in the pleasures of good company. In truth, it may be trifling; but trifling as it is, a man of parts, and experience of the world, will give an agreeable turn to it. *L'art de badiner agréablement* is by no means to be despised.

An engaging address, and turn to gallantry, is often of very great service to foreign ministers. Women have, directly, or indirectly, a good deal to say in most Courts. The late Lord Stafford [1] governed, for a considerable time, the Court of Berlin, and made his own fortune, by being well with Madame de Wartemberg, the first King of Prussia's mistress. I could name many other instances of that kind. That sort of agreeable *caquet de femmes*, the necessary fore-runner of closer conferences, is only to be got by frequenting women of the first fashion, *et qui donnent le ton*. Let every other book then give way to this great and necessary book, the World; of which there are so many various readings, that it requires a great deal of time and attention to understand it well: contrary to all other books, you must not stay at home, but go abroad to read it; and when you seek it abroad, you will not find it in booksellers' shops and stalls, but in Courts, in *hôtels*, at entertainments, balls, assemblies, spectacles, etc. Put yourself upon the foot of an easy, domestic, but polite familiarity and intimacy, in the several French houses to which you have been introduced. Cultivate them, frequent them, and show a desire

[1] Thomas Wentworth Lord Raby first Earl of Strafford of the second creation. He died in 1739.

of becoming *enfant de la maison*. Get acquainted as much as you can with *les gens de cour*; and observe, carefully, how politely they can differ, and how civilly they can hate; how easy and idle they can seem in the multiplicity of their business; and how they can lay hold of the proper moments to carry it on, in the midst of their pleasures. Courts, alone, teach versatility and politeness; for there is no living there without them. Lord Albemarle has, I hear, and am very glad of it, put you into the hands of Messieurs de Bissy. Profit by that, and beg of them to let you attend them in all the companies of Versailles and Paris. One of them, at least, will naturally carry you to Madame de la Valières, unless she is discarded by this time, and Gelliot [1] retaken. Tell them frankly, *que vous cherchez à vous former, que vous êtes en main de maîtres, s'ils veulent bien s'en donner la peine.* Your profession has this agreeable peculiarity in it, which is, that it is connected with, and promoted by pleasures; and it is the only one in which a thorough knowledge of the world, polite manners, and an engaging address, are absolutely necessary. If a lawyer knows his law, a parson his divinity, and a *financier* his calculations, each may make a figure and a fortune in his profession, without great knowledge of the world, and without the manners of gentlemen. But your profession throws you into all the intrigues, and cabals, as well as pleasures, of Courts; in those windings and labyrinths, a knowledge of the world, a discernment of characters, a suppleness and versatility of mind, and an elegancy of manners, must be your clue; you must know how to soothe and lull the monsters that guard, and how to address and gain the fair that keep, the golden fleece. These are the arts and the accomplishments absolutely necessary for a foreign minister; in which it must be owned, to our shame, that most other nations out-do the English; and, *cæteris paribus*, a French minister will get the better of an English one, at any third Court in Europe. The French have something more *liant*, more insinuating, and engaging in their manner, than we have. An English minister shall have resided seven years at a Court, without having made any one personal connection there, or without being intimate and domestic in any one house. He is always the English minister, and never naturalised. He receives his orders, demands an audience, writes an acccount of it to his Court, and his business is done. A French minister, on the contrary, has not been six weeks at a Court, without having, by a thousand

[1] A famous opera-singer at Paris.

little attentions, insinuated himself into some degree of favour with the Prince, his wife, his mistress, his favourite, and his minister. He has established himself upon a familiar and domestic footing, in a dozen of the best houses of the place, where he has accustomed the people to be not only easy, but unguarded before him; he makes himself at home there, and they think him so. By these means he knows the interior of those Courts, and can almost write prophecies to his own, from the knowledge he has of the characters, the humours, the abilities, or the weaknesses, of the actors. The Cardinal d'Ossat[1] was looked upon at Rome as an Italian, and not as a French Cardinal; and Monsieur d'Avaux,[2] wherever he went, was never considered as a foreign minister, but as a native, and a personal friend. Mere plain truth, sense, and knowledge, will by no means do alone in Courts; art and ornaments must come to their assistance. Humours must be flattered; the *mollia tempora* must be studied and known; confidence, acquired by seeming frankness, and profited of by silent skill. And, above all, you must gain and engage the heart, to betray the understanding to you. *Hæ tibi erunt artes.*

The death of the Prince of Wales,[3] who was more beloved for his affability and good-nature, than esteemed for his steadiness and conduct, has given concern to many, and apprehensions to all. The great difference of the ages of the King and Prince George, presents the prospect of a minority; a disagreeable prospect for any nation! But it is to be hoped, and is most probable, that the King, who is now perfectly recovered of his late indisposition, may live to see his grandson of age.[4] He is, seriously, a most hopeful boy; gentle and good-natured, with good sound sense. This event has made all sorts of people here historians, as well as politicians. Our histories are rummaged for all the particular circumstances of the six minorities we have had since the conquest, viz. those of Henry III, Edward III, Richard II, Henry VI, Edward V, and Edward VI; and the reasonings, the speculations, the conjectures, and the predictions, you will easily imagine, must

[1] Arnaud d'Ossat, afterwards cardinal, negotiated at Rome the reconciliation of Henri IV with the Pope. His *Correspondence*, which first appeared in 1624, has been several times reprinted. He died in 1604.
[2] Jean Antoine, Comte d'Avaux, was the plenipotentiary of France at the Conferences of Nimeguen, and afterwards ambassador in Holland until the war in 1688. His *Lettres et Négociations* were published at The Hague in 1710.
[3] Frederick, Prince of Wales, died March 20, 1751.
[4] George III was twenty-two when he succeeded in 1760.

be innumerable and endless, in this nation, where every porter is a consummate politician. Doctor Swift says, very humorously, "Every man knows that he understands religion and politics, though he never learned them; but many people are conscious they do not understand many other sciences, from having never learned them." Adieu!

MY DEAR FRIEND,　　　　　　London, April 22, O.S. 1751.

I apply to you now as to the greatest *virtuoso* of this, or perhaps any other age; one whose superior judgment and distinguishing eye hindered the King of Poland from buying a bad picture at Venice, and whose decisions in the realms of *virtù* are final and without appeal. Now to the point: I have had a catalogue sent me, *d'une vente à l'aimable de tableaux des plus grands maîtres appartenans au Sieur Araignon Apéren, valet-de-chambre de la Reine, sur le quai de la Mégisserie au coin de l'Arche Marion.* There I observe two large pictures of Titian, as described in the enclosed page of the catalogue, No. 18, which I should be glad to purchase upon two conditions: the first is, that they be undoubted originals of Titian in good preservation; and the other, that they come cheap. To ascertain the first (but without disparaging your skill), I wish you would get some undoubted connoisseurs to examine them carefully; and if, upon such critical examination, they should be unanimously allowed to be undisputed originals of Titian, and well preserved, then comes the second point, the price; I will not go above two hundred pounds sterling for the two together; but as much less as you can get them for. I acknowledge that two hundred pounds seems to be a very small sum for two undoubted Titians of that size; but, on the other hand, as large Italian pictures are now out of fashion at Paris, where fashion decides of everything, and as these pictures are too large for common rooms, they may, possibly, come within the price above limited. I leave the whole of this transaction (the price excepted, which I will not exceed) to your consummate skill and prudence, with proper advice joined to them. Should you happen to buy them for that price, carry them to your own lodgings, and get a frame made to the second, which I observe has none, exactly the same with the other frame, and have the old one new gilt; and then get them carefully packed up, and sent me by Rouen.

I hear much of your conversing with *les beaux esprits* at Paris;

I am very glad of it; it gives a degree of reputation, especially at Paris; and their conversation is generally instructive, though sometimes affected. It must be owned, that the polite conversation of the men and women of fashion at Paris, though not always very deep, is much less futile and frivolous than ours here. It turns at least upon some subject, something of taste, some point of history, criticism, and even philosophy, which, though probably not quite so solid as Mr. Locke's, is however better, and more becoming rational beings, than our frivolous dissertations upon the weather or upon whist. Monsieur Duclos[1] observes, and I think very justly, *qu'il y a à présent en France une fermentation universelle de la raison qui tend à se développer*. Whereas, I am sorry to say, that here that fermentation seems to have been over some years ago, the spirit evaporated, and only the dregs left. Moreover *les beaux esprits* at Paris are commonly well-bred, which ours very frequently are not; with the former your manners will be formed; with the latter, wit must generally be compounded for at the expense of manners. Are you acquainted with Marivaux, who has certainly studied, and is well acquainted with the heart; but who refines so much upon its *plis et replis*, and describes them so affectedly, that he often is unintelligible to his readers, and sometimes so I dare say to himself?

Do you know *Crébillon le fils*? He is a fine painter, and a pleasing writer; his characters are admirable and his reflections just. Frequent these people, and be glad, but not proud, of frequenting them; never boast of it as a proof of your own merit, nor insult, in a manner, other companies, by telling them affectedly what you, Montesquieu, and Fontenelle were talking of the other day; as I have known many people do here, with regard to Pope and Swift, who had never been twice in company with either; nor carry into other companies the tone of those meetings of *beaux esprits*. Talk literature, taste, philosophy, etc., with them, *à la bonne heure*; but then with the same ease, and more *enjouement*, talk *pompons, moires*, etc., with Madame de Blot, if she requires it. Almost every subject in the world has its proper time and place; in which no one is above or below discussion. The point is, to talk well upon the subject you talk upon; and the most trifling, frivolous subjects will still give a man of parts an opportunity of showing them.

[1] He also wrote *l'Histoire de Louis XI, Mémoires Sécrets des Regnes de Louis XIV et de Louis XV*. Rousseau used to say of his character, that he was *un homme droit et adroit*.

L'usage du grande monde can alone teach that. This was the distinguishing characteristic of Alcibiades, and a happy one it was; that he could occasionally, and with so much ease, adopt the most different, and even the most opposite habits and manners, that each seemed natural to him. Prepare yourself for the great world, as the *athletæ* used to do for their exercises; oil (if I may use that expression) your mind and your manners, to give them the necessary suppleness and flexibility; strength alone will not do, as young people are too apt to think.

How do your exercises go on? Can you manage a pretty vigorous *sauteur* between the pillars? Are you got into stirrups yet? *Faites-vous assaut aux armes?* But above all, what does Marcel say of you? Is he satisfied? Pray be more particular in your accounts of yourself; for, though I have frequent accounts of you from others, I desire to have your own too. Adieu!

Yours truly and tenderly.

My Dear Friend,   London, May 6, O.S. 1751.

The best authors are always the severest critics of their own works; they revise, correct, file, and polish them, till they think they have brought them to perfection. Considering you as my work, I do not look upon myself as a bad author, and am therefore a severe critic. I examine narrowly into the least inaccuracy or inelegancy, in order to correct, not to expose them, and that the work may be perfect at last. You are, I know, exceedingly improved in your air, address, and manners, since you have been at Paris; but still there is, I believe, room for farther improvement, before you come to that perfection which I have set my heart upon seeing you arrive at; and till that moment I must continue filing and polishing. In a letter that I received by last post, from a friend of yours at Paris, there was this paragraph: *Sans flatterie, j'ai l'honneur de vous assurer que Monsieur Stanhope réussit ici au delà de ce qu'on attendroit d'une personne de son âge; il voit très bonne compagnie, et ce petit ton, qu'on regardoit d'abord comme un peu décidé et un peu brusque, n'est rien moins que cela, parcequ'il est l'effet de la franchise, accompagnée de la politesse et de la déférence. Il s'étudie à plaire, et il y réussit. Madame de Puisieux[1] en parloit l'autre jour avec complaisance et intérêt: vous en serez content à tous égards.* This is extremely well, and I rejoice at it; one little

[1] The Marquis de Puisieux was at this time Minister of Foreign Affairs.

circumstance only may, and I hope will, be altered for the better. Take pains to undeceive those who thought that *petit ton un peu décidé et un peu brusque*; as it is not meant so, let it not appear so. Compose your countenance to an air of gentleness and *douceur*, use some expressions of diffidence of your own opinion, and deference to other people's; such as *s'il m'est permis de le dire—je croirois—ne seroit-ce pas plutôt comme cela? Au moins j'ai tout lieu de me défier de moi-même;* such mitigating, engaging words do by no means weaken your argument; but, on the contrary, make it more powerful, by making it more pleasing. If it is a quick and hasty manner of speaking that people mistake *pour décidé et brusque,* prevent their mistakes for the future, by speaking more deliberately, and taking a softer tone of voice; as in this case you are free from the guilt, be free from the suspicion too. Mankind, as I have often told you, is more governed by appearances, than by realities; and, with regard to opinion, one had better be really rough and hard, with the appearance of gentleness and softness, than just the reverse. Few people have penetration enough to discover, attention enough to observe, or even concern enough to examine, beyond the exterior; they take their notions from the surface, and go no deeper; they commend, as the gentlest and best-natured man in the world, that man who has the most engaging exterior manner, though possibly they have been but once in his company. An air, a tone of voice, a composure of countenance to mildness and softness, which are all easily acquired, do the business; and without farther examination, and possibly with the contrary qualities, that man is reckoned the gentlest, the modestest, and the best-natured man alive. Happy the man who, with a certain fund of parts and knowledge, gets acquainted with the world early enough to make it his bubble, at an age when most people are the bubbles of the world! for that is the common case of youth. They grow wiser, when it is too late; and ashamed and vexed at having been bubbles so long, too often turn knaves at last. Do not therefore trust to appearances and outside yourself, but pay other people with them; because you may be sure that nine in ten of mankind do, and ever will, trust to them.

This is by no means a criminal or blameable simulation, if not used with an ill intention. I am by no means blameable in desiring to have other people's good word, good will, and affection, if I do not mean to abuse them. Your heart, I know, is good, your sense is sound, and your knowledge extensive.

What then remains for you to do? Nothing but to adorn those fundamental qualifications, with such engaging and captivating manners, softness, and gentleness, as will endear you to those who are able to judge of your real merit, and which always stand in the stead of merit with those who are not. I do not mean by this to recommend to you *le fade doucereux*, the insipid softness of a gentle fool; no, assert your own opinion, oppose other people's when wrong; but let your manner, your air, your terms, and your tone of voice, be soft and gentle, and that easily and naturally, not affectedly. Use palliatives when you contradict; such as, *I may be mistaken, I am not sure, but I believe, I should rather think,* etc. Finish any argument or dispute with some little good-humoured pleasantry, to show that you are neither hurt yourself, nor meant to hurt your antagonist; for an argument kept up a good while often occasions a temporary alienation on each side. Pray observe particularly, in those French people who are distinguished by that character, *cette douceur de mœurs et de manières,* which they talk of so much, and value so justly; see in what it consists; in mere trifles, and most easy to be acquired, where the heart is really good. Imitate, copy it, till it becomes habitual and easy to you. Without a compliment to you, I take it to be the only thing you now want; nothing will sooner give it you than a real passion, or, at least, *un goût vif,* for some woman of fashion; and, as I suppose that you have either the one or the other by this time, you are consequently in the best school. Besides this, if you were to say to Lady Hervey, Madame Monconseil, or such others as you look upon to be your friends, *On dit que j'ai un certain petit de trop décidé et trop brusque, l'intention pourtant n'y est pas; corrigez-moi, je vous en supplie, et châtiez-moi même publiquement quand vous me trouverez sur le fait. Ne me passez rien, poussez votre critique jusqu'à l'excès; un juge aussi éclairé est en droit d'être sévère, et je vous promets que le coupable tâchera de se corriger.*

Yesterday I had two of your acquaintances to dine with me, Baron B. and his companion Monsieur S. I cannot say of the former, *qu'il est pétri de grâces*; and I would rather advise him to go and settle quietly at home, than to think of improving himself by farther travels. *Ce n'est pas le bois dont on en fait.* His companion is much better, though he has a strong *tocco di tedesco.* They both spoke well of you, and so far I liked them both. *Comment vont nos affaires avec l'aimable petite Blot?*

*Se prête-t-elle à vos fleurettes, êtes vous censé être sur les rangs?
Madame Dupin est-elle votre Madame de Lursay, et fait-elle
quelquefois des nœuds? Seriez-vous son Meilcour? Elle a, dit
on, de la douceur, de l'esprit, des manières; il y a à apprendre
dans un tel apprentissage.* A woman like her, who has always
pleased, and often been pleased, can best teach the art of
pleasing—that art without which *ogni fatica è vana.* Marcel's
lectures are no small part of that art; they are the engaging
forerunner of all other accomplishments. Dress is also an
article not to be neglected, and I hope you do not neglect it;
it helps in the *premier abord*, which is often decisive. By dress,
I mean your clothes being well made, fitting you, in the fashion
and not above it; your hair well done, and a general cleanliness
and spruceness in your person. I hope you take infinite care
of your teeth; the consequences of neglecting the mouth are
serious, not only to one's self but to others. In short, my dear
child, neglect nothing; a little more will complete the whole.
Adieu! I have not heard from you these three weeks, which
I think a great while.

MY DEAR FRIEND,   London, May 10, O.S. 1751.

I received yesterday, at the same time, your letters of the
4th and the 11th, N.S., and being much more careful of my
commissions than you are of yours, I do not delay one moment
sending you my final instructions concerning the pictures.
The man you allow to be a Titian, and in good preservation;
the woman is an indifferent and a damaged picture; but, as
I want them for furniture for a particular room, companions
are necessary; and therefore I am willing to take the woman,
for better for worse, upon account of the man; and if she is not
too much damaged, I can have her tolerably repaired, as many
a fine woman is, by a skilful hand here; but then I expect the
lady should be, in a manner, thrown into the bargain with
the man; and in this state of affairs, the woman being worth
little or nothing, I will not go above fourscore *louis* for the two
together.

As for the Rembrandt you mention, though it is very cheap
if good, I do not care for it. I love *la belle nature*; Rembrandt
paints caricatures. Now for your own commissions, which you
seem to have forgotten. You mention nothing of the patterns
which you received by Monsieur Tollot, though I told you in
a former letter, which you must have had before the date of

your last, that I should stay till I received the patterns pitched
upon by your ladies; for as to the instructions which you sent
me in Madame Monconseil's hand, I could find no mohairs in
London that exactly answered that description. I shall,
therefore, wait till you send me (which you may easily do in a
letter) the patterns chosen by your three Graces.

I would, by all means, have you go now and then, for two or
three days, to Maréchal Coigny's,[1] at Orli; it is but a proper
civility to that family, which has been particularly civil to you;
and, moreover, I would have you familiarise yourself with,
and learn the interior and domestic manners of, people of that
rank and fashion. I also desire that you will frequent Versailles
and St. Cloud, at both which Courts you have been received
with distinction. Profit by that distinction, and familiarise
yourself at both. Great Courts are the seats of true good-
breeding; you are to live at Courts, lose no time in learning
them. Go and stay sometimes at Versailles for three or four
days, where you will be domestic in the best families, by means
of your friend Madame de Puisieux, and mine, L'Abbé de la
Ville. Go to the King's and the Dauphin's levées, and distinguish yourself from the rest of your countrymen, who, I dare
say, never go there when they can help it. Though the young
Frenchman of fashion may not be worth forming intimate
connections with, they are well worth making acquaintance of;
and I do not see how you can avoid it, frequenting so many
good French houses as you do, where, to be sure, many of
them come. Be cautious how you contract friendships, but be
desirous, and even industrious, to obtain an universal acquaintance. Be easy, and even forward, in making new acquaintances;
that is the only way of knowing manners and characters in
general, which is at present your great object. You are *enfant
de famille* in three Ministers' houses; but I wish you had a
footing, at least, in thirteen; and that I should think you might
easily bring about by that common chain which, to a certain
degree, connects those you do not with those you do know.
For instance, I suppose that neither Lord Albemarle nor Marquis
de St. Germain would make the least difficulty to present you
to Comte Caunitz, the Nuncio, etc. *Il faut être rompu au monde*,
which can only be done by an extensive, various, and almost
universal acquaintance.

[1] François Comte de Coigny distinguished himself by his victories over
the Imperial forces at Parma and at Guastalla in 1734. He was raised to
the rank of Maréchal in 1741, and to a dukedom in 1747, and died in 1759.

When you have got your emaciated Philomath, I desire that his triangles, rhomboids, etc., may not keep you one moment out of the good company you would otherwise be in. Swallow all your learning in the morning, but digest it in company in the evenings. The reading of ten new characters is more your business now than the reading of twenty old books; showish and shining people always get the better of all others, though ever so solid. If you would be a great man in the world when you are old, shine and be showish in it while you are young; know everybody and endeavour to please everybody—I mean exteriorly, for fundamentally it is impossible. Try to engage the heart of every woman, and the affections of almost every man, you meet with. Madame Monconseil assures me that you are most surprisingly improved in your air, manners, and address; go on, my dear child, and never think that you are come to a sufficient degree of perfection; *nil actum reputans si quid superesset agendum*; and in those shining parts of the character of a gentleman, there is always something remaining to be acquired. Modes and manners vary in different places and at different times; you must keep pace with them, know them, and adopt them, wherever you find them. The great usage of the world, the knowledge of characters, the *brillant d'un galant homme*, is all that you now want. Study Marcel and the *beau monde* with great application, but read Homer and Horace only when you have nothing else to do. Pray who is *la belle Madame de Case*, whom I know you frequent? I like the epithet given her very well; if she deserves it, she deserves your attention too. A man of fashion should be gallant to a fine woman, though he does not make love to her, or may be otherwise engaged. *On lui doit des politesses, on fait l'éloge de ses charmes, et il n'en est ni plus ni moins pour cela:* it pleases, it flatters; you get their good word, and you lose nothing by it. These *gentillesses* should be accompanied, as indeed everything else should, with *un air, un ton de douceur et de politesse*.

Les Grâces must be of the party, or it will never do; and they are so easily had, that it is astonishing to me everybody has them not; they are sooner gained than any woman of common reputation and decency. Pursue them but with care and attention, and you are sure to enjoy them at last: without them, I am sure, you will never enjoy anybody else. You observe, truly, that Mr. —— is *gauche*; it is to be hoped that will mend with keeping company; and is yet pardonable in him, as just come from school. But reflect what you would think of a man, who had been any time in the world, and yet should be so awkward. For God's sake therefore, now think of nothing but shining, and even distinguishing yourself in the most polite Courts, by your air, your address, your manners, your politeness, your *douceur*, your graces. With those advantages (and not without them) take my word for it, you will get the better of all rivals, in business as well as in *ruelles*. Adieu. Send me your patterns by the next post, and also your instructions to Grevenkop about the seal, which you seem to have forgotten.

MY DEAR FRIEND,   Greenwich, June 6, O.S. 1751.

Solicitous and anxious as I have ever been to form your heart, your mind, and your manners, and to bring you as near perfection as the imperfection of our natures will allow, I have exhausted, in the course of our correspondence, all that my own mind could suggest, and have borrowed from others whatever I thought could be useful to you; but this has necessarily been interruptedly, and by snatches. It is now time, and you are of an age to review, and to weigh in your own mind, all that you have heard, and all that you have read, upon these subjects; and to form your own character, your conduct, and your manners, for the rest of your life, allowing for such improvements as a farther knowledge of the world will naturally give you. In this view, I would recommend to you to read, with the greatest attention, such books as treat particularly of those subjects, reflecting seriously upon them, and then comparing the speculation with the practice. For example, if you read in the morning some of La Rochefoucault's maxims, consider them, examine them well, and compare them with the real characters you meet with in the evening. Read La Bruyère in the morning, and see in the evening whether his pictures are like. Study the heart and the mind of man, and begin with your own. Meditation and reflection must lay the foundation of that knowledge; but experience and practice must, and alone can, complete it. Books, it is true, point out the operations of the mind, the sentiments of the heart, the influence of the passions—and so far they are of previous use; but without subsequent practice, experience, and observation, they are as ineffectual, and would even lead you into as many errors, in fact, as a map would do, if you were to take your notions of the towns and provinces from their delineations in it. A man would reap very little benefit by his travels, if he made them only in his closet upon a map of the whole world. Next to the two books that I have already mentioned, I do not know a better for you to read, and seriously reflect upon, than *Avis d'une mère à un fils, par la Marquise de Lambert*.[1] She was a woman of a superior understanding and knowledge of the world, had always kept the best company, was solicitous that her son should make a figure and a fortune in the world, and knew better than anybody how to point out the means. It is very short, and will take you much less time to read than you ought to employ in reflecting upon it after you have read it. Her son was in the army; she wished he might rise there; but she well knew that, in order to rise, he must first please. She says to him, therefore, *à l'égard de ceux dont vous dépendez, le premier mérite est de plaire*. And, in another place, *Dans les emplois subalternes vous ne vous soutenez que par les agrémens. Les maîtres sont comme les maîtresses; quelque service que vous leur ayez rendu, ils cessent de vous aimer quand vous cessez de leur plaire*. This, I can assure you, is at least as true in Courts as in camps, and possibly more so. If to your merit and knowledge you add the art of pleasing, you may very probably come in time to be Secretary of State; but, take my word for it, twice your merit and knowledge, without the art of pleasing, would, at most, raise you to the *important post* of Resident at Hamburgh or Ratisbon.[2] I need not tell you now, for I often have, and your own discernment must have told you, of what numberless little ingredients that art of pleasing is compounded, and how the want of the least of them lowers the whole; but the principal ingredient is, undoubtedly, *la douceur dans les manières*; nothing will give you this more than keeping company with your superiors. Madame Lambert tells her son, *que vos liaisons soient avec des personnes au dessus de vous, par là vous vous accoutumez au respect et à la politesse; avec ses égaux on se néglige, l'esprit s'assoupit*. She advises him, too, to frequent those people, and to see their inside; *il est bon d'approcher les hommes, de les voir à découvert, et avec leur mérite de tous les jours*. A happy expression! It was for this reason that I have so

---

[1] The volume which Lord Chesterfield mentions appeared in 1727, and the collected works of the Marquise de Lambert were published in 1748, and again in 1813. She died in 1733, at a very advanced age, *après une vie toujours infirme et une vieillesse fort souffrante*, adds M. Auger.

[2] It is remarkable that both these appointments were afterwards held by Mr. Stanhope.

often advised you to establish and domesticate yourself, where-
ever you can, in good houses of people above you, that you may
see their *everyday* character, manners, habits, etc. One must
see people undressed to judge truly of their shape; when they
are dressed to go abroad, their clothes are contrived to conceal,
or at least palliate, the defects of it—as full-bottomed wigs
were contrived for the Duke of Burgundy,[1] to conceal his
hump-back. Happy those who have no faults to disguise, nor
weaknesses to conceal! There are few, if any such; but unhappy
those who know so little of the world as to judge by outward
appearances!

Courts are the best keys to characters; there every passion
is busy, every art exerted, every character analysed; jealousy,
ever watchful, not only discovers, but exposes, the mysteries
of the trade, so that even bystanders, *y apprennent à déviner.*
There, too, the great art of pleasing is practised, taught, and
learned, with all its graces and delicacies. It is the first thing
needful there; it is the absolutely necessary harbinger of merit
and talents, let them be ever so great. There is no advancing
a step without it. Let misanthropes and would-be philosophers
declaim as much as they please against the vices, the simulation,
and dissimulation of Courts; those invectives are always the
result of ignorance, ill-humour, or envy. Let them show me
a cottage, where there are not the same vices of which they
accuse Courts; with this difference only, that in a cottage they
appear in their native deformity, and that in Courts, manners
and good-breeding make them less shocking, and blunt their
edge. No, be convinced that the good-breeding, the *tournure,
la douceur dans les manières*, which alone are to be acquired at
Courts, are not the showish trifles only which some people
call or think them; they are a solid good; they prevent a
great deal of real mischief; they create, adorn, and strengthen
friendships; they keep hatred within bounds; they promote
good-humour and good-will in families, where the want of good-
breeding and gentleness of manners is commonly the original
cause of discord. Get then, before it is too late, an habit of
these *mitiores virtutes*; practise them upon every the least
occasion, that they may be easy and familiar to you upon the
greatest; for they lose a great degree of their merit if they seem
laboured, and only called in upon extraordinary occasions.
I tell you truly, this is now the only doubtful part of your

[1] Louis, the eldest grandson of Louis XIV, and the pupil of Fénélon:
he died in the prime of life, to the great grief of the nation, in 1712.

character with me; and it is for that reason that I dwell upon it so much, and inculcate it so often. I shall soon see whether this doubt of mine is founded; or rather, I hope I shall soon see that it is not.

This moment I receive your letter of the 9th, N.S. I am sorry to find that you have had, though ever so slight, a return of your Carniolan disorder; and I hope your conclusion will prove a true one, and that this will be the last. I will send the mohairs by the first opportunity. As for the pictures, I am already so full, that I am resolved not to buy one more, unless by great accident I should meet with something surprisingly good, and as surprisingly cheap.

I should have thought that Lord ——, at his age, with his parts and address, need not have been reduced to keep an opera whore in such a place as Paris, where so many women of fashion generously serve as volunteers. I am still more sorry that he is in love with her; for that will take him out of good company, and sink him into bad; such as fiddlers, pipers, and *id genus omne*; most unedifying and unbecoming company for a man of fashion.

Lady Chesterfield makes you a thousand compliments. Adieu. my dear child!

MY DEAR FRIEND, Greenwich, June 13, O.S. 1751.

Les bienséances are a most necessary part of the knowledge of the world. They consist in the relations of persons, things, time, and place; good sense points them out, good company perfects them (supposing always an attention and a desire to please), and good policy recommends them.

Were you to converse with a king, you ought to be as easy and unembarrassed as with your own valet-de-chambre; but yet every look, word, and action, should imply the utmost respect. What would be proper and well-bred with others, much your superiors, would be absurd and ill-bred with one so very much so. You must wait till you are spoken to; you must receive, not give, the subject of conversation; and you must ever take care that the given subject of such conversation do not lead you into any impropriety. The art would be to carry it, if possible, to some indirect flattery; such as commending those virtues in some other person, in which that Prince either thinks he does, or at least would be thought by others to excel.

Almost the same precautions are necessary to be used with ministers, generals, etc. who expect to be treated with very near the same respect as their masters, and commonly deserve it better. There is, however, this difference, that one may begin the conversation with them, if on their side it should happen to drop, provided one does not carry it to any subject, upon which it is improper either for them to speak or be spoken to. In these two cases, certain attitudes and actions would be extremely absurd, because too easy, and consequently disrespectful. As for instance, if you were to put your arms across in your bosom, twirl your snuff-box, trample with your feet, scratch your head, etc., it would be shockingly ill-bred in that company; and, indeed, not extremely well-bred in any other. The great difficulty in those cases, though a very surmountable one by attention and custom, is to join perfect inward ease with perfect outward respect.

In mixed companies with your equals (for in mixed companies all people are to a certain degree equal) greater ease and liberty are allowed; but they too have their bounds within *bienséance*. There is a social respect necessary; you may start your own subject of conversation with modesty, taking great care, however, *de ne jamais parler de cordes dans la maison d'un pendu*. Your words, gestures, and attitudes, have a greater degree of latitude, though by no means an unbounded one. You may have your hands in your pockets, take snuff, sit, stand, or occasionally walk, as you like; but I believe you would not think it very *bienséant* to whistle, put on your hat, loosen your garters or your buckles, lie down upon a couch, or go to bed and welter in an easy chair. These are negligences and freedoms which one can only take when quite alone; they are injurious to superiors, shocking and offensive to equals, brutal and insulting to inferiors. That easiness of carriage and behaviour, which is exceedingly engaging, widely differs from negligence and inattention, and by no means implies that one may do whatever one pleases; it only means that one is not to be stiff, formal, embarrassed, disconcerted, and ashamed, like country bumpkins, and people who have never been in good company; but it requires great attention to, and a scrupulous observation of *les bienséances*; whatever one ought to do, is to be done with ease and unconcern; whatever is improper must not be done at all.

In mixed companies also, different ages and sexes are to be differently addressed. You would not talk of your pleasures

to men of a certain age, gravity, and dignity; they justly expect
from young people a degree of deference and regard. You
should be full as easy with them as with people of your own
years; but your manner must be different; more respect must
be implied; and it is not amiss to insinuate, that from them
you expect to learn. It flatters and comforts age, for not
being able to take a part in the joy and titter of youth. To
women you should always address yourself with great outward
respect and attention, whatever you feel inwardly; their sex
is by long prescription entitled to it; and it is among the duties
of *bienséance*; at the same time that respect is very properly
and very agreeably mixed with a degree of *enjouement,* if you
have it; but then, that *badinage* must either directly or indirectly tend to their praise, and even not be liable to a malicious
construction to their disadvantage. But here too great attention must be had to the difference of age, rank, and situation.
A *Maréchale* of fifty must not be played with like a young
coquette of fifteen; respect and *serious enjouement,* if I may
couple those two words, must be used with the former, and
mere *badinage, zesté même d'un peu de polissonnerie,* is pardonable
with the latter.

Another important point of *les bienséances,* seldom enough
attended to, is, not to run your own present humour and disposition indiscriminately against everybody; but to observe,
conform to, and adopt theirs. For example, if you happened
to be in a high good-humour and a flow of spirits, would you
go and sing a *pont-neuf,* or cut a caper, to la Maréchale de
Coigny, the Pope's Nuncio, or Abbé Sallier, or to any person
of natural gravity and melancholy, or who at that time should
be in grief? I believe not; as, on the other hand, I suppose,
that if you were in low spirits, or real grief, you would not choose
to bewail your situation with *la petite Blot.* If you cannot
command your present humour and disposition, single out
those to converse with who happen to be in the humour nearest
to your own.

Loud laughter is extremely inconsistent with *les bienséances,*
as it is only the illiberal and noisy testimony of the joy of the
mob at some very silly thing. A gentleman is often seen, but
very seldom heard, to laugh. Nothing is more contrary to *les
bienséances* than horse-play, or *jeux de main* of any kind whatever, and has often very serious, sometimes very fatal consequences. Romping, struggling, throwing things at one another's
head, are the becoming pleasantries of the mob, but degrade a

gentleman; *giuoco di mano, giuoco de villano*, is a very true saying, among the few true sayings of the Italians.

Peremptoriness and decision in young people is *contraire aux bienséances*; they should seldom seem to assert, and always use some softening, mitigating expression—such as *s'il m'est permis de le dire*; *je croirois plutôt*; *si j'ose m'expliquer*, which soften the manner, without giving up, or even weakening the thing. People of more age and experience expect, and are entitled to, that degree of deference.

There is a *bienséance* also with regard to people of the lowest degree; a gentleman observes it with his footman, even with the beggar in the street. He considers them as objects of compassion, not of insult; he speaks to neither *d'un ton brusque*, but corrects the one coolly, and refuses the other with humanity. There is no one occasion in the world, in which *le ton brusque* is becoming a gentleman. In short, *les bienséances* are another word for *manners*, and extend to every part of life. They are propriety; the Graces should attend in order to complete them. The Graces enable us to do, genteelly and pleasingly, what *les bienséances* require to be done at all. The latter are an obligation upon every man; the former are an infinite advantage and ornament to any man. May you unite both!

Though you dance well, do not think that you dance well enough, and consequently not endeavour to dance still better. And though you should be told that you are genteel, still aim at being genteeler. If Marcel should, do not you be satisfied. Go on; court the Graces all your life-time. You will find no better friends at Court; they will speak in your favour, to the hearts of princes, ministers, and mistresses.

Now that all tumultuous passions and quick sensations have subsided with me, and that I have no tormenting cares nor boisterous pleasures to agitate me, my greatest joy is to consider the fair prospect you have before you, and to hope and believe you will enjoy it. You are already in the world, at an age when others have hardly heard of it. Your character is hitherto not only unblemished in its moral part, but even unsullied by any low, dirty, and ungentlemanlike vice, and will, I hope, continue so. Your knowledge is sound, extensive, and avowed, especially in everything relative to your destination. With such materials to begin, what then is wanting? Not fortune, as you have found by experience. You have had, and shall have, fortune sufficient to assist your merit and your industry; and, if I can help it, you never shall have enough to make you negligent of either. You have too *mens sana in corpore sano*—the greatest blessing of all. All therefore that you want is as much in your power to acquire, as to eat your breakfast when set before you. It is only that knowledge of the world, that elegancy of manners, that universal politeness, and those graces, which keeping good company, and seeing variety of places and characters, must inevitably, with the least attention on your part, give you. Your foreign destination leads to the greatest things, and your Parliamentary situation will facilitate your progress. Consider then this pleasing prospect as attentively for yourself, as I consider it for you. Labour on your part to realise it, as I will on mine to assist and enable you to do it. *Nullum numen abest, si sit prudentia.*

Adieu, my dear child! I count the days till I have the pleasure of seeing you. I shall soon count the hours, and at last the minutes, with increasing impatience.

P.S. The mohairs are this day gone from hence for Calais, recommended to the care of Madame Morel, and directed, as desired, to the Comptroller-General. The three pieces come to six hundred and eighty French livres.

My Dear Friend,   London, June 24, O.S. 1751.

Air, address, manners, and graces, are of such infinite advantage to whoever has them, and so peculiarly and essentially necessary for you, that now, as the time of our meeting draws near, I tremble for fear I should not find you possessed of them; and, to tell you the truth, I doubt you are not yet sufficiently convinced of their importance. There is, for instance, your intimate friend, Mr. H[ayes], who, with great merit, deep knowledge, and a thousand good qualities, will never make a figure in the world while he lives. Why? Merely for want of those external and showish accomplishments which he began the world too late to acquire; and which, with his studious and philosophical turn, I believe he thinks are not worth his attention. He may very probably make a figure in the republic of letters; but he had ten thousand times better make a figure as a man of the world and of business in the republic of the United Provinces; which, take my word for it, he never will.

As I open myself, without the least reserve, whenever I think that my doing so can be of any use to you, I will give you a short account of myself when I first came into the world, which was at the age you are of now, so that (by the way) you have got the start of me in that important article by two or three years at least. At nineteen, I left the university of Cambridge, where I was an absolute pedant; when I talked my best, I quoted Horace; when I aimed at being facetious, I quoted Martial; and when I had a mind to be a fine gentleman, I talked Ovid. I was convinced that none but the ancients had common sense; that the classics contained everything that was either necessary, useful, or ornamental to men; and I was not without thoughts of wearing the *toga virilis* of the Romans, instead of the vulgar and illiberal dress of the moderns. With these excellent notions, I went first to the Hague, where, by the help of several letters of recommendation, I was soon introduced into all the best company, and where I very soon discovered that I was totally mistaken in almost every one notion I had entertained. Fortunately I had a strong desire to please (the mixed result of good-nature, and a vanity by no means blameable), and was sensible that I had nothing but the desire. I therefore resolved, if possible, to acquire the means too. I studied attentively and minutely the dress, the air, the manner, the address, and the turn of conversation of all those whom I found to be the people in fashion, and most generally allowed to please. I imitated them as well as I could; if I heard that one man was reckoned remarkably genteel, I carefully watched his dress, motions, and attitudes, and formed my own upon them. When I heard of another whose conversation was agreeable and engaging, I listened and attended to the turn of it. I addressed myself, though *de très mauvaise grâce*, to all the most fashionable fine ladies; confessed and laughed with them at my own awkwardness and rawness, recommending myself as an object for them to try their skill in forming.

By these means, and with a passionate desire of pleasing every body, I came by degrees to please some; and I can assure you, that what little figure I have made in the world, has been much more owing to that passionate desire I had of pleasing universally, than to any intrinsic merit or sound knowledge I might ever have been master of. My passion for pleasing was so strong (and I am very glad it was so), that I own to you fairly, I wished to make every woman I saw in love with me, and every man I met with admire me. Without this passion for the object, I should never have been so attentive to the means; and I own I cannot conceive how it is possible for any man of good-nature and good sense to be without this passion.

Does not good-nature incline us to please all those we converse with, of whatever rank or station they may be? And does not good sense and common observation show of what infinite use it is to please? Oh! but one may please by the good qualities of the heart, and the knowledge of the head, without that fashionable air, address, and manner, which is mere tinsel. I deny it. A man may be esteemed and respected, but I defy him to please without them. Moreover, at your age, I would not have contented myself with barely pleasing; I wanted to shine and to distinguish myself in the world as a man of fashion and gallantry, as well as business. And that ambition or vanity, call it what you please, was a right one; it hurt nobody, and made me exert whatever talents I had. It is the spring of a thousand right and good things.

I was talking you over the other day with one very much your friend, and who had often been with you, both at Paris and in Italy. Among the innumerable questions which you may be sure I asked him concerning you, I happened to mention your dress (for, to say the truth, it was the only thing of which I thought him a competent judge), upon which he said that you dressed tolerably well at Paris; but that in Italy you dressed so ill, that he used to joke with you upon it, and even to tear your clothes. Now, I must tell you, that at your age it is as ridiculous not to be very well dressed, as at my age it would be if I were to wear a white feather and red-heeled shoes. Dress is one of the various ingredients that contribute to the art of pleasing; it pleases the eyes at least, and more especially of women. Address yourself to the senses if you would please; dazzle the eyes, soothe and flatter the ears of mankind; engage their heart, and let their reason do its worst against you. *Suaviter in modo* is the great secret. Whenever you find yourself engaged insensibly in favour of anybody of no superior merit or distinguished talent, examine and see what it is that has made those impressions upon you: you will find it to be that *douceur*, that gentleness of manners, that air and address, which I have so often recommended to you; and from thence draw this obvious conclusion, that what pleases you in them will please others in you; for we are all made of the same clay, though some of the lumps are a little finer, and some a little coarser; but, in general, the surest way to judge of others is to examine and analyse one's self thoroughly. When we meet, I will assist you in that analysis, in which every man wants some assistance against his own self-love. Adieu!

My Dear Friend,   Greenwich, July 15, O.S. 1751.

As this is the last, or the last letter but one, that I think I shall write before I have the pleasure of seeing you here, it may not be amiss to prepare you a little for our interview, and for the time we shall pass together. Before kings and princes meet, ministers on each side adjust the important points of precedence, arm-chairs,[1] right hand and left, etc., so that they know previously what they are to expect, what they have to trust to; and it is right they should; for they commonly envy or hate, but most certainly distrust each other. We shall meet upon very different terms; we want no such preliminaries; you know my tenderness, I know your affection. My only object, therefore, is to make your short stay with me as useful as I can to you; and yours, I hope, is to co-operate with me. Whether, by making it wholesome, I shall make it pleasant to you, I am not sure. Emetics and cathartics I shall not administer, because I am sure you do not want them; but for alteratives you must expect a great many; and I can tell you, that I have a number of *nostrums*, which I shall communicate to nobody but yourself.

To speak without a metaphor, I shall endeavour to assist your youth with all the experience that I have purchased, at the price of seven-and-fifty years. In order to this, frequent reproofs, corrections, and admonitions will be necessary; but then, I promise you, that they shall be in a gentle, friendly, and secret manner; they shall not put you out of countenance in company, nor out of humour when we are alone. I do not expect, that, at nineteen, you should have that knowledge of the world, those manners, that dexterity, which few people have at nine-and-twenty. But I will endeavour to give them you; and I am sure you will endeavour to learn them, as far as your youth, my experience, and the time we shall pass together will allow. You may have many inaccuracies (and to be sure you have, for who has not at your age?), which few people will tell you of, and some nobody can tell you of but

---

[1] These questions of arm-chairs in visits of ceremony were at this period frequently and warmly debated, especially in the Germanic Empire. The *Memoirs* of the Margravine of Bayreuth give an account of several such, as, for instance, at Frankfort in 1741: "Comme il n'y avoit point d'exemple qu'une fille de Roi et une Impératrice se fussent trouvées ensemble, je ne savois point les prétentions que je devois exercer." She held a conference with two Prussian ministers of State on this most important subject. "Ilp furent d'avis l'un et l'autre que je ne pouvois prétendre le fauteuil, mais que cependant ils insisteroient pour me le faire obtenir!" (*Mem.*, vol. ii, p. 344.

myself. You may possibly have others too, which eyes less interested, and less vigilant than mine, do not discover; all those you shall hear of, from one whose tenderness for you will excite his curiosity, and sharpen his penetration. The smallest inattention, or error in manners, the minutest inelegancy of diction, the least awkwardness in your dress and, carriage, will not escape my observation, nor pass without amicable correction.

Two of the most intimate friends in the world can freely tell each other their faults, and even their crimes; but cannot possibly tell each other of certain little weaknesses, awkwardness, and blindnesses of self-love; to authorize that unreserved freedom, the relation between us is absolutely necessary. For example, I had a very worthy friend, with whom I was intimate enough to tell him his faults; he had but few; I told him of them, he took it kindly of me, and corrected them. But then, he had some weaknesses that I could never tell him of directly, and which he was so little sensible of himself, that hints of them were lost upon him. He had a scrag neck, of about a yard long; notwithstanding which, bags being in fashion, truly he would wear one to his wig, and did so; but never behind him, for, upon every motion of his head, his bag came forwards over one shoulder or the other. He took it into his head too, that he must, occasionally, dance minuets, because other people did; and he did so, not only extremely ill, but so awkward, so disjointed, so slim, so meagre, was his figure, that, had he danced as well as ever Marcel did, it would have been ridiculous in him to have danced at all. I hinted these things to him as plainly as friendship would allow, and to no purpose; but to have told him the whole, so as to cure him, I must have been his father, which, thank God, I am not. As fathers commonly go, it is seldom a misfortune to be fatherless; and, considering the general run of sons, as seldom a misfortune to be childless. You and I form, I believe, an exception to that rule; for, I am persuaded, that we would neither of us change our relation, were it in our power. You will, I both hope and believe, be not only the comfort, but the pride of my age; and, I am sure, I will be the support, the friend, the guide of your youth. Trust me without reserve; I will advise you without private interest, or secret envy. Mr. Harte will do so too; but still there may be some little things proper for you to know, and necessary for you to correct, which even his friendship would not let him tell you of so freely as I should;

and some of which he may possibly not be so good a judge of as I am, not having lived so much in the great world.

One principal topic of our conversation will be, not only the purity but the elegancy of the English language, in both which you are very deficient. Another will be the constitution of this country, which I believe you know less of than of most other countries in Europe. Manners, attentions, and address will also be the frequent subjects of our lectures; and whatever I know of that important and necessary art, the art of pleasing, I will unreservedly communicate to you. Dress too (which, as things are, I can logically prove requires some attention) will not always escape our notice. Thus, my lectures will be more various, and in some respects more useful than Professor Mascow's; and therefore, I can tell you, that I expect to be paid for them; but, as possibly you would not care to part with your ready money, and as I do not think that it would be quite handsome in me to accept it, I will compound for the payment, and take it in attention and practice.

Pray remember to part with all your friends, acquaintances, and mistresses (if you have any) at Paris, in such a manner as may make them not only willing, but impatient to see you there again. Assure them of your desire of returning to them; and do it in a manner that they may think you in earnest, that is, *avec onction et une espèce d'attendrissement*. All people say pretty nearly the same things upon those occasions; it is the manner only that makes the difference, and that difference is great.

Avoid, however, as much as you can charging yourself with commissions in your return from hence to Paris; I know by experience that they are exceedingly troublesome, commonly expensive, and very seldom satisfactory at last to the persons who give them; some you cannot refuse, to people to whom you are obliged, and would oblige in your turn; but as to common fiddle-faddle commissions, you may excuse yourself from them with truth, by saying that you are to return to Paris through Flanders, and see all those great towns; which I intend you shall do, and stay a week or ten days at Brussels.

Adieu! A good journey to you, if this is my last; if not, I can repeat again what I shall wish constantly.[1]

---

[1] Soon after the date of this letter Mr. Stanhope rejoined his father in England, and remained with him until November 15, on which day he set out on his return to Paris, having been appointed an attaché to Lord Albemarle's embassy. Lord Chesterfield's first impressions on seeing him, as to his manners and graces (or rather as to the want of them) are described in a letter to Madame de Monconseil of October 7, 1751.

My Dear Friend,   London, December 19, O.S. 1751.

You are now entered upon a scene of business, where I hope you will one day make a figure. Use does a great deal, but care and attention must be joined to it. The first thing necessary in writing letters of business is extreme clearness and perspicuity; every paragraph should be so clear and unambiguous, that the dullest fellow in the world may not be able to mistake it, nor obliged to read it twice in order to understand it. This necessary clearness implies a correctness, without excluding an elegancy of style. Tropes, figures, antitheses, epigrams, etc., would be as misplaced and as impertinent in letters of business, as they are sometimes (if judiciously used) proper and pleasing in familiar letters, upon common and trite subjects. In business, an elegant simplicity, the result of care, not of labour, is required. Business must be well, not affectedly, dressed, but by no means negligently. Let your first attention be to clearness, and read every paragraph after you have written it, in the critical view of discovering whether it is possible that any one man can mistake the true sense of it; and correct it accordingly.

Our pronouns and relatives often create obscurity or ambiguity; be therefore exceedingly attentive to them, and take care to mark out with precision their particular relations. For example: Mr. Johnson acquainted me that he had seen Mr. Smith, who had promised him to speak to Mr. Clarke, to return him (Mr. Johnson) those papers which he (Mr. Smith) had left some time ago with him (Mr. Clarke); it is better to repeat a name, though unnecessarily, ten times, than to have the person mistaken once. *Who*, you know, is singly relative to persons, and cannot be applied to things; *which* and *that* are chiefly relative to things, but not absolutely exclusive of persons; for one may say, the man *that* robbed or killed such-a-one; but it is much better to say, the man *who* robbed or killed. One never says, the man or the woman *which*. *Which* and *that*, though chiefly relative to things, cannot be always used indifferently as to things; and the εὐφονία must sometimes determine their place. For instance: The letter *which* I received from you, *which* you referred to in your last, *which* came by Lord Albemarle's messenger, and *which* I showed to such-a-one: I would change it thus: The letter *that* I received from you, *which* you referred to in your last, *that* came by Lord Albemarle's messenger, and *which* I showed to such-a-one.

Business does not exclude (as possibly you wish it did) the

usual terms of politeness and good-breeding, but, on the contrary, strictly requires them; such as, *I have the honour to acquaint your Lordship; Permit me to assure you; If I may be allowed to give my opinion,* etc. For the Minister abroad, who writes to the Minister at home, writes to his superior; possibly to his patron, or at least to one who he desires should be so.

Letters of business will not only admit of, but be the better for *certain graces*; but then, they must be scattered with a sparing and a skilful hand; they must fit their places exactly. They must decently adorn without encumbering, and modestly shine without glaring. But as this is the utmost degree of perfection in letters of business, I would not advise you to attempt those embellishments till you have first laid your foundation well.

Cardinal d'Ossat's letters are the true letters of business; those of Monsieur D'Avaux are excellent; Sir William Temple's are very pleasing, but I fear too affected. Carefully avoid all Greek or Latin quotations; and bring no precedents from the *virtuous Spartans, the polite Athenians, and the brave Romans.* Leave all that to futile pedants. No flourishes, no declamation. But (I repeat it again) there is an elegant simplicity and dignity of style absolutely necessary for good letters of business; attend to that carefully. Let your periods be harmonious, without seeming to be laboured; and let them not be too long, for that always occasions a degree of obscurity. I should not mention correct orthography, but that you very often fail in that particular, which will bring ridicule upon you; for no man is allowed to spell ill. I wish too that your handwriting were much better, and I cannot conceive why it is not, since every man may certainly write whatever hand he pleases. Neatness in folding up, sealing, and directing your packets, is by no means to be neglected; though I dare say you think it is. But there is something in the exterior, even of a packet, that may please or displease; and consequently worth some attention.

You say that your time is very well employed, and so it is, though as yet only in the outlines, and first *routine* of business. They are previously necessary to be known; they smooth the way for parts and dexterity. Business requires no conjuration nor supernatural talents, as people unacquainted with it are apt to think. Method, diligence, and discretion, will carry a man of good strong common sense much higher than the finest parts, without them, can do. *Par negotiis, neque supra,*[1] is the

[1] Tacitus, *Annals,* vi, 39.

true character of a man of business; but then it implies ready attention, and no *absences*; and a flexibility and versatility of attention from one object to another, without being engrossed by any one.

Be upon your guard against the pedantry and affectation of business, which young people are apt to fall into, from the pride of being concerned in it young. They look thoughtful, complain of the weight of business, throw out mysterious hints, and seem big with secrets which they do not know. Do you on the contrary never talk of business but to those with whom you are to transact it; and learn to seem *vacuus* and idle when you have the most business. Of all things, the *volto sciolto* and the *pensieri stretti* are necessary. Adieu!

MY DEAR FRIEND,   London, January 23, O.S. 1752.

Have you seen the new tragedy of *Varon*,[1] and what do you think of it? Let me know, for I am determined to form my taste upon yours. I hear that the situations and incidents are well brought on, and the catastrophe unexpected and surprising, but the verses bad. I suppose it is the subject of all the conversations at Paris, where both women and men are judges and critics of all such performances; such conversations, that both form and improve the taste and whet the judgment, are surely preferable to the conversations of our mixed companies here; which, if they happen to rise above bragg and whist, infallibly stop short of everything either pleasing or instructive. I take the reason of this to be, that (as women generally give the tone to the conversation) our English women are not near so well informed and cultivated as the French; besides that they are naturally more serious and silent.

I could wish there were a treaty made between the French and the English theatres, in which both parties should make considerable concessions. The English ought to give up their notorious violations of all the unities, and all their massacres, racks, dead bodies, and mangled carcasses, which they so frequently exhibit upon their stage. The French should engage to have more action and less declamation; and not to cram and crowd things together to almost a degree of impossibility, from a too scrupulous adherence to the unities. The English should restrain the licentiousness of their poets, and the French

[1] In the *Dictionnaire des Anonymes par Barbier* the tragedy of *Varon* is said to have bee writtenn by the Vicomte de Grave.

enlarge the liberty of theirs; their poets are the greatest slaves in their country, and that is a bold word; ours are the most tumultuous subjects in England, and that is saying a good deal. Under such regulations one might hope to see a play in which one should not be lulled to sleep by the length of a monotonical declamation, nor frightened and shocked by the barbarity of the action. The unity of time extended occasionally to three or four days, and the unity of place broke into, as far as the same street, or sometimes the same town; both which, I will affirm, are as probable as four-and-twenty hours and the same room.

More indulgence too, in my mind, should be shown, than the French are willing to allow, to bright thoughts and to shining images; for though, I confess, it is not very natural for a hero or a princess to say fine things in all the violence of grief, love, rage, etc., yet I can as well suppose that, as I can that they should talk to themselves for half-an-hour, which they must necessarily do or no tragedy could be carried on, unless they had recourse to a much greater absurdity, the choruses of the ancients. Tragedy is of a nature, that one must see it with a degree of self-deception; we must lend ourselves a little to the delusion; and I am very willing to carry that complaisance a little farther than the French do.

Tragedy must be something bigger than life, or it would not affect us. In nature, the most violent passions are silent; in Tragedy they must speak, and speak with dignity too. Hence the necessity of their being written in verse, and, unfortunately for the French, from the weakness of their language, in rhymes. And for the same reason, Cato, the Stoic, expiring at Utica, rhymes masculine and feminine at Paris, and fetches his last breath at London in most harmonious and correct blank verse.

It is quite otherwise with comedy; which should be mere common life, and not one jot bigger. Every character should speak upon the stage, not only what it would utter in the situation there represented, but in the same manner in which it would express it. For which reason I cannot allow rhymes in comedy, unless they were put into the mouth and came out of the mouth of a mad poet. But it is impossible to deceive one's self enough (nor is it the least necessary in comedy) to suppose a dull rogue of a usurer cheating, or *gros Jean* blundering in the finest rhymes in the world.

As for operas, they are essentially too absurd and extravagant to mention; I look upon them as a magic scene, contrived to please the eyes and the ears at the expense of the understanding; and I consider singing, rhyming and chiming heroes, and princesses and philosophers, as I do the hills, the trees, the birds, and the beasts, who amicably joined in one common country dance to the irresistible tune of Orpheus's lyre. Whenever I go to an opera, I leave my sense and reason at the door with my half-guinea, and deliver myself up to my eyes and my ears.

Thus I have made you my poetical confession; in which I have acknowledged as many sins against the established taste in both countries, as a frank heretic could have owned against the established church in either; but I am now privileged by my age to taste and think for myself, and not to care what other people think of me in those respects; an advantage which youth, among its many advantages, has not. It must occasionally and outwardly conform, to a certain degree, to established tastes, fashions, and decisions. A young man may, with a becoming modesty, dissent, in private companies, from public opinions and prejudices; but he must not attack them with warmth, nor magisterially set up his own sentiments against them. Endeavour to hear and know all opinions; receive them with complaisance; form your own with coolness, and give in with modesty.

I have received a letter from Sir John Lambert, in which he requests me to use my interest to procure him the remittance of Mr. Spencer's [1] money, when he goes abroad; and also desires to know to whose account he is to place the postage of my letters. I do not trouble him with a letter in answer, since you can execute the commission. Pray make my compliments to him, and assure him that I will do all I can to procure him Mr. Spencer's business; but that his most effectual way will be by Messrs. Hoare, who are Mr. Spencer's cashiers; and who will undoubtedly have their choice whom they will give him his credit upon. As for the postage of the letters, your purse and mine being pretty near the same, do you pay it over and above your next draught.

Your relations, the Princes B[orghese], will soon be with

[1] This was John Spencer, the only son of the Hon. John Spencer, son of the statesman, Charles, third Earl of Sunderland by Anne, daughter and co-heiress of the Duke of Marlborough. His son was elected M.P. for Warwick; in 1761 he was created Viscount Spencer, and, in 1765, Earl Spencer. In 1755 he married a daughter of the Right Hon. Stephen Poyntz, and was great-grandfather of John Poyntz Spencer (born 1835).

you at Paris; for they leave London this week; whenever you converse with them, I desire it may be in Italian; that language not being yet familiar enough to you.

By our printed papers, there seems to be a sort of compromise between the King and the Parliament, with regard to the affairs of the hospitals, by taking them out of the hands of the Archbishop of Paris,[1] and placing them in Monsieur d'Argenson's [2]; if this be true, that compromise, as it is called, is clearly a victory on the side of the Court, and a defeat on the part of the Parliament; for if the Parliament had a right, they had it as much to the exclusion of Monsieur d'Argenson as of the Archbishop.

Adieu.

MY DEAR FRIEND,   London, April 13, O.S. 1752.

I receive this moment your letter of the 19th, N.S. with the enclosed pieces relative to the present dispute between the King and the Parliament. I shall return them by Lord Huntingdon, whom you will soon see at Paris, and who will likewise carry you the piece, which I forgot in making up the packet I sent you by the Spanish Ambassador. The representation of the Parliament is very well drawn, *suaviter in modo, fortiter in re*. They tell the king very respectfully, that in a certain case, *which they should think it criminal to suppose,* they would not obey him. This has a tendency to what we call here Revolution principles.

I do not know what the Lord's anointed, his viceregent upon earth, divinely appointed by him, and accountable to none but him for his actions, will either think or do, upon these symptoms of reason and good sense, which seem to be breaking out all over France; but this I foresee, that before the end of this century, the trade of both King and priest will not be half so good a one as it has been. Duclos, in his *Reflections*, has observed, and very truly, *qu'il y a un germe de raison qui commence à se développer en France.* A *développement* that must prove fatal to regal and papal pretensions. Prudence may, in many cases, recommend an occasional submission to either;

---

[1] Christophe de Beaumont, raised to that dignity in 1746, and famous in after years for his opposition to the Court and his controversy with Rousseau.

[2] Marc Pierre de Voyer, Comte d'Argenson, born in 1696, was at this period Ministre de la Guerre. It was he who, when the Abbé Desfontaines was apologising for his frequent publication of libels, and had added, "Il faut bien que je vive!" drily replied, "Je n'en vois pas la nécessité!"

but when that ignorance, upon which an implicit faith in both could only be founded, is once removed, God's viceregent, and Christ's vicar, will only be obeyed and believed, as far as what the one orders, and the other says, is conformable to reason and truth.

I am very glad (to use a vulgar expression) that *you make as if you* were not well, though you really are; I am sure it is the likeliest way to keep so. Pray leave off entirely your greasy, heavy pastry, fat creams, and indigestible dumplings; and then you need not confine yourself to white meats, which I do not take to be one jot wholesomer than beef, mutton, and partridge.

Voltaire sent me from Berlin his History *du Siècle de Louis XIV*. It came at a very proper time; Lord Bolingbroke had just taught me how history should be read; Voltaire shows me how it should be written. I am sensible that it will meet with almost as many critics as readers. Voltaire must be criticised; besides, every man's favourite is attacked; for every prejudice is exposed, and our prejudices are our mistresses; reason is at best our wife, very often heard indeed, but seldom minded. It is the history of the human understanding, written by a man of parts, for the use of men of parts. Weak minds will not like it, even though they do not understand it; which is commonly the measure of their admiration. Dull ones will want those minute and uninteresting details, with which most other histories are encumbered. He tells me all I want to know, and nothing more. His reflections are short, just, and produce others in his readers. Free from religious, philosophical, political, and national prejudices, beyond any historian I ever met with, he relates all those matters as truly and as impartially, as certain regards, which must always be to some degree observed, will allow him; for one sees plainly, that he often says much less than he would say, if he might. He has made me much better acquainted with the times of Louis XIV than the innumerable volumes which I had read could do; and has suggested this reflection to me, which I had never made before —His vanity, not his knowledge, made him encourage all, and introduce many arts and sciences in his country. He opened in a manner the human understanding in France, and brought it to its utmost perfection; his age equalled in all, and greatly exceeded in many things (pardon me, pedants!) the Augustan. This was great and rapid; but still it might be done, by the encouragement, the applause, and the rewards of a vain, liberal, and magnificent Prince. What is much more surprising, is, that he stopped the operations of the human mind, just where he pleased; and seemed to say, "thus far shalt thou go, and no farther." For, a bigot to his religion, and jealous of his power, free and rational thoughts upon either never entered into a French head during his reign; and the greatest geniuses that ever any age produced, never entertained a doubt of the Divine right of Kings, or the infallibility of the Church. Poets, orators, and philosophers, ignorant of their natural rights, cherished their chains; and blind active faith triumphed, in those great minds, over silent and passive reason. The reverse of this seems now to be the case in France; reason opens itself; fancy and invention fade and decline.

I will send you a copy of this history by Lord Huntingdon, as I think it very probable that it is not allowed to be published and sold at Paris. Pray read it more than once, and with attention, particularly the second volume, which contains short, but very clear accounts of many very interesting things, which are talked of by everybody, though fairly understood by very few. There are two very puerile affectations, which I wish this book had been free from; the one is, the total subversion of all the old established French orthography; the other is, the not making use of any one capital letter throughout the whole book, except at the beginning of a paragraph. It offends my eyes to see rome, paris, france, cæsar, henry the 4th, etc., begin with small letters; and I do not conceive, that there can be any reason for doing it half so strong as the reason of long usage is to the contrary. This is an affectation below Voltaire [1]; whom, I am not ashamed to say, that I admire and delight in, as an author, equally in prose and in verse.

I had a letter a few days ago, from Monsieur du Boccage, in which he says, *Monsieur Stanhope s'est jetté dans la politique, et je crois qu'il y réussira*; you do very well, it is your destination; but remember, that to succeed in great things, one must first learn to please in little ones. Engaging manners and address must prepare the way for superior knowledge and abilities to act with effect. The late Duke of Marlborough's manners and address prevailed with the first King of Prussia to let his troops remain in the army of the Allies, when neither their representations, nor his own share in the common cause, could do it. The Duke of Marlborough had no new matter to urge to him, but had a manner which he could not, and did not, resist. Voltaire,

---

[1] This affectation has been judiciously corrected in the subsequent editions.

among a thousand little delicate strokes of that kind, says of the Duke de la Feuillade,[1] *qu'il était l'homme le plus brillant et le plus aimable du Royaume, et quoique gendre du Ministre, il avoit pour lui la faveur publique.* Various little circumstances of that sort will often make a man of great real merit be hated, if he has not address and manners to make him be loved. Consider all your own circumstances seriously, and you will find, that, of all the arts, the art of pleasing is the most necessary for you to study and possess. A silly tyrant said, *oderint modo timeant*; a wise man would have said, *modo ament nihil timendum est mihi.* Judge from your own daily experience, of the efficacy of that pleasing *je ne sçais quoi*, when you feel, as you and everybody certainly does, that in men it is more engaging than knowledge, in women than beauty.

I long to see Lord and Lady —— (who are not yet arrived), because they have lately seen you; and I always fancy that I can fish out something new concerning you from those who have seen you last; not that I shall much rely upon their accounts, because I distrust the judgment of Lord and Lady —— in those matters about which I am most inquisitive. They have ruined their own son, by what they called and thought, loving him. They have made him believe that the world was made for him, not he for the world; and unless he stays abroad a great while, and falls into very good company, he will expect, what he will never find, the attentions and complaisance from others which he has hitherto been used to from papa and mamma. This, I fear, is too much the case of Mr. ——, who, I doubt, will be run through the body, and be near dying, before he knows how to live. However you may turn out, you can never make me any of these reproaches. I indulged no silly womanish fondness for you: instead of inflicting my tenderness upon you, I have taken all possible methods to make you deserve it; and thank God, you do; at least, I know but one article in which you are different from what I could wish you, and you very well know what that is. I want that I and all the world should like you as well as I love you. Adieu.

My Dear Friend,   London, April 30, O.S. 1752.

Avoir du monde is, in my opinion, a very just and happy expression for having address, manners, and for knowing how to behave properly in all companies; and it implies very truly,

[1] See Voltaire's *Siècle de Louis XIV*, ch. xix.

that a man that has not these accomplishments, is not of the world. Without them, the best parts are inefficient, civility is absurd, and freedom offensive. A learned parson, rusting in his cell at Oxford or Cambridge, will reason admirably well upon the nature of man; will profoundly analyse the head, the heart, the reason, the will, the passions, the senses, the sentiments, and all those subdivisions of we know not what; and yet, unfortunately, he knows nothing of man, for he has not lived with him, and is ignorant of all the various modes, habits, prejudices, and tastes, that always influence and often determine him. He views man as he does colours in Sir Isaac Newton's prism, where only the capital ones are seen; but an experienced dyer knows all their various shades and gradations, together with the result of their several mixtures. Few men are of one plain, decided colour; most are mixed, shaded, and blended; and vary as much, from different situations, as changeable silks do from different lights.

The man *qui a du monde* knows all this from his own experience and observation; the conceited cloister philosopher knows nothing of it from his own theory; his practice is absurd and improper, and he acts as awkwardly as a man would dance who had never seen others dance, nor learned of a dancing-master, but who had only studied the notes by which dances are now pricked down as well as tunes. Observe and imitate, then, the address, the arts, and the manners of those *qui ont du monde*: see by what methods they first make, and afterwards improve, impressions in their favour. Those impressions are much oftener owing to little causes than to intrinsic merit, which is less volatile, and has not so sudden an effect. Strong minds have undoubtedly an ascendant over weak ones, as Galigaia Maréchale d'Ancre very justly observed, when, to the disgrace and reproach of those times, she was executed [1] for having governed Mary of Medicis by the arts of witchcraft and magic. But then ascendant is to be gained by degrees, and by those arts only which experience and the knowledge of the world teaches; for few are mean enough to be bullied, though most are weak enough to be bubbled. I have often seen people of superior, governed by people of much inferior, parts, without knowing or even suspecting that they were so governed. This can only happen when those people of inferior parts have more worldly dexterity and experience than those they govern. They see the weak and unguarded part, and apply to it: they

[1] On July 8, 1617.

take it, and all the rest follows. Would you gain either men or women, and every man of sense desires to gain both, *il faut du monde*. You have had more opportunities than ever any man had, at your age, of acquiring *ce monde*; you have been in the best companies of most countries, at an age when others have hardly been in any company at all. You are master of all those languages which John Trott seldom speaks at all, and never well; consequently you need be a stranger nowhere. This is the way, and the only way, of having the *du monde*; but, if you have it not, and have still any coarse rusticity about you, may one not apply to you the *rusticus expectat* of Horace?

This knowledge of the world teaches us more particularly two things, both which are of infinite consequence, and to neither of which nature inclines us; I mean, the command of our temper, and of our countenance. A man who has no *monde* is inflamed with anger, or annihilated with shame, at every disagreeable incident; the one makes him act and talk like a madman, the other makes him look like a fool. But a man who has *du monde*, seems not to understand what he cannot or ought not to resent. If he makes a slip himself, he recovers it by his coolness, instead of plunging deeper by his confusion, like a stumbling horse. He is firm, but gentle; and practises that most excellent maxim, *suaviter in modo, fortiter in re*. The other is the *volto sciolto e pensieri stretti*. People, unused to the world, have babbling countenances; and are unskilful enough to show, what they have sense enough not to tell. In the course of the world, a man must very often put on an easy, frank countenance, upon very disagreeable occasions; he must seem pleased, when he is very much otherwise; he must be able to accost and receive with smiles, those whom he would much rather meet with swords. In Courts he must not turn himself inside out. All this may, nay must be done, without falsehood and treachery; for it must go no farther than politeness and manners, and must stop short of assurances and professions of simulated friendship. Good manners, to those one does not love, are no more a breach of truth, than "your humble servant," at the bottom of a challenge is; they are universally agreed upon, and understood to be things of course. They are necessary guards of the decency and peace of society; they must only act defensively; and then not with arms poisoned with perfidy. Truth, but not the whole truth, must be the invariable principle of every man, who has either religion, honour, or prudence. Those who violate it, may be cunning, but they are not able. Lies and perfidy are the refuge of fools and cowards. Adieu!

P.S. I must recommend to you again, to take your leave of all your French acquaintance, in such a manner as may make them regret your departure, and wish to see and welcome you at Paris again; where you may possibly return before it is very long. This must not be done in a cold, civil manner, but with at least seeming warmth, sentiment, and concern. Acknowledge the obligations you have to them, for the kindness they have shown you during your stay at Paris; assure them that, wherever you are, you shall remember them with gratitude; wish for opportunities of giving them proofs of your *plus tendre et respectueux souvenir*; beg of them, in case your good fortune should carry you to any part of the world where you could be of any the least use to them, that they would employ you without reserve. Say all this, and a great deal more, emphatically and pathetically; for you know *si vis me flere*——.[1] This can do you no harm, if you never return to Paris; but if you do, as probably you may, it will be of infinite use to you. Remember too, not to omit going to every house, where you have ever been once, to take leave, and recommend yourself to their remembrance. The reputation which you leave at one place, where you have been, will circulate, and you will meet with it at twenty places, where you are to go. That is a labour never quite lost.

This letter will show you, that the accident which happened to me yesterday,[2] and of which Mr. Grevenkop gives you an account, has had no bad consequences. My escape was a great one.

MY DEAR FRIEND,   London, May 11, O.S. 1752.

I break my word by writing this letter; but I break it on the allowable side, by doing more than I promised. I have pleasure in writing to you; and you may possibly have some profit in reading what I write; either of the motives were sufficient for me, both I cannot withstand. By your last, I calculate that you will leave Paris this day se'nnight; upon that supposition, this letter may still find you there.

---

[1] "Si vis me flere, dolendum est. Primum ipsi tibi."
HORACE, *De Arte Poetica.*

[2] A fall from his horse in Hyde Park.

Colonel Perry arrived here two or three days ago, and sent me a book from you, *Cassandra* [1] abridged. I am sure it cannot be too much abridged. The spirit of that most voluminous work, fairly extracted, may be contained in the smallest *duodecimo*; and it is most astonishing that there ever could have been people idle enough to write or read such endless heaps of the same stuff. It was, however, the occupation of thousands in the last century; and is still the private, though disavowed, amusement of young girls, and sentimental ladies. A love-sick girl finds in the captain with whom she is in love all the courage and all the graces of the tender and accomplished Oroondates; and many a grown-up sentimental lady talks delicate Clelia to the hero, whom she would engage to eternal love, or laments with her that love is not eternal.

> Ah! qu'il est doux d'aimer, si l'on aimoit toujours!
> Mais hélas! il n'est point d'éternelles amours. [2]

It is, however, very well to have read one of those extravagant works (of all which La Calprenède's are the best), because it is well to be able to talk with some degree of knowledge upon all those subjects that other prople talk sometimes upon; and I would by no means have anything that is known to others be totally unknown to you. It is a great advantage for any man to be able to talk or to hear, neither ignorantly nor absurdly, upon any subject; for I have known people, who have not said one word, hear ignorantly and absurdly; it has appeared in their inattentive and unmeaning faces. This, I think, is as little likely to happen to you as to anybody of your age; and if you will but add a versatility and easy conformity of manners, I know no company in which you are likely to be *de trop*.

This versatility is more particularly necessary for you at this time, now that you are going to so many different places; for though the manners and customs of the several Courts of Germany are in general the same, yet every one has its parti-

[1] *Cassandre*, a romance in ten volumes by Gautier de Costes, Seigneur de la Calprenède; he also wrote *Cléopâtre* in twelve volumes. He died in 1663.

[2] Two lines from the *Clélie* of Mademoiselle de Scudéry, which are ridiculed by Boileau in his ingenious dialogue, *Les Héros de Roman*. They are addressed by Lucretia to Brutus, and the reply of Brutus, which Boileau also quotes, is equally mawkish:

> Permettez-moi d'aimer, merveille de nos jours,
> Vous verrez qu'on peut voir d'éternelles amours.

Well might the Pluton of Boileau's dialogue exclaim: "Je ne sais tantôt plus où j'en suis. Lucrèce amoureuse! Lucrèce coquette! Et Brutus son galant!"

cular characteristic—some peculiarity or other, which distinguishes it from the next. This you should carefully attend to, and immediately adopt. Nothing flatters people more, nor makes strangers so welcome, as such an occasional conformity.

I do not mean by this that you should mimic the air and stiffness of every awkward German Court; no, by no means; but I mean that you should only cheerfully comply and fall in with certain local habits—such as ceremonies, diet, turn of conversation, etc. People who are lately come from Paris, and who have been a good while there, are generally suspected, and especially in Germany, of having a degree of contempt for every other place. Take great care that nothing of this kind appear, at least outwardly, in your behaviour; but commend whatever deserves any degree of commendation, without comparing it with what you may have left, much better, of the same kind at Paris. As, for instance, the German kitchen is, without doubt, execrable, and the French delicious; however, never commend the French kitchen at a German table, but eat of what you can find tolerable there, and commend it, without comparing it to anything better. I have known many British Yahoos, who, though while they were at Paris conformed to no one French custom, as soon as they got anywhere else, talked of nothing but what they did, saw, and eat at Paris.

The freedom of the French is not to be used indiscriminately at all the Courts in Germany, though their easiness may and ought; but that, too, at some places more than others. The Courts at Manheim and Bonn, I take to be a little more unbarbarised than some others; that of Mayence, an ecclesiastical one, as well as that of Treves (neither of which is much frequented by foreigners), retains, I conceive, a great deal of the Goth and Vandal still. There, more reserve and ceremony are necessary, and not a word of the French. At Berlin, you cannot be too French. Hanover, Brunswick, Cassel, etc. are of the mixed kind, *un peu décrottés, mais pas assez.*

Another thing which I most earnestly recommend to you, not only in Germany, but in every part of the world where you may ever be, is, not only real, but seeming attention to whomever you speak to, or to whoever speaks to you. There is nothing so brutally shocking, nor so little forgiven, as a seeming inattention to the person who is speaking to you; and I have known many a man knocked down for (in my opinion) a much slighter provocation than that shocking inattention which I mean. I have seen many people who, while you are speaking to them, instead of looking at, and attending to you, fix their eyes upon the ceiling, or some other part of the room, look out of the window, play with a dog, twirl their snuff-box, or pick their nose. Nothing discovers a little, futile, frivolous mind more than this, and nothing is so offensively ill-bred; it is an explicit declaration on your part that every, the most trifling, object deserves your attention more than all that can be said by the person who is speaking to you. Judge of the sentiments of hatred and resentment which such treatment must excite in every breast where any degree of self-love dwells, and I am sure I never yet met with that breast where there was not a great deal. I repeat it again and again (for it is highly necessary for you to remember it) that sort of vanity and self-love is inseparable from human nature, whatever may be its rank or condition; even your footman will sooner forget and forgive a beating, than any manifest mark of slight and contempt. Be therefore, I beg of you, not only really, but seemingly and manifestly, attentive to whoever speaks to you; nay more, take their tone, and tune yourself to their unison. Be serious with the serious, gay with the gay, and trifle with the triflers. In assuming these various shapes, endeavour to make each of them seem to sit easy upon you, and even to appear to be your own natural one. This is the true and useful versatility, of which a thorough knowledge of the world at once teaches the utility, and the means of acquiring.

I am very sure, at least I hope, that you will never make use of a silly expression, which is the favourite expression, and the absurd excuse of all fools and blockheads. *I cannot do such a thing*—a thing by no means either morally or physically impossible. I *cannot* attend long together to the same thing, says one fool; that is, he is such a fool that he will not. I remember a very awkward fellow, who did not know what to do with his sword, and who always took it off before dinner, saying, that he could not possibly dine with his sword on; upon which I could not help telling him, that I really believed he could, without any probable danger either to himself or others. It is a shame and an absurdity for any man to say that he cannot do all those things which are commonly done by all the rest of mankind.

Another thing, that I must earnestly warn you against, is laziness; by which more people have lost the fruit of their travels, than, perhaps, by any other thing. Pray be always in motion. Early in the morning go and see things; and the rest of the day go and see people. If you stay but a week at a

place, and that an insignificant one, see, however, all that is
to be seen there; know as many people, and get into as many
houses, as ever you can.

I recommend to you likewise, though probably you have
thought of it yourself, to carry in your pocket a map of Germany, in which the post-roads are marked; and also some
short book of travels through Germany. The former will
help to imprint in your memory situations and distances; and
the latter will point out many things for you to see, that might
otherwise possibly escape you; and which, though they may
in themselves be of little consequence, you would regret not
having seen, after having been at the places where they were.

Thus warned and provided for your journey, God speed you;
Felix faustumque sit! Adieu.

MY DEAR FRIEND,   London, May 31, O.S. 1752.

The world is the book, and the only one to which, at present,
I would have you apply yourself; and the thorough knowledge
of it will be of more use to you, than all the books that ever
were read. Lay aside the best book whenever you can go
into the best company; and depend upon it, you change for the
better. However, as the most tumultuous life, whether of
business or pleasure, leaves some vacant moments every day,
in which a book is the refuge of a rational being, I mean now to
point out to you the method of employing those moments
(which will and ought to be but few) in the most advantageous
manner.

Throw away none of your time upon those trivial futile books,
published by idle or necessitous authors, for the amusement of
idle and ignorant readers; such sort of books swarm and buzz
about one every day; flap them away, they have no sting.
Certum pete finem, have some one object for those leisure
moments, and pursue that object invariably till you have
attained it; and then take some other. For instance, considering your destination, I would advise you to single out the most
remarkable and interesting eras of modern history, and confine
all your reading to that era. If you pitch upon the Treaty of
Munster (and that is the proper period to begin with, in the
course which I am now recommending), do not interrupt it
by dipping and deviating into other books, unrelative to it;
but consult only the most authentic histories, letters, memoirs,
and negotiations, relative to that great transaction; reading

and comparing them with all that caution and distrust which
Lord Bolingbroke recommends to you, in a better manner and
in better words than I can.[1] The next period, worth your
particular knowledge, is the Treaty of the Pyrenees; which
was calculated to lay, and in effect did lay, the foundation of
the succession of the House of Bourbon to the Crown of Spain.
Pursue that in the same manner, singling, out of the millions
of volumes written upon that occasion, the two or three most
authentic ones; and particularly letters, which are the best
authorities in matters of negotiation. Next come the Treaties
of Nimeguen and Ryswick, postscripts in a manner to those
of Munster and the Pyrenees. Those two transactions have
had great light thrown upon them by the publication of many
authentic and original letters and pieces. The concessions
made at the Treaty of Ryswick, by the then triumphant Louis
the Fourteenth, astonished all those who viewed things only
superficially; but, I should think, must have been easily
accounted for by those who knew the state of the kingdom
of Spain, as well as of the health of its king, Charles the Second,
at that time.

The interval between the conclusion of the peace of Ryswick,
and the breaking out of the great war in 1702, though a short,
is a most interesting one. Every week of it almost produced
some great event. Two Partition Treaties, the death of the
King of Spain, his unexpected Will, and the acceptance of it
by Louis the Fourteenth, in violation of the second treaty of
partition, just signed and ratified by him; Philip the Fifth,
quietly and cheerfully received in Spain, and acknowledged as
King of it by most of those Powers who afterwards joined in an
alliance to dethrone him. I cannot help making this observation upon that occasion. That character has often more to do
in great transactions, than prudence and sound policy; Louis
the Fourteenth gratified his personal pride, by giving a Bourbon
King to Spain, at the expense of the true interest of France;
which would have acquired much more solid and permanent
strength by the addition of Naples, Sicily, and Lorraine, upon
the foot of the second Partition Treaty; and I think it was

---

[1] See Lord Bolingbroke's fourth Letter on the Study of History. He
warns us that, "History becomes very often a lying panegyric or a lying
satire; for different nations, or different parties in the same nation, belie
one another without respect to truth, as they murder one another without
regard to right. . . . But different religions have not been so barbarous
to one another as sects of the same religion; and, in like manner, nation
has had better quarter from nation than party from party."

fortunate for Europe that he preferred the Will. It is true, he might hope to influence his grandson; but he could never expect that his Bourbon posterity in France should influence his Bourbon posterity in Spain; he knew too well how weak the ties of blood are among men, and how much weaker still they are among Princes.

The *Memoirs* of Count Harrach, and of Las Torres, give a good deal of light into the transactions of the Court of Spain, previous to the death of that weak King; and the letters of the Maréchal d'Harcourt, then the French Ambassador in Spain, of which I have authentic copies in manuscript, from the year 1698 to 1701, have cleared up that whole affair to me. I keep that book for you. It appears by those letters, that the imprudent conduct of the House of Austria, with regard to the King and Queen of Spain, and Madame Berlips, her favourite, together with the knowledge of the Partition Treaty, which incensed all Spain, were the true and only reasons of the Will in favour of the Duke of Anjou. Cardinal Portocarrero, nor any of the Grandees, were bribed by France, as was generally reported and believed at that time; which confirms Voltaire's anecdote upon that subject.[1] Then opens a new scene and a new century; Louis the Fourteenth's good fortune forsakes him, till the Duke of Marlborough and Prince Eugene make him amends for all the mischief they had done him, by making the Allies refuse the terms of peace offered by him at Gertruydenberg. How the disadvantageous peace of Utrecht was afterwards brought on, you have lately read; and you cannot inform yourself too minutely of all those circumstances, that treaty being the freshest source from whence the late transactions of Europe have flowed.

The alterations which have since happened, whether by wars or treaties, are so recent, that all the written accounts are to be helped out, proved, or contradicted, by the oral ones of almost every informed person, of a certain age or rank in life. For the facts, dates, and original pieces of this century, you will find them in Lamberti, till the year 1715, and after that time in Rousset's *Recueil*.

I do not mean that you should plod hours together in researches of this kind; no, you may employ your time more usefully; but I mean, that you should make the most of the moments you do employ, by method, and the pursuit of one single object at a

---

[1] *Siècle de Louis XIV*, ch. xvi, which contains a brief, but clear, and for the most part exact, account of these transactions.

time; not should I call it a digression from that object, if, when you meet with clashing and jarring pretensions of different Princes to the same thing, you had immediately recourse to other books, in which those several pretensions were clearly stated; on the contrary, that is the only way of remembering those contested rights and claims; for, were a man to read *tout de suite*, Schwederus's *Theatrum Pretensionum*, he would only be confounded by the variety, and remember none of them; whereas, by examining them occasionally, as they happen to occur, either in the course of your historical reading, or as they are agitated in your own times, you will retain them, by connecting them with those historical facts which occasioned your inquiry. For example, had you read, in the course of two or three folios of Pretensions, those, among others of the two Kings of England and Prussia to Ost Frise, it is impossible that you should have remembered them; but now that they are become the debated object at the Diet at Ratisbon, and the topic of all political conversations, if you consult both books and persons concerning them, and inform yourself thoroughly, you will never forget them as long as you live. You will hear a great deal of them on one side, at Hanover; and as much on the other side, afterwards, at Berlin; hear both sides, and form your own opinion; but dispute with neither.

Letters from foreign Ministers to their Courts, and from their Courts to them, are, if genuine, the best and most authentic records you can read, as far as they go. Cardinal d'Ossat's, President Jeannin's,[1] D'Estrades,[2] Sir William Temple's, will not only inform your mind, but form your style; which, in letters of business, should be very plain and simple, but at the same time exceedingly clear, correct and pure.

All that I have said may be reduced to these two or three plain principles: 1st. That you should now read very little, but converse a great deal; 2dly. To read no useless unprofitable books; and 3dly. That those which you do read may all tend to

---

[1] The President Jeannin, born in 1540, had attached himself to the party of the league, but afterwards became one of the most able and upright ministers of Henry IV, and was entrusted by that great monarch with several important missions to the States-General in the years 1607, 1608, and 1609. His *Négociations* were first published in 1656, by his grandson, l'Abbé Castille.—M.

[2] Godefroi, Comte d'Estrades, a Maréchal of France, distinguished himself in the course of a long life (1607 to 1686) by his skilful negotiations in various countries, especially in Germany and Holland. In 1709 his *Lettres et Mémoires* appeared in five volumes; but a far more complete edition, extending to nine volumes, followed in 1743.

a certain object, and be relative to, and consequential to, each other. In this method, half-an-hour's reading every day will carry you a great way. People seldom know how to employ their time to the best advantage till they have too little left to employ; but if, at your age, in the beginning of life, people would but consider the value of it, and put every moment to interest, it is incredible what an additional fund of knowledge and pleasure such an economy would bring in. I look back with regret upon that large sum of time, which in my youth I lavished away idly, without either improvement or pleasure. Take warning betimes, and enjoy every moment; pleasures do not commonly last so long as life, and therefore should not be neglected; and the longest life is too short for knowledge, consequently every moment is precious.

I am surprised at having received no letter from you since you left Paris. I still direct this to Strasburg, as I did my two last. I shall direct my next to the post-house at Mayence, unless I receive, in the meantime, contrary instructions from you. Adieu! Remember *les attentions*; they must be your passports into good company.

MY DEAR FRIEND,　　　　　　　London, September 29, 1752.

There is nothing so necessary, but at the same time there is nothing more difficult (I know it by experience) for you young fellows, than to know how to behave yourselves prudently towards those whom you do not like. Your passions are warm, and your heads are light; you hate all those who oppose your views, either of ambition or love; and a rival, in either, is almost a synonymous term for an enemy. Whenever you meet such a man, you are awkwardly cold to him, at best; but often rude, and always desirous to give him some indirect slap. This is unreasonable; for one man has as good a right to pursue an employment, or a mistress, as another; but it is, into the bargain, extremely imprudent; because you commonly defeat your own purpose by it, and while you are contending with each other, a third often prevails. I grant you, that the situation is irksome; a man cannot help thinking as he thinks, nor feeling what he feels; and it is a very tender and sore point to be thwarted and counterworked in one's pursuits at Court, or with a mistress; but prudence and abilities must check the effects, though they cannot remove the cause. Both the pretenders make themselves disagreeable to their mistress, when they spoil the company by their pouting, or their sparring; whereas, if one of them has command enough over himself (whatever he may feel inwardly) to be cheerful, gay, and easily and unaffectedly civil to the other, as if there were no manner of competition between them, the lady will certainly like him the best, and his rival will be ten times more humbled and discouraged; for he will look upon such a behaviour as a proof of the triumph and security of his rival; he will grow outrageous with the lady, and the warmth of his reproaches will probably bring on a quarrel between them. It is the same in business; where he who can command his temper and his countenance the best, will always have an infinite advantage over the other. This is what the French call *un procédé honnête et galant*, to *pique* yourself upon showing particular civilities to a man, to whom lesser minds would in the same case show dislike, or perhaps rudeness. I will give you an instance of this in my own case; and pray remember it, whenever you come to be, as I hope you will, in a like situation.

When I went to the Hague, in 1744,[1] it was to engage the Dutch to come roundly into the war, and to stipulate their quotas of troops, etc.; your acquaintance, the Abbé de la Ville, was there on the part of France, to endeavour to hinder them from coming into the war at all. I was informed, and very sorry to hear it, that he had abilities, temper, and industry. We could not visit, our two masters being at war; but the first time I met him at a third place, I got somebody to present me to him; and I told him, that though we were to be national enemies, I flattered myself we might be, however, personal friends; with a good deal more of the same kind, which he returned in full as polite a manner. Two days afterwards I went, early in the morning, to solicit the deputies of Amsterdam, where I found l'Abbé de la Ville, who had been beforehand with me; upon which I addressed myself to the Deputies, and said, smilingly, *Je suis bien fâché, Messieurs, de trouver mon ennemi avec vous; je le connois déjà assez pour le craindre; la partie n'est pas égale, mais je me fie à vos propres intérêts contre les talens de mon ennemi; et au moins si je n'ai pas eu le premier mot j'aurai le dernier aujourd'hui.* They smiled; the Abbé was pleased with the compliment, and the manner of it, stayed about

---

[1] According to the present style of computation, Lord Chesterfield should have said 1745. But until the passing of his own Act, in 1751, the civil, ecclesiastical, and legal year was reckoned as commencing only on March 25. See Sir Harris Nicolas's valuable *Chronology of History*, p. 38, ed. 1833.

a quarter of an hour, and then left me to my Deputies, with whom I continued upon the same tone, though in a very serious manner, and told them that I was only come to state their own true interests to them, plainly and simply, without any of those arts, which it was very necessary for my friend to make use of to deceive them. I carried my point, and continued my *procédé* with the Abbé; and by this easy and polite commerce with him, at third places, I often found means to fish out from him whereabouts he was.

Remember, there are but two *procédés* in the world for a gentleman and a man of parts; either extreme politeness or knocking down. If a man, notoriously and designedly insults and affronts you, knock him down; but if he only injures you, your best revenge is to be extremely civil to him in your outward behaviour, though at the same time you counterwork him, and return him the compliment, perhaps with interest. This is not perfidy nor dissimulation; it would be so, if you were at the same time, to make professions of esteem and friendship to this man, which I by no means recommend, but, on the contrary, abhor. All acts of civility are, by common consent, understood to be no more than a conformity to custom, for the quiet and conveniency of society, the *agrémens* of which are not to be disturbed by private dislikes and jealousies. Only women and little minds pout and spar for the entertainment of the company, that always laughs at, and never pities them. For my own part, though I would by no means give up any point to a competitor, yet I would pique myself upon showing him rather more civility than to another man. In the first place, this *procédé* infallibly makes all *les rieurs* of your side, which is a considerable party; and in the next place, it certainly pleases the object of the competition, be it either man or woman; who never fail to say, upon such occasion, that *they must own you have behaved yourself very handsomely in the whole affair.* The world judges from the appearances of things, and not from the reality, which few are able, and still fewer are inclined, to fathom; and a man who will take care always to be in the right in those things, may afford to be sometimes a little in the wrong in more essential ones; there is a willingness, a desire to excuse him. With nine people in ten, good-breeding passes for good-nature, and they take attentions for good offices. At courts there will be always coldnesses, dislikes, jealousies, and hatred, the harvest being but small in proportion to the number of labourers; but then, as they arise often, they die soon, unless they are perpetuated by the manner in which they have been carried on, more than by the matter which occasioned them. The turns and vicissitudes of courts frequently make friends of enemies and enemies of friends; you must labour, therefore, to acquire that great and uncommon talent, of hating with good-breeding, and loving with prudence; to make no quarrel irreconcilable, by silly and unnecessary indications of anger; and no friendship dangerous in case it breaks, by a wanton, indiscreet, and unreserved confidence.

Few (especially young) people know how to love, or how to hate; their love is an unbounded weakness, fatal to the person they love; their hate is a hot, rash, and imprudent violence, always fatal to themselves. Nineteen fathers in twenty, and every mother who had loved you half as well as I do, would have ruined you; whereas I always made you feel the weight of my authority, that you might one day know the force of my love. Now, I both hope and believe, my advice will have the same weight with you from choice, that my authority had from necessity. My advice is just eight-and-thirty years older than your own, and consequently, I believe you think, rather better. As for your tender and pleasurable passions, manage them yourself; but let me have the direction of all the others. Your ambition, your figure, and your fortune, will, for some time at least, be rather safer in my keeping than in your own. Adieu!

MY DEAR FRIEND,   London, May 27, 1753.

I have this day been tired, jaded, nay tormented, by the company of a most worthy, sensible, and learned man, a near relation of mine, who dined and passed the evening with me. This seems a paradox, but is a plain truth; he has no knowledge of the world, no manners, no address; far from talking without book, as is commonly said of people who talk sillily, he only talks by book; which, in general conversation, is ten times worse. He has formed in his own closet, from books, certain systems of everything, argues tenaciously upon those principles, and is both surprised and angry at whatever deviates from them. His theories are good, but unfortunately are all impracticable. Why? Because he has only read and not conversed. He is acquainted with books and an absolute stranger to men. Labouring with his matter, he is delivered of it with pangs; he hesitates, stops in his utterance, and always expresses himself inelegantly. His actions are all ungraceful; so that, with all his merit and knowledge, I would rather converse six hours with the most frivolous tittle-tattle woman, who knew something of the world, than with him.

The preposterous notions of a systematical man, who does not know the world, tire the patience of a man who does. It would be endless to correct his mistakes, nor would he take it kindly; for he has considered everything deliberately, and is very sure that he is in the right. Impropriety is a characteristic, and a never-failing one, of these people. Regardless, because ignorant, of customs and manners, they violate them every moment. They often shock, though they never mean to offend; never attending either to the general character, or the particular distinguishing circumstances of the people to whom, or before whom, they talk; whereas the knowledge of the world teaches one, that the very same things which are exceedingly right and proper in one company, time, and place, are exceedingly absurd in others. In short, a man who has great knowledge from experience and observation, of the characters, customs, and manners of mankind, is a being as different from and as superior to a man of mere book and systematical knowledge, as a well-managed horse is to an ass. Study, therefore, cultivate and frequent men and women; not only in their outward, and consequently guarded, but in their interior, domestic, and consequently less disguised characters and manners.

Take your notions of things as by observation and experience you find they really are, and not as you read that they are or should be; for they never are quite what they should be. For this purpose, do not content yourself with general and common acquaintance; but, wherever you can, establish yourself, with a kind of domestic familiarity, in good houses. For instance, go again to Orli for two or three days, and so at two or three *reprises*. Go and stay two or three days at a time at Versailles, and improve and extend the acquaintance you have there. Be at home at St. Cloud; and whenever any private person of fashion invites you to pass a few days at his country-house, accept of the invitation. This will necessarily give you a versatility of mind, and a facility to adopt various manners and customs; for everybody desires to please those in whose house they are; and people are only to be pleased in their own way. Nothing is more engaging than a cheerful and easy conformity to people's particular manners, habits, and even weaknesses; nothing (to use a vulgar expression) should come amiss to a young fellow. He should be, for good purposes, what Alcibiades was commonly for bad ones, a Proteus, assuming with ease, and wearing with cheerfulness, any shape. Heat, cold, luxury, abstinence, gravity, gaiety, ceremony, easiness, learning, trifling, business, and pleasure, are modes which he should be able to take, lay aside, or change occasionally, with as much ease as he would take or lay aside his hat. All this is only to be acquired by use and knowledge of the world, by keeping a great deal of company, analysing every character, and insinuating yourself into the familiarity of various acquaintance. A right, a generous ambition to make a figure in the world, necessarily gives the desire of pleasing; the desire of pleasing points out, to a great degree, the means of doing it; and the art of pleasing is, in truth, the art of rising, of distinguishing one's self, of making a figure and a fortune in the world. But without pleasing, without the Graces, as I have told you a thousand times, *ogni fatica è vana*.

You are now but nineteen, an age at which most of your countrymen are illiberally getting drunk in port at the University. You have greatly got the start of them in learning; and, if you can equally get the start of them in the knowledge and manners of the world, you may be very sure of outrunning them in Court and Parliament, as you set out so much earlier than they. They generally begin but to see the world at one-and-twenty; you will by that age have seen all Europe. They set out upon their travels unlicked cubs, and in their travels they only lick one another, for they seldom go into any other company. They know nothing but the English world, and the worst part of that too, and generally very little of any but the English language; and they come home at three or four-and-twenty refined and polished (as is said in one of Congreve's plays) like Dutch skippers from a whale-fishing.

The care which has been taken of you, and (to do you justice) the care you have taken of yourself, has left you, at the age of nineteen only, nothing to acquire but the knowledge of the world, manners, address, and those exterior accomplishments. But they are great and necessary acquisitions, to those who have sense enough to know their true value; and your getting them before you are one-and twenty, and before you enter upon the active and shining scenes of life, will give you such an advantage over your contemporaries, that they cannot overtake you; they must be distanced. You may probably be placed about a young prince, who will probably be a young king. There all the various arts of pleasing, the engaging address, the

versatility of manners, the *brillant*, the Graces, will outweigh
and yet outrun all solid knowledge and unpolished merit. Oil
yourself, therefore, and be both supple and shining for that
race, if you would be first or early at the goal. Ladies will
most probably too have something to say there; and those who
are best with them will probably be best somewhere else.
Labour this great point, my dear child, indefatigably; attend
to the very smallest parts, the minutest graces, the most trifling
circumstances, that can possibly concur in forming the shining
character of a complete Gentleman, *un galant homme, un homme
de cour*, a man of business and pleasure; *estimé des hommes,
recherché des femmes, aimé de tout le monde.* In this view, observe
the shining part of every man of fashion who is liked and
esteemed; attend to, and imitate that particular accomplish-
ment for which you hear him chiefly celebrated and distinguished; then collect those various parts, and make yourself
a mosaic of the whole. No one body possesses everything,
and almost everybody possesses some one thing worthy of
imitation; only choose your models well; and, in order to do
so, choose by your ear more than by your eye. The best
model is always that which is most universally allowed to be
the best, though in strictness it may possibly not be so. We
must take most things as they are, we cannot make them what
we would, nor often what they should be; and, where moral
duties are not concerned, it is more prudent to follow than to
attempt to lead. Adieu!

My Dear Friend,   London, December 25, 1753.

Yesterday again I received two letters at once from you,
the one of the 7th, the other of the 15th, from Manheim.

You never had in your life so good a reason for not writing,
either to me or to anybody else, as your sore finger lately fur-
nished you. I believe it was painful, and I am glad it is cured;
but a sore finger, however painful, is a much lesser evil than
laziness of either body or mind, and attended by fewer ill
consequences.

I am very glad to hear that you were distinguished at the
Court of Manheim from the rest of your countrymen and fellow-
travellers; it is a sign that you had better manners and address
than they; for take it for granted, the best-bred people will
always be the best received wherever they go. Good manners
are the settled medium of social, as *specie* is of commercial life;

returns are equally expected for both; and people will no more advance their civility to a bear than their money to a bankrupt. I really both hope and believe that the German Courts will do you a great deal of good; their ceremony and restraint being the proper correctives and antidotes for your negligence and inattention. I believe they would not greatly relish your weltering in your own laziness, and an easy chair, nor take it very kindly if, when they spoke to you, or you to them, you looked another way, as much as to say ——. As they give so they require attention; and, by the way, take this maxim for an undoubted truth: That no young man can possibly improve in any company for which he has not respect enough to be under some degree of restraint.

I dare not trust to Meyssonier's report of his Rhenish, his Burgundy not having answered either his account or my expectations. I doubt, as a wine-merchant, he is the *perfidus caupo*, whatever he may be as a banker. I shall therefore venture upon none of his wine; but delay making my provision of old hock till I go abroad myself next spring; as I told you in the utmost secrecy in my last,[1] that I intend to do; and then, probably, I may taste some that I like, and go upon sure ground. There is commonly very good both at Aix-la-Chapelle and Liege; where I formerly got some excellent, which I carried with me to Spa, where I drank no other wine.

As my letters to you frequently miscarry, I will repeat in this that part of my last which related to your future motions. Whenever you shall be tired of Berlin, go to Dresden, where Sir Charles Williams will be, who will receive you with open arms. He dined with me to-day, and sets out for Dresden in about six weeks. He spoke of you with great kindness, and impatience to see you again. He will trust and employ you in business (and he is now in the whole secret of importance) till we fix our place to meet in; which probably will be Spa.

Wherever you are, inform yourself minutely of, and attend particularly to, the affairs of France; they grow serious, and, in my opinion, will grow more and more so every day. The King is despised, and I do not wonder at it; but he has brought it about to be hated at the same time, which seldom happens to the same man. His Ministers are known to be as disunited as incapable; he hesitates between the Church and the Parliaments, like the ass in the fable, that starved between two hampers of hay; too much in love with his mistress to part

[1] That letter is missing.

with her, and too much afraid for his soul to enjoy her; jealous of the Parliaments who would support his authority; and a devoted bigot to the Church that would destroy it.

The people are poor, consequently discontented; those who have religion are divided in their notions of it; which is saying that they hate one another. The Clergy never do forgive; much less will they forgive the Parliament; the Parliament never will forgive them. The Army must, without doubt, take, in their own minds at least, different parts in all these disputes, which, upon occasion, would break out. Armies, though always the supporters and tools of absolute power for the time being, are always the destroyers of it too; by frequently changing the hands in which they think proper to lodge it. This was the case of the Prætorian bands, who deposed and murdered the monsters they had raised to oppress mankind. The Janissaries in Turkey, and the regiments of Guards in Russia, do the same now. The French nation reasons freely, which they never did before, upon matters of religion and government, and begin to be *spregiudicati*; the officers do so too; in short, all the symptoms which I have ever met with in history, previous to great changes and revolutions in Government, now exist, and daily increase in France. I am glad of it; the rest of Europe will be the quieter, and have time to recover.

England, I am sure, wants rest; for it wants men and money; the Republic of the United Provinces wants both still more; the other Powers cannot well dance, when neither France nor the Maritime Powers can, as they used to do, pay the piper, The first squabble in Europe that I foresee will be about the Crown of Poland, should the present King die; and therefore I wish his Majesty a long life and a merry Christmas. So much for foreign politics; *à propos* of them, pray take care, while you are in those parts of Germany, to inform yourself correctly of all the details, discussions, and agreements which the several wars, confiscations, bans, and treaties, occasioned between the Bavarian and Palatine Electorates; they are interesting and curious.

I shall not, upon the occasion of the approaching New Year, repeat to you the wishes which I continue to form for you; you know them all already; and you know that it is absolutely in your own power to satisfy most of them. Among many other wishes, this is my most earnest one: That you would open the New Year with a most solemn and devout sacrifice to the Graces; who never reject those that supplicate them with fervour; without them, let me tell you, that your friend, Dame Fortune, will stand you in little stead; may they all be your friends! Adieu!

MY DEAR FRIEND,   London, February 26, 1754.

I have received your letters of the 4th from Munich, and of the 11th from Ratisbon; but I have not received that of the 31st of January, to which you refer in the former. It is to this negligence and uncertainty of the post, that you owe your accidents between Munich and Ratisbon; for, had you received my letters regularly, you would have received one from me, before you left Munich, in which I advised you to stay, since you were so well there. But at all events, you were in the wrong to set out from Munich in such weather and such roads; since you could never imagine that I had set my heart so much upon your going to Berlin, as to venture your being buried in the snow for it. Upon the whole, considering all, you are very well off. You do very well, in my mind, to return to Munich, or, at least, to keep within the circle of Munich, Ratisbon, and Manheim, till the weather and the roads are good; stay at each or any of those places as long as ever you please; for I am extremely indifferent about your going to Berlin.

As to our meeting, I will tell you my plan, and you may form your own accordingly. I propose setting out from hence the last week in April, then drinking the Aix-la-Chapelle waters for a week, and from thence being at Spa about the 15th of May, where I shall stay two months at most, and then returning straight to England. As I both hope and believe that there will be no mortal at Spa during my residence there, the fashionable season not beginning till the middle of July, I would by no means have you come there at first, to be locked up with me and some few *Capucins*, for two months, in that miserable hole; but I would advise you to stay where you like best, till about the first week in July, and then to come and pick me up at Spa, or meet me upon the road at Liege or Brussels. As for the intermediate time, should you be weary of Manheim and Munich, you may, if you please, go to Dresden to Sir Charles Williams, who will be there before that time; or you may come for a month or six weeks to the Hague; or, in short, go or stay wherever you like best. So much for your motions.

As you have sent for all the letters directed to you at Berlin, you will receive from thence volumes of mine, among which you will easily perceive that some were calculated for a supposed perusal previous to your opening them. I will not repeat anything contained in them, excepting, that I desire you will send me a warm and cordial letter of thanks for Mr. Eliot; who has, in the most friendly manner imaginable, fixed you at his own borough of Liskeard, where you will be elected, jointly with him, without the least opposition or difficulty. I will forward that letter to him into Cornwall, where he now is.

Now, that you are to be soon a man of business, I heartily wish you would immediately begin to be a man of method; nothing contributing more to facilitate and despatch business, than method and order. Have order and method in your accounts, in your reading, in the allotment of your time; in short, in everything. You cannot conceive how much time you will save by it, nor how much better everything you do will be done. The Duke of Marlborough [1] did by no means spend, but he slatterned himself into that immense debt, which is not yet near paid off. The hurry and confusion of the Duke of Newcastle do not proceed from his business, but from his want of method in it. Sir Robert Walpole, who had ten times the business to do, was never seen in a hurry, because he always did it with method.

The head of a man who has business and no method nor order, is properly that *rudis indigestaque moles quam dixere chaos*. As you must be conscious that you are extremely negligent and slatternly, I hope you will resolve not to be so for the future. Prevail with yourself, only to observe good method and order for one fortnight; and I will venture to assure you, that you will never neglect them afterwards, you will find such conveniency and advantage arising from them. Method is the great advantage that lawyers have over other people, in speaking in Parliament; for, as they must necessarily observe it in their pleadings in the Courts of Justice, it becomes habitual to them everywhere else. Without making you a compliment, I can tell you with pleasure, that order, method, and more activity of mind, are all that you want, to make, some day or other, a considerable figure in business. You have more useful knowledge, more discernment of characters, and much more discretion, than is common at your age; much more, I am sure, than I had at that age. Experience you cannot yet have,

[1] Charles Spencer, fourth Earl of Sunderland, succeeded, in 1733, as heir in the female line, to the Dukedom of Marlborough. At his death, in 1758, he had attained high military rank, and even perhaps military reputation.

and therefore trust in the mean time to mine. I am an old traveller; and well acquainted with all the bye as well as the great roads; I cannot misguide you from ignorance, and you are very sure I shall not from design.

I can assure you, that you will have no opportunity of subscribing yourself, my Excellency's etc.[1] Retirement and quiet were my choice some years ago, while I had all my senses, and health and spirits enough to carry on business; but now I have lost my hearing, and find my constitution declining daily, they are become my necessary and only refuge. I know myself (no common piece of knowledge, let me tell you), I know what I can, what I cannot, and consequently what I ought to do. I ought not, and therefore will not, return to business, when I am much less fit for it than I was when I quitted it. Still less will I go to Ireland, where, from my deafness and infirmities, I must necessarily make a different figure from that which I once made there. My pride would be too much mortified by that difference. The two important senses of seeing and hearing should not only be good, but quick, in business; and the business of a Lord-Lieutenant of Ireland (if he will do it himself) requires both those senses in the highest perfection. It was the Duke of Dorset's not doing the business himself, but giving it up to favourites, that has occasioned all this confusion in Ireland; and it was my doing the whole myself, without either favourite, minister, or mistress, that made my administration so smooth and quiet. I remember, when I named the late Mr. Liddel[2] for my secretary, everybody was much surprised at it; and some of my friends represented to me, that he was no man of business, but only a very genteel, pretty young fellow; I assured them, and with truth, that that was the very reason why I chose him; for that I was resolved to do all the business myself, and

---

[1] This passage shows that some overture was made, or expected to be made, to Lord Chesterfield to resume the Lord-Lieutenancy of Ireland. Already, in 1750, he had refused the offer of a high Cabinet office, the Presidency of the Council. "Lord Chesterfield has declined it," writes Horace Walpole; "for he says he cannot hear causes as he is grown deaf" (To Sir H. Mann, December 19, 1750). A subsequent letter from Walpole shows that Lord Chesterfield gave another reason for his refusal: "He said he would not be President, because he would not be between two fires"—meaning the Pelham brothers. He added: "The two brothers are like Arbuthnot's Lindamira and Indamora; the latter was a peaceable, tractable gentlewoman, but her sister was always quarrelling and kicking; and as they grew together there was no parting them!" (Walpole to Mann, December 22, 1750). On Lord Chesterfield's refusal, the office was conferred upon Lord Granville.

[2] Richard Liddel, Esq., Member of Parliament for Bossiney, in Cornwall. He died in June 1746.

without even the suspicion of having a minister; which the Lord-Lieutenant's secretary, if he is a man of business, is always supposed, and commonly with reason, to be.

Moreover, I look upon myself now to be *emeritus* in business, in which I have been near forty years together; I give it up to you; apply yourself to it, as I have done, for forty years, and then I consent to your leaving it for a philosophical retirement, among your friends and your books. Statesmen and beauties are very rarely sensible of the gradations of their decay; and, too sanguinely hoping to shine on in their meridian, often set with contempt and ridicule. I retired in time, *uti conviva satur*; or, as Pope says, still better, *"Ere tittering youth shall shove you from the stage."* My only remaining ambition is to be the councillor and minister of your rising ambition. Let me see my own youth revived in you; let me be your Mentor, and with your parts and knowledge, I promise you, you shall go far. You must bring, on your part, activity and attention, and I will point out to you the proper objects for them. I own, I fear but one thing for you, and that is what one has generally the least reason to fear from one of your age; I mean your laziness; which, if you indulge, will make you stagnate in a contemptible obscurity all your life. It will hinder you from doing anything that will deserve to be written, or from writing anything that may deserve to be read; and yet one or other of these two objects should be at least aimed at by every rational being.

I look upon indolence as a sort of *suicide*; for the man is effectually destroyed, though the appetites of the brute may survive. Business by no means forbids pleasures; on the contrary, they reciprocally season each other; and I will venture to affirm, that no man enjoys either in perfection, that does not join both. They whet the desire for each other. Use yourself, therefore, in time, to be alert and diligent in your little concerns; never procrastinate, never put off till to-morrow, what you can do to-day; and never do two things at a time; pursue your object, be it what it will, steadily and indefatigably; and let any difficulties (if surmountable) rather animate than slacken your endeavours. Perseverance has surprising effects.

I wish you would use yourself to translate, every day, only three or four lines, from any book, in any language, into the correctest and most elegant English that you can think of; you cannot imagine how it will insensibly form your style, and give you an habitual elegancy; it would not take you up a quarter of an hour in a day. This letter is so long, that it will hardly leave you that quarter of an hour, the day you receive it. So good-night.

MY DEAR FRIEND,   Bath, November 15, 1756.

I received yours yesterday morning, together with the Prussian papers, which I have read with great attention. If Courts could blush, those of Vienna and Dresden ought, to have their falsehoods so publicly and so undeniably exposed. The former will, I presume, next year, employ a hundred thousand men, to answer the accusation; and if the Empress of the two Russias is pleased to argue in the same cogent manner, their logic will be too strong for all the King of Prussia's rhetoric. I well remember the Treaty so often referred to in those pieces, between the two Empresses in 1746. The King was strongly pressed by the Empress Queen to accede to it. Wasner [1] communicated it to me for that purpose. I asked him if there were no secret articles; suspecting that there were some, because the ostensible Treaty was a mere harmless defensive one. He assured me there were none. Upon which I told him, that as the King had already defensive alliances with those two Empresses, I did not see of what use his accession to this Treaty, *if merely a defensive one*, could be, either to himself or the other contracting parties; but that, however, if it was only desired as an indication of the King's good will, I would give him an Act, by which his Majesty should accede to that Treaty, as far, but no farther, as at present he stood engaged to the respective Empresses, by the defensive alliances subsisting with each. This offer by no means satisfied him; which was a plain proof of the secret articles now brought to light, and into which the Court of Vienna hoped to draw us. I told Wasner so, and after that I heard no more of his invitation.

I am still bewildered in the changes at Court, of which I find that all the particulars are not yet fixed. Who would have thought, a year ago, that Mr. Fox, the Chancellor, and the Duke of Newcastle, should all three have quitted together? nor can I yet account for it; explain it to me, if you can. I cannot see, neither, what the Duke of Devonshire and Fox, whom I looked upon as intimately united, can have quarrelled about, with relation to the Treasury; inform me, if you know. I never doubted of the prudent versatility of your Vicar of Bray; but

[1] The Imperial Minister in England.

I am surprised at O'Brien Wyndham's [1] going out of the Treasury, where I should have thought that the interest of his brother-in-law, George Grenville, would have kept him.

Having found myself rather worse, these two or three last days, I was obliged to take some *ipecacuanha* last night; and, what you will think odd, for a vomit, I brought it all up again in about an hour, to my great satisfaction and emolument, which is seldom the case in restitutions.

You did well to go to the Duke of Newcastle,[2] who, I suppose, will have no more levées; however, go from time to time, and leave your name at his door, for you have obligations to him Adieu.

My Dear Friend,   Blackheath, September 1, 1763.

Great news! The King sent for Mr. Pitt, last Saturday, and the conference lasted a full hour; on the Monday following another conference lasted much longer; and yesterday a third, longer than either. You take for granted, that the treaty was concluded and ratified; no such matter, for this last conference broke it entirely off; and Mr. Pitt and Lord Temple went yesterday evening to their respective country houses. Would you know what it broke off upon, you must ask the newsmongers, and the coffee-houses; who, I dare say, know it all very minutely; but I, who am not apt to know anything that I do not know, honestly and humbly confess, that I cannot tell you; probably one party asked too much, and the other would grant too little.[3] However, the King's dignity was not, in my mind, much consulted, by their making him sole Plenipotentiary of a treaty, which they were not, in all events, determined to conclude. It ought surely to have been begun by some inferior agent, and his Majesty should only have appeared in rejecting or ratifying it. Louis XIV never sate down before a town in person, that was not sure to be taken.

However, *ce qui est différé n'est pas perdu*; for this matter must be taken up again, and concluded before the meeting of the Parliament, and probably upon more disadvantageous terms

[1] Percy O'Brien Wyndham was second son of Sir William Wyndham. A few days after the date of this letter, he was created Earl of Thomond, in the peerage of Ireland.
[2] He had at last, most unwillingly, resigned.
[3] The most authentic account of this transaction is given by Lord Hardwicke in a letter to his son, Lord Royston, September 4, 1763. See notes to the *Chatham Correspondence*, vol. ii, pp. 236-42. See also Lord Macaulay's *Essay on Pitt*.

to the present Ministers, who have tacitly admitted, by this late negotiation, what their enemies have loudly proclaimed, that they are not able to carry on affairs. So much *de re politicâ*.

I have at last done the best office that can be done, to most married people; that is, I have fixed the separation between my brother and his wife[1]; and the definitive treaty of peace will be proclaimed in about a fortnight; for the only solid and lasting peace, between a man and his wife, is, doubtless, a separation. God bless you!

MY DEAR FRIEND,   Blackheath, September 30, 1763.

You will have known, long before this, from the Office, that the departments are not cast as you wished; for Lord Halifax, as senior, had of course his choice, and chose the Southern, upon account of the colonies. The Ministry, such as it is, is now settled *en attendant mieux*; but, in my opinion, cannot, as they are, meet the Parliament.

The only, and all the efficient people they have, are in the House of Lords; for, since Mr. Pitt has firmly engaged Charles Townshend to him, there is not a man of the Court side, in the House of Commons, who has either abilities or words enough to call a coach. Lord Bute is certainly playing *un dessous de cartes*, and I suspect that it is with Mr. Pitt; but what that *dessous* is, I do not know, though all the coffee-houses do most exactly.

The present inaction, I believe, gives you leisure enough for *ennui*, but it gives you time enough too for better things; I mean, reading useful books; and, what is still more useful, conversing with yourself some part of every day. Lord Shaftesbury recommends self-conversation[1] to all authors; and I would recommend it to all men; they would be the better for it. Some people have not time, and fewer have inclination, to enter into that conversation; nay, very many dread it, and fly to the most trifling dissipations, in order to avoid it; but if a man would allot half an hour every night, for this self-conversation, and recapitulate with himself whatever he has done, right or wrong, in the course of the day, he would be both the better and the wiser for it. My deafness gives me more than sufficient time

---

[1] Shaftesbury uses the words "self-examination" and "self-inspection" (*Characteristics*, i, 168 and 196), but not, I think, "self-conversation."— Note by Dr. Hill, in *The Worldly Wisdom of Lord Chesterfield*.

for self-conversation; and I have found great advantages from it.

My brother, and Lady Stanhope, are at last finally parted. I was the negotiator between them; and had so much trouble in it, that I would much rather negotiate the most difficult point of the *jus publicum Sacri Romani Imperii*, with the whole Diet of Ratisbon, then negotiate any point with any woman. If my brother had had some of those self-conversations, which I recommend, he would not, I believe, at past sixty, with a crazy, battered constitution, and deaf into the bargain, have married a young girl, just turned of twenty, full of health, and consequently of desires. But who takes warning by the fate of others? This, perhaps, proceeds from a negligence of self-conversation. God bless you!

My Dear Friend,   Bath, December 18, 1763.

I received your letter this morning, in which you reproach me with not having written to you this week. The reason was, that I did not know what to write. There is that sameness in my life here, that *every day is still but as the first.* I see very few people; and, in the literal sense of the word, I hear nothing.

Mr. Luther and Mr. Conyers [1] I hold to be two very ingenious men; and your image of the two men ruined, one by losing his law-suit, and the other by carrying it, is a very just one. To be sure they felt in themselves uncommon talents for business and speaking, which were to reimburse them!

Lord Northumberland is rightly served for taking for his own man another man's man. Hamilton [2] most notoriously belonged always to Lord Holland, who, I dare say, has his reasons for putting Hamilton upon all this.

Harte has a great poetical work to publish before it be long; he has shown me some parts of it. He has entitled it *Emblems*; but I persuaded him to alter that name, for two reasons; the first was, because they were not emblems, but fables; the second was, that, if they had been emblems, Quarles had degraded and vilified that name to such a degree, that it is impossible to make use of it after him; so they are to be called Fables, though

---

[1] William Harvey, member for Essex, having died in November 1763, a new writ was ordered, and Mr. John Luther was elected. His unsuccessful competitor was Mr. Conyers.

[2] This was Single-speech Hamilton, who had been chosen by Lord Halifax, and continued by Lord Northumberland, as Secretary, during their Lord Lieutenancies of Ireland; but he had a quarrel with the latter. This paragraph was formerly suppressed.

Moral Tales would, in my mind, be the properest name. If you ask me what I think of those I have seen, I must say that *sunt plura bona, quædam mediocria, et quædam——*.

Your report of future changes, I cannot think is wholly groundless; for it still runs strongly in my head, that the mine we talked of will be sprung at, or before, the end of the Session.

I have got a little more strength, but not quite the strength of Hercules. . . . So good-night, and God bless you!

MY DEAR FRIEND,   London, December 27, 1765.

I arrived here from Bath last Monday, rather, but not much better than when I went thither. My rheumatic pains, in my legs and hips, plague me still; and I must never expect to be quite free from them.

You have, to be sure, had from the Office an account of what the Parliament did, or rather did not do, the day of their meeting; and the same point will be the great object at their next meeting; I mean the affair of our American Colonies, relatively to the late imposed Stamp Duty; which our Colonists absolutely refuse to pay. The Administration are for some indulgence and forbearance to those froward children of their mother country; the Opposition are for taking vigorous, as they call them, but I call them violent measures; not less than *les dragonades*; and to have the tax collected by the troops we have there. For my part, I never saw a froward child mended by whipping; and I would not have the mother country become a step-mother. Our trade to America brings in, *communibus annis*, two millions a-year; and the Stamp Duty is estimated at but one hundred thousand pounds a-year; which I would by no means bring into the stock of the Exchequer, at the loss, or even the risk of a million a-year to the national stock.

I do not tell you of the Garter given away yesterday, because the newspapers will; but I must observe, that the Prince of Brunswick's riband is a mark of great distinction to that family; which, I believe, is the first (except our own Royal Family) that has ever had two blue ribands at a time; but it must be owned they deserve them.

One hears of nothing now, in town, but the separation of men and their wives. Will Finch the ex-Vice Chamberlain,[1]

---

[1] Mr. Finch married in 1746 Lady Charlotte Fermor.

Lord Warwick,[1] your friend Lord Bolingbroke.[2] I wonder at none of them for parting; but I wonder at many for still living together; for in this country, it is certain, that marriage is not well understood.

I have this day sent Mr. Larpent two hundred pounds for your Christmas-box, which I suppose he will inform you of by this post. Make this Christmas as merry a one as you can; for *pour le peu de bon tems qui nous reste, rien n'est si funeste qu'un noir chagrin*. For the new years, God send you many, and happy ones!

Adieu.

[1] Francis Greville, first Earl of Warwick, married in 1742 Elizabeth, daughter of Lord Archibald Hamilton.
[2] Frederick, second Viscount Bolingbroke, married Lady Diana Spencer, daughter of the Duke of Marlborough. A divorce ensued in 1768, and Lady Diana became the wife of the Hon. Topham Beauclerk.

LETTERS TO OTHER RELATIVES

TO HIS GODSON—PHILIP STANHOPE

A series of 236 letters was addressed by Lord Chesterfield to Philip Stanhope, his godson and distant kinsman, who became his heir and successor to the earldom. They were first published in the *Edinburgh Magazine and Review*, February to May 1774 (others published 1890), probably from copies made by Dr. Dodd; they were reprinted in a Dublin edition of the Letters to his Son in 1776; in the supplementary quarto volume to Maty's edition of Chesterfield's *Works*, by B. W., of the Inner Temple; and in Lord Mahon's edition of 1845.

MY DEAR LITTLE BOY,   Bath, October 31, 1765.

Our correspondence has hitherto been very desultory and various. My letters have had little or no relation to each other, and I endeavoured to suit them to your age and passion for variety. I considered you as a child, and trifled with you accordingly; and, though I cannot yet look upon you as a man, I shall consider you as being capable of some serious reflections. You are now above half a man, for before your present age is doubled you will be quite a man: therefore, *paulo majora canamus.*

You already know your religious and moral duties, which, indeed are exceedingly simple and plain; the former consist in fearing and loving your Creator, and in observing His laws, which He has written in every man's heart, and which your conscience will always remind you of, if you give it but a fair hearing; the latter, I mean your moral duties, are fully contained in these few words, *Do as you would be done by.* Your classical knowledge, others more able than myself will instruct you in. There remains, therefore, nothing in which I can be useful to you, except to communicate to your youth and inexperience what a long observation and knowledge of the world enables me to give you.

I shall then, for the future, write you a series of letters, which I desire you will read twice over, and keep by you, upon the *duty,* the *utility,* and the *means* of pleasing—that is, of being what the French call *aimable*; an art which, it must be owned, they possess almost exclusively; they have studied it the most, and they practise it the best. I shall, therefore, often borrow their expressions in the former letters, as answering my ideas better than any I can find in my own language.

Remember this, and fix it in your mind, that whoever is not *aimable*, is in truth *nobody at all* with regard to the general intercourse of life; his learning is pedantry, and even his virtues have no lustre. Perhaps my subject may oblige me to say things above your present *forte*; but, in proportion as your understanding opens and extends itself, you will understand them; and then *hæc olim meminisse juvabit*.

I presume you will not expect elegancy, or even accuracy, in letters of this kind, which I write singly for your use. I give you my matter just as it occurs to me. May it be useful to you, for I do not mean it for public perusal.

P.S. If you were in this place, it would quite turn your little head; here would be so much of your dear variety, that you would think rather less, if possible, than most of the company who saunter away their whole time and do nothing.

MY DEAR LITTLE BOY,   Bath, November 7, 1765.

The desire of being pleased is universal; the desire of pleasing should be so too; it is included in that great and fundamental principle of morality, of doing to others what one wishes they should do to us. There are, indeed, some moral duties of a much higher nature, but none of a more amiable; and I do not hesitate to place it at the head of what Cicero calls the *leniores virtutes*.

The benevolent and feeling heart performs this duty with pleasure, and in a manner that gives it at the same time; but the great, the rich, the powerful, too often bestow their favours upon their inferiors in the manner they bestow their scraps upon their dogs, so as neither to oblige man nor dogs. It is no wonder if favours, benefits, and even charities thus bestowed ungraciously, should be as coldly and faintly acknowledged. Gratitude is a burden upon our imperfect nature, and we are but too willing to ease ourselves of it, or at least to lighten it as much as we can.

The *manner*, therefore, of conferring favours or benefits, is, as to pleasing, almost as important as the matter itself. Take care, then, never to throw away the obligations, which perhaps you may have it in your power to confer upon others by an air of insolent protection, or by a cold and comfortless manner, which stifles them in their birth. Humanity inclines, religion requires, and our moral duties oblige us, as far as we are able, to relieve the distresses and miseries of our fellow-creatures; but this is not all, for a true heartfelt benevolence and tenderness will prompt us to contribute what we can to their ease, their amusement, and their pleasure, as far as innocently we may. Let us, then, not only scatter benefits, but even strew flowers for our fellow-travellers, in the rugged ways of this wretched world!

There are some, and but too many in this country particularly, who, without the least visible taint of ill-nature or malevolence, seem to be totally indifferent, and do not show the least desire to please; as, on the other hand, they never designedly offend. Whether this proceeds from a lazy, negligent, and listless disposition, from a gloomy and melancholy nature, from ill-health and low spirits, or from a secret and sullen pride, arising from the consciousness of their boasted liberty and independency, is hard to determine, considering the various movements of the human heart, and the wonderful errors of the human mind; but, be the cause what it will, that neutrality, which is the effect of it, makes these people, as neutralities do, despicable, and mere blanks in society. They would surely be roused from their indifference, if they would seriously consider the infinite *utility of pleasing*, which I shall do in my next.

MY DEAR LITTLE BOY,   Bath, November 13, 1765.

As the *utility* of pleasing seems to be almost a self-evident proposition, I shall rather hint it to you than dwell upon it. The person who manifests a constant desire to please, places his, perhaps, small stock of merit at great interest. What vast returns, then, must real merit, when thus adorned, necessarily bring in? A prudent usurer would with transport place his last shilling at such interest, and upon so solid a security.

The man who is amiable will make almost as many friends as he does acquaintances; I mean in the current acceptation of the word, but not such sentimental friends as Pylades or Orestes, Nisus and Euryalus, etc.; but he will make people in general wish him well, and inclined to serve him in anything not inconsistent with their own interest.

Civility is the essential article towards pleasing, and is the result of good-nature and of good-sense; but good-breeding is the decoration, the lustre of civility, and only to be acquired by a minute attention to, and experience of, good company. A good-natured ploughman or fox-hunter may be intentionally as civil as the politest courtier, but their manner often degrades and vilifies their matter; whereas, in good-breeding, the *manner* always adorns and dignifies the *matter* to such a degree that I have often known it give currency to base coin. We may truly say, in this case, *materiem superat opus*.

Civility is often attended by a ceremoniousness, which good breeding corrects, but will not quite abolish. A certain degree of ceremony is a necessary outwork of manners, as well as of religion; it keeps the forward and petulant at a proper distance, and is a very small restraint to the sensible and to the well-bred part of the world. We find, in the *Tale of a Tub*, that Peter had too much pomp and ceremony, Jack too little; but Martin's conduct seems to be a good rule for both worship and manners, and good-sense and good-breeding pursue this true medium. In my next, I shall consider the *means* of pleasing.

P.S. I am very sorry I can send you no venison this year, but I have no doe venison this time, the season has been so unfavourable. You must celebrate your natal day this year without it, which you will do best by reflecting that you are now ten years old, and that you have no time to lose in trifling childish dissipation. You must apply now or never.

MY DEAR LITTLE BOY,   Bath, November 25, 1765.

Carefully avoid an argumentative and disputative turn, which too many people have, and some even value themselves upon, in company; and, when your opinion differs from others, maintain it only with modesty, calmness, and gentleness; but never be eager, loud, or clamorous; and, when you find your antagonist beginning to grow warm, put an end to the dispute by some genteel *badinage*: for, take it for granted, if the two best friends in the world dispute with eagerness, upon the most trifling subject imaginable, they will, for the time, find a momentary alienation from each other. Disputes upon any subject are a sort of trial of the understanding, and must end in the mortification of one or other of the disputants. On the other hand, I am far from meaning that you should give an universal assent to all that you hear said in company; such an assent would be mean, and in some cases criminal; but blame with indulgence, and correct with *douceur*.

It is impossible for a man of sense not to have a contempt for fools, and for a man of honour not to have an abhorrence of knaves; but you must gain upon yourself, so as not to discover either in their full extent. They are, I fear, too great a majority to contend with; and their number makes them formidable, though not respectable. They commonly hang together, for the mutual use they make of each other. Show them a reserved civility, and let them not exist with regard to you. Do not play off the fool, as is too commonly done by would-be wits, nor shock the knave unnecessarily, but have as little as possible to do with either; and remember always, that whoever contracts a friendship with a knave or a fool, has something bad to do or to conceal. A young man, especially at his first entering into the world, is generally judged of by the company he keeps—and it is a very fair way of judging; and though you will not at first be able to make your way, perhaps, into the best company, it is always in your power to avoid bad. It may be, that you will ask me how I define *good* and *bad* company? and I will do it as well as I can, for it is of the greatest importance to know the difference.

Good company consists of a number of people of a certain fashion (I do not mean birth), of whom the majority are reckoned to be people of sense, and of decent characters—in short, of those who are allowed universally to be, and are called, good company. It is possible, nay probable, that a fool or two may sneak, or a knave or two intrude into such company; the former, in hopes of getting the reputation of a little common sense, and the latter, that of some common honesty. But, *ubi plura nitent*, like Horace, you must not be offended *paucis maculis*.

Bad company is, whatever is not generally allowed to be good company; but there are several gradations in this, as well as in the other; and it will be impossible for you, in the common course of life, not to fall sometimes into bad company; but get out of it as soon and as well as you can. There are some companies so blasted and scandalous, that to have been with them twice would hurt your character, both as to virtue and parts; such is the company of bullies, sharpers, jockies, and low debauchees either in wine or women, not to mention fools. On the other hand, do not, while young, declaim and preach against them like a Capuchin. You are not called upon to be a repairer of wrongs, or a reformer of manners. Let your own be pure, and leave others to the contempt or indignation they deserve.

There is a third sort of company, which, without being scandalous, is vilifying and degrading. I mean, what is called *low* company, which young men of birth and fashion, at their first appearance in the world, are too apt to like, from a degree of bashfulness, *mauvaise honte*, and laziness, which is not easily rubbed off. If you sink into this sort of company but for one year, you will never emerge from it, but remain as obscure and insignificant as they are themselves. Vanity is also a great inducement to keep low company; for a man of quality is sure to be the first man in it, and to be admired and flattered, though, perhaps, the greatest fool in it. Do not think I mean, by low company, people of no birth; for birth goes for nothing with me, nor, I hope, with you; but I mean, by low company, obscure, insignificant people, unknown and unseen in the polite part of the world, and distinguished by no one particular merit or talent, unless, perhaps, by soaking and sotting out their evenings; for drinking is generally the dull and indecent occupation of such company.

There is another sort of company which I wish you to avoid in general, though now and then (but seldom) there may be no harm in seeing it. I mean the company of wags, witlings, buffoons, mimics, and merry fellows, who are all of them commonly the dullest fellows in the world with the strongest animal spirits. If from mere curiosity you go into such company, do not wear in it a severe, philosophical face of contempt of their illiberal mirth, but content yourself with acting a very inferior part in it; contract no familiarity with any of the performers, which would give them claims upon you that you could not with decency either satisfy or reject. Call none of them by their Christian names, as Jack, Frank, etc., but use rather a more ceremonious civility with them than with your equals, for nothing keeps forward and petulant puppies at a proper distance so effectually as a little ceremony.

My Dear Little Boy,   Bath, December 4, 1765.

Bad company is much more easily defined than good; what is bad must strike everybody at first sight; folly, knavery, and profligacy can never be mistaken for wit, honour, and decency. Bad company have *fœnum in cornu, longe fuge*; but in good, there are several gradations from good to the best; merely good, is rather free from objections than deserving of praise. Aim at the best: but what is the best? I take it to be those societies of men or women, or a mixture of both, where great politeness, good-breeding, and decency, though, perhaps, not always virtue, prevail.

Women of fashion and character—I do not mean absolutely unblemished—are a necessary ingredient in the composition of good company; the *attention* which they require, and which is always paid them by well-bred men, keeps up politeness, and gives a habit of good-breeding; whereas men, when they live together without the lenitive of women in company, are apt to grow careless, negligent, and rough among one another. In company, every woman is every man's superior, and must be addressed with respect—nay more, with flattery—and you need not fear making it too strong. Such flattery is not mean on your part, nor pernicious to them, for it can never give them a greater opinion of their beauty or their sense than they had before; therefore, make the dose strong—it will be greedily swallowed.

Women stamp the character, fashionable or unfashionable, of all young men at their first appearance in the world. Bribe them with minute attention, good-breeding, and flattery. I have often known their proclamation give a value and currency to base coin enough, and, consequently, it will add a lustre to the truest sterling. Women, though otherwise called sensible, have all of them, more or less, weaknesses, singularities, whims and humours, especially vanity; study attentively all their failings, gratify them as far as you can—nay, flatter them, and sacrifice your own little humours to them. Young men are too apt to show a dislike, not to say an aversion and contempt, for ugly and old women, which is both impolitic and injudicious; for there is a respectful politeness due to the whole sex. Besides, the ugly and the old, having the least to do themselves, are jealous of being despised, and never forgive it; and I could suppose cases, in which you would desire their friendship, or at least their neutrality. Let it be a rule with you never to show that contempt which very often you will have, and with reason, for a human creature, for it will never be forgiven. An injury is sooner pardoned than an insult.

My Dear Little Boy,   Bath, December 18, 1765.

If God gives you wit, which I am not sure that I wish you unless He gives you at the same time, at least an equal portion of judgment to keep it in good order, wear it like your sword in the scabbard, and do not brandish it to the terror of the whole company. If you have real wit, it will flow spontaneously, and you need not aim at it; for, in that case, the rule of the Gospel is reversed, and it will prove—seek, and you shall *not* find. Wit is so shining a quality that everybody admires it; most people aim at it, all people fear it, and few love it unless in themselves. A man must have a good share of wit himself to endure a great share in another. When wit exerts itself in satire, it is a most malignant distemper. Wit, it is true, may be shown in satire; but satire does not constitute wit, as many imagine. A man of real wit will find a thousand better occasions of showing it.

Abstain, therefore, most carefully from satire, which, though it fall on no particular person in company, and momentarily, from the malignancy of the human heart, pleases all, yet, upon reflection, it frightens all too. Every one thinks it may be his turn next, and will hate you for what he finds you could say of him, more than be obliged to you for what you do not say. Fear and hatred are next-door neighbours. The more wit you have, the more good-nature and politeness you must show, to induce people to pardon your superiority; for that is no easy matter. Learn to shrink yourself to the size of the company you are in. Take their tone, whatever it may be, and excel in it if you can; but never pretend to give the tone. A free conversation will no more bear a dictator, than a free government will.

The character of a man of wit is a shining one that every man would have, if he could, though it is often attended with some inconveniences; the dullest Alderman ever aims at it, cracks his dull joke, and thinks, or at least hopes, that it is wit; but the denomination of *a wit* is always formidable, and very often ridiculous. These *titular wits* have commonly much less wit than petulance and presumption; they are at best the *rieurs de leur quartier,* in which narrow sphere they are at once feared and admired.

You will perhaps ask me, and justly, how, considering the delusion of self-love and vanity, from which no man living is absolutely free, how you shall know whether you have wit or not. To which the best answer I can give you is, not to trust to the voice of your own judgment, for it will deceive you, nor to your ears, which will always greedily receive flattery, if you are worth being flattered; but trust only to your eyes, and read in the countenance of good company their approbation or dislike of what you say. Observe, carefully, too, whether you are sought for, solicited, and in a manner pressed into good company. But even all this will not absolutely ascertain your wit; therefore do not, upon this encouragement, flash your wit in people's faces à *ricochets*, in the shape of *bon mots*, epigrams, small repartees.

Appear to have rather less than more wit than you really have. A wise man will live as much within his wit as his income. Content yourself with good sense and reason, which at the long-run are ever sure to please everybody who has either; if wit comes into the bargain, welcome it, but never invite it. Bear this truth always in your mind, that you may be admired for your wit, if you have any; but that nothing but good sense and good qualities can make you be loved; they are substantial, every day's wear. Wit is for *les jours de gala*, where people go chiefly to be stared at.

P.S. I received your last letter, which is very well written. I shall see you next week, and bring you some pretty things from hence; because I am told you are a very good boy, and have learned very well.

MY DEAR LITTLE BOY, Bath, January 21, 1766.

I have more than once recommended to you, in the course of our correspondence, attention; but I shall frequently recur to that subject, which is as inexhaustible as it is important. Attend carefully, in the first place, to human nature in general, which is pretty much the same in all human creatures, and varies chiefly by modes, habits, education, and example. Analyse, and, if I may use the expression, anatomize it; study your own, and that will lead you to know other people's; carefully observe the words, the looks, and gestures of the whole company you are in, and retain all their little singularities, humours, tastes, affections, and antipathies; which will enable you to please or avoid them occasionally as your judgment may direct you.

I will give you the most trifling instance of this that can be imagined, and yet will be sure to please. If you invite anybody to dinner, you should take care to provide those things which you have observed them to like more particularly, and not to have those things which you know they have an antipathy to. These trifling things go a great way in the Art of Pleasing, and the more so, from being so trifling, that they are flattering proofs of your regard for those persons. These things are what the French call *des attentions*; which, to do them justice, they study and practise more than any people in Europe.

Attend to, and look at whoever speaks to you, and never seem *distrait* or *rêveur*, as if you did not hear them at all; for nothing is more contemptuous, and consequently more shocking. It is true, you will by this means often be obliged to attend to things not worth anybody's attention; but it is a necessary sacrifice to be made to good manners in society. A minute attention is also necessary to time, place, and character; a *bon mot* in one company is not so in another, but, on the contrary, may prove offensive. Never joke with those whom you observe to be at the time pensive and grave; and, on the other hand, do not preach and moralise in a company full of mirth and gaiety. Many people come into company full of what they intend to say in it themselves, without the least regard to others; and thus charged up to the muzzle are resolved to let it off at any rate. I knew a man who had a story about a gun, which he thought a good one and that he told it very well. He tried all means in the world to turn the conversation upon guns; but, if he failed in his attempt, he started in his chair, and said he heard a gun fired; but when the company assured him they heard no such thing, he answered, perhaps then I was mistaken; but, however, since we are talking of guns, —and then told his story, to the great indignation of the company.

Become, as far as with innocence and honour you can, all things to all men, and you will gain a great many. Have *des prévenances* too, and say or do what you judge beforehand will be most agreeable to them, without their hinting at or expecting it. It would be endless to specify the numberless opportunities a man has of pleasing, if he will but make use of them; your own good sense will suggest them to you, and your good-nature, and even your interest, will induce you to practise them. Great attention is to be had to times and seasons; for example, at meals talk often, but never long at a time; for the frivolous bustle of servants, and often the more frivolous conversation of the guests, which chiefly turns upon kitchen-stuff, and cellar-stuff, will not bear any long reasonings or relations. Meals are and were always reckoned the moments of relaxation of the mind, and sacred to easy mirth and social cheerfulness. Conform to this custom, and furnish your quota of good-humour; but be not induced by example to the frequent excess of gluttony or intemperance; the former inevitably produces dulness, the latter madness.

Observe the *à propos* in everything you say or do. In conversing with those who are much your superiors, however easy and familiar you may and ought to be with them, preserve the respect that is due to them. Converse with your equals with an easy familiarity, and at the same time with great civility and decency. But too much familiarity, according to the old saying, often breeds contempt, and sometimes quarrels. I know nothing more difficult in common behaviour than to fix due bounds to familiarity; too little implies an unsociable formality, too much destroys friendly and social intercourse. The best rule I can give you to manage familiarity is, never to be more familiar with anybody than you would be willing and even glad that he should be with you. On the other hand, avoid that uncomfortable reserve and coldness which is generally the shield of cunning, or the protection of dulness. The Italian maxim is a wise one, *il volto sciolto, i pensieri stretti*; that is, let your countenance be open and your thoughts be close. To your inferiors you should use a hearty benevolence in your words and actions, instead of a refined politeness, which would be apt to make them suspect that you rather laughed at them. For example, your civility to a mere country gentleman must be in a very different way to what you would use to a man of the world: your reception of him should seem hearty, and rather coarse, to relieve him from the embarrassment of his own *mauvaise honte*.

Have attention even in the company of fools; for, though they are fools, they may, perhaps, drop or repeat something worth your knowing, and which you may profit by. Never talk your best in the company of fools; for they would not understand you, and would perhaps suspect that you jeered them, as they commonly call it; but talk only the plainest common sense to them, and very gravely, for there is no jesting nor *badinage* with them. Upon the whole, with attention, and *les attentions*, you will be sure to please; without them, you will be sure to offend.

MY DEAR LITTLE BOY, [Undated.]

Carefully avoid all affectation either of body or of mind. It is a very true and a very trite observation that no man is ridiculous for being what he really is, but for affecting to be what he is not. No man is awkward by nature, but by affecting to be genteel. I have known many a man of common sense pass generally for a fool, because he affected a degree of wit that God had denied him. A ploughman is by no means awkward in the exercise of his trade, but would be exceedingly ridiculous if he attempted the air and graces of a man of fashion. You learned to dance, but it was not for the sake of dancing; it was to bring your air and motions back to what they would naturally have been, if they had had fair play, and had not been warped in your youth by bad examples, and awkward imitations of other boys.

Nature may be cultivated and improved, both as to the body and the mind; but it is not to be extinguished by art; and all endeavours of that kind are absurd, and an inexpressible fund for ridicule. Your body and mind must be at ease, to be agreeable; but affectation is a particular restraint, under which no man can be genteel in his carriage, or pleasing in his conversation. Do you think your notions would be easy or graceful, if you wore the clothes of another man much slenderer or taller than yourself? Certainly not; it is the same thing with the mind, if you affect a character that does not fit you, and that nature never intended for you. But do not mistake, and think that it follows from hence, that you should exhibit your whole character to the public, because it is your natural one. No; many things must be suppressed, and many things concealed, in the best character. Never force nature; but it is by no means necessary to show it all.

Here discretion must come to your assistance, that sure and safe guide through life; discretion, that necessary companion to reason, and the useful *garde-fou*, if I may use the expression, to wit and imagination. Discretion points out the *à propos*, the *decorum*, the *ne quid nimis*, and will carry a man with moderate parts further than the most shining parts would without it. It is another word for judgment, though not quite synonymous to it. Judgment is not upon all occasions required, but discretion always is. Never affect nor assume a particular character; for it will never fit you, but will probably give you a ridicule; leave it to your conduct, your virtues, your morals, and your manners, to give you one. Discretion will teach you to have particular attention to your *mœurs*, which we have no one word in our language to express exactly. *Morals* are too much, *manners* too little. *Decency* comes the nearest to it, though rather short of it. Cicero's word *decorum* is properly the thing; and I see no reason why that expressive word should not be adopted and naturalized in our language; I have never scrupled using it in that sense.

A propos of words. Study your own language more carefully than most people do; get a habit of speaking it with propriety and elegance; for nothing is more disagreeable than to hear a gentleman talk the barbarisms, the solecisms, and the vulgarisms of porters. Avoid, on the other hand, a stiff and formal accuracy, especially what the women call hard words, when plain ones as expressive are at hand. The French make it their study *bien narrer*, but are apt *narrer trop*, and with too affected an elegancy.

The three commonest topics of conversation are religion, politics, and news. All people think they understand the two first perfectly, though they never studied either; and are therefore very apt to talk both dogmatically and ignorantly, consequently with warmth. But religion is by no means a proper subject of conversation in a mixed company; it should only be treated among a very few people of learning, for mutual instruction. It is too awful and respectable a subject to become a familiar one. Therefore never mingle yourself in it any further, than to express an universal toleration and indulgence to all errors in it, if conscientiously entertained; for, every man has as good a right to think as he does, as you have to think as you do; nay, in truth, he cannot help it.

As for politics, they are still more universally understood; and, as every one thinks his private interest more or less concerned in them, nobody hesitates to pronounce decisively upon them, not even the ladies, the copiousness of whose eloquence is more to be admired than the conclusiveness of their logic.

It will be impossible for you to avoid engaging in these conversations, for there are hardly any others; but take care to do it coolly, and with great good-humour; and whenever you find that the company begin to be heated, and noisy for the good of their country, be only a patient hearer, unless you can interpose by some agreeable *badinage*, and restore good-humour to the company. And here I cannot help observing to you, that nothing is more useful either to put off or to parry disagreeable and puzzling affairs, than a good-humoured and genteel *badinage*; I have found it so by long experience. But this *badinage* must not be carried to *mauvaise plaisanterie*; it must be light, without being frivolous; sensible, without being sententious; and, in short, have that *je ne sçais quoi* which everybody feels, and nobody can describe.

I shall now for a time suspend the course of these Letters; but as the subject is inexhaustible, I shall occasionally resume it. In the meantime, believe, that a man, who does not generally please is nobody; and that a constant endeavour to please, will infallibly please to a certain degree at least.

<hr />

(*To be Delivered after his own Death.*[1])

MY DEAR BOY,

You will have received by my will solid proofs of my esteem and affection. This paper is not a will, and only conveys to you my most earnest requests, for your good alone, which requests, from your gratitude for my past care, from your good heart, and your good sense, I persuade myself, you will observe as punctually as if you were obliged by law to do so. They are not the dictates of a peevish, sour old fellow, who affects to give good rules, when he can no longer give bad examples, but the advice of an indulgent and tender friend (I had almost said parent), and the result of the long experience of one *hackneyed in the ways of life*, and calculated only to assist and guide your unexperienced youth.

You will probably come to my title and estate too soon, and at an age at which you will be much less fit to conduct yourself with discretion than you were at ten years old. This I know is a very unwelcome truth to a sprightly young fellow, and will hardly be believed by him, but it is nevertheless a truth, and a truth which I most sincerely wish, though I cannot reasonably hope, that you may be firmly convinced of. At that critical period of life, the dangerous passions are busy, impetuous, and stifle all reflection, the spirits high, the examples in general bad. It is a state of continual ebriety for six or seven years at least, and frequently attended by fatal and permanent consequences, both to body and mind. Believe yourself then to be drunk, and as drunken men, when reeling, catch hold of the next thing in their way to support them, do you, my dear boy, hold by the rails of my experience. I hope they will hinder you from falling, though perhaps not from staggering a little sometimes.

<hr />

[1] First printed in *Letters from a Celebrated Nobleman to his Heir* (London and Brighthelmstone, 1783).

As to your religious and moral obligations I shall say nothing, because I know that you are thoroughly informed of them, and hope that you will scrupulously observe them, for if you do not you can neither be happy here nor hereafter.

I suppose you of the age of one-and-twenty, and just returned from your travels much fuller of fire than reflection; the first impressions you give of yourself, at your first entrance upon the great stage of life in your own country, are of infinite consequence, and to a great degree decisive of your future character. You will be tried first by the grand jury of Middlesex, and if they find a Bill against you, you must not expect a very favourable verdict from the many petty juries who will try you again in Westminster.

Do not set up a tawdry, flaunting equipage, nor affect a grave one; let it be the equipage of a sensible young fellow, and not the gaudy one of a thoughtless young heir; a frivolous *éclat* and profusion will lower you in the opinion of the sober and sensible part of mankind. Never wear over-fine clothes; be as fine as your age and rank require, but do not distinguish yourself by any uncommon magnificence or singularity of dress. Follow the example of Martin, and equally avoid that of Peter or Jack.[1] Do not think of shining by any one trifling circumstance, but shine in the aggregate, by the union of great and good qualities, joined to the amiable accomplishments of manners, air and address.

At your first appearance in town, make as many acquaintances as you please, and the more the better, but for some time contract no friendships. Stay a little and inform yourself of the characters of those young fellows with whom you must necessarily live more or less, but connect yourself intimately with none but such whose moral characters are unblemished. For it is a true saying, *tell me who you live with and I will tell you what you are*; and it is equally true, that, when a man of sense makes a friend of a knave or a fool he must have something bad to do, or to conceal. A good character will be soiled at least by frequent contact with a bad one.

Do not be seduced by the fashionable word *spirit*. A man of spirit in the usual acceptation of that word is, in truth, a creature of strong and warm animal life, with a weak understanding; passionate, wrong-headed, captious, jealous of his mistaken honour, and suspecting intended affronts, and, which is worse, willing to fight in support of his wrong head. Shun this kind

[1] In Swift's *Tale of a Tub.*

of company, and content yourself with a cold, steady firmness and resolution. By the way, a woman of spirit is *mutatis mutandis*, the duplicate of this man of spirit; a scold and a vixen.

I shall say little to you against gaming, for my example cries aloud to you DO NOT GAME. Gaming is rather a rage than a passion; it will break in upon all your rational pleasures, and perhaps with some stain upon your character, if you should happen to win; for whoever plays deep must necessarily lose his money or his character. I have lost great sums at play, and am sorry I lost them, but I should now be much more sorry if I had won as much. As it is, I can only be accused of folly, to which I plead guilty. But as in the common intercourse of the world you will often be obliged to play at social games, observe strictly this rule: Never sit down to play with men only, but let there always be a woman or two of the party, and then the loss or the gain cannot be considerable.

Do not be in haste to marry, but look about you first, for the affair is important. There are but two objects in marriage, love or money. If you marry for love, you will certainly have some very happy days, and probably many very uneasy ones, if for money, you will have no happy days and probably no uneasy ones; in this latter case let the woman at least be such a one that you can live decently and amicably with, otherwise it is a robbery; in either case, let her be of an unblemished and unsuspected character, and of a rank not indecently below your own.

You will doubtless soon after your return to England be a Member of one of the two Houses of Parliament; there you must take pains to distinguish yourself as a speaker. The task is not very hard if you have common sense, as I think you have, and a great deal more. The *Pedarii Senatores*, who were known only by their feet, and not by their heads, were always the objects of general contempt. If on your first, second or third attempt to speak, you should fail, or even stop short, from that trepidation and concern, which every modest man feels upon those occasions, do not be discouraged, but persevere; it will do at last. Where there is a certain fund of parts and knowledge, speaking is but a knack, which cannot fail of being acquired by frequent use. I must however add this caution, never write down your speeches beforehand; if you do you may perhaps be a good declaimer, but will never be a debater. Prepare and digest your matter well in your own thoughts. and *Verba non invita sequantur*. But if you can properly introduce into your speech a shining declamatory period or two which the audience may carry home with them, like the favourite song of an opera, it will have a good effect. The late Lord Bolingbroke had accustomed himself so much to a florid eloquence even in his common conversation (which anybody with care may do) that his real *extempore* speeches seemed to be studied. Lord Mansfield was, in my opinion, the next to him in undeviating eloquence, but Mr. Pitt carried with him, unpremeditated, the strength of thunder, and the splendour of lightning. The best matter in the world if ill-dressed and ungracefully spoken, can never please. Conviction or conversion are equally out of the question in both Houses, but he will come the nearest to them who pleases the most. In that, as in everything else, sacrifice to the Graces. Be very modest in your *exordium*, and as strong as you can be in your *peroratio*.

I can hardly bring myself to caution you against drinking, because I am persuaded that I am writing to a rational creature, a gentleman, and not to a swine. However, that you may not be insensibly drawn into that beastly custom of even sober drinking and sipping, as the sots call it, I advise you to be of no club whatsoever. The object of all clubs is either drinking or gaming, but commonly both. A sitting member of a drinking club is not indeed always drunk, perhaps seldom quite so, but he is certainly never quite sober, and is *beclareted* next morning with the guzzle of the preceding evening. A member of a gaming club should be a cheat, or he will soon be a beggar.

You will and you ought to be in some employment at Court.[1] It is the best school for manners, and whatever ignorant people may think or say of it, no more the seat of vice than a village is; human nature is the same everywhere, the modes only are different. In the village they are coarse; in the Court they are polite; like the different clothes in the two several places, frieze in the one, and velvet in the other.

Be neither a servile courtier nor a noisy patriot; custom, that governs the world instead of reason, authorises a certain latitude in political matters not always consistent with the strictest morality, but in all events remember *servare modum, finemque tueri*.

Be not only tender and jealous of your moral, but of your political, character. In your political warfare, you will necessarily make yourself enemies, but make them only your political

[1] In 1798 he was appointed Master of the Horse.

and temporary, not personal, enemies. Pursue your own principles with steadiness, but without personal reflection or acrimony, and behave yourself to those who differ from you with all the politeness and good humour of a gentleman, for in the frequent jumble of political atoms, the hostile and the amicable ones often change places.

In business be as able as you can, but do not be cunning; cunning is the dark sanctuary of incapacity. Every man can be cunning if he pleases, by simulation, dissimulation, and in short by lying. But that character is universally despised and detested, and justly too; no truly great man was ever cunning. Preserve a dignity of character by your virtue and veracity. You are by no means obliged to tell all that you know and think, but you are obliged by all the most sacred ties of morality and prudence, never to say anything contrary to what you know or think to be true. Be master of your countenance, and let not every fool who runs read it. One of the fundamental rules, and almost the only honest one of Italian politics, is *Volto sciolto e pensieri stretti*, an open countenance and close thoughts.

Never be proud of your rank or birth, but be as proud as you please of your character. Nothing is so contrary to true dignity as the former kind of pride. You are, it is true, of a noble family, but whether of a very ancient one or not I neither know nor care, nor need you, and I dare say there are twenty fools in the House of Lords who could out-descend you in pedigree. That sort of stately pride is the standing jest of all people who can make one; but dignity of character is universally respected. Acquire and preserve that most carefully. Should you be unfortunate enough to have vices, you may, to a certain degree, even dignify them by a strict observance of decorum; at least they will lose something of their natural turpitude.

Carefully avoid every singularity that may give a handle to ridicule, for ridicule (with submission to Lord Shaftesbury [1]), though not founded upon truth, will stick for some time, and if thrown by a skilful hand perhaps for ever. Be wiser and better than your contemporaries, but seem to take the world as it is, and men as they are, for you are too young to be a *censor morum*; you would be an object of ridicule. Act contrary to many Churchmen, practise virtue, but do not preach it whilst you are young.

If you should ever fill a great station at Court, take care

[1] Referring to his saying that "ridicule is the best test of truth."

above all things to keep your hands clean and pure from the infamous vice of corruption, a vice so infamous that it degrades even the other vices that may accompany it. Accept no present whatever; let your character in that respect be transparent and without the least speck, for as avarice is the vilest and dirtiest vice in private, corruption is so in public life. I call corruption the taking of a sixpence more than the just and known salary of your employment, under any pretence whatsoever. Use what power and credit you may have at Court in the service of merit rather than of kindred, and not to get pensions and reversions for yourself or your family, for I call that also, what it really is, scandalous pollution, though of late it has been so frequent that it has almost lost its name.

Never run in debt, for it is neither honest nor prudent, but on the contrary, live so far within your annual income as to leave yourself room sufficient for acts of generosity and charity. Give nobly to indigent merit, and do not refuse your charity even to those who have no merit but their misery. Voltaire expresses my thought much better than I can myself:

> *Répandez vos bienfaits avec magnificence,*
> *Même aux moins vertueux ne les refusez pas,*
> *Ne vous informez pas de leur reconnoissance:*
> *Il est grand, il est beau, de faire des ingrats.*

Such expense will do you more honour, and give you more pleasure, than the idle profusion of a modish and *erudite* luxury.

These few sheets will be delivered to you by Dr. Dodd at your return from your travels, probably long after I shall be dead; read them with deliberation and reflection, as the tender and last testimonies of my affection for you. They are not the severe and discouraging dictates of an old parent, but the friendly and practicable advice of a sincere friend, who remembers that he has been young himself and knows the indulgence that is due to youth and inexperience. Yes, I have been young, and a great deal too young. Idle dissipation and innumerable indiscretions, which I am now heartily ashamed and repent of, characterized my youth. But if my advice can make you wiser and better than I was at your age, I hope it may be some little atonement.

God bless you!   CHESTERFIELD.

TO HIS SON'S WIDOW—MRS. EUGENIA
STANHOPE [1]

MADAM,
London, March 16, 1769.

A troublesome and painful inflammation in my eyes obliges me to use another hand than my own, to acknowledge the receipt of your letter from Avignon, of the 27th past.

I am extremely surprised that Mrs. du Bouchet should have any objection to the manner in which your late husband desired to be buried, and which you, very properly, complied with. All I desire, for my own burial, is not to be buried alive; but how or where, I think, must be entirely indifferent to every rational creature.

I have no commission to trouble you with, during your stay at Paris; from whence, I wish you and the boys a good journey home; where I shall be very glad to see you all, and assure you of my being, with great truth,

Your faithful humble servant.

MADAM,
Wednesday (1769).

The last time I had the pleasure of seeing you, I was so taken up in playing with the boys, that I forgot their more important affairs. How soon would you have them placed at school? When I know your pleasure as to that, I will send to Monsieur Perny, to prepare everything for their reception. In the mean time, I beg that you will equip them thoroughly with clothes, linen, etc., all good, but plain; and give me the

---

[1] "The affliction (the news of his son's death) of itself was sufficient (to Lord Chesterfield), but it was enhanced by another scarcely less distressing piece of intelligence. It was announced by a lady, who took this first opportunity of acquainting the earl that she had been married to Mr. Stanhope several years, and had two children (sons) by him, which were then with her. Whatever Lord Chesterfield's feelings might be at receiving this authentic information of a clandestine engagement, contracted by his son so long before, concealed with so much art and industry, and brought to light at such an instant, he did not confound the innocent with the guilty, but took upon himself the care of providing for the children."— Maty's *Memoirs*, p. 352.

account, which I will pay; for I do not intend, that, from this time forwards, the two boys should cost you one shilling.

I am with great truth, yours, etc.

MADAM,   Thursday Morning (1769).

As some day must be fixed for sending the boys to school, do you approve of the 8th of next month? by which time the weather will probably be warm and settled, and you will be able to equip them completely.

I will, upon that day, send my coach to you, to carry you and the boys to Loughborough House, with all their immense baggage. I must recommend to you, when you leave them there, to suppress, as well as you can, the overflowings of maternal tenderness; which would grieve the poor boys the more, and give them a terror of their new establishment. I am with great truth,   Yours, etc.

MADAM,   Bath, October 11, 1769.

Nobody can be more willing or ready to obey orders than I am; but then I must like the orders and the orderer. Your orders and yourself come under this description; and therefore I must give you an account of my arrival and existence, such as it is, here. I got hither last Sunday, the day after I left London, less fatigued than I expected to have been; and now crawl about this place upon my three legs, but am kept in countenance by many of my fellow crawlers: the last part of the Sphynx's riddle approaches, and I shall soon end, as I began, upon all fours.

When you happen to see either Monsieur or Madame Perny, I beg you will give them this *melancholic* proof of my caducity, and tell them, that the last time I went to see the boys, I carried the Michaelmas quarterage in my pocket, and when I was there I totally forgot it; but assure them, that I have not the least intention to bilk them, and will pay them faithfully, the two quarters together, at Christmas.

I hope our two boys are well; for then I am sure you are so.

I am, etc.

MADAM,   Bath, October 28, 1769.

Your kind anxiety for my health and life, is more than, in my opinion, they are both worth: without the former, the latter is a burden; and, indeed, I am very weary of it. I think I have got some benefit by drinking these waters, and by bathing, for my old, stiff, rheumatic limbs; for I believe I could now outcrawl a snail, or perhaps even a tortoise.

I hope the boys are well. Phil, I dare say, has been in some scrapes; but he will get triumphantly out of them, by dint of strength and resolution. I am, etc.

MADAM, Bath, November 5, 1769.

I remember very well the paragraph which you quote from a letter of mine to Mrs. du Bouchet, and see no reason yet to retract that opinion, *in general*, which at least nineteen widows in twenty had authorised. I had not then the pleasure of your acquaintance; I had seen you but twice or thrice; and I had no reason to think that you would deviate, as you have done, from other widows, so much, as to put perpetual shackles upon yourself, for the sake of your children; but (if I may use a vulgarism) one swallow makes no summer: five righteous were formerly necessary to save a city, and they could not be found; so, till I find four more such righteous widows as yourself, I shall entertain my former notions of widowhood in general.

I can assure you that I drink here very soberly and cautiously, and at the same time keep so cool a diet, that I do not find the least symptom of heat, much less of inflammation. By the way, I never had that complaint, in consequence of having drank these waters; for I have had it but four times, and always in the middle of summer. Mr. Hawkins is timorous, even to *minuties*, and my sister delights in them.

Charles will be a scholar, if you please; but our little Philip, without being one, will be something or other as good, though I do not yet guess what. I am not of the opinion generally entertained in this country, that man lives by Greek and Latin alone; that is, by knowing a great many words of two dead languages, which nobody living knows perfectly, and which are of no use in the common intercourse of life. Useful knowledge, in my opinion, consists of modern languages, history, and geography; some Latin may be thrown in to the bargain, in compliance with custom and for closet amusement.

You are, by this time, certainly tired with this long letter, which I could prove to you from Horace's own words (for I am a *scholar*) to be a bad one; he says, that water-drinkers can write nothing good; so I am, with real truth and esteem,

Yours, etc.

TO CHARLES AND PHILIP STANHOPE

Bath, October 27, 1771.

I received, a few days ago, two of the best written letters that I ever saw in my life; the one signed Charles Stanhope, the other Philip Stanhope. As for you, Charles, I did not wonder at it; for you will take pains, and are a lover of letters; but you idle rogue, you Phil, how came you to write so well, that one can almost say of you two, *et cantare pares et respondere parati*? Charles will explain this Latin to you.

I am told, Phil, that you have got a nick-name at school, from your intimacy with Master Strangeways; and that they call you Master *Strangerways*; for to be sure, you are a strange boy. Is this true?

Tell me what you would have me bring you both from hence, and I will bring it you, when I come to town. In the mean time, God bless you both!

TO LORD HUNTINGDON

My DEAR LORD,   London, November 25, O.S. 1751.

I was very glad to find by the last letter you honoured me with that your time for leaving Paris was at last fixed. For though I look upon that place to be the best in Europe for forming a young man of quality, yet you have now had so much, though you wanted so much less of it than other people, and as you have a good deal still to do abroad, and, as your predecessor Hastings says in *Jane Shore*, "but a little time to do it in," it is time to set about it.

If (as I suppose was the case) Mlle Lang prevailed with you to pass this winter at Paris, the cause was at your age, a very justifiable one; I believe I should do the same at mine, without half so many or so good reasons for it, as I dare say you had. Her situation, and degree of character made your connection with her for a time not unbecoming. It is the duration of those connections that makes them disgraceful, when the influence of the lady is supposed to be extended from the senses to the understanding and conduct of her friend.

Since you take the trouble of going to Spain, where probably you will never go again, I would advise you to see it all when you are there. If from Madrid you go down southward to Seville, and from thence come up again through Granada and Valentia to Barcelona, you will have seen the best parts of Spain, and particularly those that are dignified by the remains of Roman, Gothic and Moorish antiquities. From Barcelona (if you are not sea sick) your passage by sea to Geneva or Leghorn will be short and pleasant in the autumn. Mr. Keene, the King's Ambassador at Madrid, will, I am sure, show you all the attention and regard that you deserve, and consequently you will want no letters of recommendation to Madrid, nor any to any of those provinces of Spain which you propose to visit afterwards. Otherwise I would have sent you some from the Spanish Ambassador here; I spoke to him about it, and he assured me that Mr. Keene was as well-known in Spain as he was, and could do you as much, or more, service there. May I beg of you, my dear Lord, to make my compliments to M. du Clos, and to return to him my particular thanks for the great pleasure he has given me by his last performance, *Les Mémoires*, etc.? It is just what I wished for, when I had read his *Considerations* I wanted to have those just reflections exemplified and set in all their light by characters. It has done it in my mind incomparably; the pictures are finely drawn, and highly coloured, and what the Italians [call] the *costumi* are most exactly observed. I wish it had been wrote, and that I had read it, seven and thirty years ago; I think it would have saved me some vices, and many follies, which were really not my own, but adoptive ones in complaisance to *les mœurs du siècle*.

If our accounts here from Paris are true, the change of the temper and genius of the French people with regard to their Government is astonishing. They used to hug their chains and boast their servitude; they now seem to be galled by them and struggling to shake them off. If they have found out (though late) that kings are not a part of the Divinity; that they are neither anointed nor appointed by him to be the scourges of their fellow creatures; that they have no other rights but those of civil and mutual compact; but that mankind in general have natural and inherent rights which no power upon earth can legally deprive them of; if, they have at last discovered these truths, which by the way are not very abstruse ones, their natural vivacity, and their shame of so long an entertained error will probably carry them very far the other way. People are very apt to run into the opposite extreme of a detected and exploded prejudice; and *ce germe de raison qui tend à se développer en France*, as du Clos observed, will probably grow too strong for absolute power, which can only be supported by error, ignorance and prejudice. As a friend of mankind, I shall be glad if it proves so, and as a friend to my own country, I heartily wish it may; for without troubles at home France is now too powerful and formidable abroad.

Might it not be worth your while to take a Spanish master at Paris, till you go to Spain, and to take another during your stay at Madrid? It is a very easy though a very copious language; and many, not to say most of the Spaniards, even the people of quality, speak no other languages. It will moreover facilitate your learning Italian, which it resembles extremely, excepting some Moorish words. I have sent your little servant back to Paris, to profit by your example, and to form himself upon your model, if he can. Those were at least the instructions I gave him, and I think I could not give him shorter nor more useful ones. Adieu my dear Lord, without peroration. Professions are inconsistent with the truth of the friendship with which I am most faithfully and unalterably yours,

CHESTERFIELD.

MY DEAR LORD,   London, November 21, 1752.

I am sure I need not tell you how impatient I was to hear of your safe arrival at Madrid, and how pleased I was when I heard it from yourself. You have now gone through the worst part of Spain, so that in your future journies the country will at least mend upon you, though the manners and the cleanliness of the natives will not. Spain is surely the only country in Europe that has been barbarizing itself every day more and more in proportion as all the other countries have civilized themselves. Since the conquest of the people by the Romans, their most shining period is without question the time of the Moors; and ever since their expulsion, civil and ecclesiastical tyranny have acted in concert, and successfully, in scattering that general darkness and ignorance which are so necessary for their views. Their descendants the Irish, I mean the true, genuine Irish of the west and south of Ireland, are, I can assure you, full as lazy, as proud and as nasty, as their ancestors, and, though they are not civil slaves, they are the most bigoted religious ones in the world. Their priests, very near as ignorant as themselves, have only sense enough to continue them in that state of darkness, that fits them for their purposes. They now pretend, I am told, to some degree of learning at Madrid, they have a number of people there less ignorant, I suppose, than the rest, whom they call an Academy, and who have lately published a spanish dictionary in seven or eight volumes in folio, which M. Caradazal has been so good as to send me. As I look upon that nation as a phenomenon, I am very glad that you see it with your eyes, which is the only way of seeing phenomina as they really are. While you are at Madrid, and afterwards at Lisbon, it will be in your power, and I recommend it to you, to collect at those most catholic and most faithful courts, all the letters of recommendation you possibly can from nuntios, cardinals, bishops and others to their friends at Rome and other parts of Italy. A man who travels with your views, information and improvement cannot have too many letters of recommendation to every place he goes to. The very number of them gives him a degree of consideration; and you may have a great number from people of the very first rank, to Rome, Naples, and Parma. I hope you will be able to get to Barcelona in April, or at least before the excessive heats come on in Spain, where, in case of accidents, I take it for granted that their physicians are as ignorant, though perhaps less knaves than their divines.

I am just returning to Bath, where I have been trying for two months what drinking those waters, together with bathing and pumping my head, would do for me. I hear something better than when I went there, but still not well enough to think myself restored to society. I do by no means wish to be restored to that noisy, tumultuous and busy part of the world, which I had before renounced by choice, but I justly dread as the greatest of my misfortunes, the not being able to hear quietly in my own room, you, and four or five (if there be so many) such as you, who might be at once kind and idle enough to pass a few hours with me here.

Public matters here continue in the same quiet and inactive state in which the death of the late Prince of Wales put them, and are likely to continue so for some time longer. For though private interest wants no spur, faction wants a head to conduct it. There are no thoughts yet of enlarging the family of the

Prince of Wales, and I believe there will not be for some time; which I am glad of.

Lady Chesterfield would have me every time that I write to you repeat her thanks for the *corbeille* which is justly made the capital piece of her dressing room.   But I have compounded with her to repeat them only this time, and to give it under my hand as my own opinion as well as her's, that it is at once the prettiest and the finest thing of the kind that ever I saw in my life.

Adieu my dear Lord, may all pleasures and happiness attend you wherever you go.   Think sometimes of a useless old fellow who is, with the truest affection and esteem, your most faithful humble servant.

CHESTERFIELD.